MW01620554

DAN WITZ

In Plain View

30 Years of Artworks Illegal and Otherwise

Gingko Press

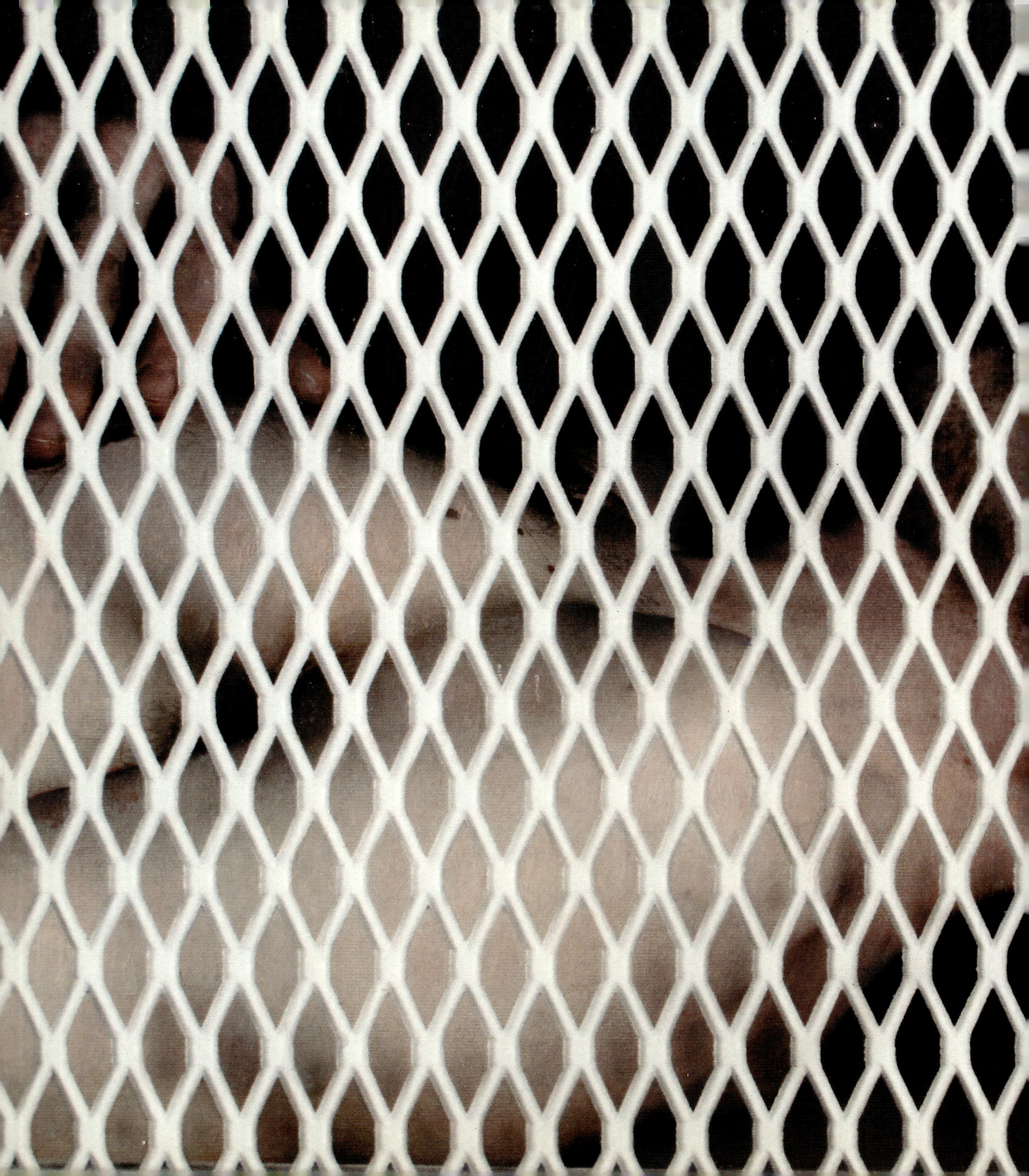

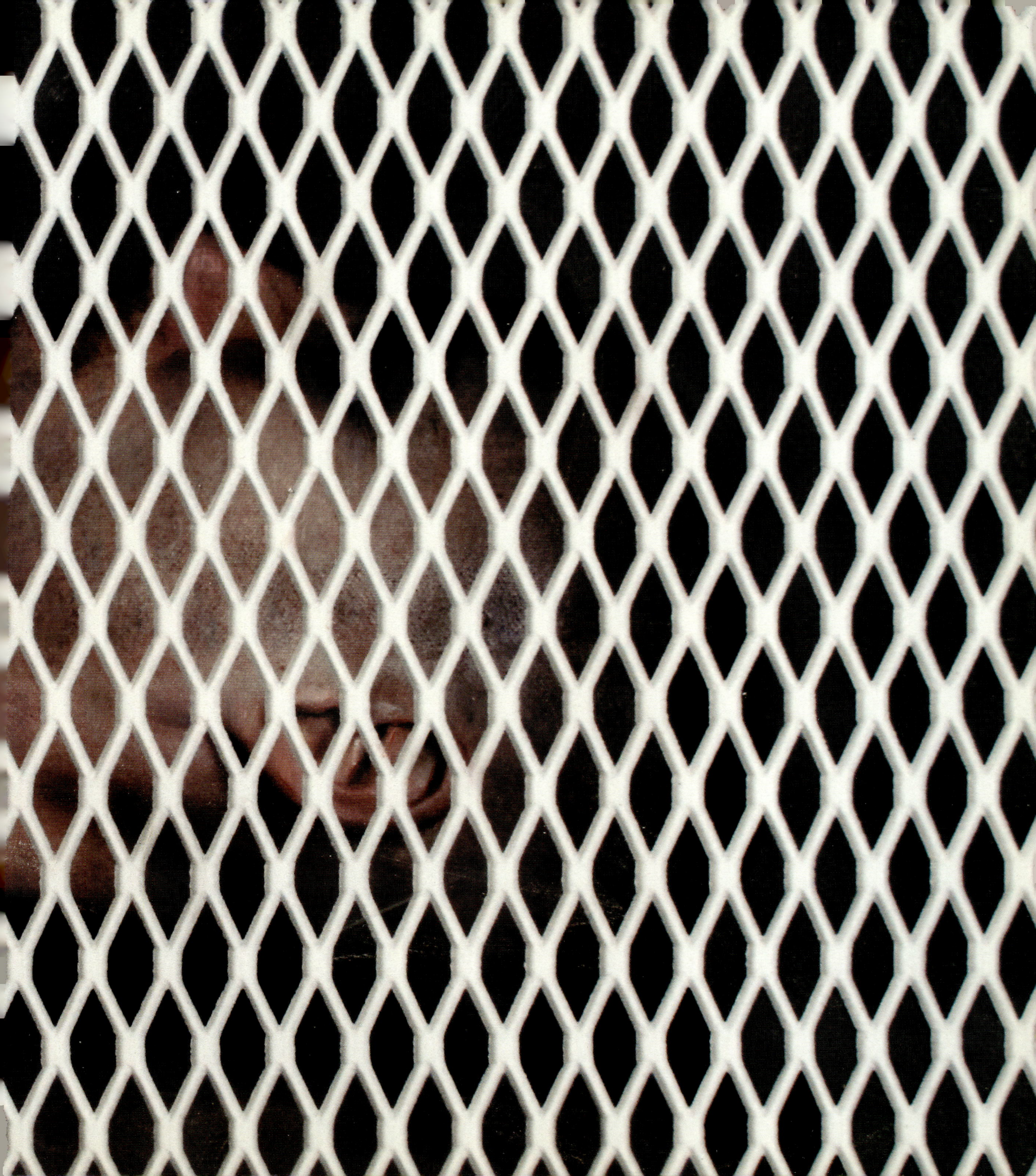

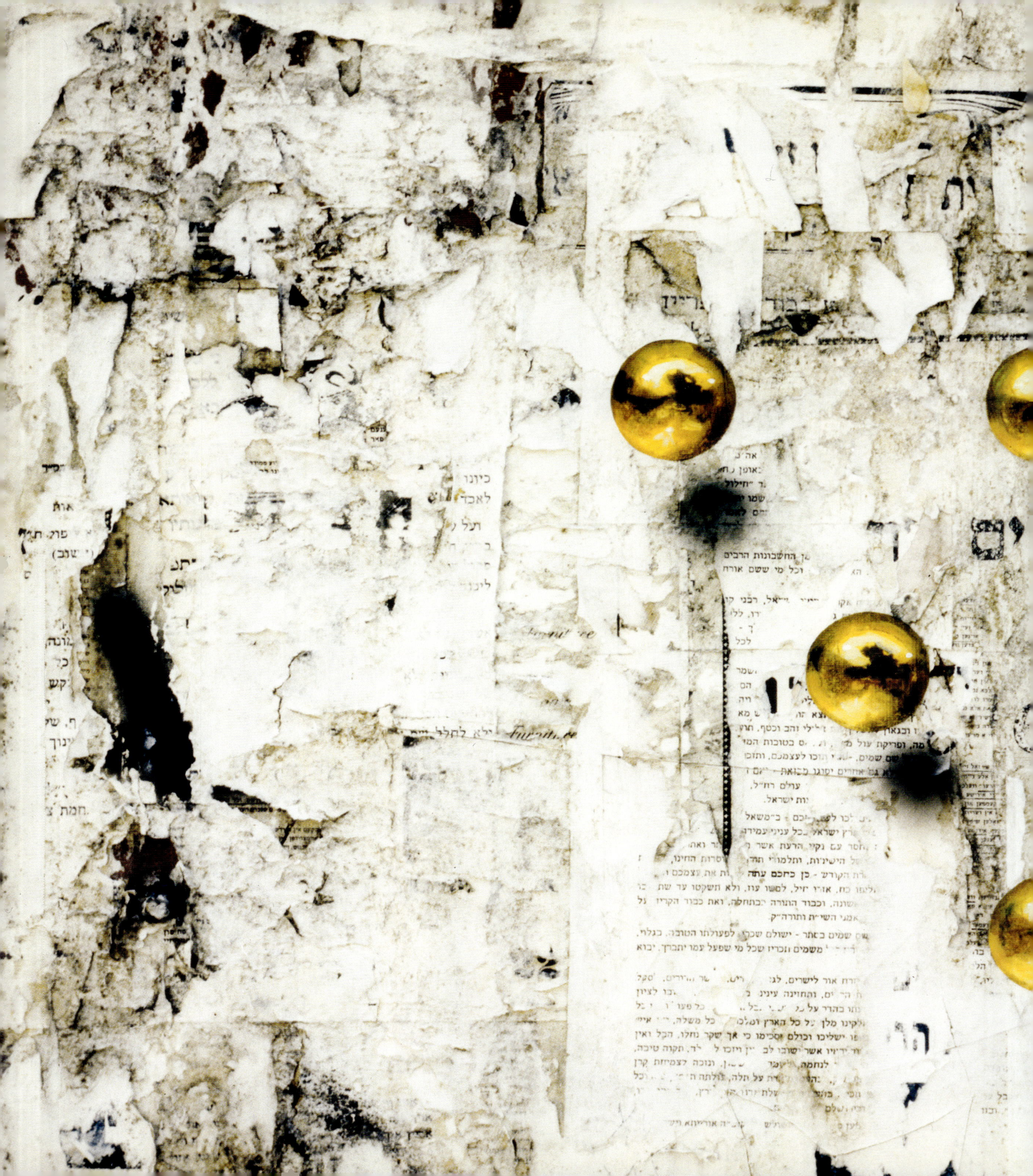

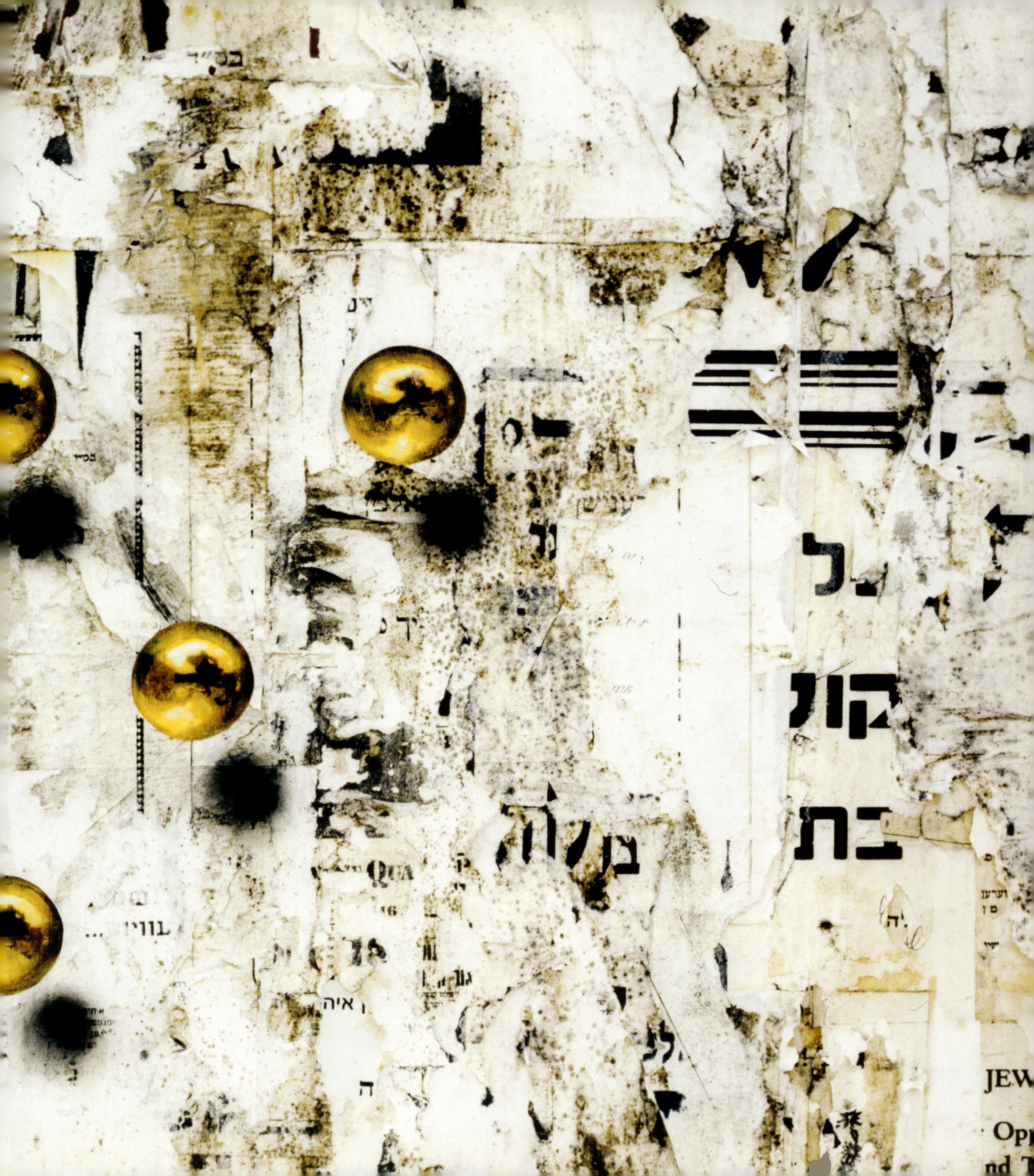

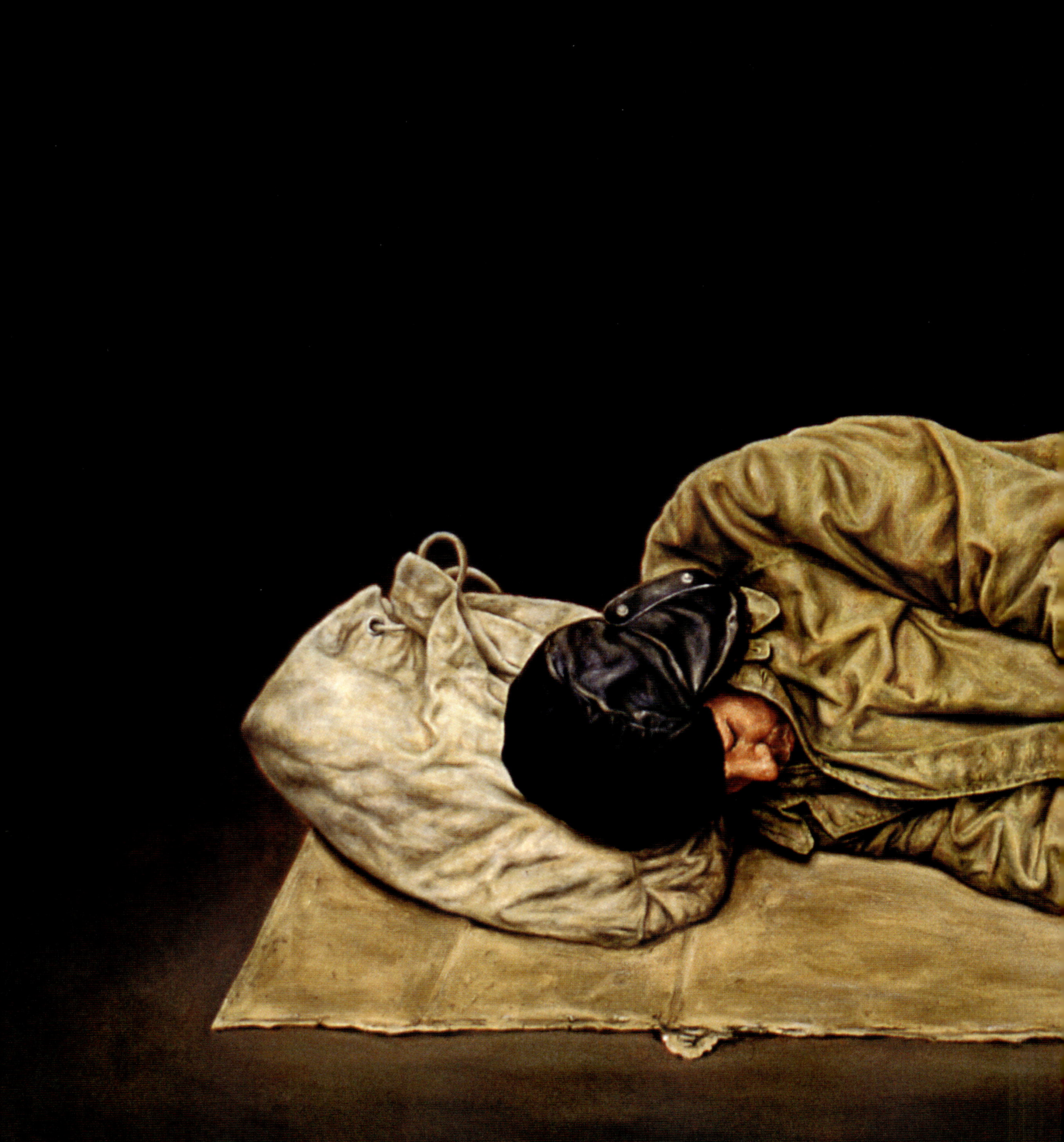

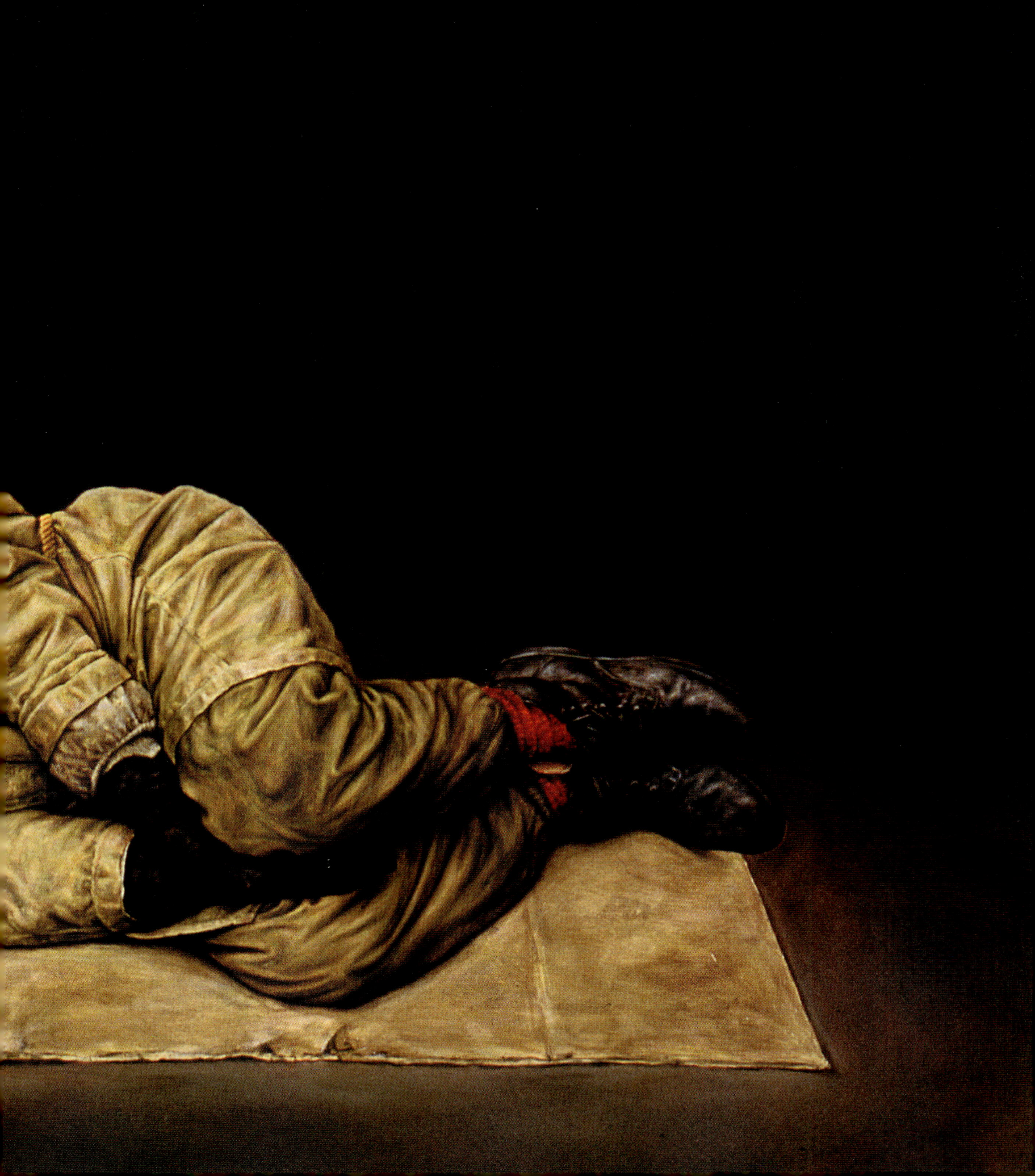

IMAGES ON PREVIOUS PAGES:

WILLIAMSBURG. BROOKLYN, 2009. // Mixed media mounted on plastic, glued to construction wall. (P.2–3)

CLYMER BETWEEN BEDFORD AND DIVISION, WILLIAMSBURG, BROOKLYN, 1997. // Mixed media on sticker paper affixed to wall (P.4–6)

SELF PORTRAIT, 1992. // Oil on canvas. Private Collection. (P.7–8)

OPPOSITE PAGE:

CIBAR (SHRINE), 2006. // Oil and digital media on Canvas. Private Collection

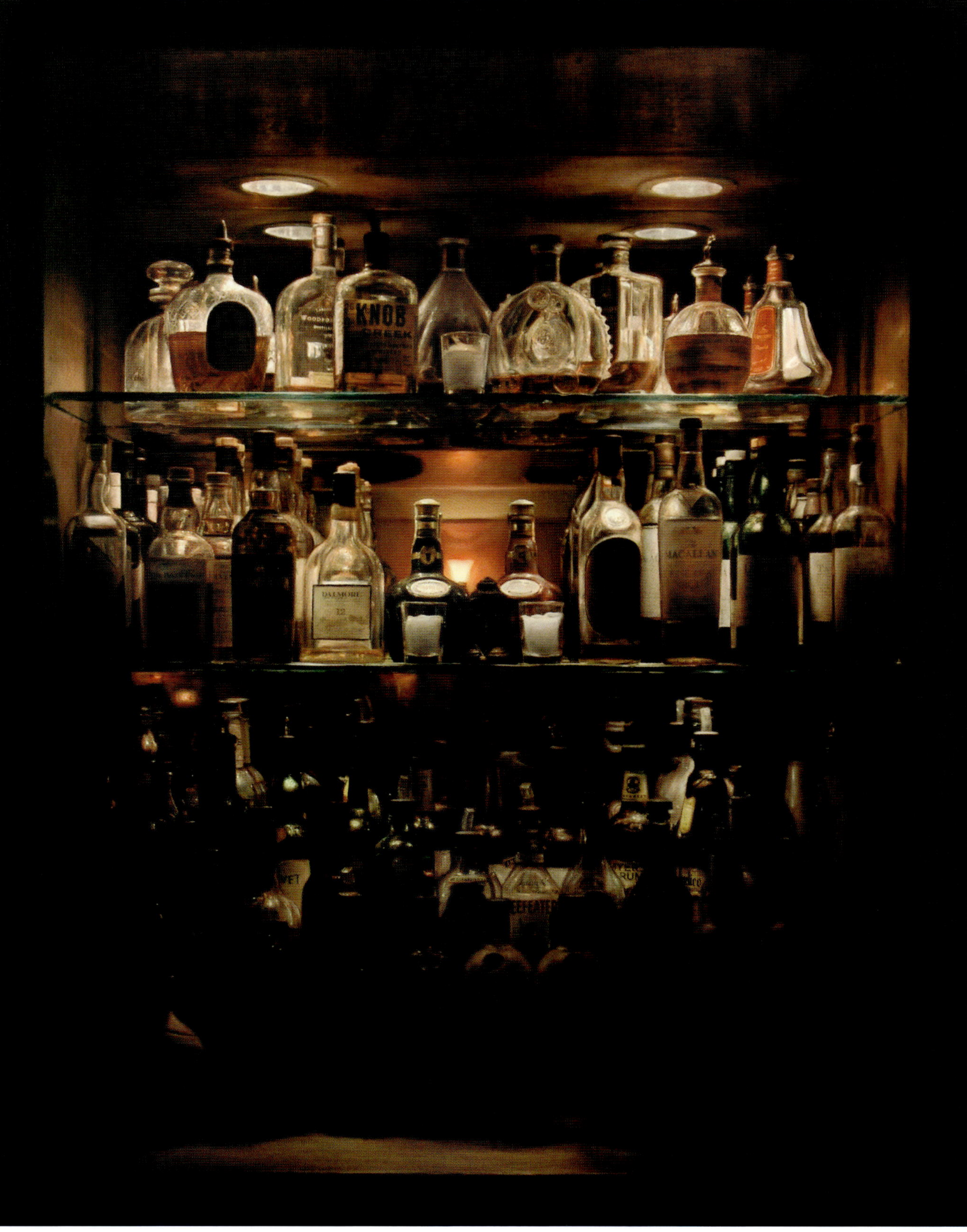
KNOB
CREEK
MACALLAN
DALMORE
12

"In an environment where virtually every moment of human attention has been transformed into an opportunity for a sales pitch, anything that goes up that's not about selling–anything that goes up which is designed to encourage thought rather than consumer behavior, is by definition subversive. It undercuts the notion that human fulfillment is something that takes place across a retail counter."

Stewart Ewen
Professor of media studies, Hunter College
From *To Be Seen,* a film by Alice Arnold.

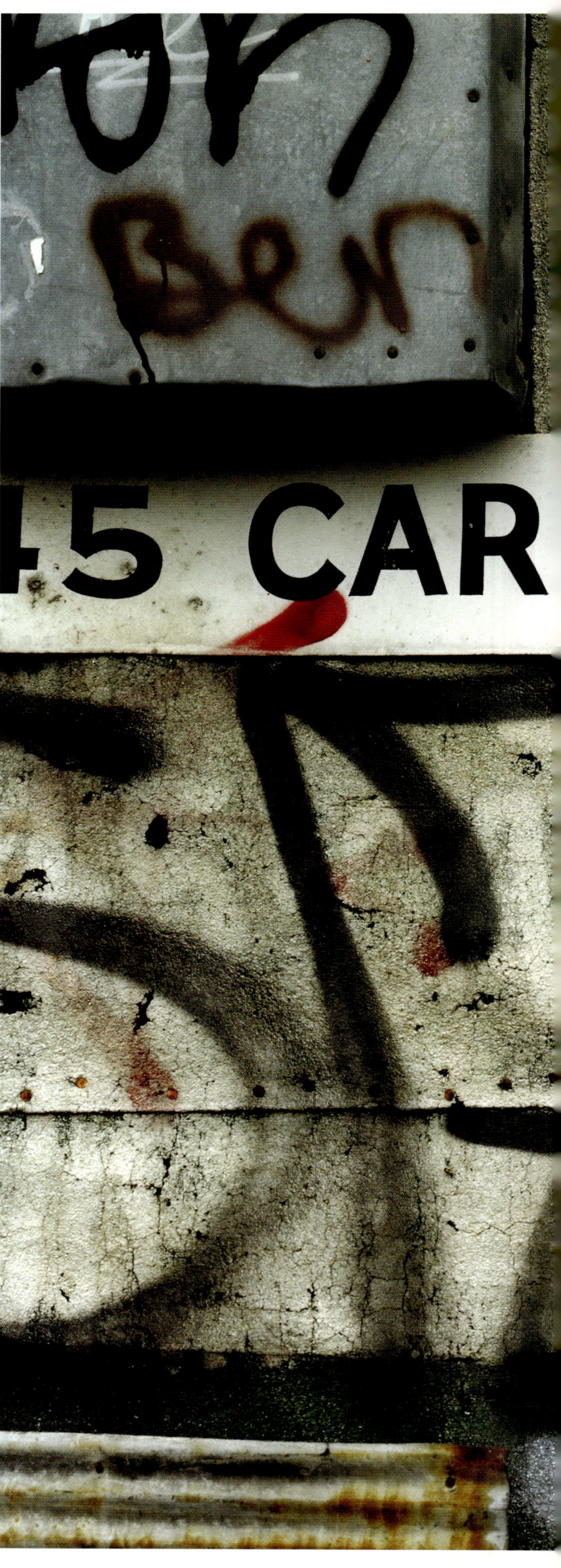

MADISON NEAR PIKE ST., NYC, 2000. // Acrylic on sticker paper and on metal wall.

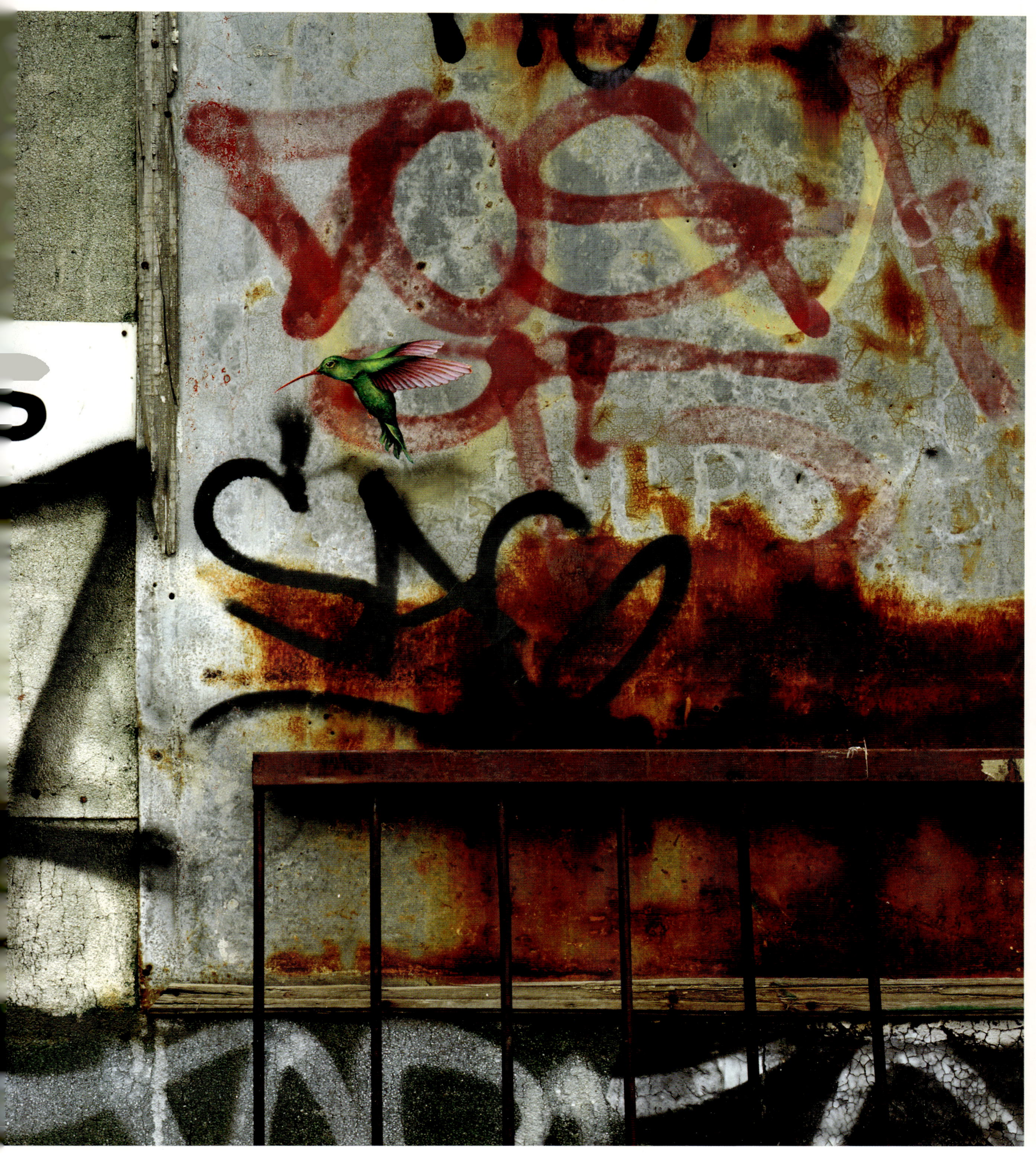

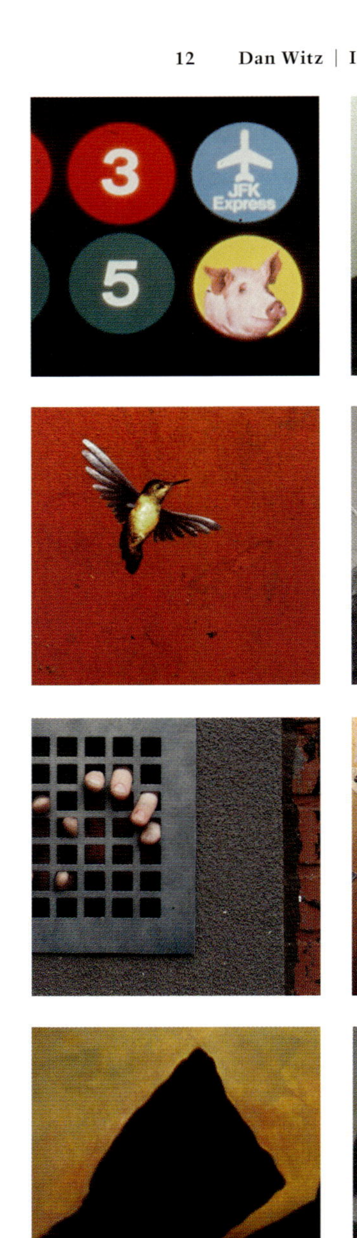
3
JFK Express
5

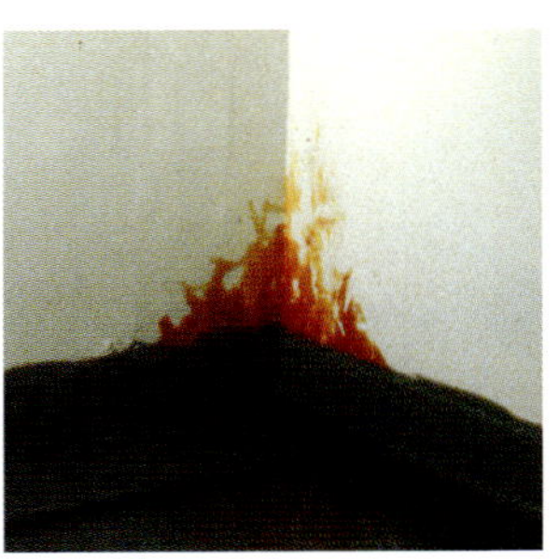

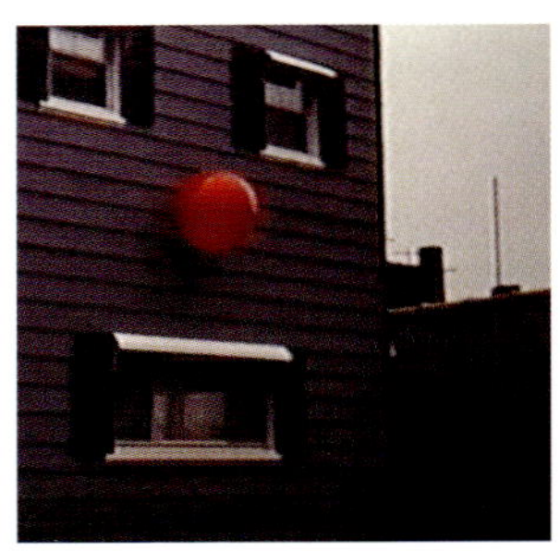

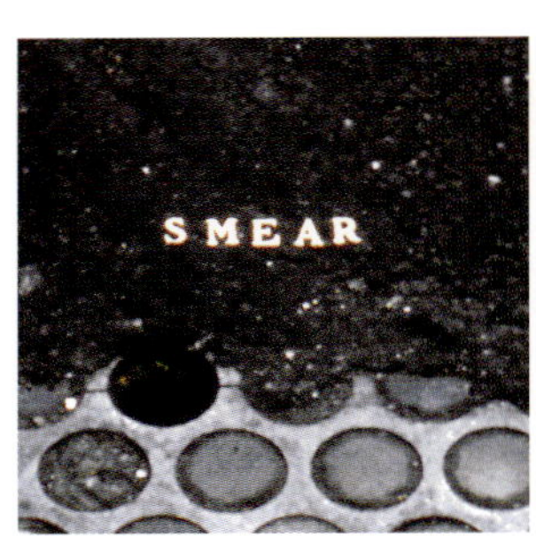
SMEAR

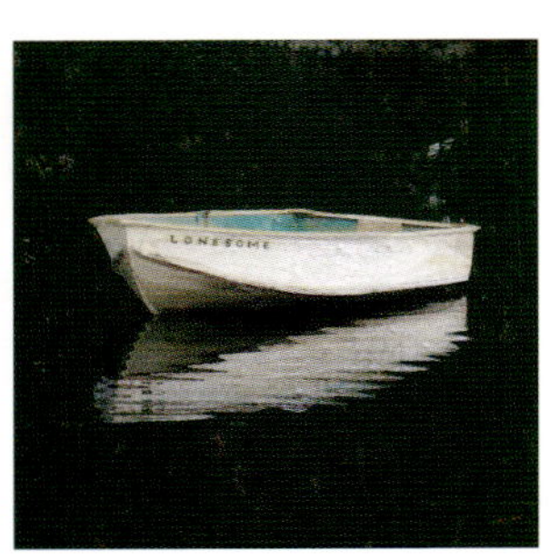

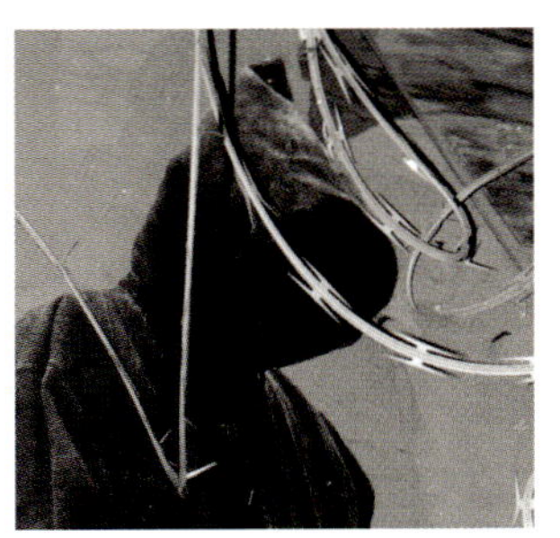

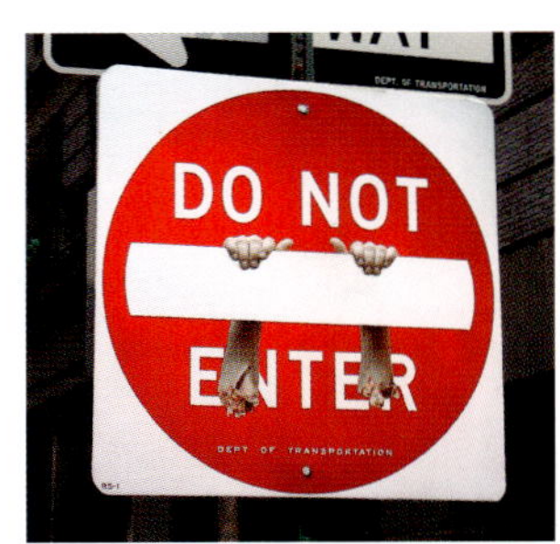
DO NOT
ENTER

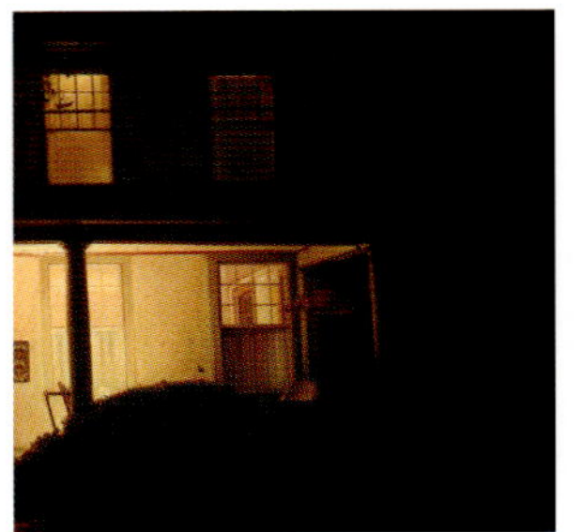

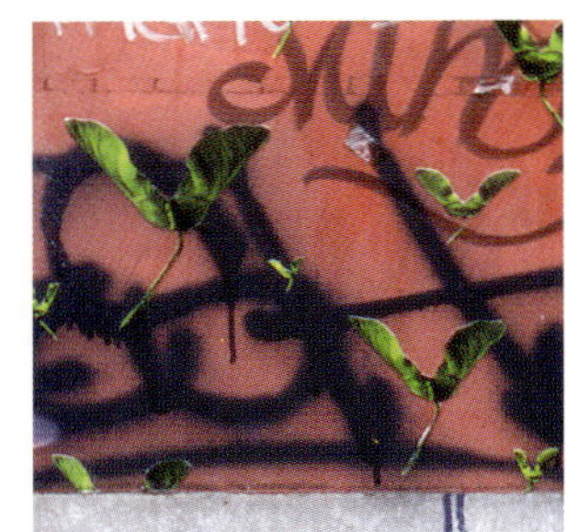

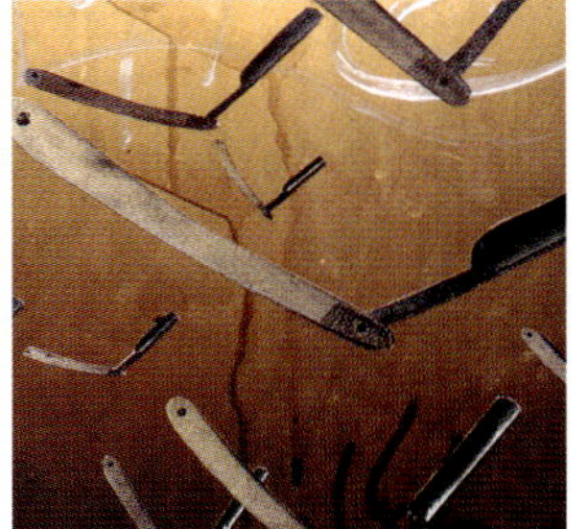

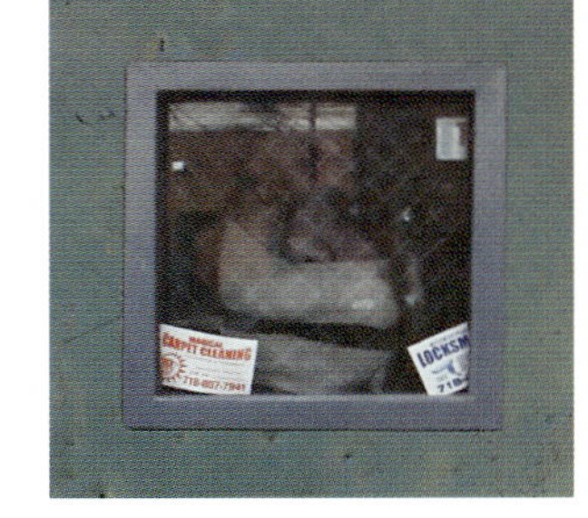

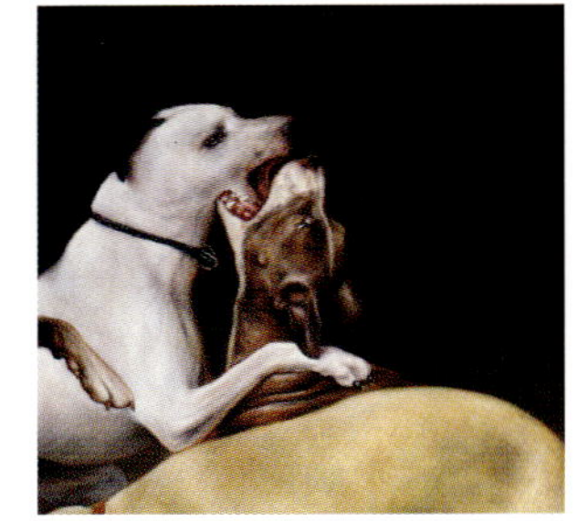

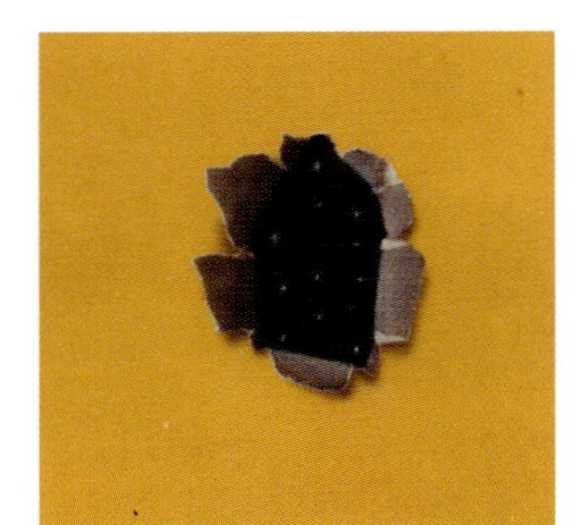

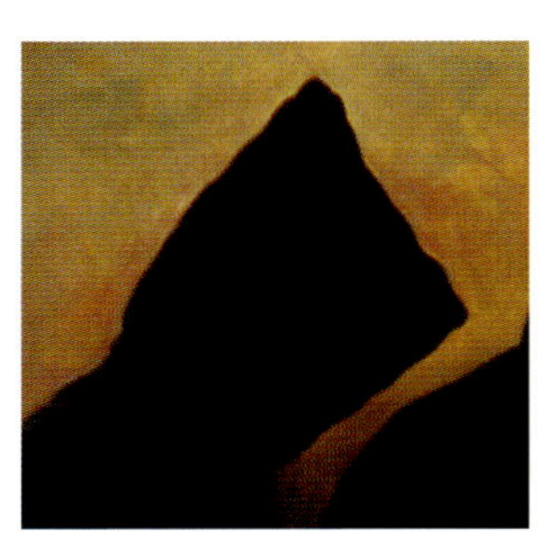

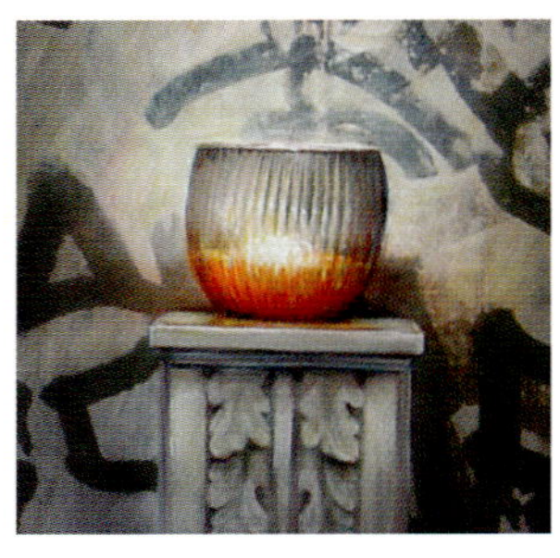

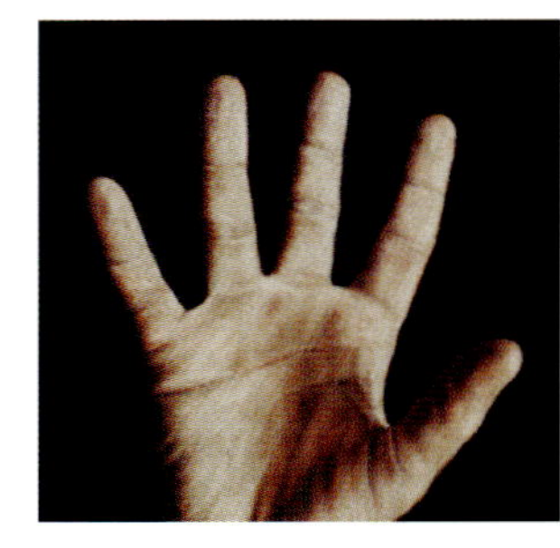

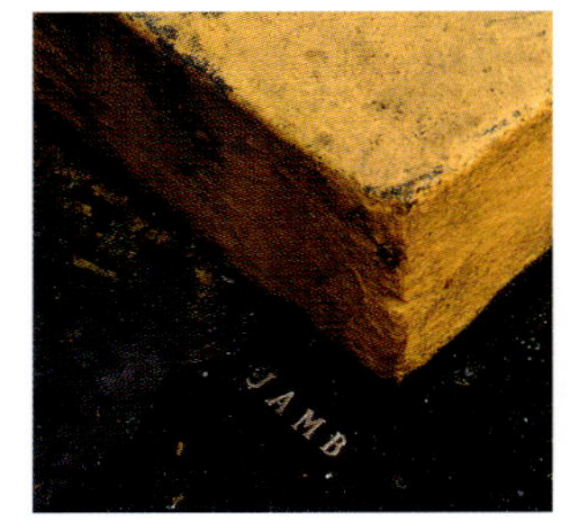
JAMB

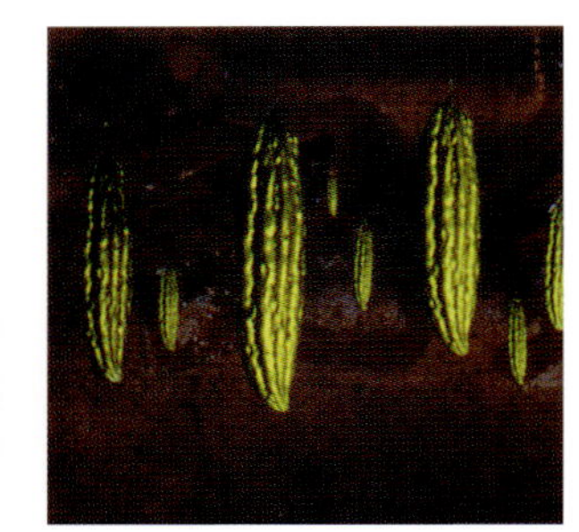

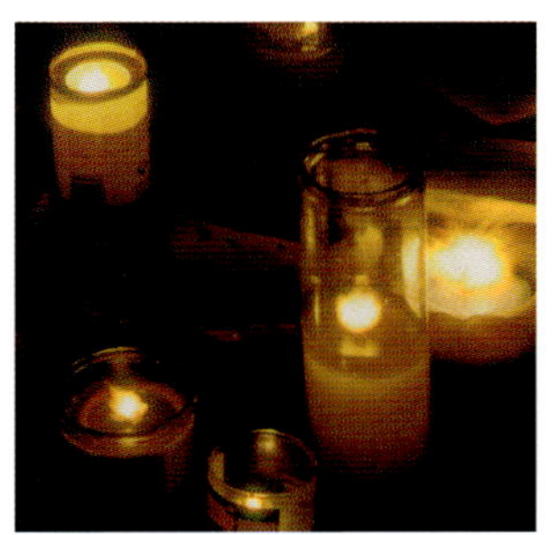

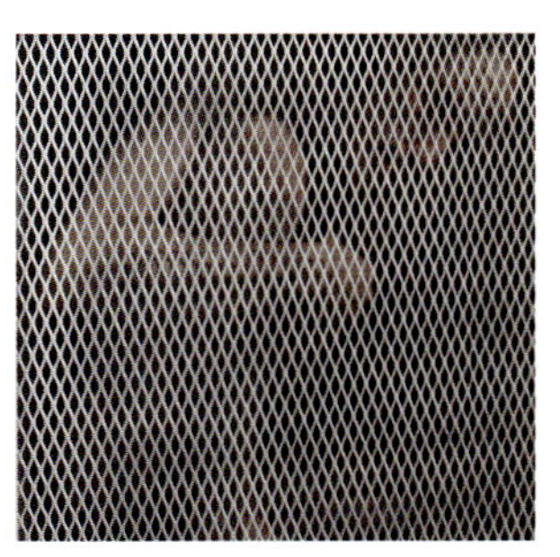

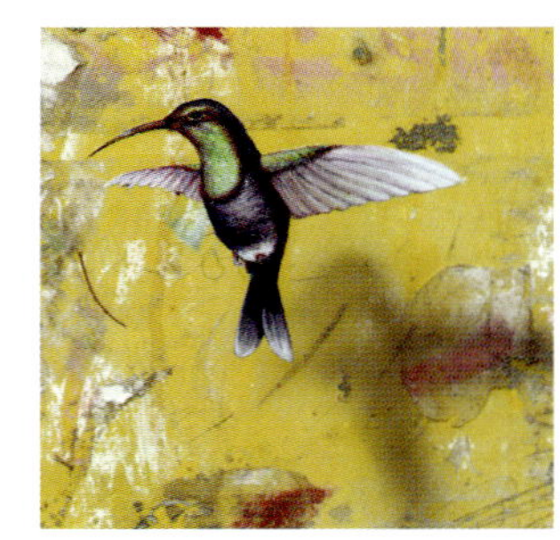

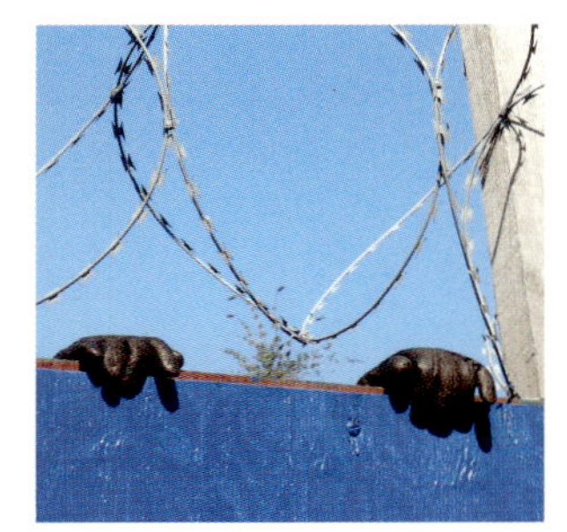

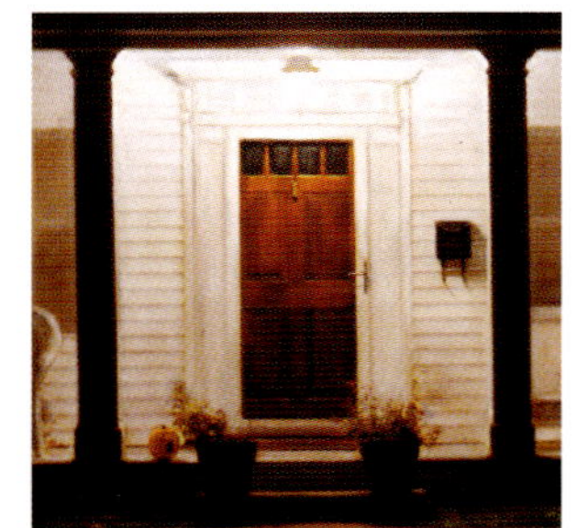

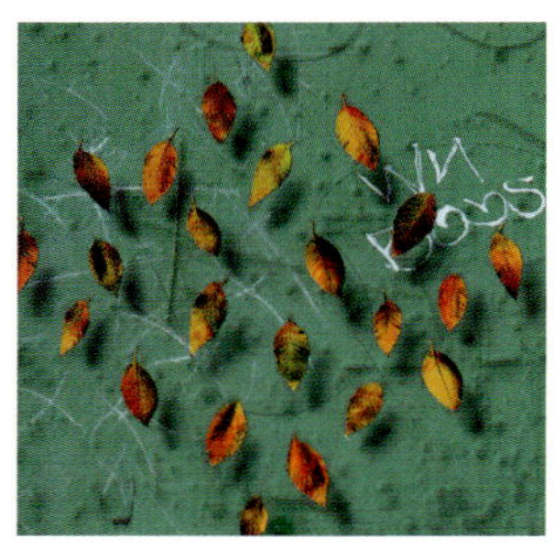

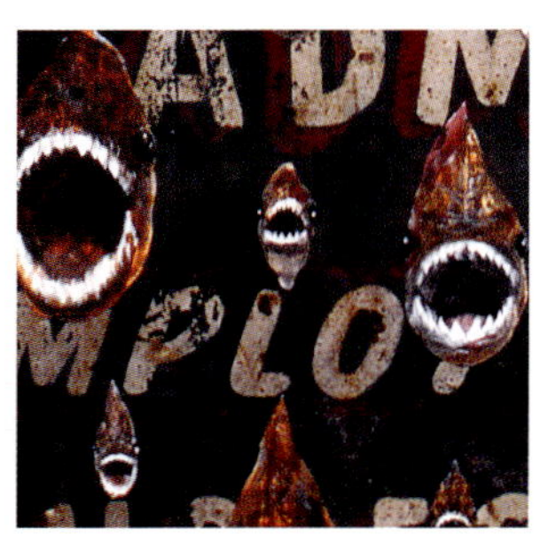

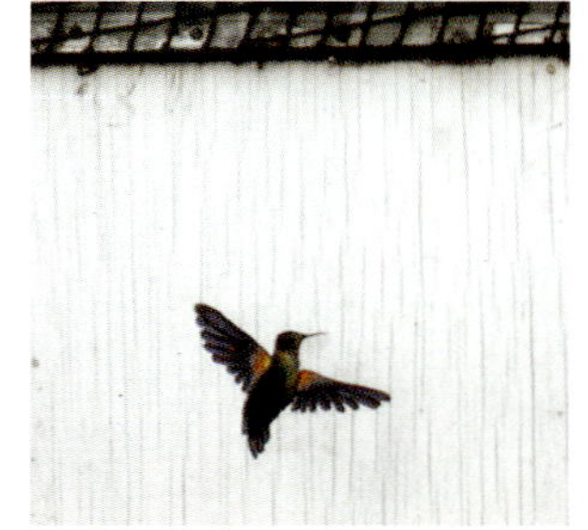

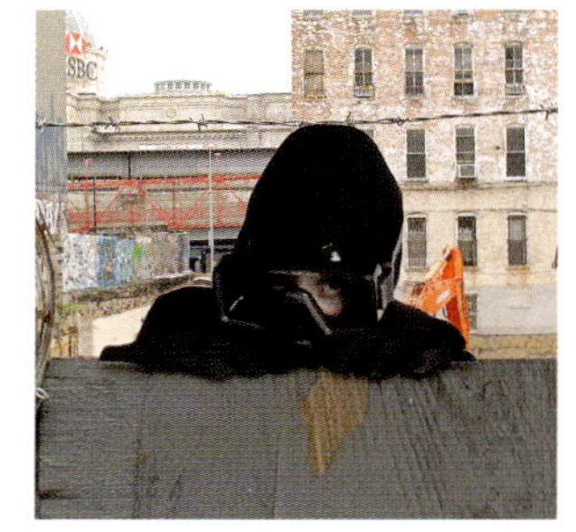

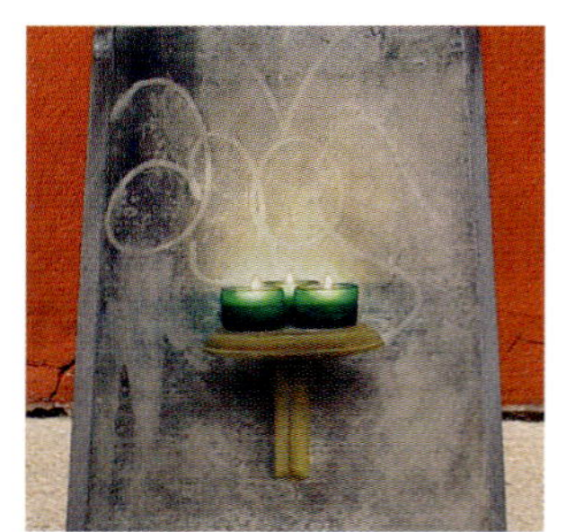

CONTENTS

INTRODUCTION

THE MANIFESTO

"When I was a little kid, there was a stream that came down from the hill at our place and would have cut across our yard, but years before, somebody went out there and covered this stream with stone, mortared the stone together so that it left a hump down through the middle of the yard, as if it were left there by a seven hundred pound mole. And when the stream dried up, my brother and I–he was in the third grade and I was in the fifth–we went down to the end of that tunnel and walked through it, lighting our way with torches. We found an old accordion under there. It was a great find, and we brought it home and tried to play it. But it wouldn't play, and we found we could get into it by opening and opening this screw and lifting the top off. We got into all the valves and bellows and everything, and there, stuck in a corner, we found a piece of paper, a sign, and it said 'WHAT THE HELL ARE YOU LOOKING IN HERE FOR, DAISY MAE?'

Ken Kesey
Interviewed in Esquire

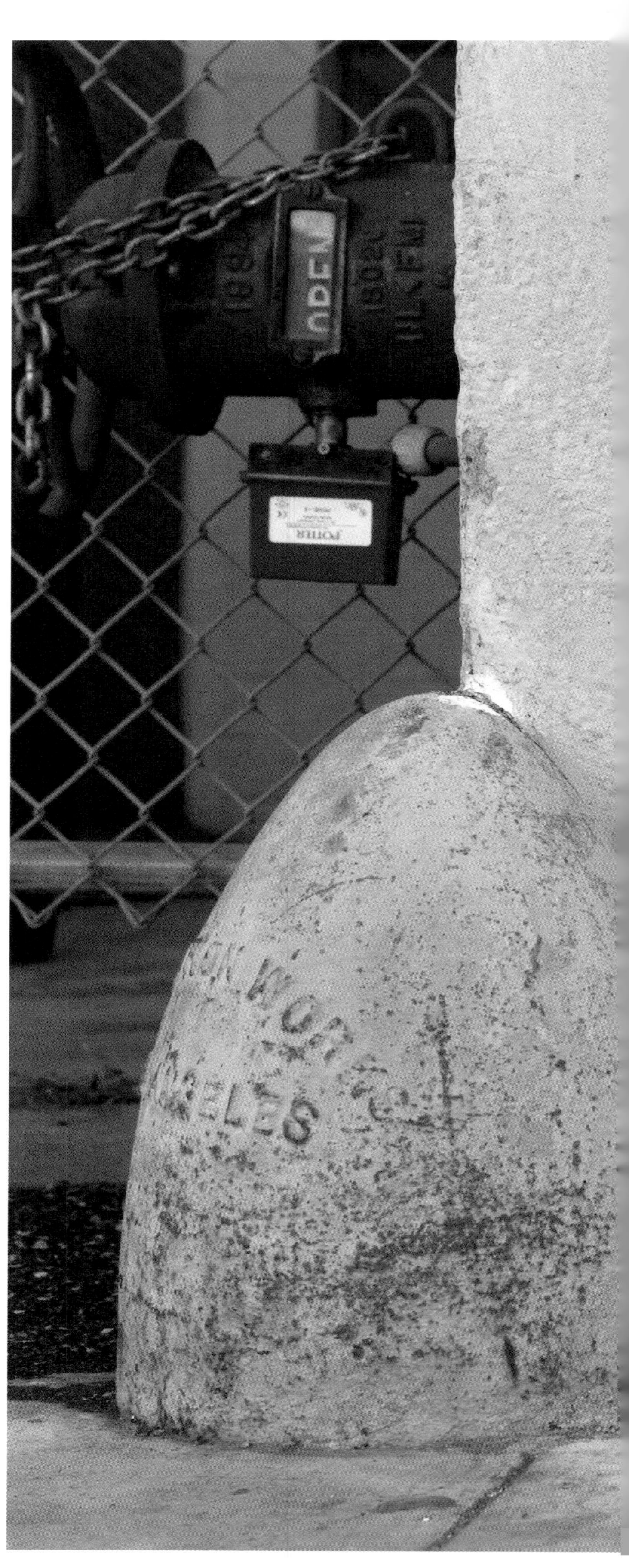

LOS ANGELES, CA, 2009. // Digital and mixed media on plastic and stucco wall.

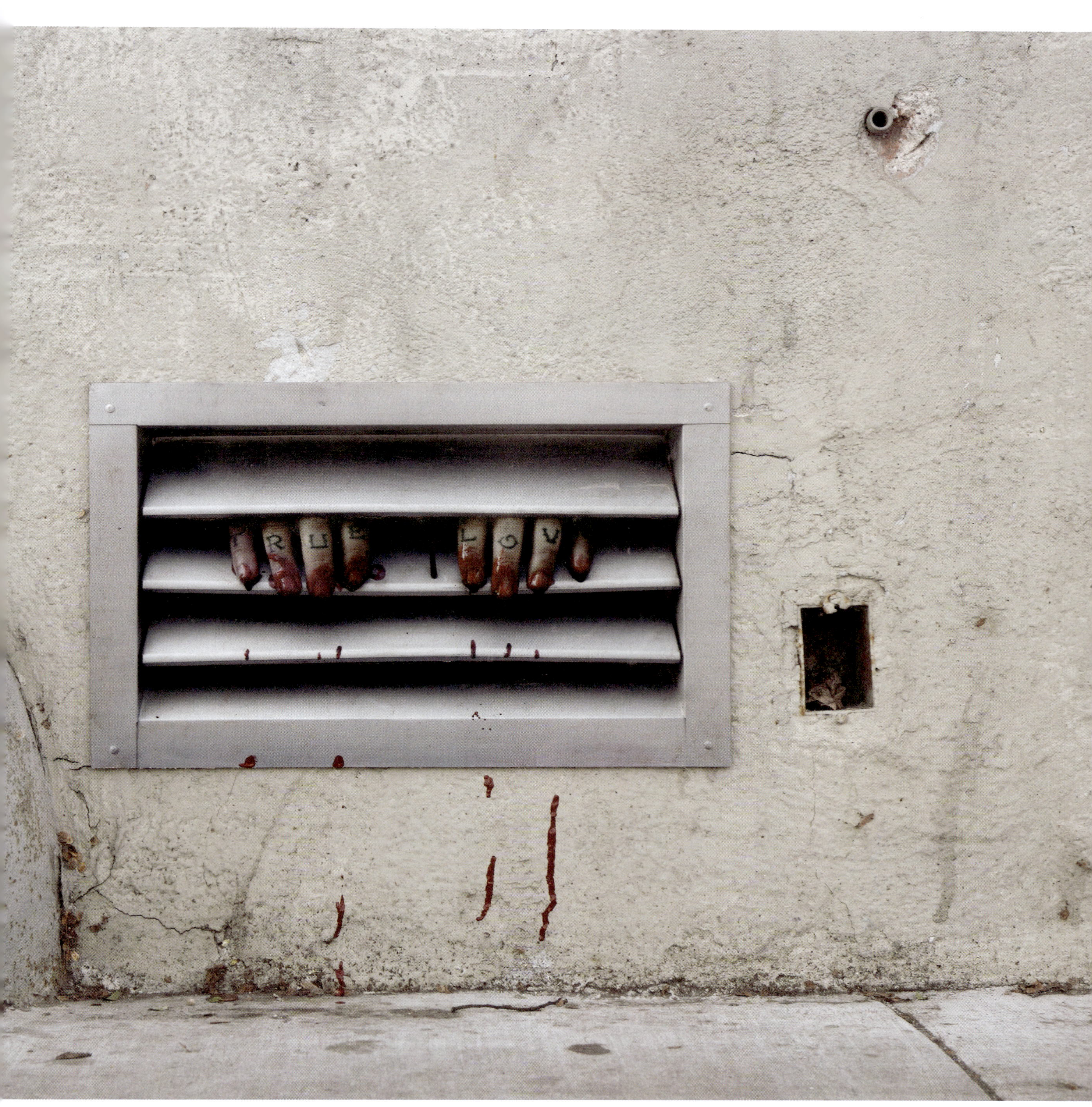
TRUE
LOV

FOREWORD

David Lopes

Exploring the mysterious and the absurd with equal probity and purpose, image-making for Dan Witz always involves a sense of wonder. His approach places equal value on paintings echoing techniques of the Dutch masters as on an ongoing visual dialogue engaging the public in pranks and visual puns. His range of expression runs from the cerebral to the visceral and from the simple gesture to complex arrangements. Witnessing the breadth and variety of Witz's work is inspiring. An approach that marries mature technique and content to a childlike curiosity and flexibility of mind yields images that are always surprising and often unsettling.

There's often a hard edge to Witz's content and approach, but cynicism is just not on his palette. On the contrary, he speaks of his proclivity for engaging the urban audience in a humorous visual repartee in monastic terms. The way the artist speaks of his "prank practice" simultaneously evokes the Merry Pranksters and Buddhist percepts. His experiences and training seem somehow incidental to his aesthetic as he refuses to be constrained in any way.

Dan's art often involves the exploration of the mysterious and enigmatic, inviting chance to play a role in any number of ways. Self-described as "congenitally restless," Witz describes a "wandering practice" and employs a motorcycle for street art actions around New York City. For missions outside of the city, the artist allows randomness to creep into his ramblings, losing himself in suburban environs, while driving around looking for source material to photograph as reference for his studio work.

A graduate of one of the finest art and architecture schools in the country, one feels that Witz took what he needed from the experience and jettisoned the rest. He began his formal art training at RISD and finished at Cooper Union. He speaks of feeling a certain amount of alienation from his fellow art school students, only really finding his groove making music in the punk and noise scene of the late '70s.

When asked about the influences and lineage of his work, the artist places emphasis on his formative experiences with music and his involvement in bands. Variety and originality were the most highly prized attributes of the music scene Witz became more involved in after graduating from Cooper Union in the early '80s. These tenets obviously had a huge impact on him as he seems perpetually engaged in inventing new forms and forums for his work. The artist's work reminds us that outsiders share a common lineage. Witz bridges Ken Kesey and the Ramones, the Situationists and R. Crumb. As punk punctured the pomposity of arena rock, Witz seems intent on bursting contemporary art-world bubbles.

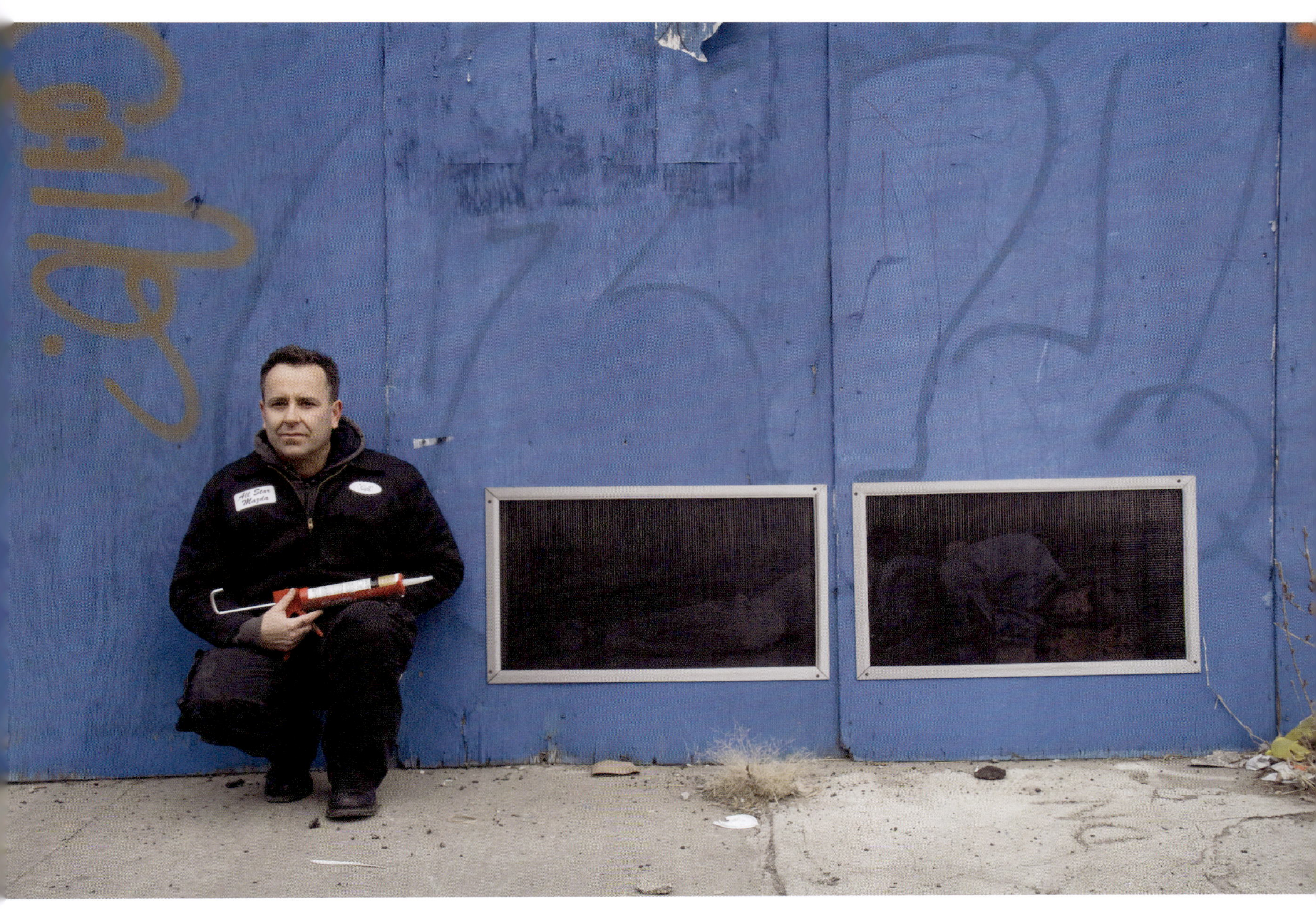

DAN WITZ // Photo by Ame Curtiss.

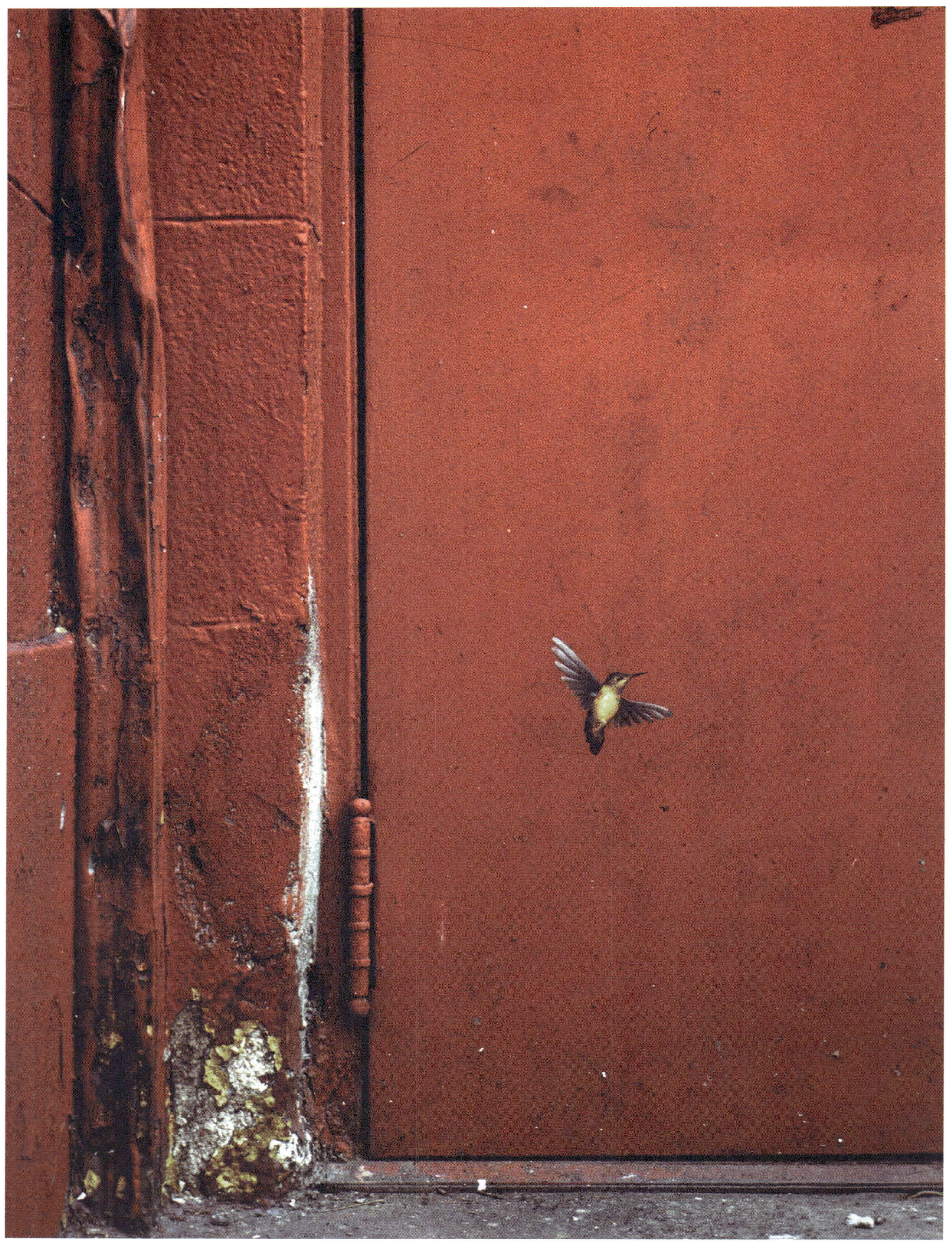

4TH ST. BETWEEN BOWERY AND 2ND AVE., NYC., 1979. // Acrylic on metal door.

INTERVIEW WITH DAN WITZ
by Marc and Sara Schiller of the

WOOSTER COLLECTIVE

When you were a kid did you have a black sketchbook?

I did! It went everywhere with me, along with my rapidograph pen. I drew compulsively in styles shamelessly derivative of R. Crumb and Raw Comix. Nothing special. I don't remember being very impressed with myself as a prodigy or anything, but I was the class artist by default. My dream was to move to New York City to be poor and struggle and find my dark side and meet the right people and make a brief meteoric career out of my suffering. Brief because I was going to die young.

You've said your creativity's connected to your rebelliousness

Well… I had this really normal, healthy childhood. Nice parents, safe home, supported. A nightmare. The worst background possible for any kind of artist. Starting around fourteen, I began rebelling, I sought out extreme situations—the stranger the better. I thought you had to have felt real pain to be authentic. So I cultivated my dark side in the hopes of making me a more interesting person, and a more interesting artist—and, maybe, attract some dark, interesting women. It wasn't until much later though that I actually did my Robert Johnson going-down-to-the-crossroads thing.

I guess I was afraid of being too ordinary. Too well adjusted. Too susceptible to the traps of comfort and security. In the early 70s that kind of apathy was widely perceived as the cause of the world's problems. It was how the Vietnam war got started, what made people sleepwalk through life and why the world was so fucked up. Art, being an artist, being awake, was going to be my rebellion against this state of affairs.

(I thought) I needed to burn that middle class midwestern programming out of me. Scorched earth policy. Drugs and drink. Romanticizing debauchery. I read Bukowski and Kerouac, William Burroughs, Hunter S. Thompson, and listened to Jim Morrison and the Velvet Underground; I idolized dead and dissipated rock stars (Jimi, Janis…), worshipped movies like Clockwork Orange and Apocalypse Now. Anything nihilistic or anarchic appealed to me. I wore black. My hair, my speech—everything about me was annoying to older people.

Also, during this time—this is embarrassing—my friends and I adopted a motto taken from a beer ad: "You only go around once in life, so grab for all the gusto you can." Schlitz, I think it was. Embarassing, not just because of that word, 'gusto', but because that's basically how I made all my decisions for the next 20 years.

When did you get your first tattoo?

17.

What was it?

A star.

A star? Does that have any meaning?

It meant I had a tattoo. In 1974 having a tattoo—even a tiny little star—was unusual. At least where I came from.

What was the influence RISD had on you?

Coming from suburban Chicago, it was a shock. The Eastern private-school culture was hugely intimidating. Everything midwestern about me was wrong—my hair, my shoes, my taste. Eager, wide-eyed me, I liked Magritte and The Grateful Dead. I wore hiking boots. Brown hiking boots. Every kid growing up in America deals with taste snobbery, but this was combative. Eventually though I had to admit they had a point. The Sex Pistols and Andy Warhol were more relevant; hippie times were over. I began to understand that style wasn't necessarily a bad thing. And rebellion was sexy. So it was quick: I cut my hair, got some black boots, and adjusted my taste in music.

Art students should know everything new that's happening. That's their job. In such a world, your identity is defined by your opinions: nothing is worse than being uninformed. Peer group scorn, or the mere risk of it, was a formative experience for me.

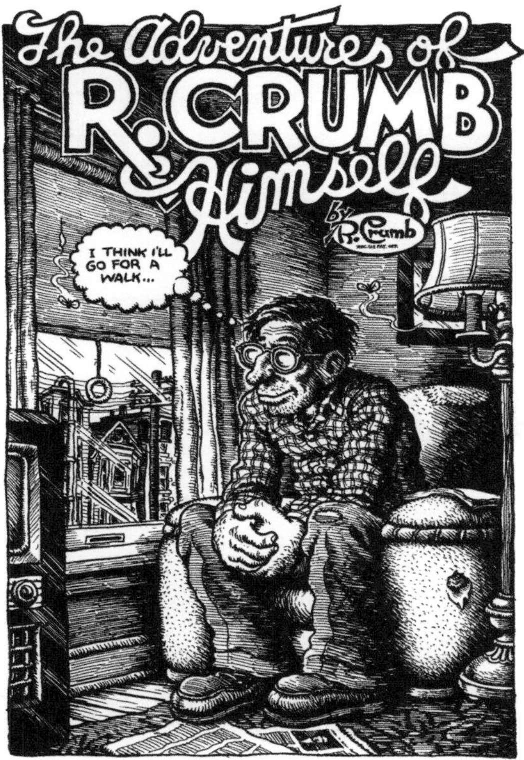

ABOVE:

THE ADVENTURES OF R.CRUMB // © Robert Crumb, 2009.

Was art school still something you were rebelling against or a place you could express yourself?

Both. Art schools back then were more anti-establishment, less explicitly about careers. Being a loser was considered acceptable, even interesting. Art was still [viewed as] an essential part of the social fabric, an agent for change. Artists had a social responsibility. There was this almost religious belief that Cubism and Modernism had changed the world, painting had freed something; art was a potent force, capable of influencing the public. It sounds quaint now, but I believed that pictures on a wall could actually change the way everyone thought.

The big discovery during this period was that there were mysteries hidden below the surface of everyday life, forces of subtle power. It was an artist's job to bring these to light, and these universal truths would re-connect us with ourselves and help the world become a better place. Anyway, I bought it.

Besides the politics, did you learn drawing and the basics?

Definitely. And photography. And carpentry. And oil painting technique. And color theory. And anatomy. A lot of useful things.

So, if this was the era of conceptual art, how did your influence move from R. Crumb and Raw Comix to painterly realism? How and why did your technique get so realistic, so technical?

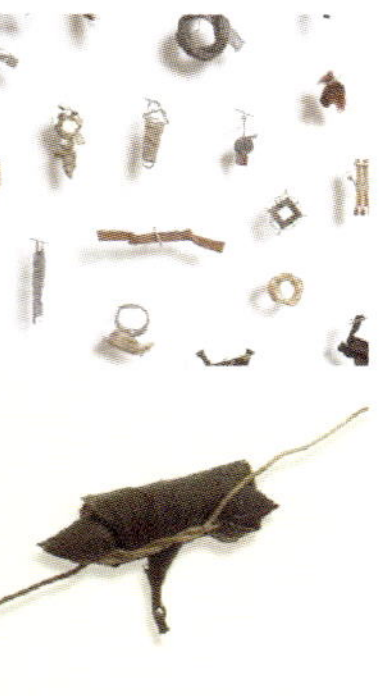

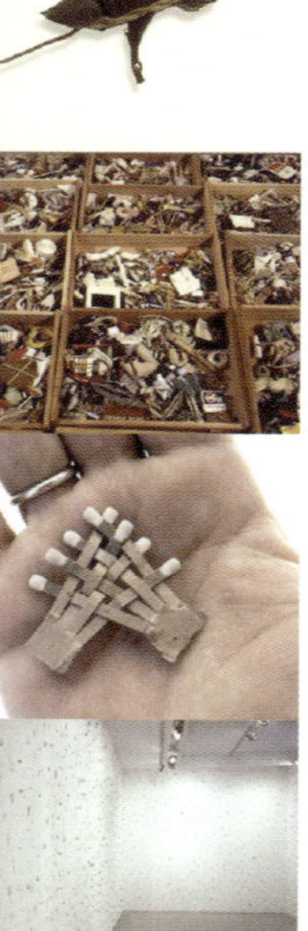

This was later, after I moved to New York: I was at Cooper Union but spending more time exploring the city, in bars and clubs, hanging around the art–punk scene. That group despised successful artists. "Posers", they called them. Personally, still wanting to be successful, I tried to keep an open mind. I did my time in museums and video rooms. Mostly, though, I found the art of the time unrewarding and dull. Apparently the goal was to be removed from ordinary life, to be beyond regular people's access, and if you wanted the entrance code you had to work really hard to get it. Why? I understood reductionism but what was wrong with letting people in? What good is art that makes people feel unworthy and left out? I still don't know. This was the beginning of a life-long aversion to anything exclusionary. Or boring. Especially boring. For me, that was the worst thing art could be. If you couldn't dance to it (metaphorically, I mean) then fuck it.

And, since that was the status quo, I was happy to rebel against it. Realism, accessibility seemed really seditious at the time. That suited me fine.

Mostly, I just wanted to make the kind of art I wanted to see. I look back and see that developing my own style had a lot to do with rejection – rebelling against whatever there was, a reaction... Mostly I defined myself by what I didn't want to be.

When did the street start influencing you?

Back then, Providence was the costume jewelry capital of the world. Walking around I'd find all this tiny metal stuff laying on the ground—fittings, ball bearings, odd, tiny, inscrutable things—robot flotsam. When my pockets got full, I'd set up these ordered displays on window ledges or other flat surfaces. Carefully, like in a museum cabinet or store window, I'd line the objects up or make a regimented little circle or something and leave it behind. I don't think it ever occurred to me to photograph it. I liked thinking about people coming upon them and pausing, and being mildly puzzled for a moment or two. This was also the first street art I made in New York when I transferred to Cooper Union. I still do this by the way. The stuff is mostly plastic now, which although more colorful, isn't as much fun.

Right. So you moved to New York. When was this?

1978.

What were your first impressions of New York?

Terror. The black-out and riots had just happened. If you lived outside NYC back then, you thought you'd be mugged the minute you got to town, that they'd steal the gold fillings from your teeth before you got out of Port Authority.

How was Cooper Union?

Ok. Good, I guess. Free. You've got to like that.

It's very prestigious—

Yeah, which has never meant a thing for me. For awhile after I graduated I kept an updated resume until I realized no one looked at those things. Interesting group of kids there, though. That was valuable. It was kind of a prep program for the art business, a mini-microcosm of what was waiting for us out there. These were ambitious, knowledgeable, savvy careerists. Way out of my league.

Did it push you more?

No. Or, yes, in a reactive way. I mean, I was intimidated by all the New Yorkers with their big vocabularies and cold shoulders. This was before the days when tolerance was fashionable in the art world. Or pluralism. In the painting department, you were either in their club—by then it was macho neo-expressionism—or you were locked out, invisible. Naturally, me being me, I became the opposite of a macho expressionist, painting with tiny brushes and Flemish detail. I joked at the time that I couldn't help it: I was genetically cursed with good small-motor control.

There were so many amazing things about being in New York though. A few weeks after I arrived, a girl from school invited me over to her loft in Soho. I'd never seen one of these before and instantly decided that was how I wanted to live. She put on Steve Reich's Music for 18 Musicians and this just totally blew me away. One of the strangest, most beautiful

LEFT:

GATHERING DUST // © Donald Lipski

OPPOSITE PAGE:

FOUND OBJECTS. // Re-creation of early 70s installation.

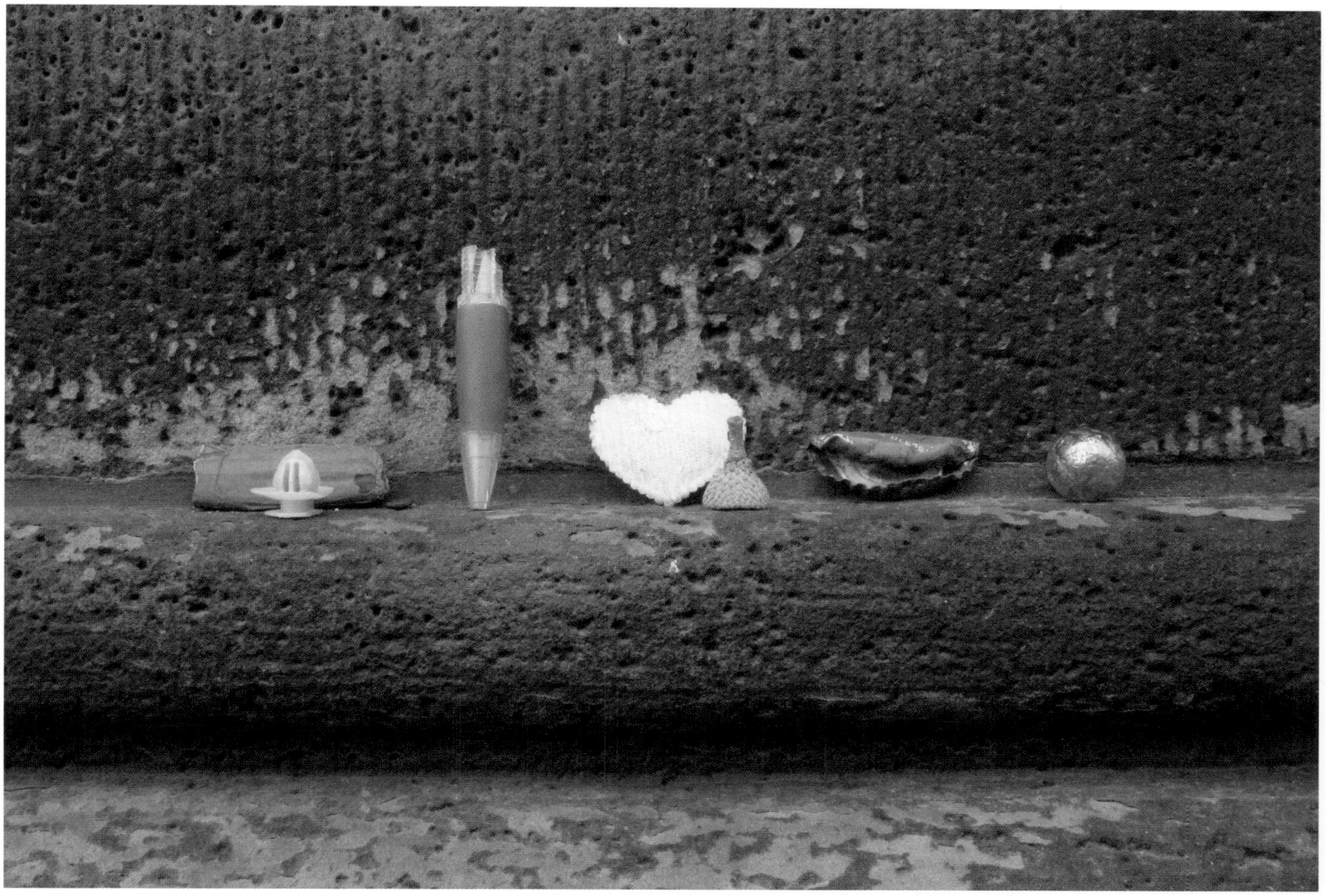

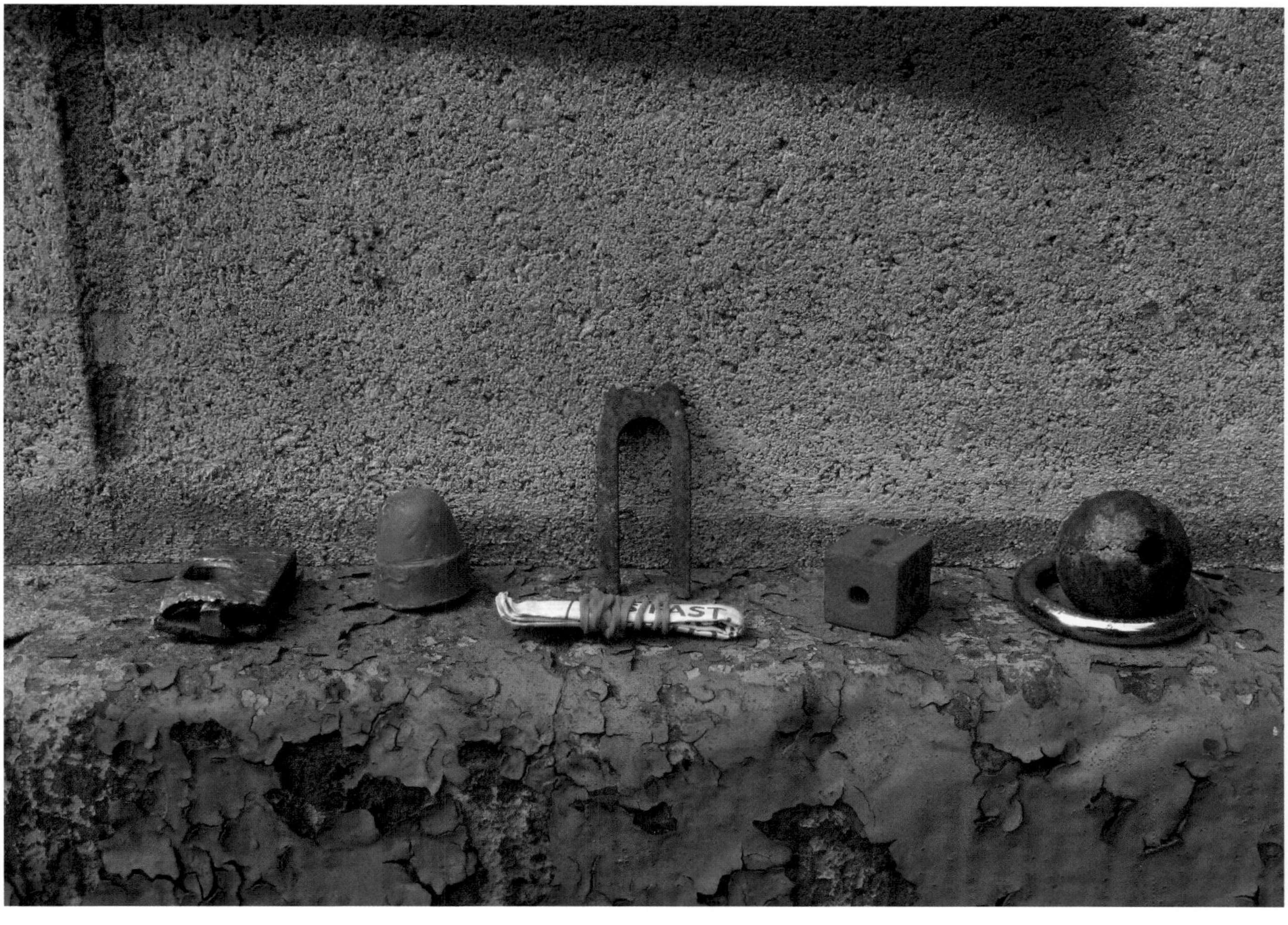

things I'd ever heard. A real goosebump experience. Totally opened something in me.

What else was inspiring you at the time? How did you get into the punk scene?

In the galleries, the ruling cabal at the time was still the minimalists, a bunch of older white dudes, Carl Andre, Donald Judd—

You didn't respect that stuff?

I tried to. Robert Ryman, Agnes Martin, Richard Serra. If nothing else, they're extreme, which I tried to like, but for the most part the minimal corporate art of the time left me cold. I'd go up to the Whitney or someplace and the only thing I'd really enjoy was looking out the window at the city. I did admire Brice Marden a bit but none of that dry reductionist stuff reflected anything that was going on in our lives. The Lower East Side, the dying city, the crime and drugs, the homeless people screaming their heads off, the graffitied trains careening by, the kids break-dancing, spinning on their heads, the vacant eyed punks walking around all strung out. I mean, trash fires, black eyes, torn fishnet stockings, rubble—all this seemed more relevant to my life. And definitely more fun.

You've mentioned that the cold post modern architecture of Cooper Union inspired you—

Yes, but not in a positive way... Cooper Union was not an especially warm and welcoming place. Painters were kept on one floor, graphic designers on another. Photographers, architects, really interesting folks, all stayed on their own turfs, no one really hung out. I was new to the city and everyone seemed so stiff and wary of each other. Also, the school itself had just been renovated in the highest post modern manner. A show piece--blazing fluorescent lights, intense angles, dehumanizing grids... theoretical architecture at its most sterile and alienating. No surprise but it was impossible to feel comfortable there. In art school, you should feel free to make a mess, to make mistakes, to be un-self conscious. But not in those studios. It was deadly.

Also I was pretty sure nobody liked me and I began to get resentful. I was living in an unheated loft with a couple of punk bands, and—it's such a garret cliché—but I was perpetually broke, cold, and lonely.

One night, I was in my studio drinking, smoking, angry, thinking, "Fuck this place, fuck these people. They're all such dicks—

Were you getting more tattoos?

No, but I had a motorcycle, which seemed to annoy everyone. And I was semi-punk, which was –hard to believe—threatening. It was ironic. I mean, the school was on St. Marks Place. CBGB's, the Mudd Club, the No New York bands -- history was being made all around them, but they were stuck in their Neo whatever-it-was-ism: I don't know, Jism-ism... Julian Schnabel was big, the 80's uber-egos ruled, and since I didn't paint that way,—the way everyone should paint—I was out, invisible, so I just said, "Fuck it, I'm gonna set this place on fire and everyone, all the stuck up New York assholes will go running out and maybe they'll finally talk to each other." So I got a palette with big blobs of yellow, orange, and red acrylic paint on it and I went up and down the back stairs painting these fast, loosely brushstroked fires. To be honest, by the time I was finished I was pretty drunk and I don't remember much about it except someone told on me and I got caught. I came into school the next day and found out I'd been expelled. At first the school officials wanted me to personally paint it out but then they decided better and had the maintenance crew do it. Which gave every one at the school an extra few days to see it.

It probably would've blown over but the guy who was acting director of the whole school was also the Dean of the Architecture Department—this very famous architectural theorist. One of those academic types who'd never had anything built. Except the renovation of Cooper Union. And he flipped out that I was desecrating his creation. Apparently, others had been grumbling about the de-humanizing effect of the building and my little stunt was the last straw, the final insult, and he lost his temper.

On this particular day I had my critical theory class, the 'an-aesthetics of boredom' I called it, where we dissected the most tedious hidden subtext of anything anyone was calling art that day. Hungover, freaked out, and, as usual, having nothing art-smart or art-school-hip to offer, just realist paintings, I decided to make the fires my piece for the "crit". The class dutifully trooped out into the stairwell and, to my surprise, everyone was into it. Suddenly, hidden subtexts I'd never thought of, and definitely hadn't planned, were getting gushing reviews. I got all this attention. Girls started noticing me. And since my expulsion was threatening to become a cause that other people dissatisfied with the working environment could rally around, I was quickly re-instated. Lucky coincidences I know, but the attention was a real revelation to me.

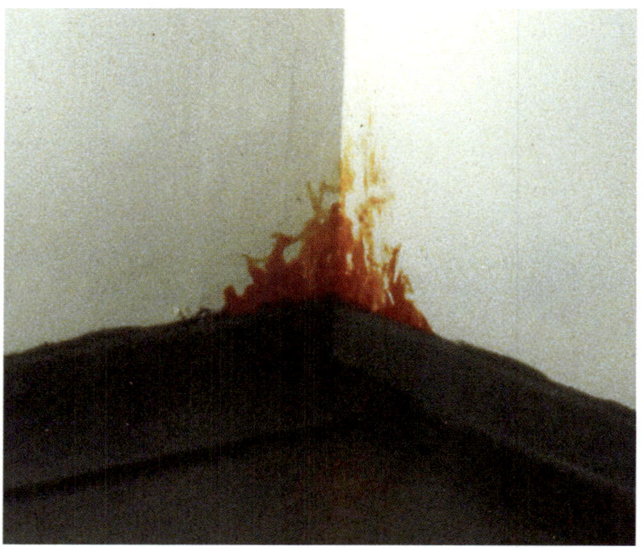

FIRES, COOPER UNION, NYC., 1978. // Acrylic paint on wall. My first public art. I painted a series of fires up and down the cold post- modern stairways at Cooper Union. A typical drunken art school prank, I figured, but I got into a lot of trouble which resulted in a lot of attention. Which really got my attention.

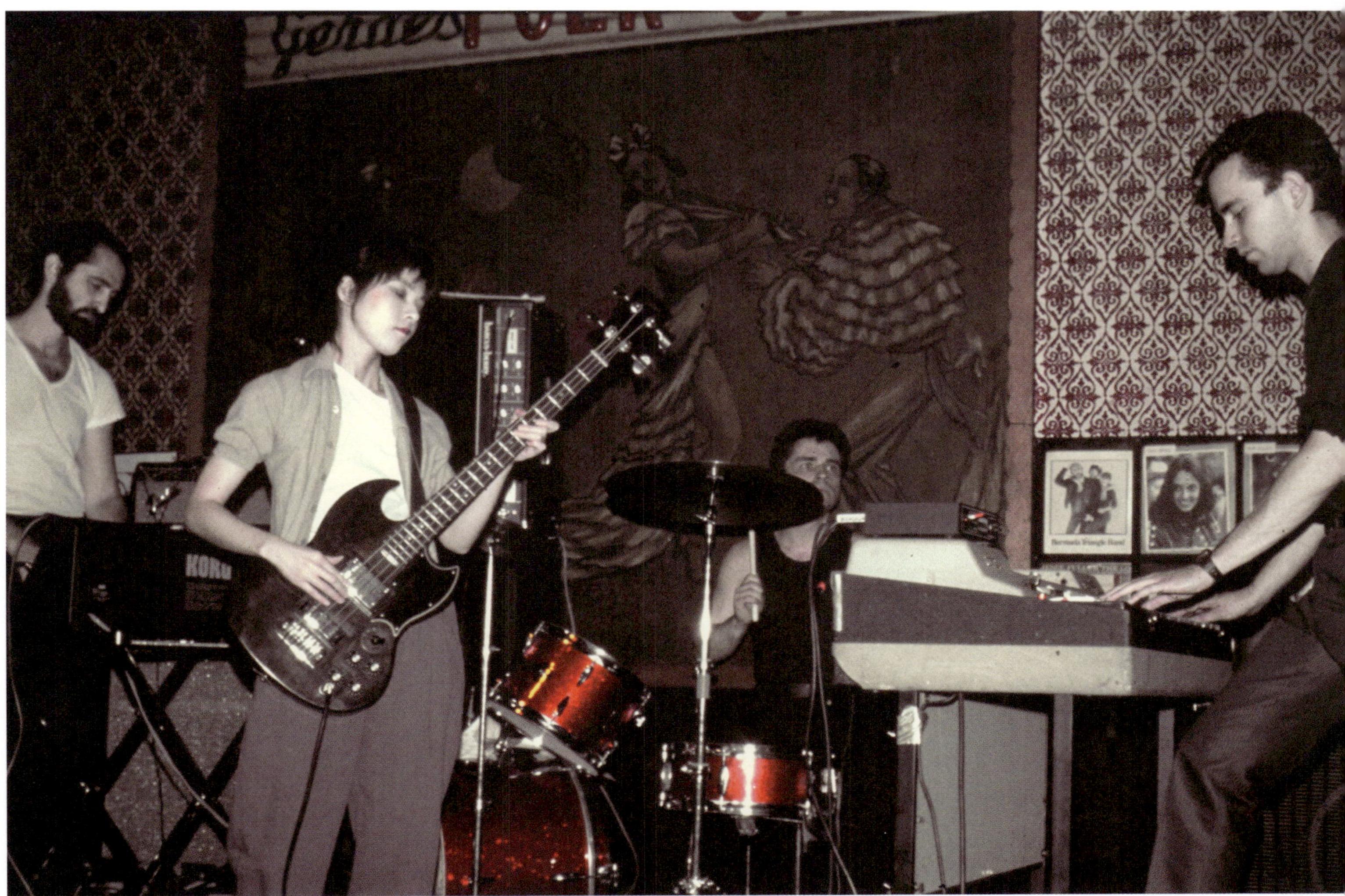

This was the early 80's?

Yeah. After I got out of school I pretty much concentrated on survival and starting a band.

Did you go see a band at that time that was so memorable, so inspiring that you decided to get up and do it yourself?

Yeah, at the time the No New York bands were starting to peak. Mars, DNA, the Contortions, Static, The Lounge Lizards. Theoretical Girls. Their ruling aesthetic was to be completely original, to never do anything anyone had ever heard or seen before. Also, since there was no chance any of them would ever get rich or famous, since there was no product being sold other than the moment, it was largely incorruptible, and very liberating to someone like me. That scene really helped me to see past my middle-class programming, especially the need to make good, and please the people in charge.

Rauschenberg once said he wanted his stuff to be somewhere in the space between art and life. These bands were actually doing that. And I wanted to get in on it.

What was the name of your band?

I was in a few. The first, Civil Defense, played out only once, at a loft party. We knew someone so our picture ended up on the cover of the East Village Eye, which totally freaked us out. We immediately started arguing and broke up. Later, my main project was EQ'd with my wife and friends of ours.

In the downtown scene back then, there were these really talented people--Rhys Chatham, Laurie Anderson, Elliot Sharp, and Glenn Branca--who used the local bands as a talent pool—or, in my case, considering my lack of musical talent, more of a labor pool. Anyway, they tapped the scene for musicians to play in their various ensembles and projects. Sometimes it even paid. Most of my friends played with someone. The guy who I admired the most was Glenn Branca. I ended up playing in a couple of his ensembles.

And painting the whole time?

Yes. That's right after I did the first big street project, the hummingbirds.

EQ'D PLAYING AT FOLK CITY, NYC., 1982. // The Bass player is my ex–wife.

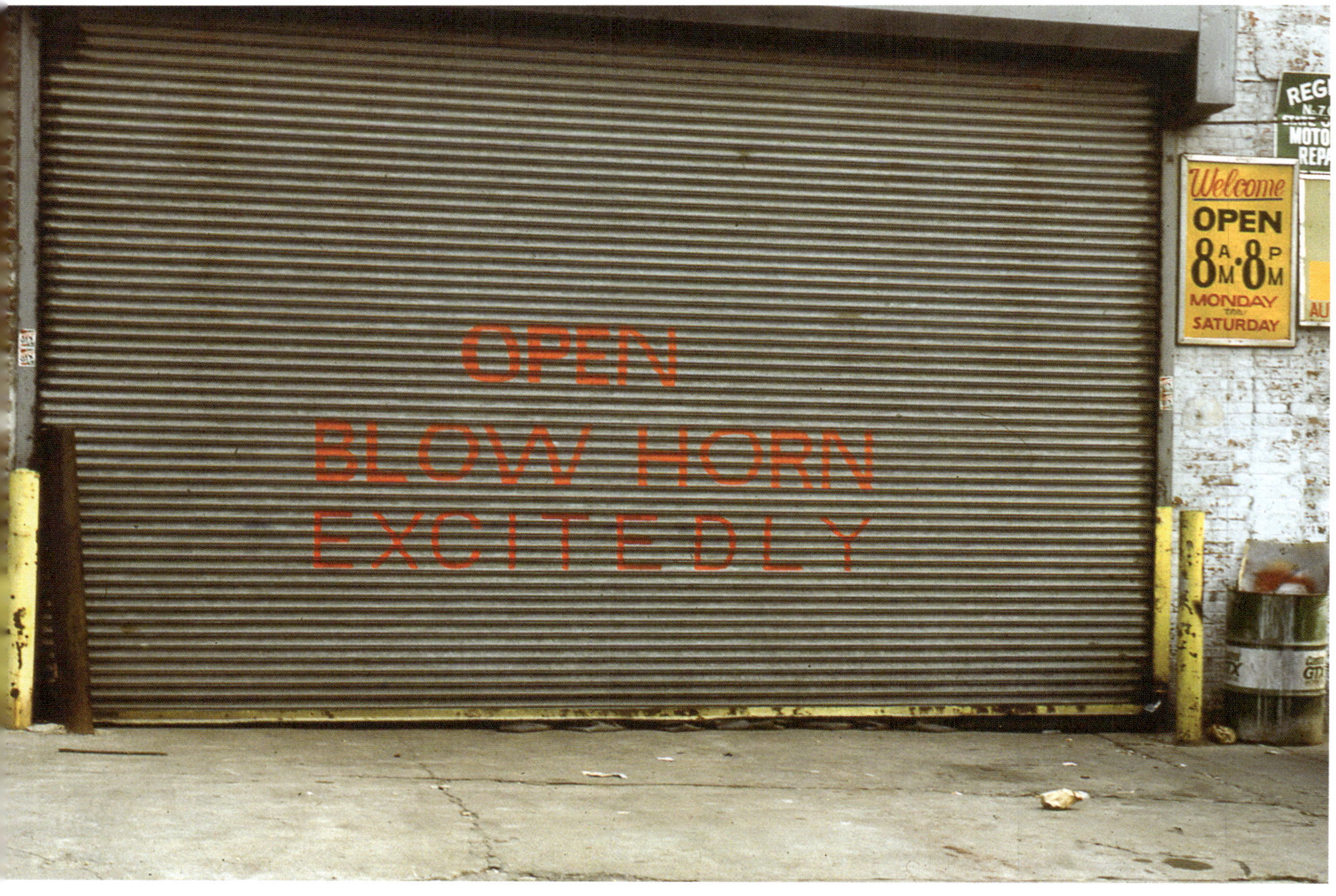

How did that develop?

I'd been doing those little ledge accumulations, the found objects. Walking for hours every day to save subway fare. Somewhere along the way I decided I wanted a tag.

Was working on the street illegal back then?

Definitely.

So there was still the risk and excitement?

For sure. Probably less the danger of getting arrested and more about getting roughed up or mugged. Random violence was common back then. Something we don't have to deal with as much today.

Did you ever get messed with by street people?

No. Close. Stuff was often happening nearby but I always managed to avoid getting involved.

How?

I'm not sure. Maybe because I've always been a kind of grungy guy. Muggers don't seem to pick me. Also, I'd travel to painting locations on my motorcycle and sit on my helmet while painting. Believe it or not, I mean I'm clearly not like this, but having a bike, being a 'biker', is an effective deterrent to predators.

And the cops? They wouldn't arrest you?

I suppose they would if they were in the mood. If you were in their face too brazen or defacing city property they'd haul you in. But, back then, they'd prioritize, they'd make judgement calls. A white guy painting a hummingbird on an acceptably decrepit surface wasn't usually important enough to make them get out of the car. I learned to show them pictures of birds I'd done, and a lot of times they'd even be, like, "cool, keep going". That really taught me a lot. How to find the outer limit of what I can get away with. I've worked that way ever since and somehow I've never been arrested.

LOWER WEST SIDE OF MANHATTAN, 1986. // Enamel on metal gate. I added the "excitedly."

You were doing them downtown?

Yes. Basically in a circle around Soho. That was where the galleries were so I didn't put any there. I wanted them to be in regular neighborhoods so real people would see them. Art types in Soho not being real people.

Were any of your friends doing street art?

Not really. Except for punk band posters. That was a big influence on me. Graffiti was getting talked about a lot. I liked it but was never really interested in trying it—the tagging concept was interesting though. I liked thinking of my hummingbirds as an anti-tag. This was something that was three inches square and took two hours to finish; like portraits they were unbelievably difficult to pull off, to bring to life, and hardly anyone would see them—and the people who would see them probably wouldn't be useful to my "career". That twisted kind of dynamic really satisfied me.

And what did the hummingbird represent?

Well, most importantly it hovered. It had a formal reason to be vibrating there. That was why I initially chose it. But then I found out more about them and it became a creature I could identify with. Fierce, elusive, high metabolisms...Also, my hummingbirds were anatomically correct but the color was a total improvisation, a response to the environment, which was a very satisfying painterly experience for me sitting out there. Also, it's kind of—if not exactly corny—then definitely anti-hip. I mean, little hummingbirds? They're so likeable, they're actually pretty--which had to be the most offensive thing art could be at that time. (Maybe, still?) In any case, the little birds fulfilled my need to be in reaction against the art establishment of the time.

How many hummingbirds did you do?

Around 50.

And did people notice them?

Yes. To my amazement. It became a kind of a word of mouth thing, but the Village Voice ran a thing, and so did NY magazine, so people knew about it.

Who else was doing stuff outside then? This is before Keith Haring?

Yes. The only street art I knew about was Charles Simonds' Little People Villages on the Lower East Side. That's an underknown piece. Basquiat was doing Samo stuff around the same time but he was considered more of a graffiti artist. I wasn't aware of John Ahearn, Rigoberto Torres, and John Fekner, older guys working up in the Bronx, until a few years after I painted the birds. I'd definitely seen the aphorism posters by Jenny Holzer; and I was very aware of Gordon Matta Clark's abandoned building interventions.. This isn't street art but I had postcards up on my wall of Sandy Skoglund's Radioactive Cats and Donald Lipski's Gathering Dust piece, which I'd seen at Artist's Space. Two pieces that influenced me a lot.

So the birds were the first thing you actually painted out doors?

The first thing of mine. I'd worked for a billboard painter before this. So I already knew how much I enjoyed being outside painting. Working as a sign painter's helper was as important a part of my art schooling as Cooper Union. My boss, Gonzalez, was probably the best technical draftsman I ever met. A natural eye. A genius. Way beyond me or anyone I've met since. To him art was silly. Effete. Realistic painting was something you figured out how to do fast and efficiently, to get the maximum effect. Time was money. A lesson I consolidated later by copying Crananch and Bosch and other 15th and 16th century masters. Not to be too precious. Not to let me get in front of the effect the painting's supposed to have. When I get that way I can still feel Gonzalez smirking over my shoulder.

And these pranks, these one-off pieces, you were doing these all along?

Yes. That was when I was touring with Branca. I couldn't sustain big projects so I'd go out and do small intervention type things. I was just beginning to understand that I was making photographs, so I would go out with a camera, careful not to be a "photographer" though. Making objects for consumption felt inappropriate, hypocritical. The photographs were, and still are, souvenirs of the real piece.

Tell us about your first show.

My first show was at an alternative performance space my band played at a lot. Inroads. I knew the guy who booked the bands so he let me put up my Birds of Manhattan photographs

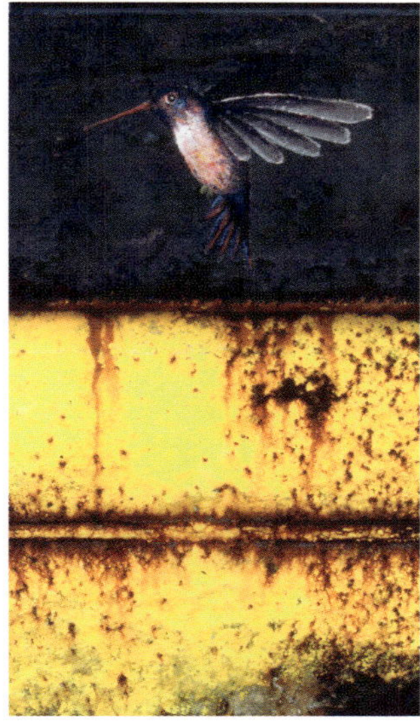

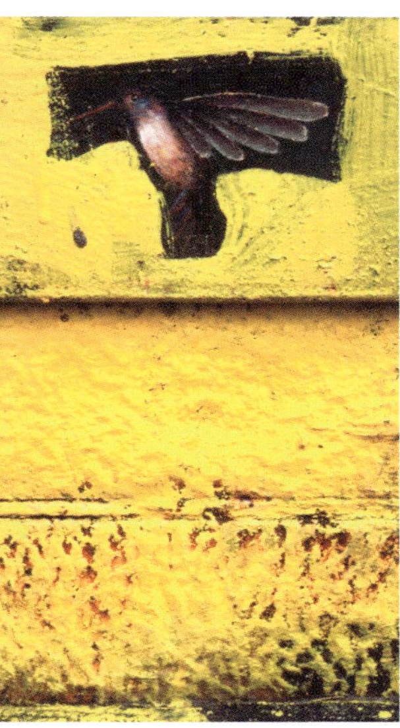

PEARL ST. BETWEEN GOLD & WATER, NYC. // Before and After (two weeks later).

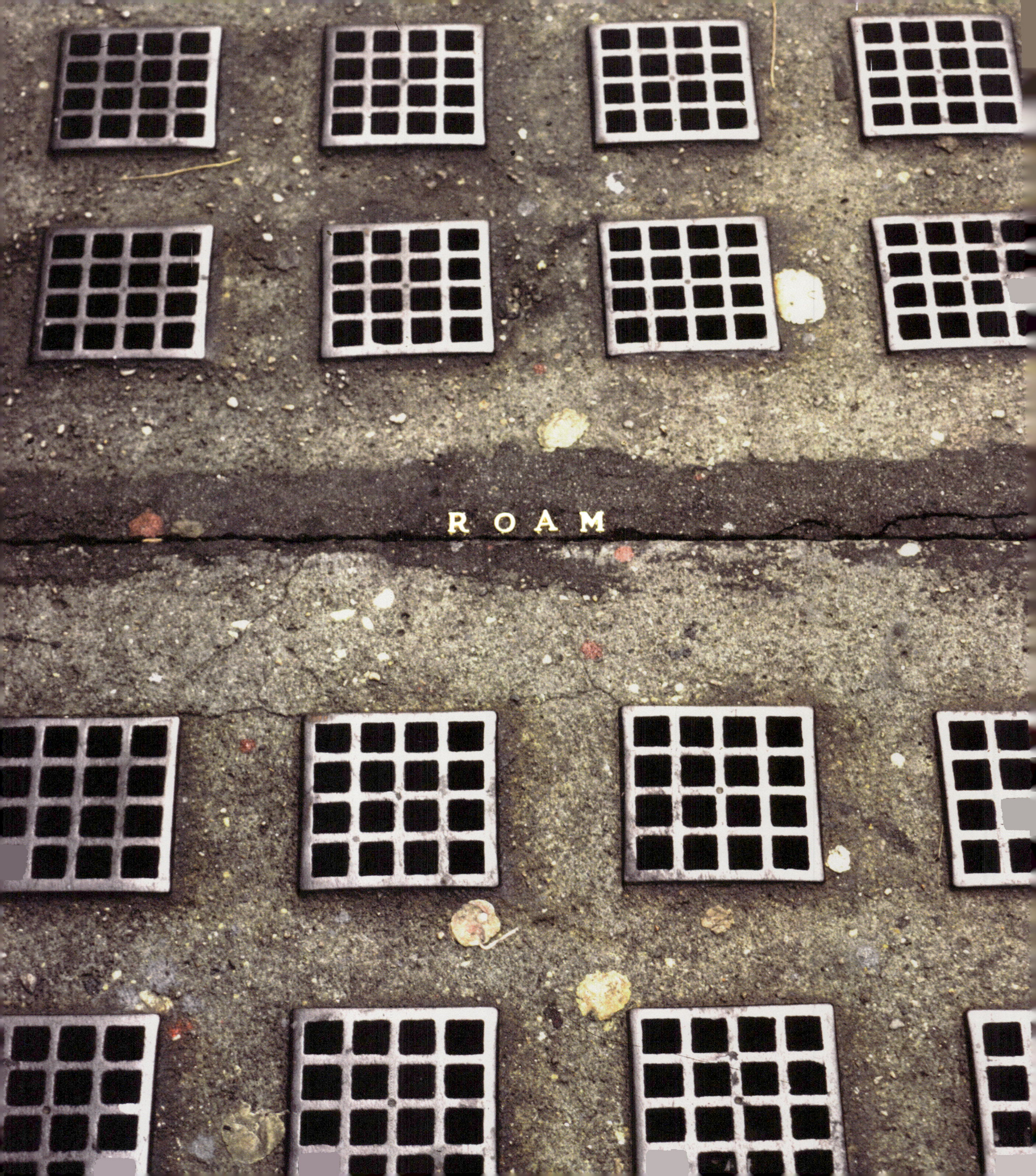
ROAM

in the lobby. The first show of my paintings was at a bar on Avenue A. The hand portraits. A kid I knew from Club 57, Carlo McCormick, came to the opening and brought an art dealer he was working for, Barry Blinderman, who was this reputable art dealer by day but a rock club dude by night. He'd seen me play. We hit it off and eventually he offerred me a show in his Soho gallery, Semaphore.

So what was the significance of the hands?

When I was touring Europe, as crazy as it was, I used to slip away to the art museums, the pre 20th century ones. I began having relationships with the old masters, a mental museum which I keep to this day. Maybe it had something to do with the contrast of my death-noise life style by night, but the light, the space, the astonishing quietude and duration of reality in those paintings...even hung over and sleep deprived as I was (or maybe because)--it was a revelation to me. I became convinced that the truth for me lay somewhere in the fusion of the two worlds.

Giotto, I remember in Florence, really affected me. The hand portraits came from that. Simple gestural, architectonic. For my portraits, I used artist's hands, my friends who were artists posed for the photos I worked from. Portraits because I think people look exactly like their hands. (And their shoes. The worn-in ones.)

And the old white guys with their shirts off?

Yeah. Still fucking hilarious. Not one of my better-selling series.

Were you still rebelling at this point?

Yes. Well, I think I was hoping to outsmart my self-sabotaging ways by making objects that were both rebellious and consumable. Something I've never had much luck at.

How did the shows go?

Okay. Nothing stellar. I did ok. Not enough to quit my day job. I never really hit it too big in the East Village scene. Even though it was pluralism personified, somehow I managed to stay on the fringe. The real story behind the East Village era was that it was more a social phenomenon than anything else, and I think my personality was a problem. Arrogant and thin skinned. Fearing the people I most wanted acceptance from, resenting them because of their power over me.

So your street art was mainly pranks at this point?

Yes. I was so overwhelmed with the bands and the full time job and getting evicted again and the shows and the paintings, I'd go out a couple times a summer and do some pranks.

POEM DOWN BROADWAY, 1980. // This one image is taken from the series. Metal letters, hammered into asphalt.

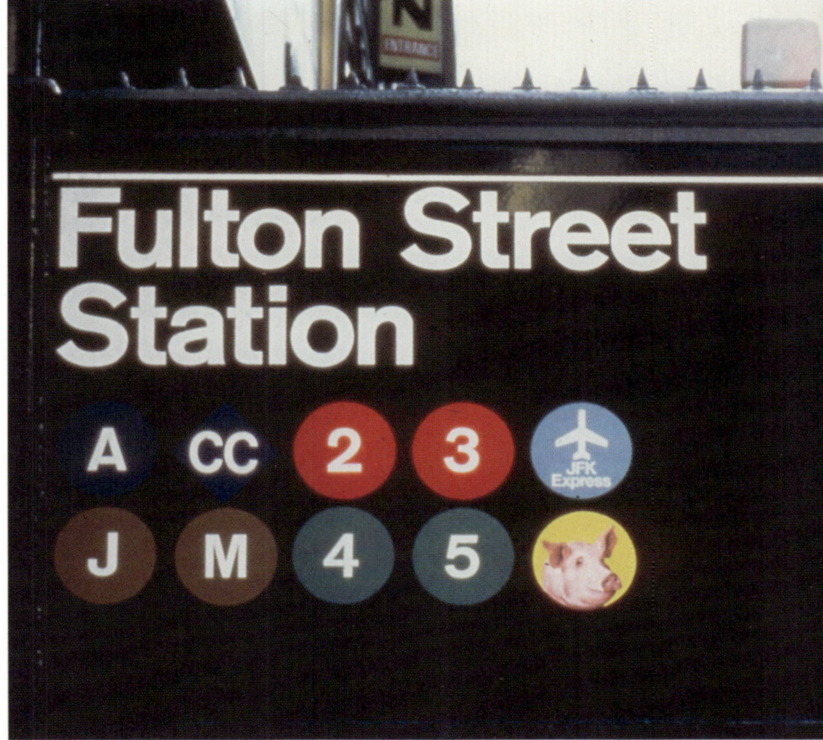

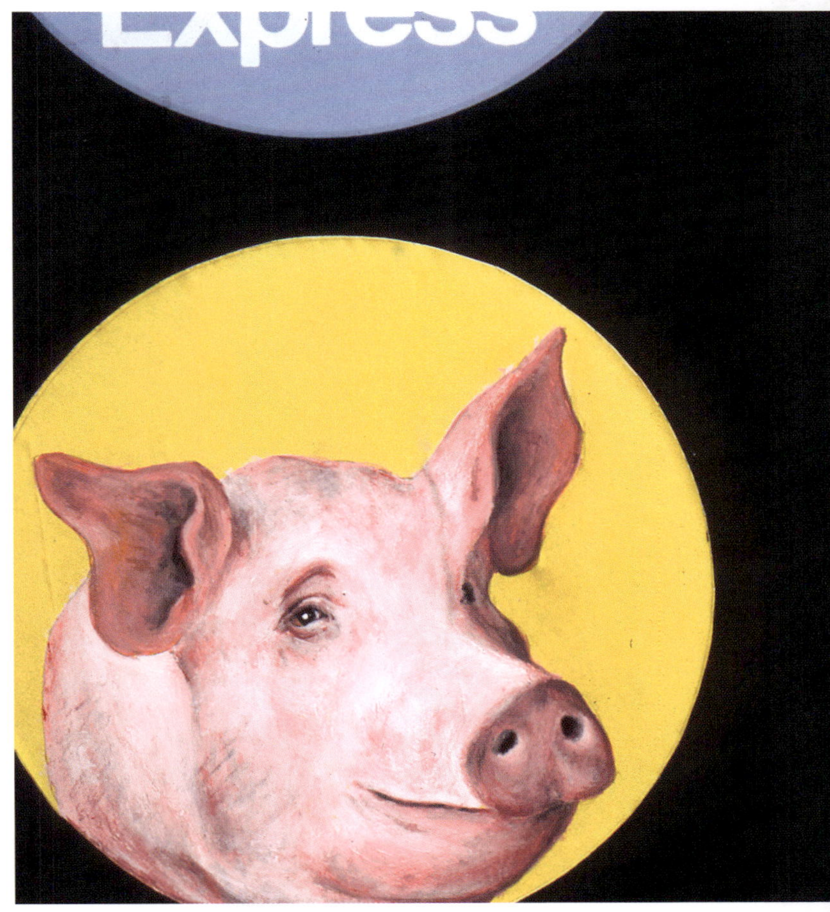

NYC., 1980. // Acrylic on sticker paper affixed to metal sign. A birthday present for my (now former) wife. She commuted from Fulton street station. The first instance of me working off site on sticker paper.

Were Keith Haring and those guys doing stuff by then?

Yes. One day I was painting uptown and this woman walked by and kinda huffily asked me, 'Who do you think you are, Keith Haring?" My first reaction was a decision not to paint uptown, then I began to wonder if my days of doing street art might be over.

So what kept you painting through all that? It seems like you were doing really well at music. Why didn't you just become a musician?

I sucked. Admittedly this was an asset in that scene, but it became pretty clear I was in danger of becoming the thing I resented most in the art world: mediocre but well connected. Knowing I was really a painter and this was a fodder phase or something, I accepted it. I remember playing somewhere, Pyramid Club on a Saturday night I think it was, and it dawned on me that I was an entertainer, I was in show business—and a bit of a hack. Honestly, maybe if there was more of a living in it, I would've stuck with it like a day job, but, fortunately, there wasn't. The truth is, I wasn't interested in music in the overall sense, in the obsessive way I was with art and art history. People I've met who are really good at what they do often seem to posess an encyclopedic knowledge of everything about their medium, they see themselves as the logical continuum of that time line, they know and are constantly gathering more information about every aspect of their field of choice. The canon, the anti-canon, trivia, anecdotes, etc. A couple of guys I played with in Branca's band were like that about music, dedicated, obsessed: they ended up forming Sonic Youth. I'm naturally that way about painting and visual art. But not music. For me being a musician was mostly about fun. I will say, performing on stage is still one of the most intense experiences I've ever had.

So then you started putting the words into the hot tar. The Poem Down Broadway. How did this idea come about?

Walking. Most of my ideas come when I'm walking around the city. After 30 years I've got a story for every street in Manhattan. I'm serious. Every street. Strangely though, whenever I'm walking along with someone and tell them this, they never ask me the story about where we are... Anyway, having a dog and walking her three times each day has been a huge help to my thinking.

For that piece the idea was to make a kind of automatic writing poem on Broadway from 96th Street to the Battery. I think I was interested in DuChamp's or John Cage's modernistic rejection strategies. Allowing chance to cancel critical intervention. Whatever. Maybe I'd been reading art magazines. It's funny. Even though I fancied myself some kind of art terrorist, using beauty and poetry as rebellion etc. I see how I secretly wanted to be accepted, to be allowed at the party. These days, I realize how lucky I was that no one was interested and that I was allowed to keep developing on my own.

What happened to the poem?

I lost it. Probably cause it wasn't very good. Suspending critical intervention can be pretty dull it turns out. What did happen, the unforeseen thing, the 'lucky' surprise about the whole project, wasn't my original concept, but the documentation photos. Since my pieces were meant to be experienced on the street I'd always tried to underplay the aesthetic object of the photos. Another received notion from art magazines, probably. But I noticed that every time I went to pick up my slides I'd get really nervous. There was no way of avoiding it. These were photographs. Like nothing I'd ever seen either, like these images were really mine.

Unintended results are always a good sign, I think. Every project I've done that's been successful has had this element of accidental revelation: a change of course that, looking back, totally feels like a lucky break. I know that platitude about the harder you work the luckier you get probably applies, but it feels more like something random and fragile, some slippery, elusive x-factor like "inspiration". I know artists who allow room for this in their conceptual process; they'll trust that more will be revealed by the process. I can't. I just try not to let fear make any decisions.

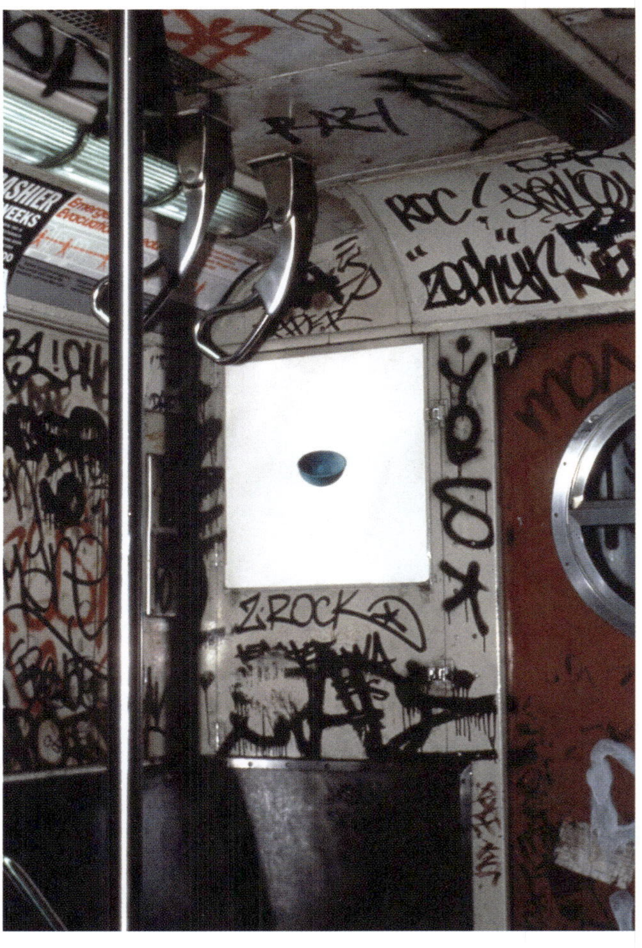

1983. // I'd been taking the cardboard from these ad spaces and using the blank sides to paint on. Eventually it occured to me to put some back up.

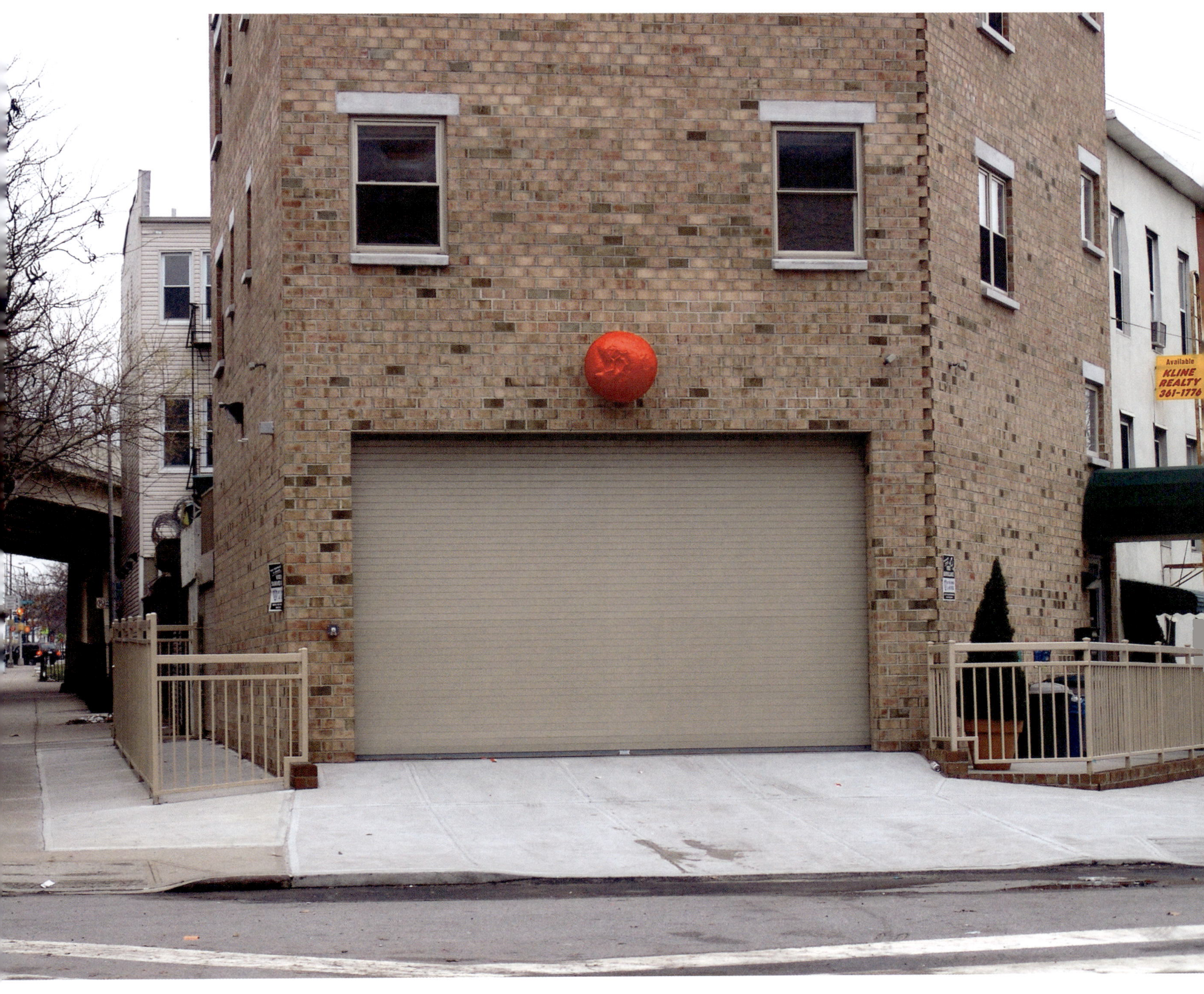

RICHARDSON ST., GREENPOINT, BROOKLYN, 2005–2006. // My first annual New Year's Eve prank.

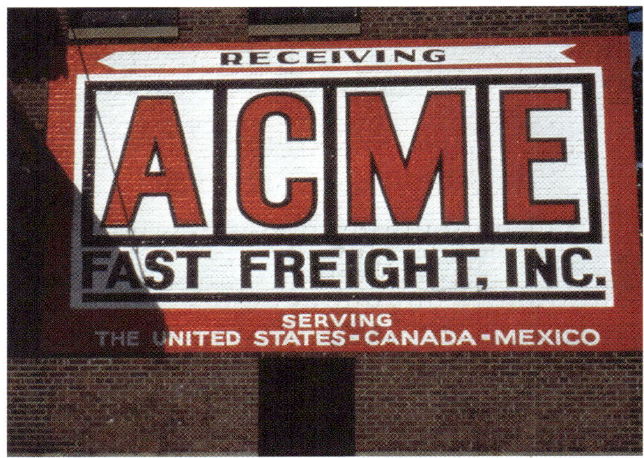

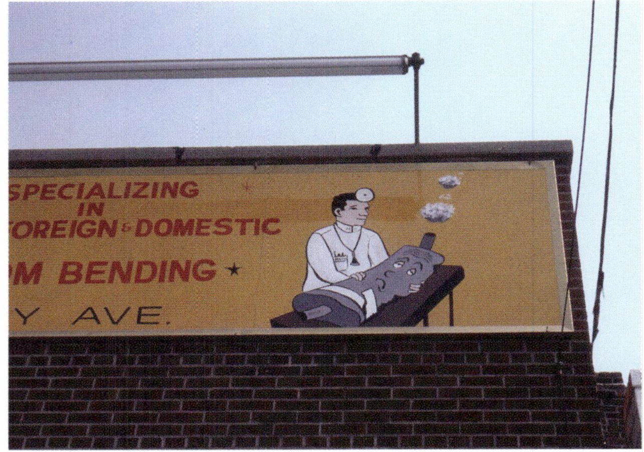

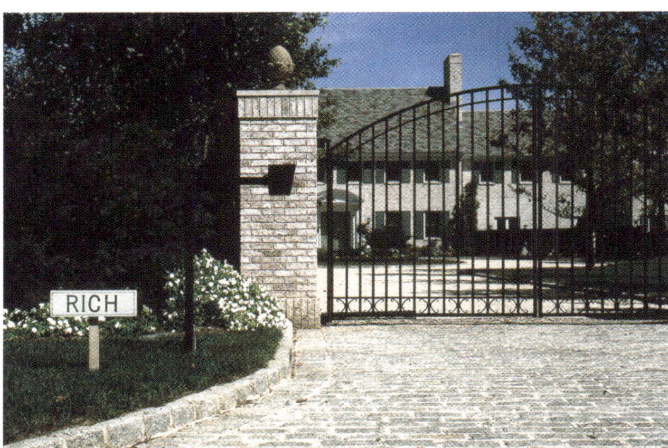

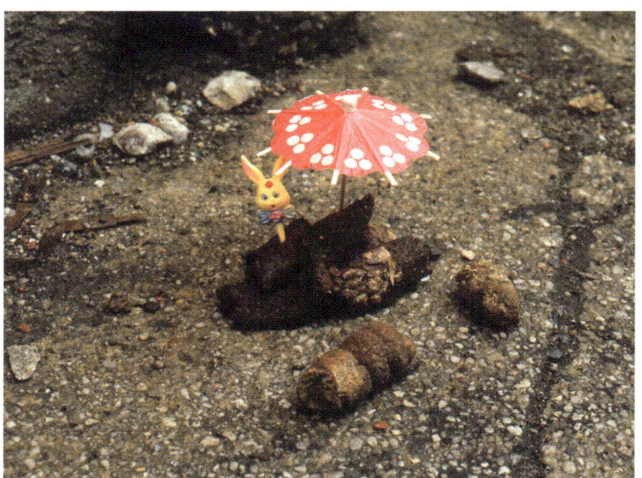

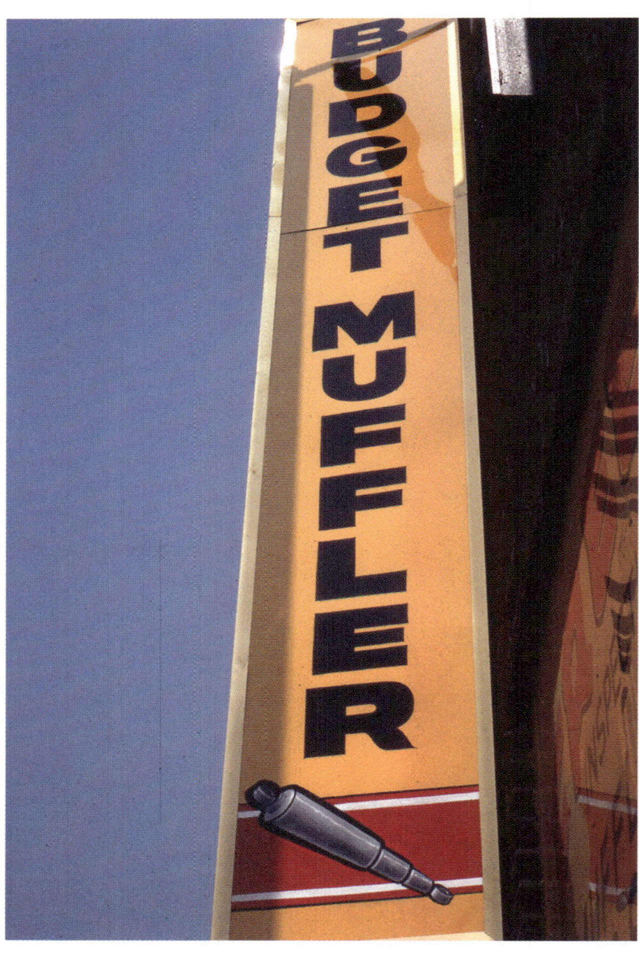

TOP:

ACME, 1978. // One of the first signs I worked on.

CENTER:

SOUTHHAMPTON, NY., 1988. // Enamel on wooden sign.

LOWER:

DUMBO, BROOKLYN, NYC., 1982. // I did this series before the city passed a law requiring us to clean up after our dogs.

BOTH IMAGES ABOVE:

1978. // My first job in New York was working for a sign painter. Mostly I carried the ladders and set up scaffolding. Unfortunately for my boss, I never really got the hang of lettering but I did learn to love painting outdoors and how to paint a straight line--with either hand. As a favor, in return for paying me so little, he'd let me paint the pictures. Still some of my proudest works.

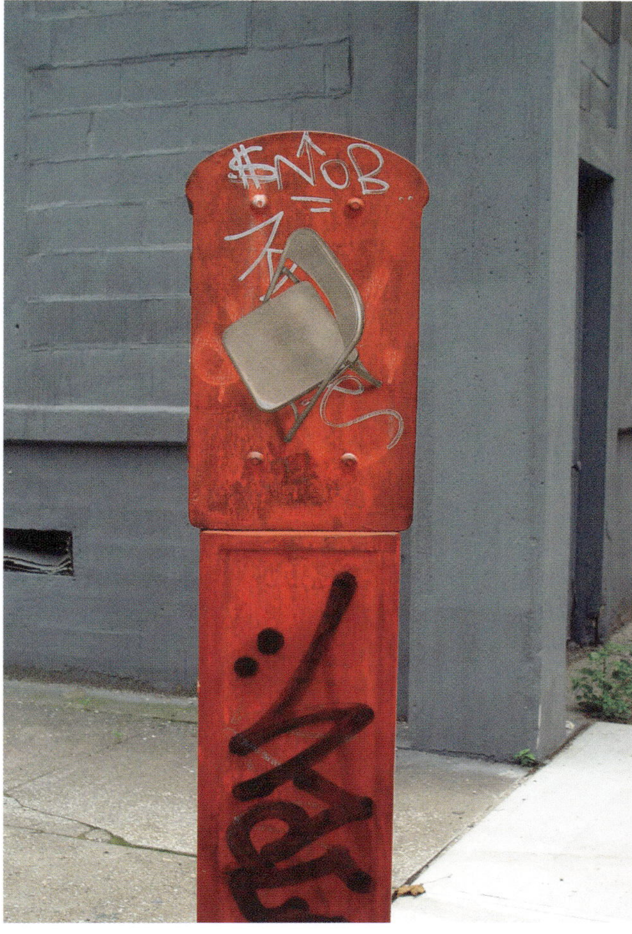

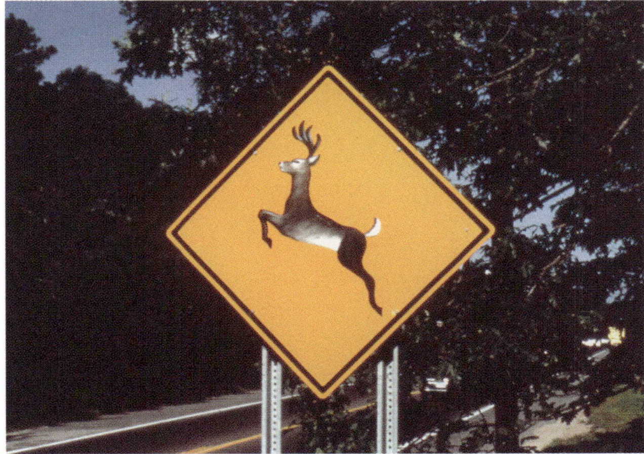

TOP:

WEST ST., GREENPOINT, BROOKLYN, 2003. // From a series of post 9/11 RIP memorials. Mixed media and acrylic on vinyl adhesive paper and acrylic on metal fire call box.

BOTTOM:

SAG HARBOR, NEW YORK, 1988. // Acrylic on vinyl sticker paper, on metal sign.

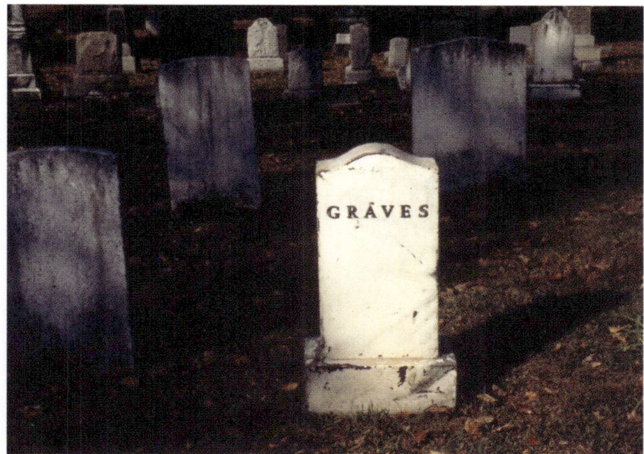

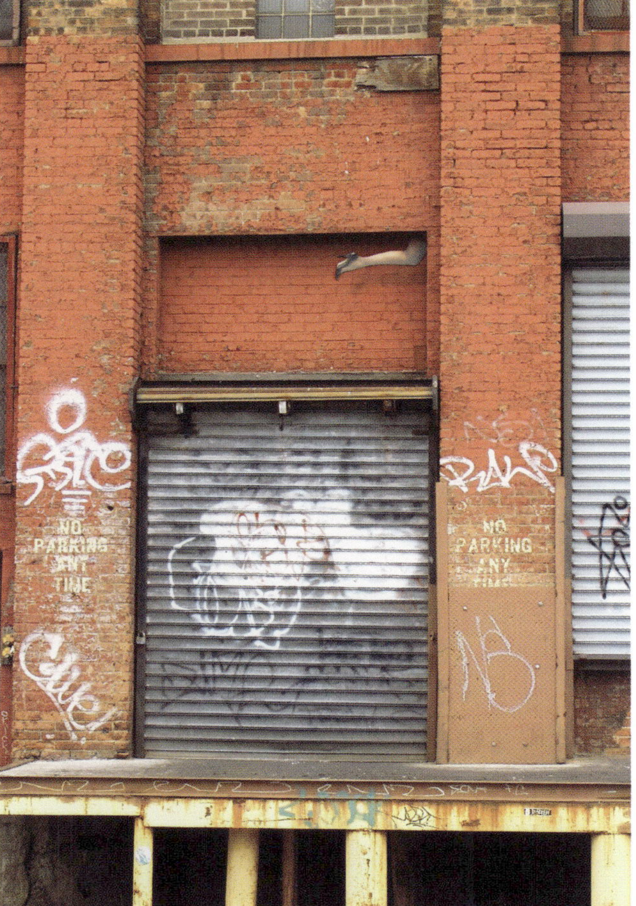

TOP:

WOODSTOCK, NEW YORK, 1987. // Prop grave stone (removed).

BOTTOM:

WILLIAMSBURG, BROOKLYN, 2005. // Acrylic and mixed media on plastic and on brick wall.

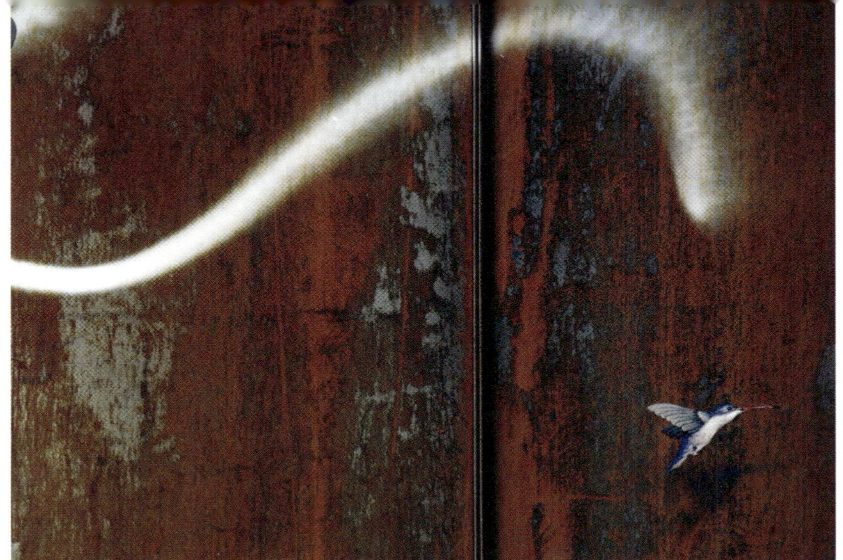

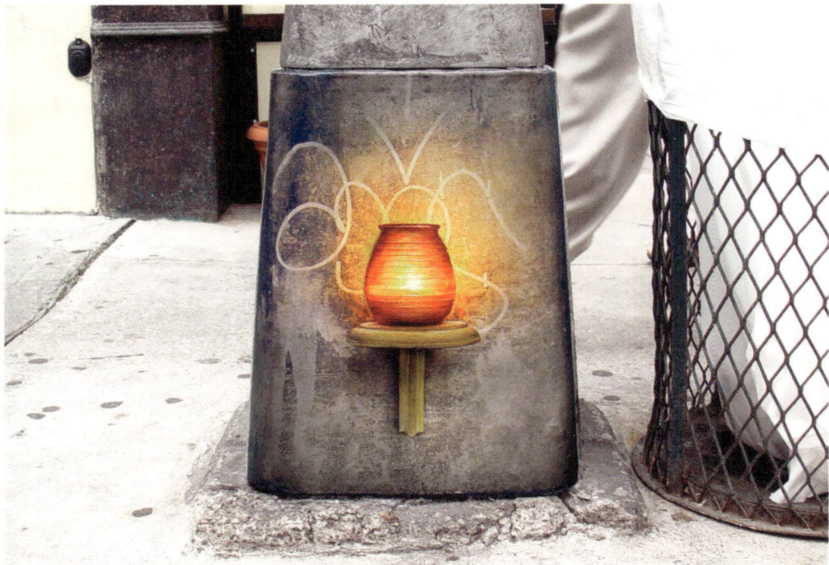

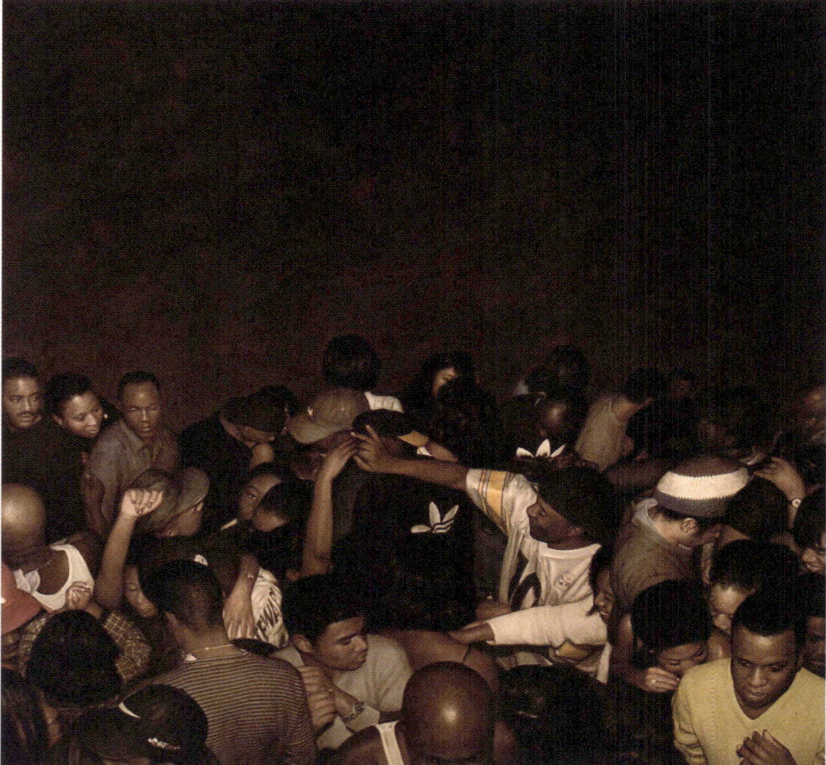

FREEMAN'S ALLEY OFF RIVINGTON, NYC., 2000.
Acrylic on vinyl sticker paper and metal shutter.

GRAND ST., NYC., 2002.
Acrylic and mixed media on lightpole.

SAPPHIRE LOUNGE, 2008.
Oil and digital media on canvas.

A lot of your work is centered around projects. Do you have one-offs that failed, that never became projects or do you usually conceive of things as projects?

The one-offs or Pranks fail or succeed. Sometimes a one off succeeds and becomes a series, usually not. I think for every project you see there's one or two that fail, or never get off the ground. It's getting better now. I've learned to be suspicious of myself when I get really clever ideas–especially after going to art shows. It wasn't always that way though. That's why I like to work in series. From start to finish things shake down and change. Sometimes the early stuff is good and fresh and the later ones mannered and contrived, and sometimes the early stuff is crude and the later ones develop and acquire that grace/luck thing...it's maddening 'cause I never know. Even while I'm in the process I don't know. I need to get some time away from it, some distance. The best I can do managing this dilemma is with another artist's cliché, "Heart on fire, Mind of Ice". Balance. That's the only way I know to survive the hellish doubts and second guessing that inevitably starts about half way into any project. The heart on fire part's easy, a given, it's the discipline though, the stick to it voice that I've had to cultivate. For me though, failure's so disheartening, so cruelly depressing, it's got the potential to shut me down completely. It's absolutely crucial that I maintain this cold calculating side, this paranoid overseer that keeps the whole contraption on track.

Were there any back then that failed?

God, yeah. The early sticker pieces... It took about 2 years to get that working. Lots of bad pieces back then: I must've cut out thousands of bright yellow American cheese food slices. Nothing from that series made it. I remember a batcave thing, with dozens of bats, sleeping upside down. Stupid. Sophomoric. Took weeks to paint. I don't think I even kept any photos.

I totally lose interest in my work after it's finished. After the actual installation or painting phase is done I'm over it, out of love, they're dead to me. It becomes an administrative problem then (photographing, archiving, etc.). Maybe editing 50 pieces down to 10 to 12 usable images each year takes its toll. Too many little deaths. So much hope, so many near misses. It's brutal. I think I protect myself by investing my self-worth in what's next. For me, the new work's always the thing. If you meet me and ask me how I am, sooner or later I'm gonna start telling you about My Next Big Thing.

So there's a gap here in the early 90's. Set that up for us.

Yeah...New York had been bottoming out for awhile by the early 90's. Especially on the Lower East Side, my neighborhood, things were pretty desperate. Crime, homelessness, addiction, HIV, it was unbelievably dismal. I had a little saying that the street was a bad dog and if you got too close to it, sooner or later it would bite you. It did. I'd found the dark side I'd naively been hoping for as a teenager. I'd had a very serious motorcycle crash in 1990; there'd been some bad relationship stuff, the end-game of my own addiction problems; my last show at Semaphore had bombed and I'd pretty much detached from the gallery scene. I was still doing street art but it was haphazard. This was a dark time for me, my trip down to the crossroads, and frankly, with all my life problems, art just seemed superfluous. A self indulgence. I mean people were dying, you know? Downtown was decimated. Every week it seemed you'd hear about another drug overdose or suicide, or some other sweet soul fading away with AIDS.

I was doing paintings as well, developing what would be my mosh pit style, but in the face of all that was going on, and my financial independence (due to the insurance settlement from the motorcycle crash), I drew inward, avoiding attention and becoming increasingly uncomfortable with my role in life and the artist's secret—that mostly what we're doing is making products for consumption by wealthy people.

Around this time, a friend of mine, Walter Robinson, the art critic, said something, an off-hand remark, which he claims not to remember, about, "artists being lackeys, making shiny baubles for rich people." This really stuck with me. My first joking response was something like, "yeah, if you're lucky," but eventually the awful truth of it really began to depress me.

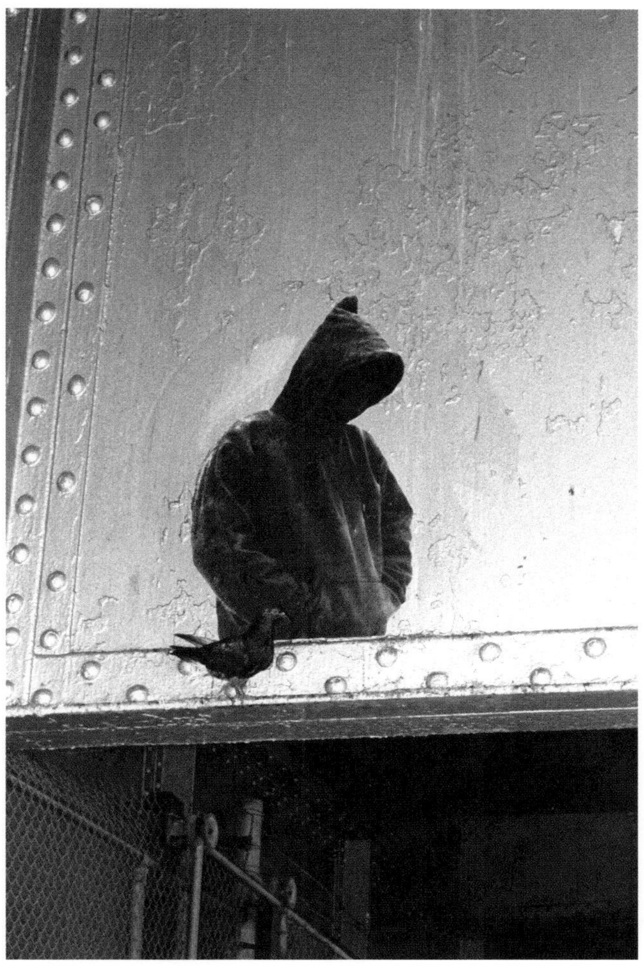

DELANCEY ST., NYC., 1994. // Silk-screened poster wheat-pasted on Williamsburg Bridge.

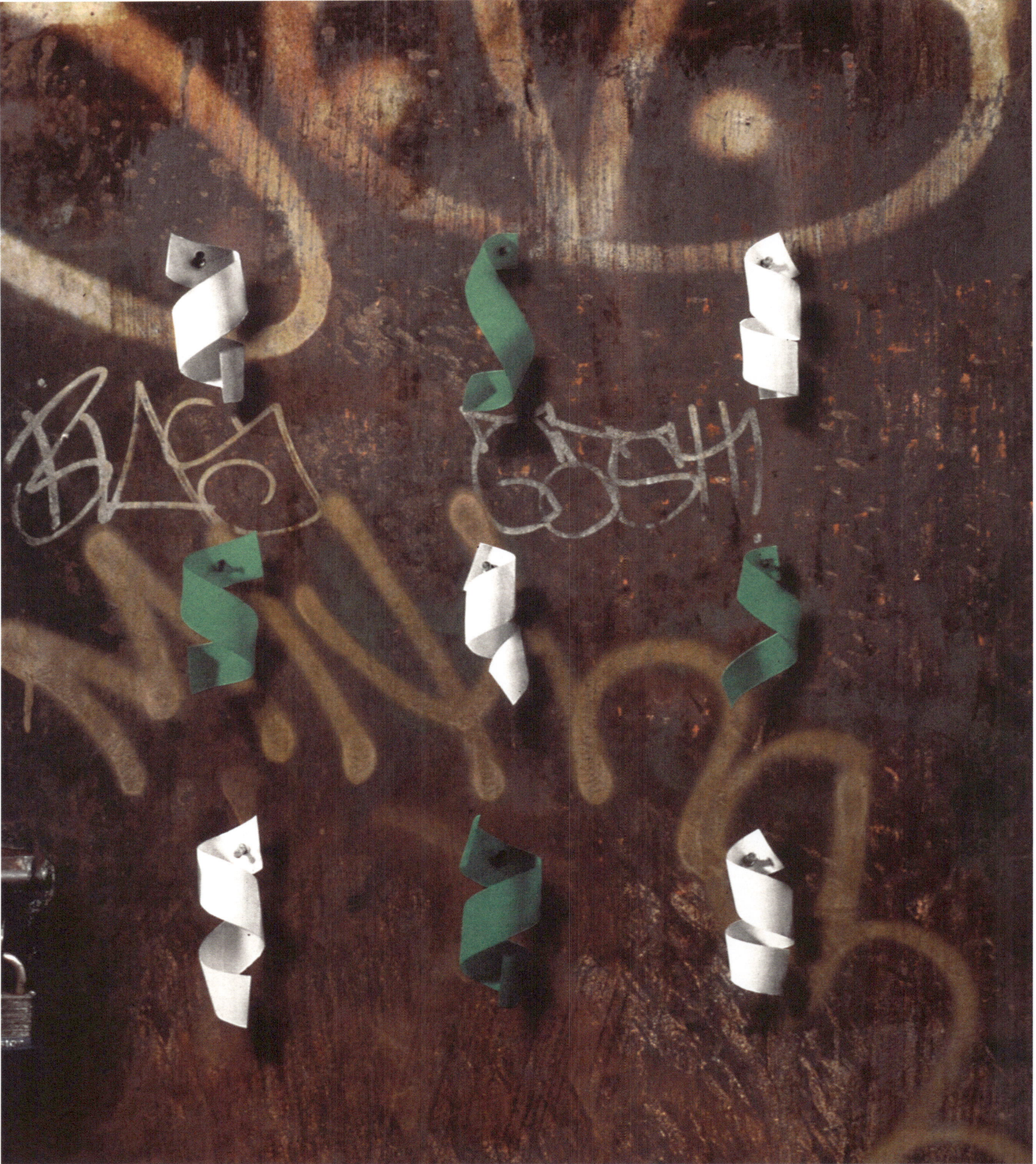

Which brings us to the hoodys. How did that come about?

Yeah, well, after all that, the question became if you can't sell your soul, what can you do to keep your soul alive? I knew that I was always happiest, most at ease with my creative self when I was working out on the street. It's uncomplicated, there's no ulterior motives, no critical static; maybe people see it, probably they don't. I could handle that. I did some prankish pieces, then the hoodys.

It's not an anti drug thing or anti drug dealer message, which is what some people thought —

Cause you put it up in drug cop spots—

Right. I think the working title was "The Plague Angel". I likened it to deer crossing signs or the X's they painted on houses that had the plague in the Middle Ages. I know I intended it as an elegy of the times and the place, an archetypal high sign.

Is it painted on the wall?

These are photo silkscreens wheat pasted on the wall. My last analog piece. The digital era is dawning...

Did this get you a lot of attention?

Yes.

How?

Magazines, newspapers... I'd really blanketed the East Side below 14th Street so most people couldn't help but be aware of them. Also, I'd put them up high with a ladder so they weren't easily removed. Getting those up was insane. Me and a friend would go out at three in the morning; we'd be creeping around these very sketchy neighborhoods, me up on a ladder obviously up to no good. Not cool. Very risky. This was when I first learned about choreographing installations, shaving seconds off the time I was exposed, regulating everything down to the smallest detail to minimize the risk. Somehow I was lucky with the cops, but even more lucky that no local vigilante saw me on the ladder and thought I was breaking and entering.

How many did you do?

Around 70, I think.

This, at a time, when, thinking about street art, people talk about Keith Haring and Jenny Holzer, but they were long past. So this was totally unique, right?

I'm trying to think... but not much was going on back then. Revs and Cost xeroxes were everywhere. Stuff like that. This is still before the cheap sticker revolution.

So, are you showing in galleries at this time?

Not really. No one was interested. At that time the whole topic of my career was very disheartening. I was struggling. You know though, all the problems I had back then, as bad as it was, now I can see how it was a good thing, how in the end it worked out to my advantage. Anyway, it forced me to figure out what made me happy creatively, to find the joy in it again.

Some artists thrive on career pressure, not me. And I have to say, having had that experience of making art purely for myself--from then on it's been easier for me to deal with the career crap, to not let it make me crazy or take the fun out of being an artist. Ambition's inevitable I think, but it's a lot simpler, cleaner, to be ambitious with the bigger picture, with art history.

The Hoodys were a turning point. Not only did it re-ignite my interest in street art, it re-set all my intentions about making art. Starting in '95, the digital era, I began doing hundreds of pieces a year. I went nuts.

Were these getting photographed, were you associated with these as well?

Oh yeah, I'm a compulsive archivist. But I didn't have a web site; the internet wasn't really a common thing in our lives yet. For the most part the work was purely anonymous. I'd show the photos in galleries and alternative spaces if I could but the response was always pretty tepid. No one seemed to get it. Commercial gallery types would be sympathetic but avoid eye contact, like I had toilet paper stuck to my shoe or something. I think they assumed I put my stuff on the street because I wanted attention and couldn't get anyone to show me. Again, I just had to let go of that, or any need for approval. Which was a lot easier than it sounds because I was having such a good time. The stickers were so labor intensive and the photos were so bizarre and surprising, I barely registered that people didn't care.

So in '96 you started adding the shadows?

Yes. A big moment for me. The whole thing broke open when I started doing that. Remember this kind of middle brow art movement in the 70's, abstract illusionism? It's a cheesy cousin of photo realism. Abstract gestural backgrounds with little blobs of paint magically floating above airbrush shadows?

Sure.

My dermatologist had one of these paintings in her waiting room. One day I was staring at it, secretly liking it, and I had a real honest to God epiphany. Like a lot of my generation I'd been a big fan of 60's custom car culture—especially the airbrush artists and pin stripers. Similarally I'd always admired tattoo artists and skater graphics, underground cartoons, Big Daddy Roth, Robert Williams, Raw Comix, all these fantastically gifted artists we'd later refer to as the inspiration for the Low-Brow movement. Anyway, it must've been one of those

TROMPE L'OEIL SERIES. 6TH ST. BETWEEN 2ND AND 3RD AVES., NYC., 1996. // Acrylic and mixed media on sticker paper and metal door.

zeitgeist visitations or something because I went straight from the dermatolgist and bought an airbrush and started getting busy with a huge new bag of trompe l'oeil—fool the eye—techniques. Kitschy maybe, but jamming with the urban backdrops, it really made sense to me.

By 95, 96, the city's getting cleaned up, gentrified. Were you feeling the pressure from the police and property owners?

Definitely. And in response my installation tactics were evolving. Not only am I spending less time exposed, but this is helping me choose where I put my work. In most neighborhoods there's an area or two that, because of location, neglect, and some mysterious village social dynamic, attracts the graffiti. These were my walls. Actually, it was after seeing the black-and-white hoody pictures that I realized how bizarrely beautiful these walls were—especially the really old surfaces with long uninterrupted accumulations of tagging. Maybe because the hoody photos were in black and white, I could really see the graffiti; I didn't take it for granted like I usually do. I was amazed by how much energy there was in it, how fresh it seemed. The gestural confidence, the swooping bravery of the writing; the way the spray paint fizzes, it's like a flare, or a sparkler--it actually glows. And the drips! Such gravity—like a force of nature. And, incredibly, this is going on everywhere in the city; it's in our faces every day, shouting. But, even me, a street artist, I hardly noticed it. Until I started integrating my trompe l'oeils with it. Then things really started acting up. The walls came alive. Layers of tagging became weirdly spatial, the walls transformed, became six feet deep.

Ok. I love these guys but maybe three years of Jackson Pollock's entire career, two years of De Kooning's and some Franz Kline's come close to the uncanny perfection of these surfaces. Rothko got the palimpsest part, but no human artist could produce such marks. "Force of nature" is the term for it: I mean it's like erosion, or a coral reef, or randon mutations in evolution. Leonardo Da Vinci has a famous quote on this, I'll look it up and send it to you.

With the trompe l'oeils was it still a rebellious theme?

Inasmuch as I was doing art on the street, yes. But, aesthetically, except for the low-brow factor, not so much. This was still my private rebellion, my pocket realms, the weird secret art I made. There was even some guilt involved, like I shouldn't be devoting so much time and resource to something so clearly obscure. I was hooked though.

So at the same time as this you were painting the mosh pit paintings?

Yes. I work in the studio during the cold weather and on the street when it's warm.

So you went to concerts and stood in the mosh pits and photographed and made the paintings from the photos?

Yeah. I went for weeks actually and took hundreds of pictures. All the group paintings are like that—massive research. I love it—shooting the pictures, waiting, being still. It's supremely fulfilling in some kind of hunter-gatherer way. For these I had the camera on a long pole and I stood on the outside of the mosh pit and held it over the center. After awhile I got to know the music and could hit the timer and count down to the climatic moment. Very thrilling when I nailed it right. I've always loved this part of my work, the chasing down and dragging home of source material. Instantly gratifying. Much more so than painting. The first of these are composed with a slide projector, then I got into scanning the pictures and working in Photoshop and that made a lot more interesting things possible.

In 2000 you painted more hummingbirds—

Yes. My farewell to Lower Manhattan. I've always wanted to develop a thesis or riff on how the greatest single influence on the development of my street art has been New York City Real Estate. I could make a graph. One vector would be real estate value and as it climbs, the other one, my time spent on site, declines. As my need for speed increases, so does my need to innovate and refine my media and other choices.

The Birds...?

Oh yeah—that year, as the eviction notices began arriving, I was so busy with lawyers etc. trying to hang onto my loft on Ludlow Street that I didn't have the time or the heart to get involved with one of my big projects. But, when the weather got warmer I couldn't help it, I had to go outside and do something. I figured it would be apt to finish my Manhattan years where I started—to close the circle with some hummingbirds.

These window paintings are from the same time?

Yeah. The Home Sweet Home Windows. When I started that series I don't think I really understood the full story of why I was so drawn to these warmly lit windows. For awhile I was working some anti-Clement Greenberg rap about how paintings really are windows (duh!), but it wasn't until I'd painted four or five of them that it dawned on me that I was so attracted to the image because of my own impending homelessness.

And that led to the World Trade Center shrines?

Right. I'd been learning how to paint light—that was my Next Big Thing—and I'd been thinking a lot about shrines, how art often functions as secular shrines, as objects that promote that kind of reverie. The week before September 11th I was actually up in the Bronx at a housing project, photographing the shrine neighbors left at the doorstep of a murdered nine year old girl (balloons, flowers, stuffed animals, photographs). I wasn't sure what I wanted to do exactly, it was just my way of researching or sketching.

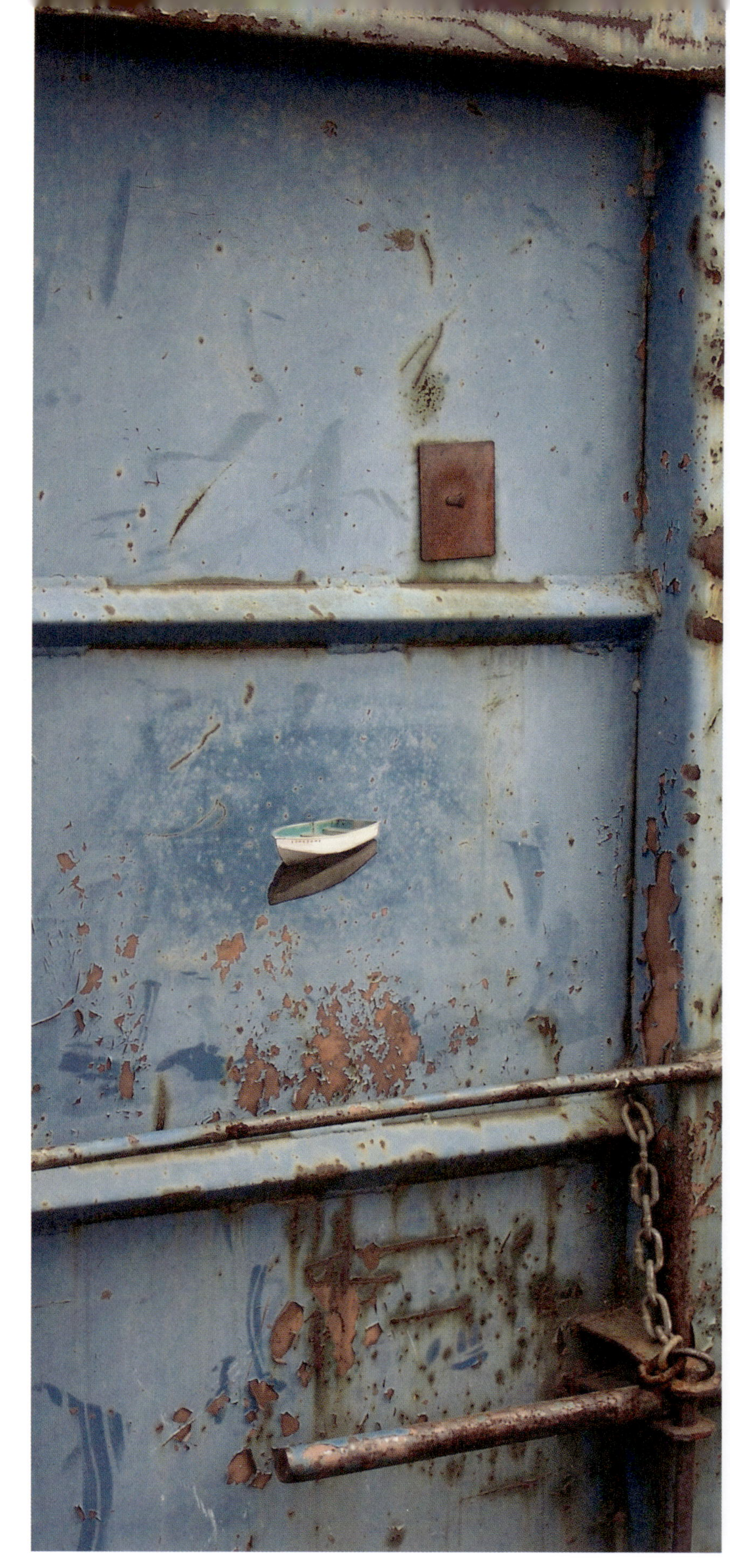

FROM THE LONESOME BOAT SERIES, NYC., 2005.
Acrylic and Digital Media on vinyl Sticker Paper on Dumpster.

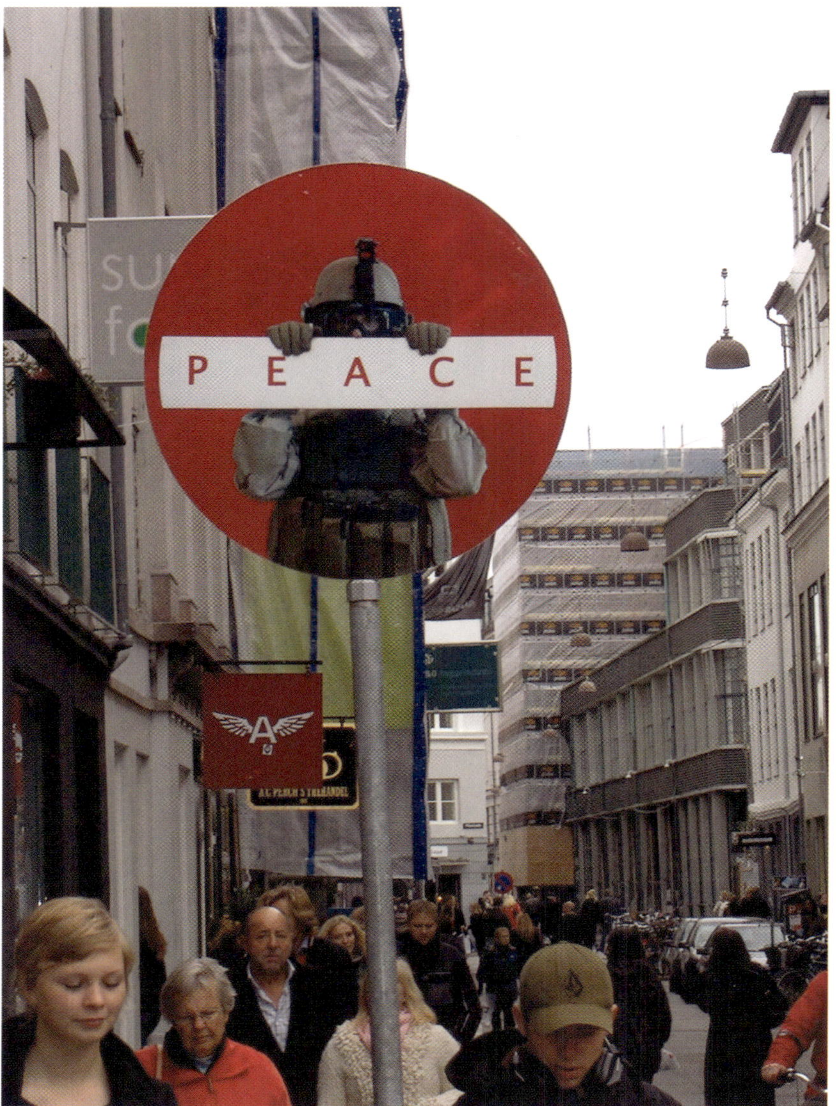

Tell us about September 11th.

For about a week after September 11th every night I lugged my large format photo equipment to Union Square Park and photographed the shrines people had left there. I wasn't sure why, I didn't have a clear idea or project in mind. I guess I was just groping in the dark, doing my best to deal with the shock like everyone else. One thing I did know: every time I put the hood on and those tiny flickering candles came into focus, I felt something eerie, a moment of communion with all those poor people who'd died.

I started out by making some paintings of the candle fields, warming up, then, gradually, I came up with the street component of it all—putting the trompe l'oeil shrines on the bases of the light poles. Getting those made was complicated and absurdly technical; there were so many steps, so many new ideas, and oddly, nothing went wrong. Every phase went as planned; it all worked, no struggle, no false turns, no frustration or drama…it was spooky. Usually, for me, there's gotta be some horrible 11th hour obstacle to overcome, but this was the most trouble free series I've ever done. Very strange.

And you put these up emanating from the World Trade Center?

Yes. A star pattern. I'd wanted to do something like that for awhile, enforce an arbitrary structure, obey a grid on a map, but it always felt too self conscious or art-smart. But for this project, I could do no wrong, it totally made sense.

And so that set me onto painting light. By this point, with my fluency at digital sampling this is getting possible. My gallery work has always been about trying to utilize what's unique about oil paint on canvas, what paintings can do that no other visual media can. I love paint's ability to create light—it's extraordinay—paint doesn't just evoke or suggest light, it actually produces the experience of light. Miraculous.

Since the early Renaissance, painters in oil have known that light, entering a painting, traveling through the magnifying lens of transparent color glazes, gathers strength then bounces off the bright white ground making their canvasses seem to glow. Oddly, this technology's been mostly lost or forgotten.

This was the first time I think we were introduced to your work. The shrines. This is when we realized there was a whole other level to street art. For us it's why we became so interested in it, it had an emotional depth that we didn't know street art could have. Because at the time there were a lot of stickers, there was some really great work, but nothing that you looked at and your breath was taken away.

When did you get a digital camera?

I'd had one for awhile but the 9/11 Shrine Series was the first of the purely digital documentations. A lot of the inspiration to get busy in the digital world came from the music I was listening to. Sampling was changing everything. Things I'd been wanting to do for years were suddenly possible with the click of a mouse. And for free. And I could do it at home. I've only really had any success sampling my own photos though.

Originally you said you were taking pictures as documentation not as art but then, starting in the 90s, you said you were selling the photos, the documents as art.

The goal is to be self supporting. I think people buy the photos to be connected, to support the concept as much as for their aesthetic value as photographs. I mean it's like the experience of the art itself. It's got to be best on the street, that's the true piece—but it's important too that there's layers and subtexts, that there's something that will walk away and stay with you… worlds within worlds…The photograph and all the internet incarnations of the piece are just supporting that. I agree that my photographs are art objects—but always with an asterisk.

When I see a movie or read something or see a band or some art that cracks me open, it stays with me. I get to carry that open feeling around with me—for awhile. Unfortunately life takes over and it fades. The blinders go back on. I've often wished I could carry around some talisman of that experience, a souvenir to remind me. People put art up in their homes for that reason. Maybe that's why I get tattooed

FROM THE DO NOT ENTER SERIES, COPENHAGEN, DENMARK, 2007. // Acrylic and digital media on plastic, affixed to metal sign.

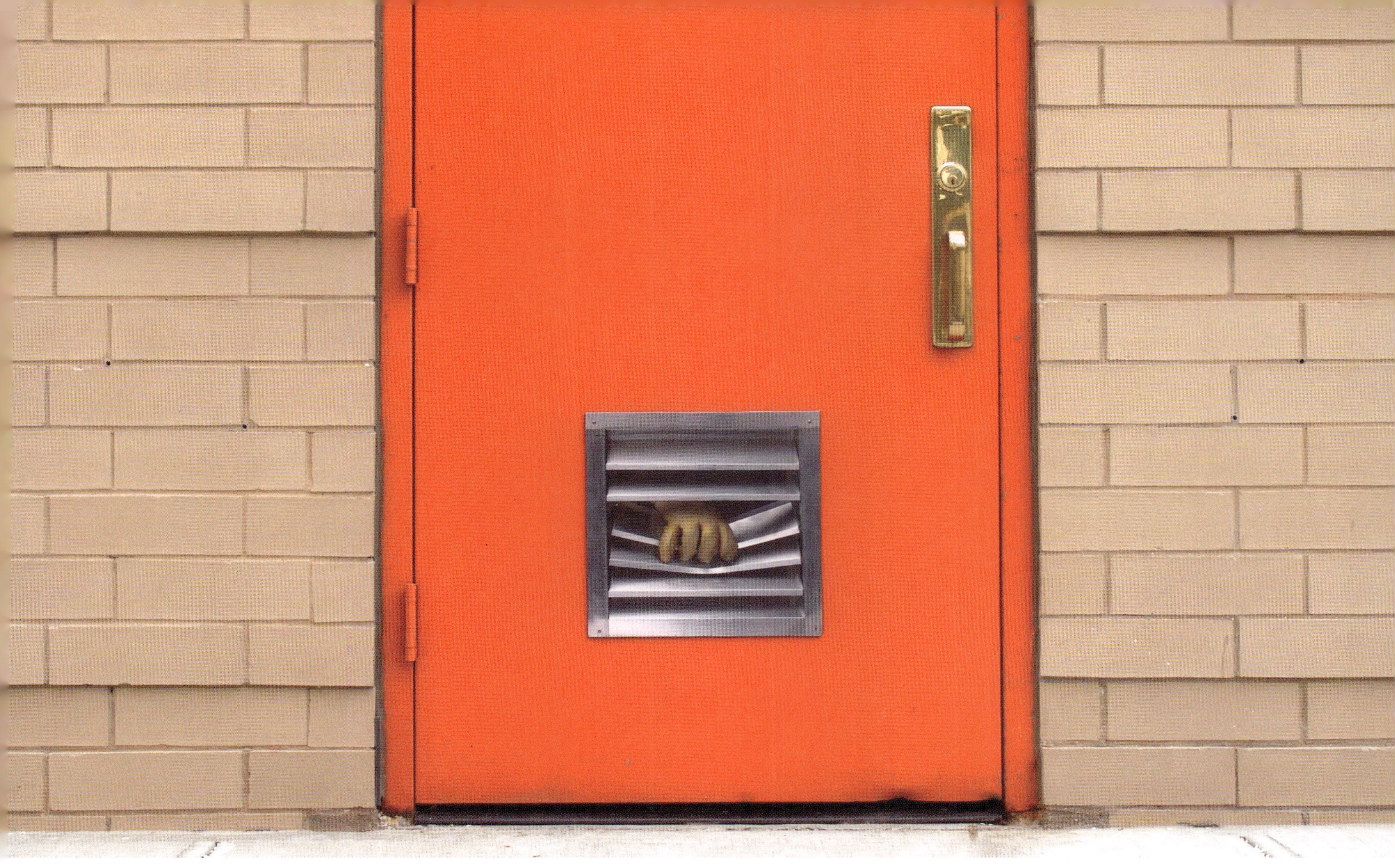

When did you start getting tattoos?

I really started getting covered about 15 years ago.

Are any of them your own designs?

A few but mostly I'm collecting the tattoo artists. I find an artist I like, we discuss what I'm thinking about and I pretty much let them do the rest. I like thinking of my tattoos as permanent notes to self. That I hardly ever read. But the messages are definitely under my skin.

Do you think there's an element of it where you're not in control of the outcome? I think it's very interesting that an artist would let another artist do art on their body permanently.

I believe that Tennesee Williams thing: for artists security is death. I'm vulnerable to the seductions of security. I guess I seek outside help to keep me uncomfortable. Every now and then I gotta get someone to stick a needle in me and deflate me—or poke me to keep me awake.

I used to say that art should be an agent for change. I wanted my work to wake people up, but as time went by I realized that it's useless trying to anticipate how people will think. Now I'm content to let doing my stuff help keep me awake—to be an agent for my own inner change. Much healthier.

When are you the happiest?

Hmmm...when I was a little kid, me and my brother used to draw together, we'd have these battles, complete with sound effects, we'd lay on the floor and draw these battle scenes and hours would go by without me knowing it. Today, before I came over here, I went out and put up some of those Do Not Enter signs. Two hours went by and I was gone like that, utterly out of my body. I'm driving around, just a big roving eye-ball, calculating risk, planning my attack, it's dirty, I'm hot—

You're in the zone—

Yes. I'm so absorbed, I'm totally relieved of my self. Very happy.

FROM THE UGLY NEW BUILDINGS SERIES. LONG ISLAND CITY, QUEENS, NY., 2008. // Mixed Media on plastic affixed to metal door.

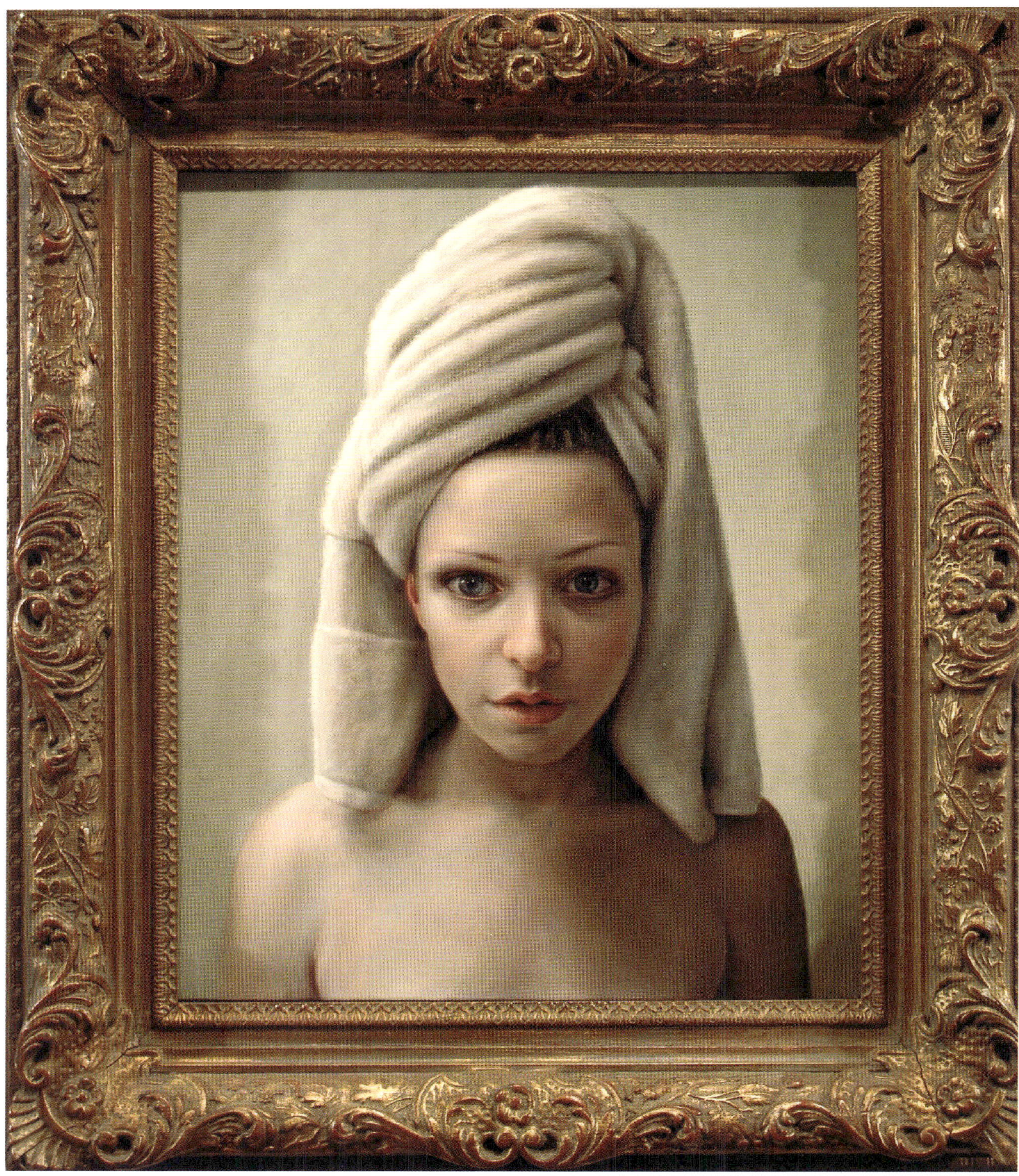

ROSY, 2006. // Private Collection. Oil and Digital Media on canvas.

Do you see this period of time as a culmination of all the time spent working on the street? Obviously now there's all this attention to street art, the media's certainly been writing about it in a different way than they have in the past. Where do you see yourself now in that continuum that started when you were a kid in Chicago?

To me this is just an interesting phase in it all. Our 15 minutes. To be honest, I've never been very good at analyzing my (so called) career. I'm trying for this conversation but in real life I know better than to get too involved. I mean, if this is a culmination then what comes next--you know? I guess if anything, all the media attention's a bit problematic.

In what way?

It adds pressure, self consciousness. I've been through it before so I recognize the pitfalls and have some ideas on how to deal with it. But on the plus side, now that there's some familiarity with what we're all doing, there's more freedom. My subject matter can be more personal, less mediated for mass consumption. Like doing a redux of the hummingbirds in 2000. Or the Man of Sorrows, or Lonesome Boats. I never would've done something as personal and obscure as that in the 80's.

The internet must have changed a lot for you. Now you can see what other people are doing, keep connected in a whole new way.

Yes. And it's so much more fair than when I started. It's not like you have to know the right people to get your work out there anymore. An artist has a chance now that if they do good work people will get to see it. You don't have to go to the right dinner parties or be charming or good looking; it doesn't matter where you went to school and who's 'taken you up'. I'm not naïve. I know that stuff still matters. I know the art busine$$ still rules. But, thanks to sites like Wooster, not with such overwhelming hegemony.

What's next?

I'm excited about working globally. The 2007 project, the signs, I can send anywhere and even have people put them up for me. Anywhere in the world. That's a radical departure. I was working in Manhattan today and I have to say I wasn't really feeling it. The city's been locked down, sanitized, a lot of what inspired my love affair with this place is gone--gentrified away. I'm not giving up though. My feeling is that I should be able to make art out of anything, anywhere. The Manhattan Mall is just another new environment, another opportunity. As a matter of fact, my next series is going to hit the Ugly New Buildings, the sterile condos sprouting up everywhere in Brooklyn and the Lower East Side. Honestly, I'm grateful for the change. Should be a blast.

Do you still work alone?

Usually. I had help in Copenhagen last week, but I really didn't need it. I like working alone. It's easier to get into that zone—

It's meditative.—

Totally. There's a lot of similarities between doing street art and performing. You have to be very present, very in the moment. Focus is crucial. I've got some kind of minor A.D.D. or something which makes it hard for me to concentrate with too much roof brain chatter going on. When I'm working alone it's no problem.

One summer though it actually helped to have someone along. I had a girlfriend, Lisa From Norway, who would ride on the back of the bike and help me. That would be our weekend fun, which we both preferred to going to the beach or whatever couples normally do on the weekend. She'd watch for cops and peel stickers and hand them to me then clean the airbrush while I was photographing. We were a team. With her there my focus was actually enhanced, it was probably the best it's ever been. Talk about happiness! I could be in the zone for hours. A few times lately, I've brought photographers along. They're careful not to interfere but I feel their presence. I make unbelievably stupid mistakes, I'm not in the zone.

Was there ever any one moment that stands out for you as a moment of creative bliss, an epiphany, that zen samadhi moment.

All the time! Take, for instance in that period doing the trompe l'oeils, I'd be out with Lisa in Sheepshead Bay or wherever, someplace desolate and beautiful. I'd put up a piece, some intricate highly rehearsed arrangement I'd been fretting about all week. I'd airbrush the shadows, and we'd both stand back and just kind of shake our heads, go 'yeah' then she'd clean the

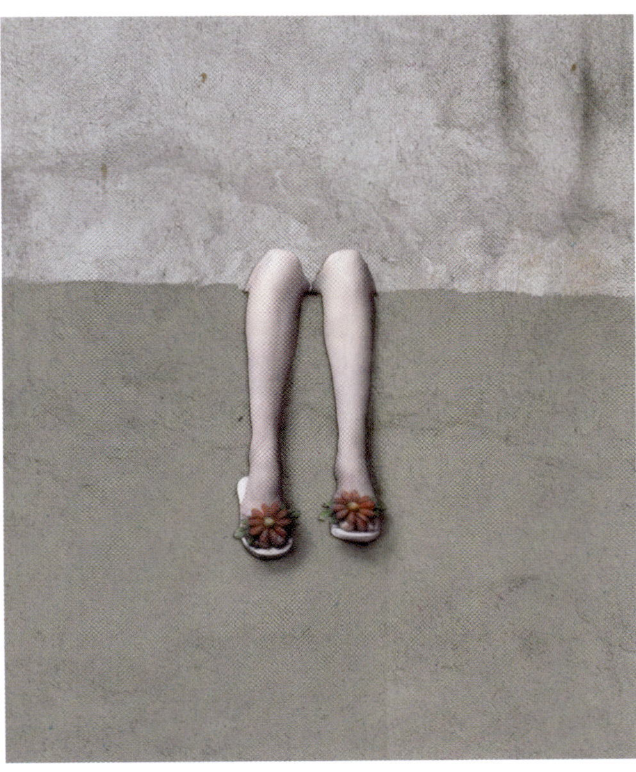

CAT, ALLEN ST., NYC., 2001 // Mixed Media on Plastic affixed to stucco wall.

airbrush and I'd take the picture. Since I was the one creating the illusion I was too close to it and never could tell if it was successful--if in fact the modules looked like they were floating or sticking out of the wall or whatever they were supposed to be doing. It wasn't until I'd put the hood on the 4x5 camera and focused the glass and saw the image upside down that I could get an idea what I'd done. That moment there—if the piece worked—BOOM!—I think I know what you mean.

Who are the other artists on the street that you like?

I don't want to offend anyone by forgetting them, so I won't get specific but I'm interested in the ones who are pushing it, doing something new.

Also, for selfish reasons I'm interested in street artists who evolve, whose work is changing and keeps on being surprising. I get a lot of energy out of that. It helps me to keep pushing.

Did you see this coming? That there'd be a lot of artists working on the street?

Yes and no. Actually, back in the 80's and 90's I always wondered why more people weren't doing it. It's so obvious...such fun. The fact that it's happening these days makes perfect sense.

In what way?

Well, let's face it: most art's been locked down. Museums and galleries are gated communities. There's cool stuff going on there but, in the age of the easy-access internet, it's just too ghetto-ized, too difficult and intimidating for the larger public to find. I think another reason why street art is so popular these days, besides the obvious easy attention and alt.fame thing, is that since it's not for sale, it can't be owned, it's not tainted, it's an alternative to Art and Culture that's become just another commodity. That gives it authenticity, credibility to anyone who's had to grow up soul-starved in the consumer wasteland. So goodbye monolithic record companies and pretentious art magazines; put your band on Myspace and stick your art up on a lamp post.

The phrase street art polarizes people. As street art gets more popular and the friction between graffiti and street art worlds ramps up, how do you feel about the word street art?

I'm staying out of that one. I haven't heard another phrase that works better. It's fine with me.

People ask us all the time, if there is a common theme in street art. Are the artists motivated by similar things?. We've always felt that street artists are so accepting of so many different people and styles and methods and processes that it's really hard to find one motivation that umbrellas everybody. One thing that we hear a lot about is a sense of street art re-claiming public space and looking at how advertising has become so pervasive in our lives. Do you see your work as a reaction to any of that? Do you think of yourself as reclaiming public space when you work?

Of course. For one of my only public-art commissions I put up huge trompe l'oeil sharpened sticks on a wall. The aim was to physically keep those vinyl banner billboards away. I'm definitely in the lineage of situationist philosophy and I'm a big believer in culture jamming and billboard liberation. I get the connections there with what I do, but it's always been kind of retroactive or below thought or intention. It wasn't until I started hanging around with you guys and heard the phrase, "corporate vandalism" that I fully understood that aspect of what I was reacting against.

How do you pick your spots? What draws you to say that's where I'm going to put a piece?

Different projects have different criteria. The hoodys needed to be local. The WTC shrines needed to span the entire metropolitan area. Sometimes it's just something aesthetic I'm attracted to, like the graffiti palimpsests I used with the trompe l'oeils or the horizontal line that becomes the top of a wall in the Kilroy Variations. With the "Floating..." series, to counteract preciousness, I put pieces on dumpsters, tractor trailers, bulldozers, freight trains—anything that would be gone the next day. I needed to let go, to send the work out into the world on its own.

The second part of the answer is: "What can I get away with?". That changes with the local economy, the weather, the time of day, the day of the week, what I'm putting up, adhesion issues, how long it takes to put up, and a dozen other variables I can't think of right now. It's a problem I enjoy. Installation strategies from just five years ago would be insanely risky these days. This need to outwit the authorities has been such an important influence on my work. It keeps me innovating and changing, it keeps my work fresh and stimulating to me. I sometimes wonder if, without the danger, I would have gotten bored years ago and quit.

I've always wondered, how do you deal with the temporality, with the fact that the artwork's ephemeral? How do you deal with the fact that 5 minutes later someone could come along and paint over one of your pieces? How do you reconcile that?

I take a picture immediately. Then say good-bye. It can be hard but you get used to it. I suppose it raises the stakes; it's part of the tension of this kind of art. And there's ways to minimize the stress. My favorite, I got from a nature show on Sea Turtles. Once a year female sea turtles lay hundreds of eggs in a hole on the beach. Amazingly though, only one or two of these survive long enough to mate and lay eggs themselves. Some don't hatch, half or more of the hatchlings get eaten by birds before they can even make it to the shoreline. In the first five minutes in the water, another half of them get killed by other predators; in their first month at sea, another half of those don't make it. By the time they mature to the age where they can reproduce, with luck, maybe only one or two survive. My solution is that the more pieces I do each year, the greater the odds are that some will survive long enough to mate and ensure the continuation of the species.

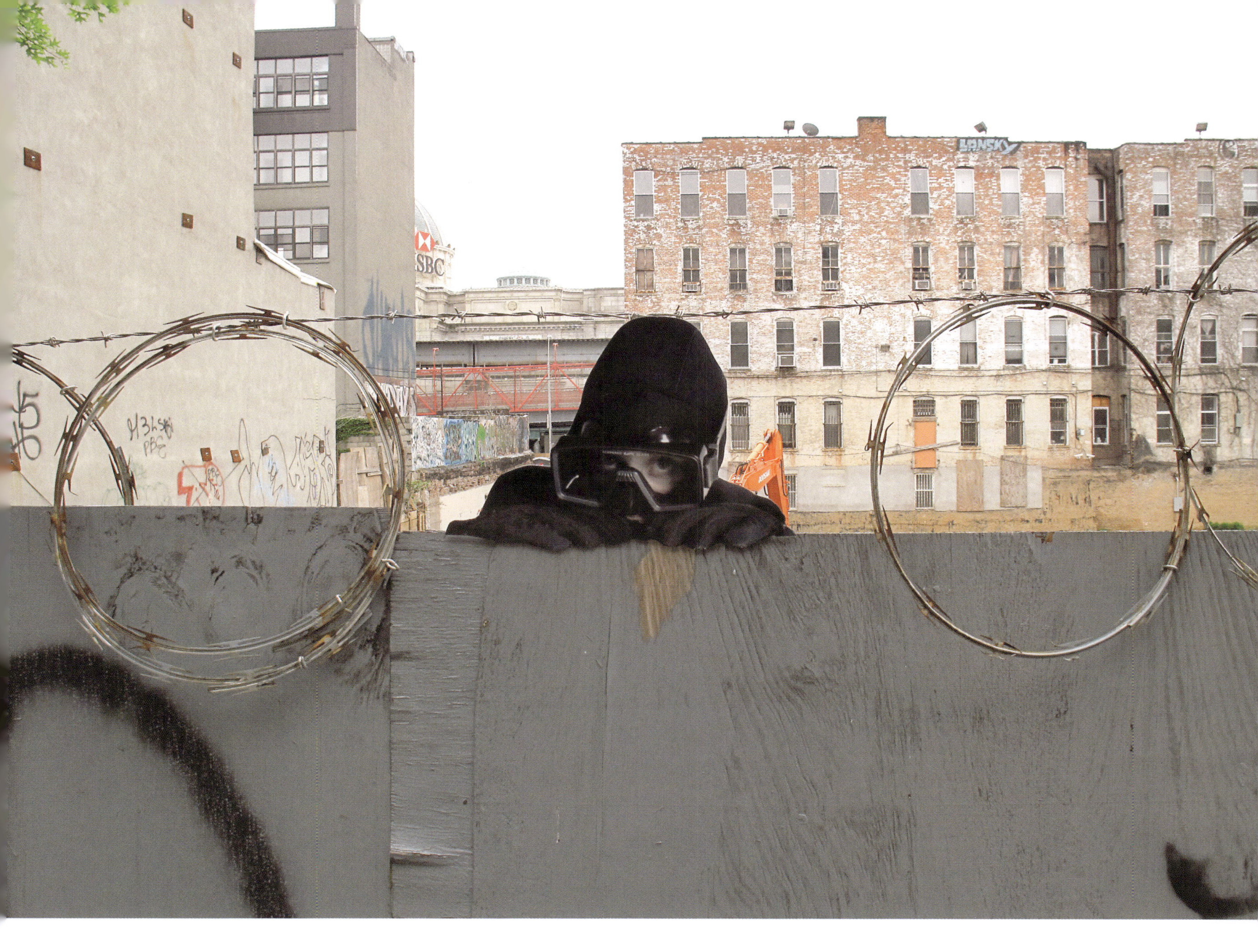

SARAH, 2008. // Mixed Media on plastic affixed to wooden construction wall.

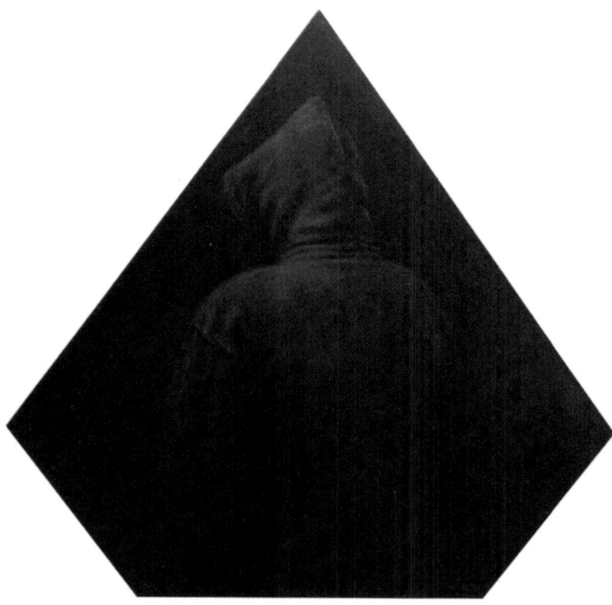

How do you decide how much creative energy to devote to street art vs fine art. Is it instinctual or are there dollars you want to earn—

Whenever I make careful thoughtful decisions based on financial considerations it always goes terribly wrong.

So it's an emotional balance and not financial?

Yes. It's not that I'm some kind of anti-materialist. I've got my feet in both worlds like you said, I just have a black thumb when it comes to the business side of art. If I could do things I knew would sell I might be tempted to try. Fortunately, I know better, I mean, I know myself well enough by now to know it wouldn't work.

Each of those baroque style group paintings takes about six months to paint. This is not a smart financial move. Obviously I could care less, I'm gonna do them anyway, except working on one painting every day for six months drives me crazy. Absolutely insane. My back goes out, my skin gets bad, my dog won't even come up to the studio because of the tense atmosphere up there. As it turns out, this problem actually works in my favor. To save my sanity, to feel better, I need to finish something. So I take a week or two off and work on the less complicated but very fulfilling night paintings. Now it happens that if I work on enough of the baroque style group paintings I end up producing enough of the night paintings each year to support myself. And my other bad habits like street art. So it works out. Sort of.

It's still early in your career but when you hear about artists or read about their careers there's certain years, periods they go through, that they're best known for. What do you feel your best years have been?

Honestly, I'm still getting used to the idea that people I've never met know about my work. But the first answer that comes to mind is now. Now is the best time. I've never been more productive and more focused. But—and I know that I'm probably the last person to know the real answer to this, and I've dealt with enough good art dealers by now to accept that I'm not the best judge of my own work, but, I have to say, undoubtedly, the time after I did the hoodies, back when no one knew who I was, the three or four years I did the trompe l'oeils, before street art was fashionable, that's the time that comes to mind as my most innovative and productive. I'm aware by the way that that's the least discussed or reproduced of my stuff. So, yeah, clearly, you're asking the wrong person.

What is influencing you now? What's inspiring you?

Bob Dylan. Brian Eno. Joe Strummer. I know. It's wrong. You were probably hoping for something cutting edge. Or at least visual. Sorry.

Something I think a lot about now, is how creative people I admire -- artists, directors, rock stars, writers, comedians -- how do they survive and have long productive careers? Especially ones that are very successful. With that kind of pressure how do they stay sane enough to keep making new and surprising work? I'm really interested in what happens to them after they get successful, how they survive psychically and manage to keep making good work with that new set of problems. So many people I respect get famous and their work starts to suck. I'm curious about the instances where that's not happening.

Is that what's fueling you? The next level?

God no. I don't think I'll ever have to worry about being so successful I start to suck.

What's to come? Are there more goals, things you want to achieve?

I've never been very goal oriented. Except to have a living situation that allows me to paint every day. Having a book like this made is good. Ummm...I'd like to make bigger paintings, maybe one day have a cool big studio? Funny. I don't know if this is good or bad, but that's probably the same answer I would've given 30 years ago.

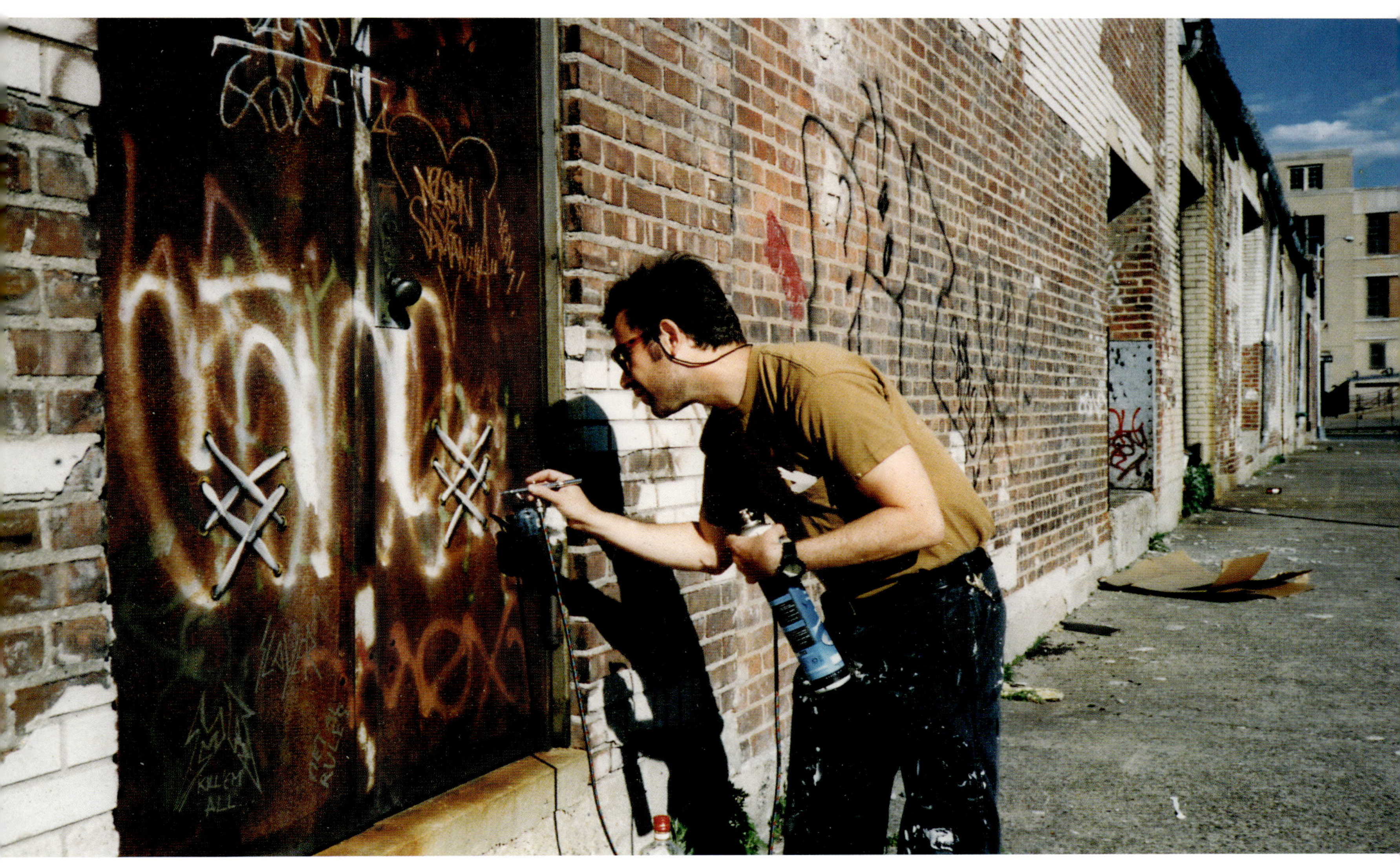

ABOVE:

N.14TH ST., WILLIAMSBURG, BROOKLYN, 1996. // Photo by Lisa Gregersen

OPPOSITE PAGE:

HOODY, 1995. // Oil on canvas. Images from my street works occasionally find their way into my paintings.

STREET ART

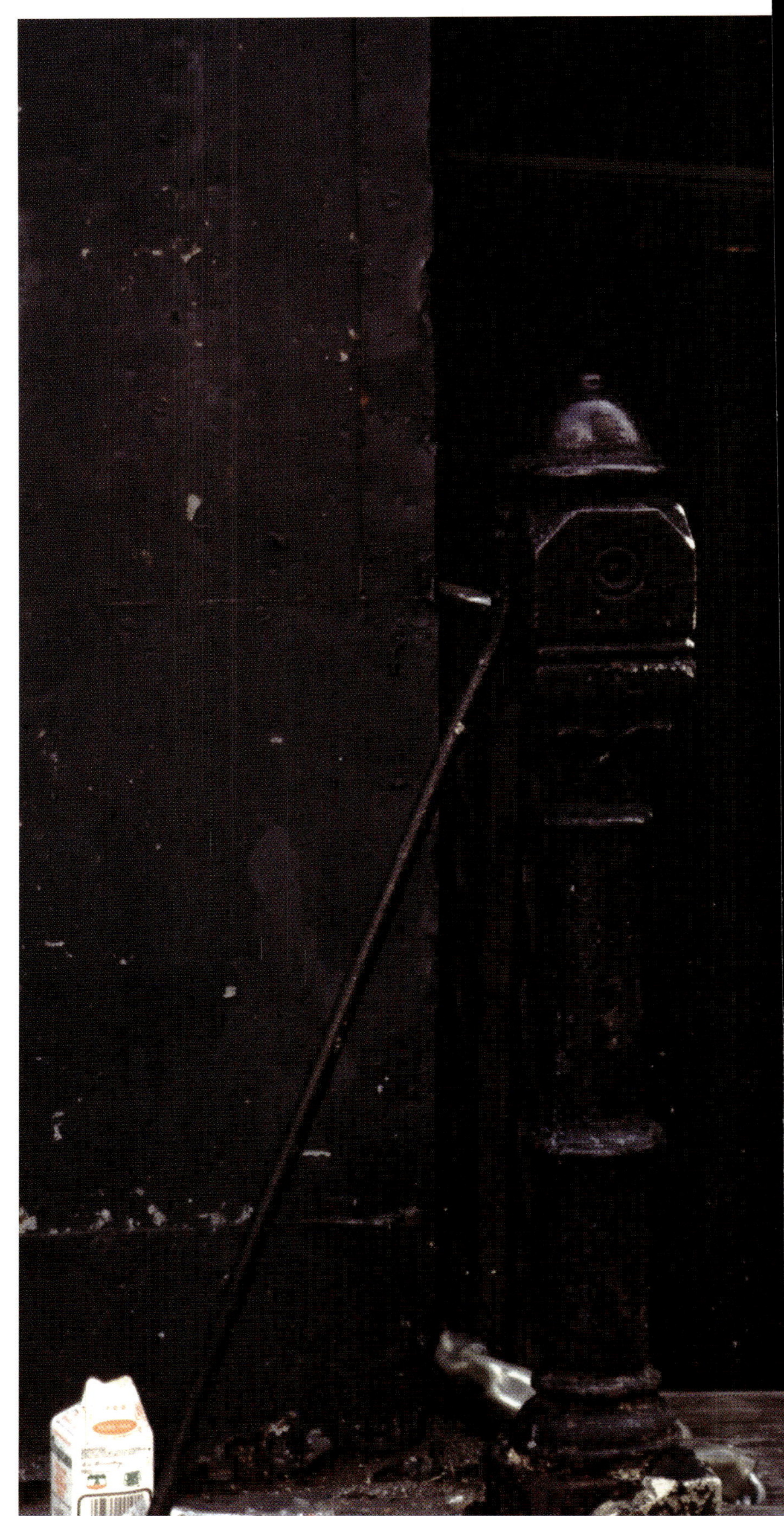

BOWERY NEAR SPRING, NYC., 1979. // Acrylic on metal.

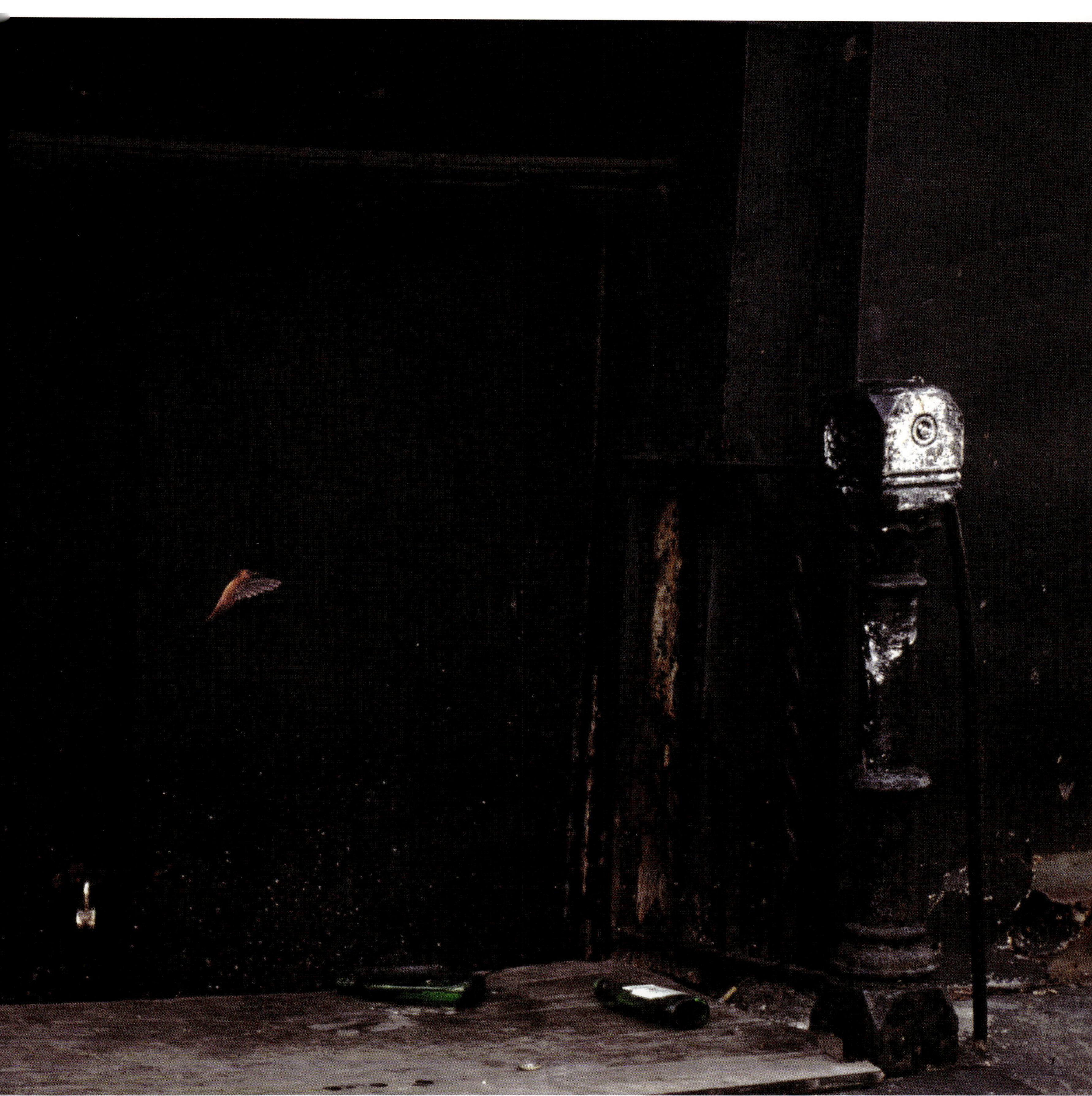

THE BIRDS OF MANHATTAN

1979

The Birds of Manhattan was the first of my large scale street art projects. I painted over 40 hummingbirds in lower Manhattan below fourteenth street. Except in Soho where all the galleries were. Each bird took about 2 hours to complete. It seems difficult to believe now but when the cops or supers caught me I never got in any serious trouble. In fact, once they saw I was painting a hummingbird, almost invariably they'd let me finish.

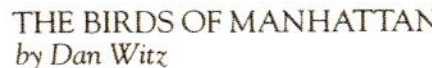

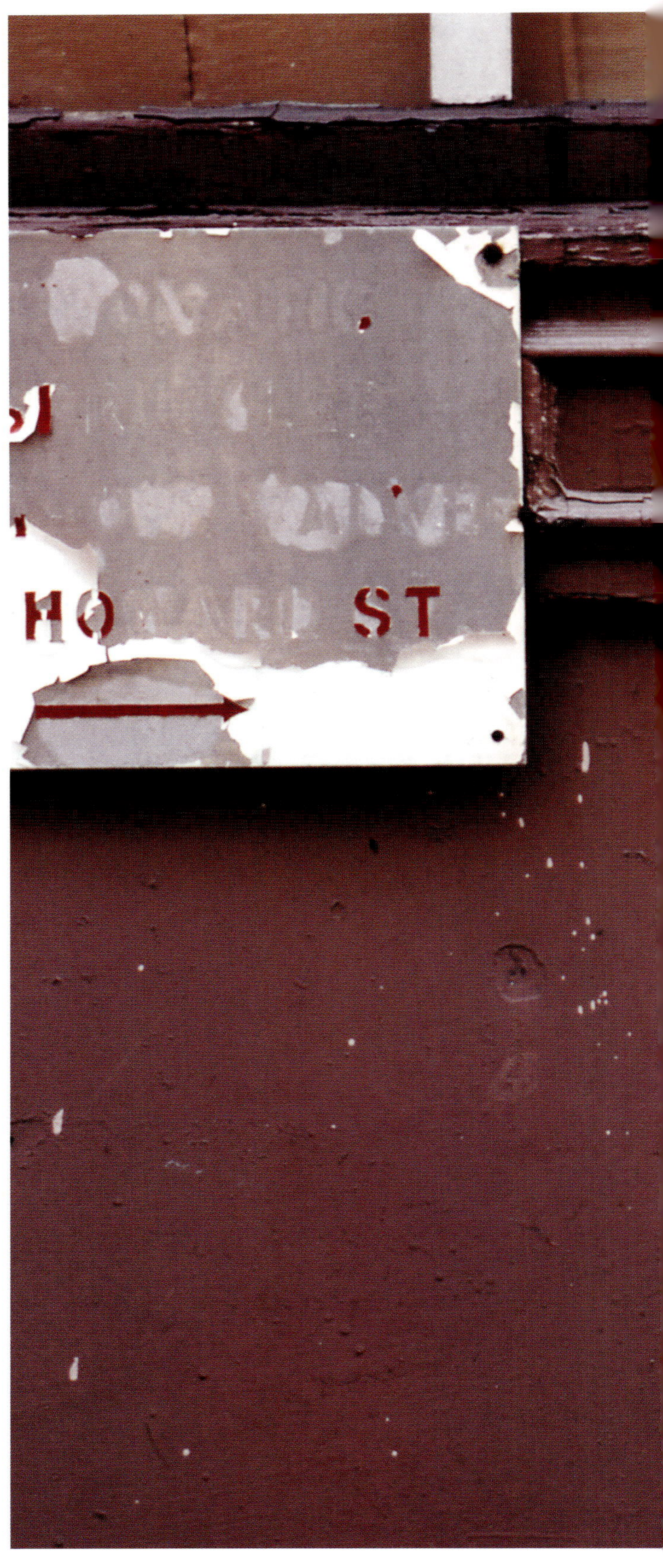

ABOVE:

***THE BIRDS OF MANHATTAN*, COVER.** 1983. // I used my NEA artist's book grant to produce this.

RIGHT:

HOWARD ST., BETWEEN BROADWAY & CROSBY, NYC., 1979. // Acrylic on Masonry Wall.

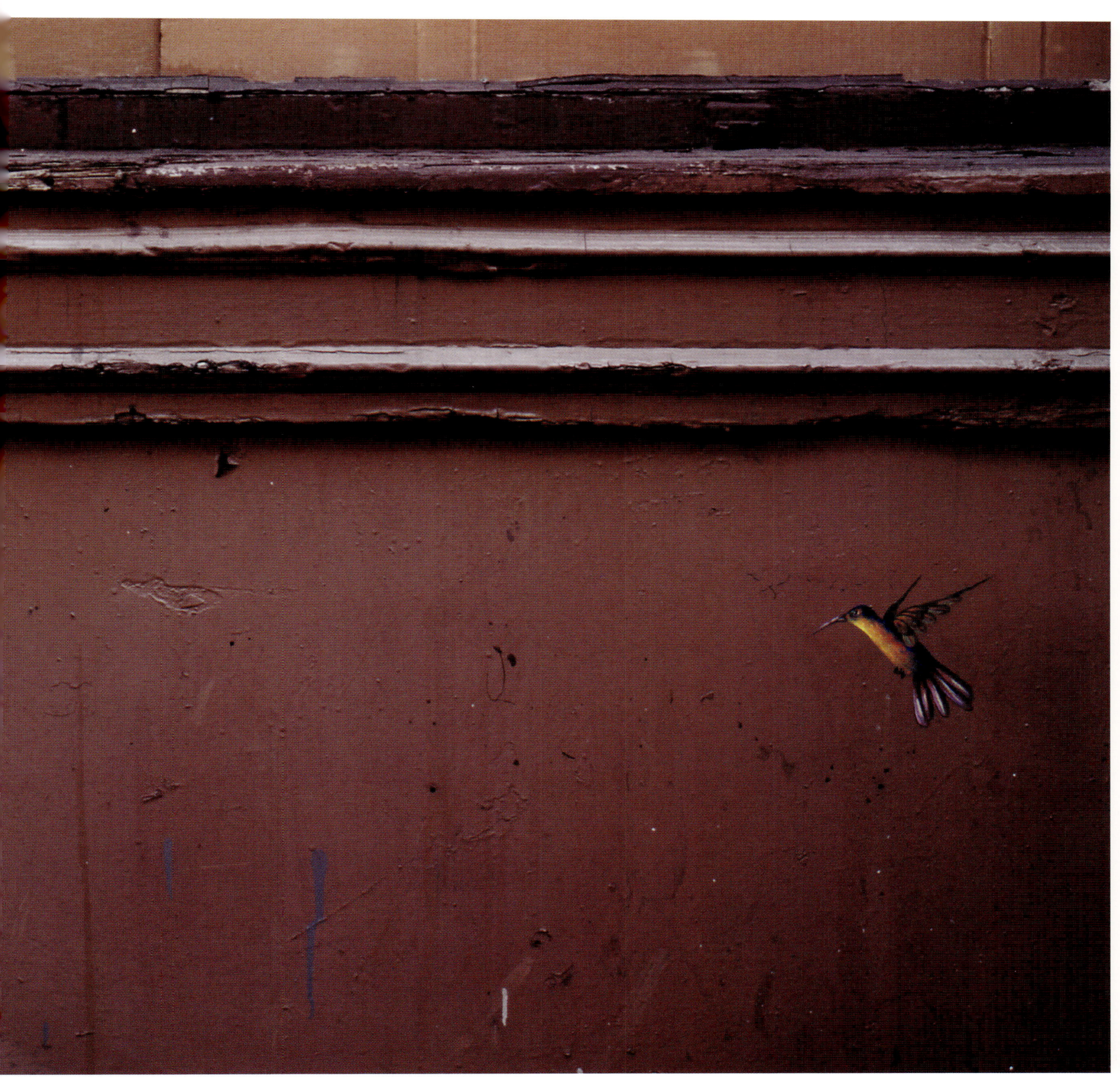

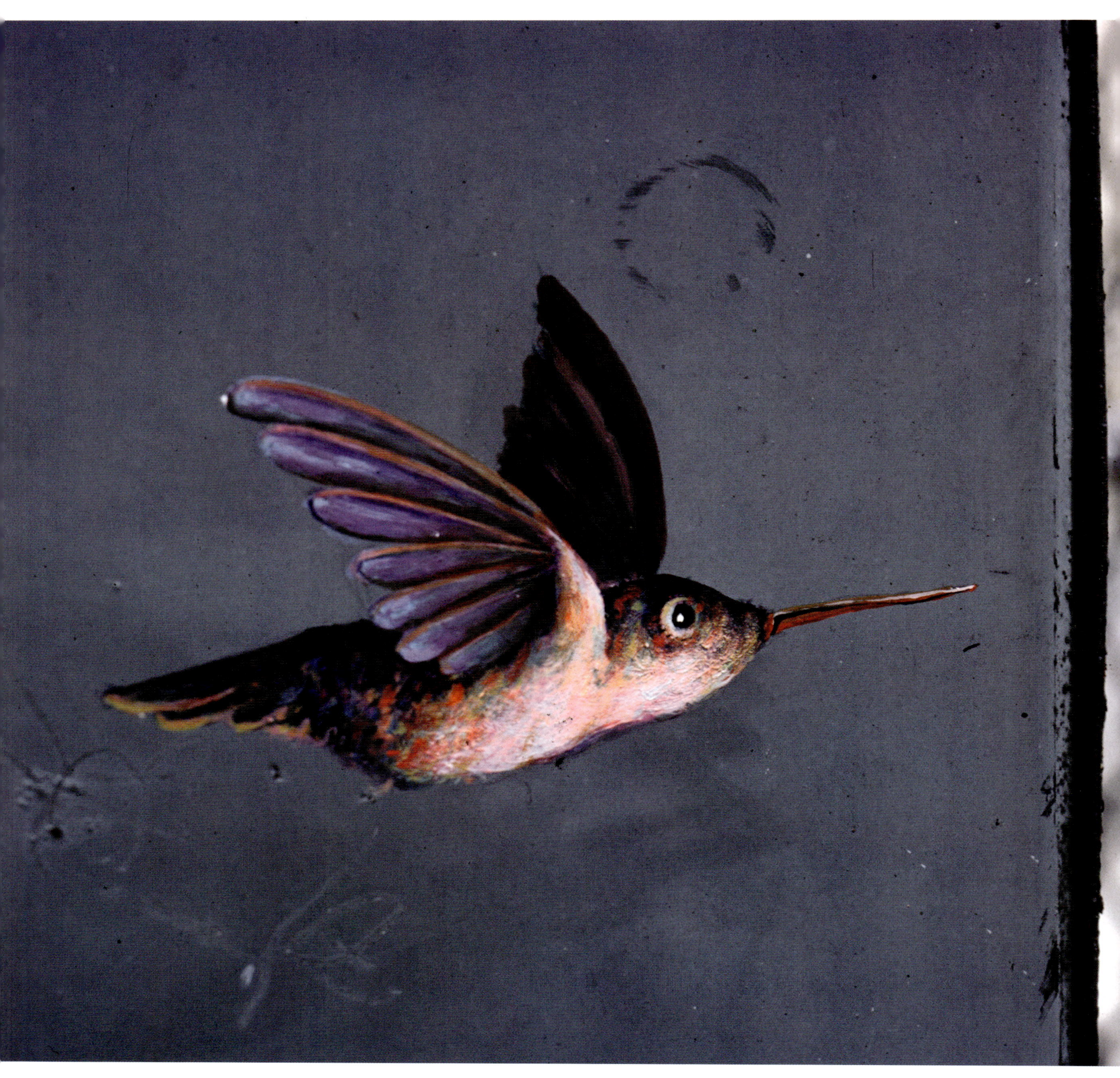

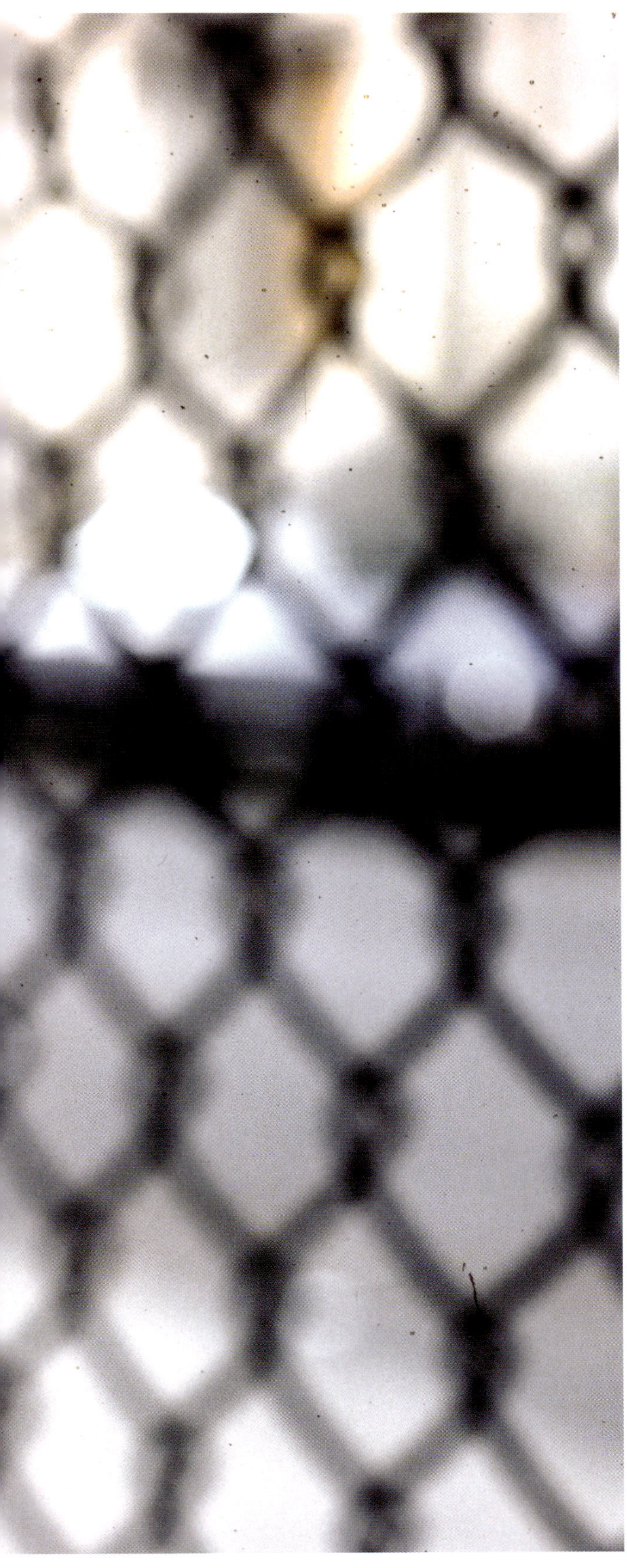

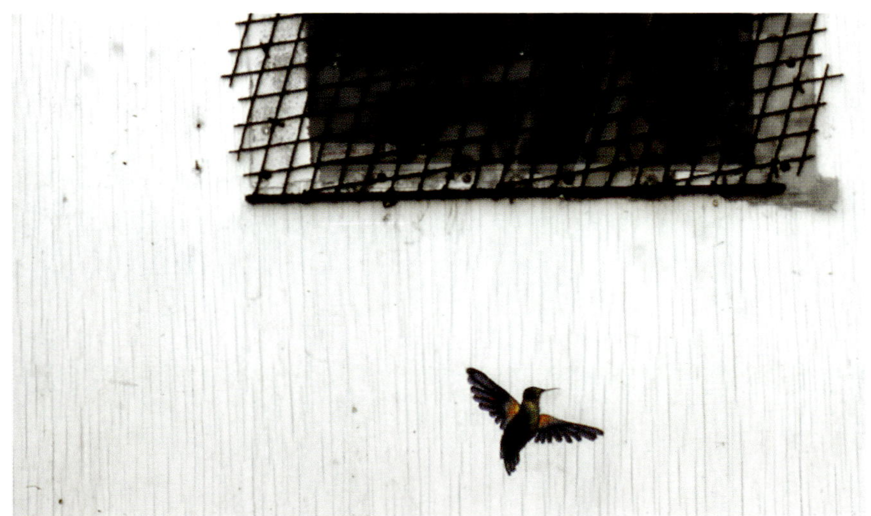

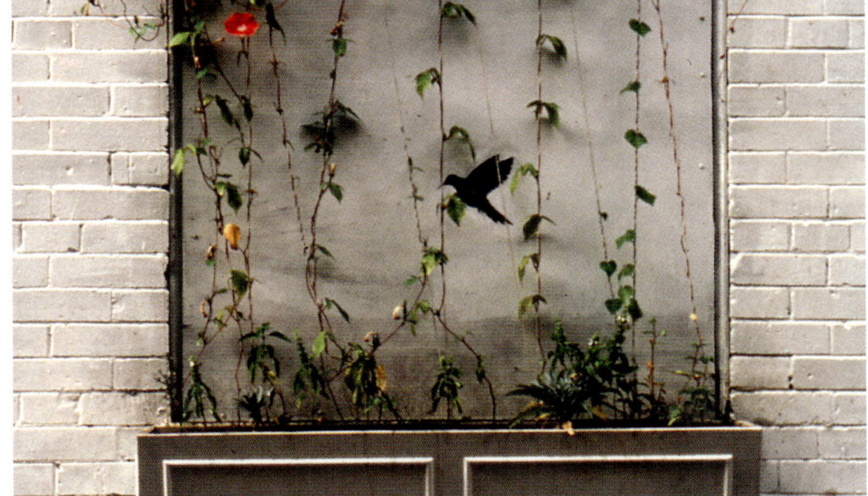

LEFT:

MULBERRY ST., NYC., 1979. // Between Broome and Grand.

TOP:

CHURCH ST., NYC., 1979. // Near Murray.

BOTTOM:

BEDFORD ST. NYC., 1979. // Near Barrow.

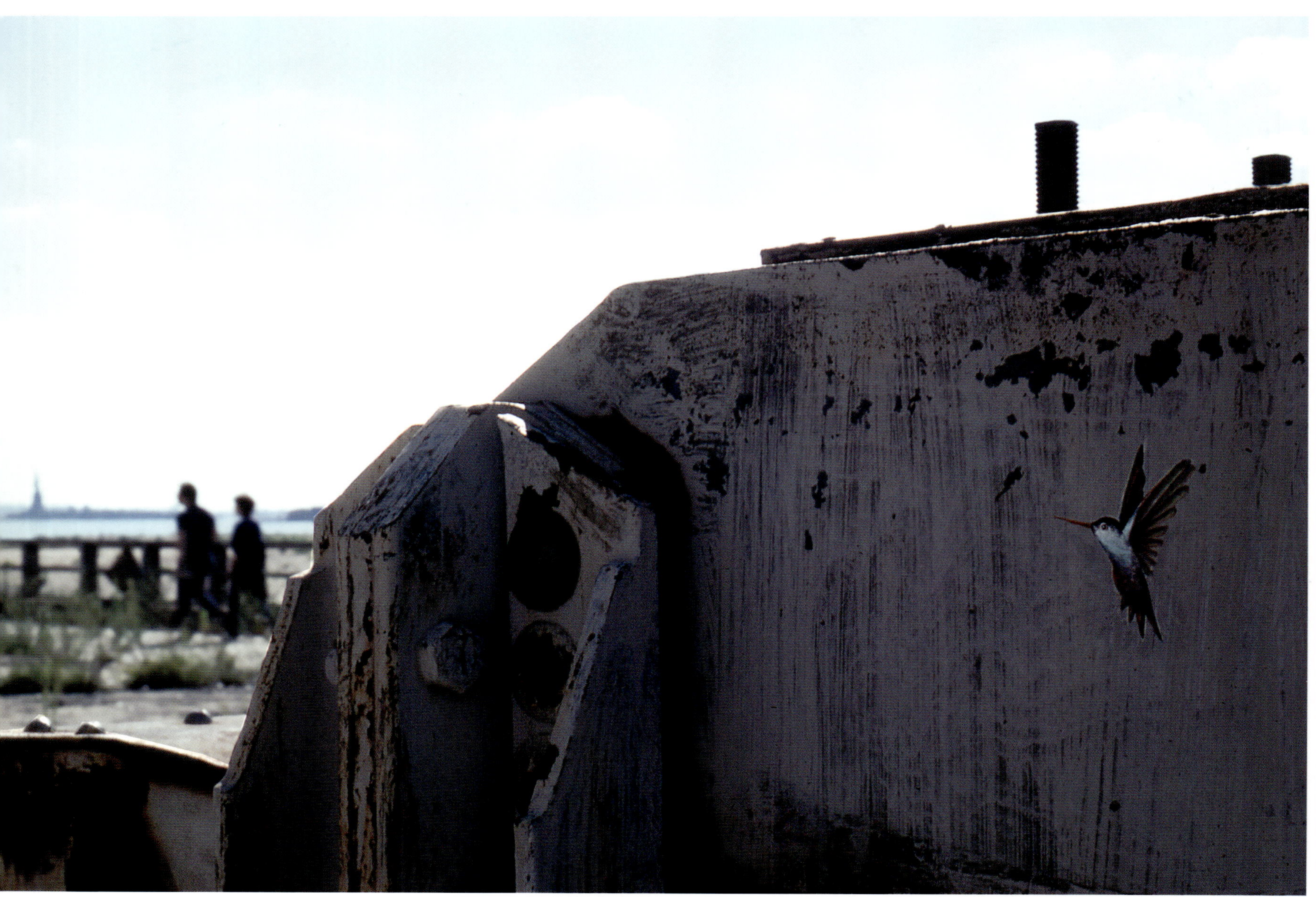

WEST SIDE HIGHWAY, NYC., 1979. // Near Chambers.

2ND ST., NYC., 1979. // Near Ave. A.

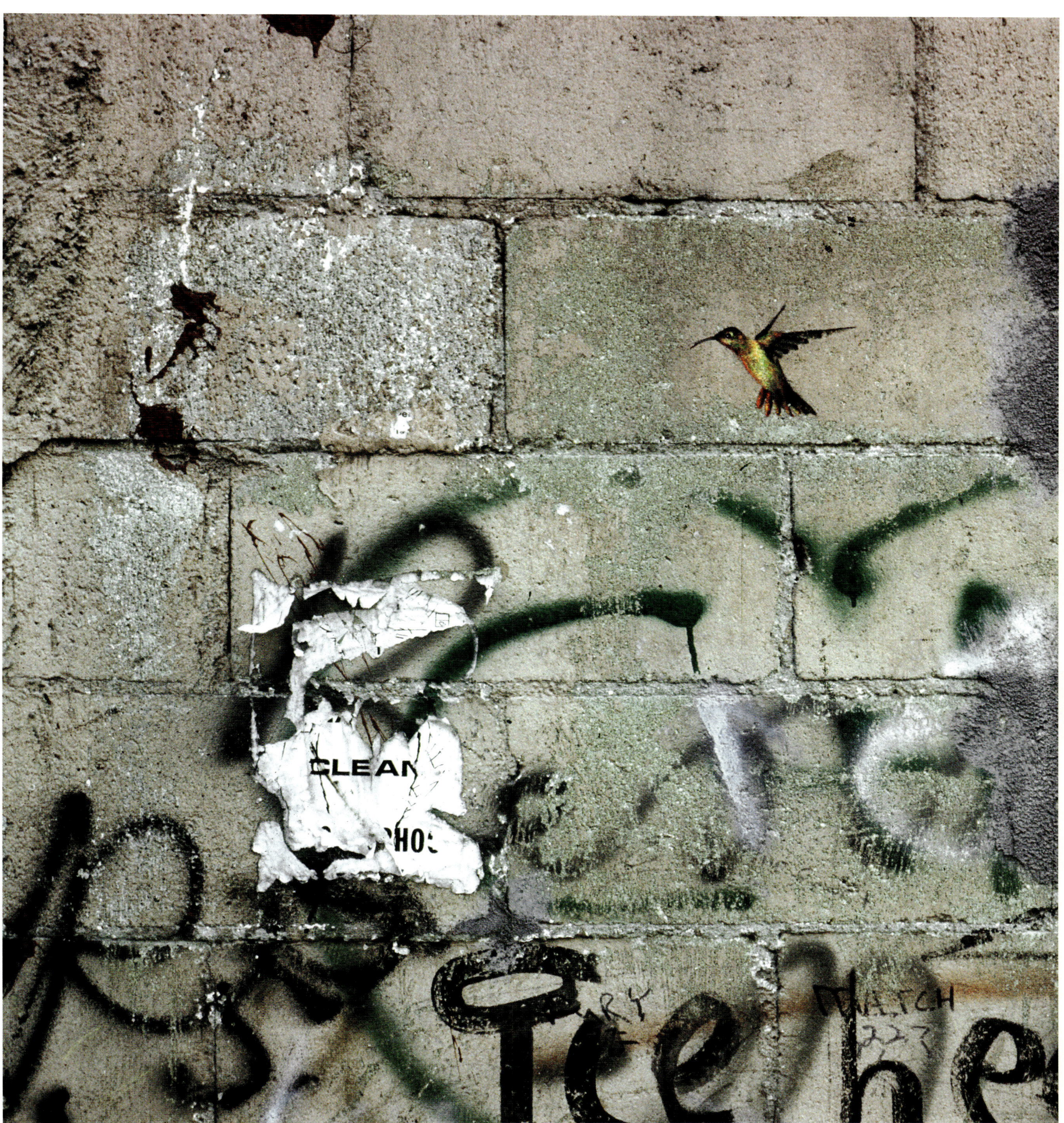

BLEEKER ST., NYC., 1979. // Between Bowery and Mott.

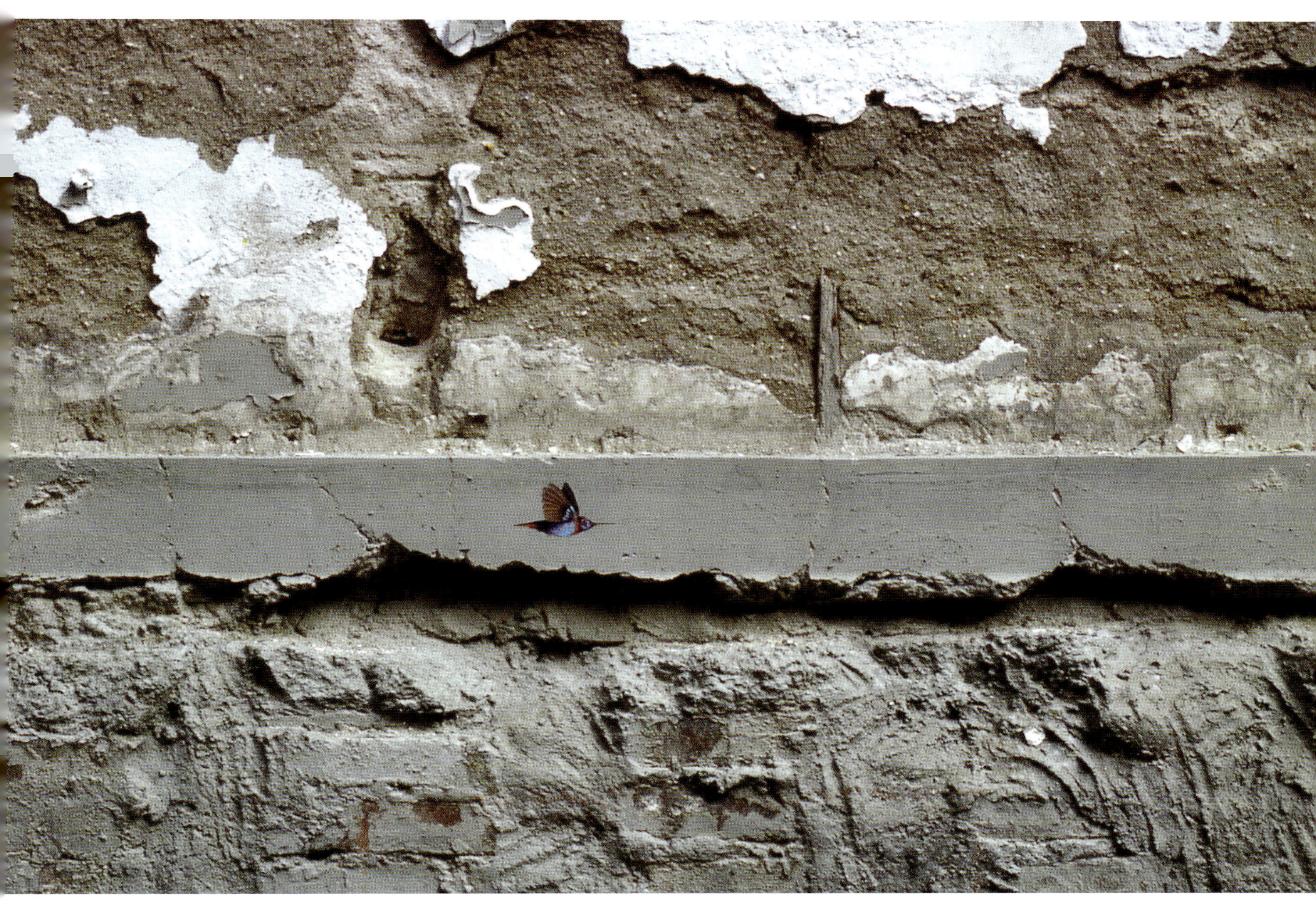

WALL ST. NYC., 1979. // Near Pine.

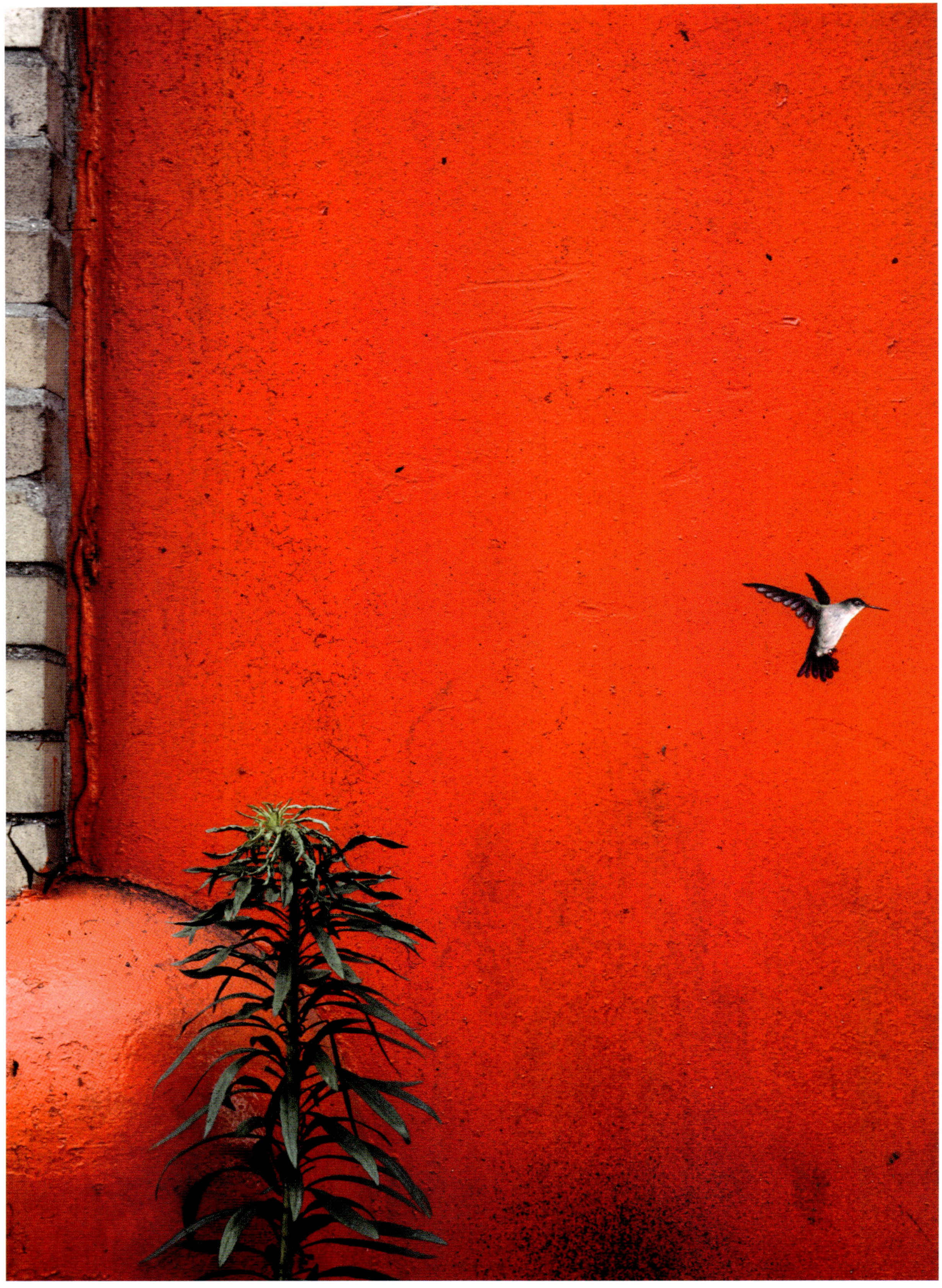

WASHINGTON ST., NYC., 1979. // Between Spring and W. Houston.

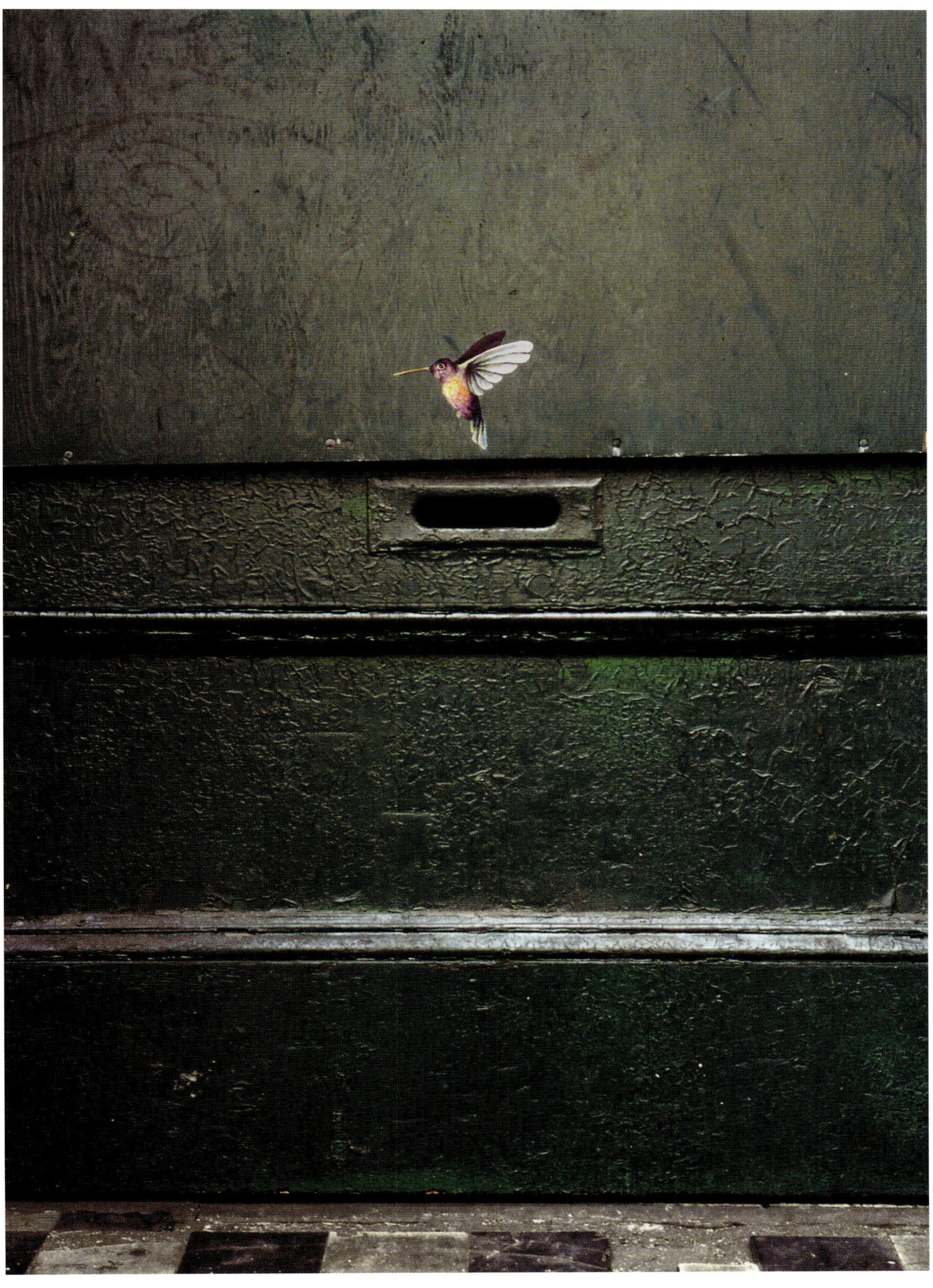

CENTRE ST. NYC., 1979. // Near Canal.

BROADWAY POEM

1980

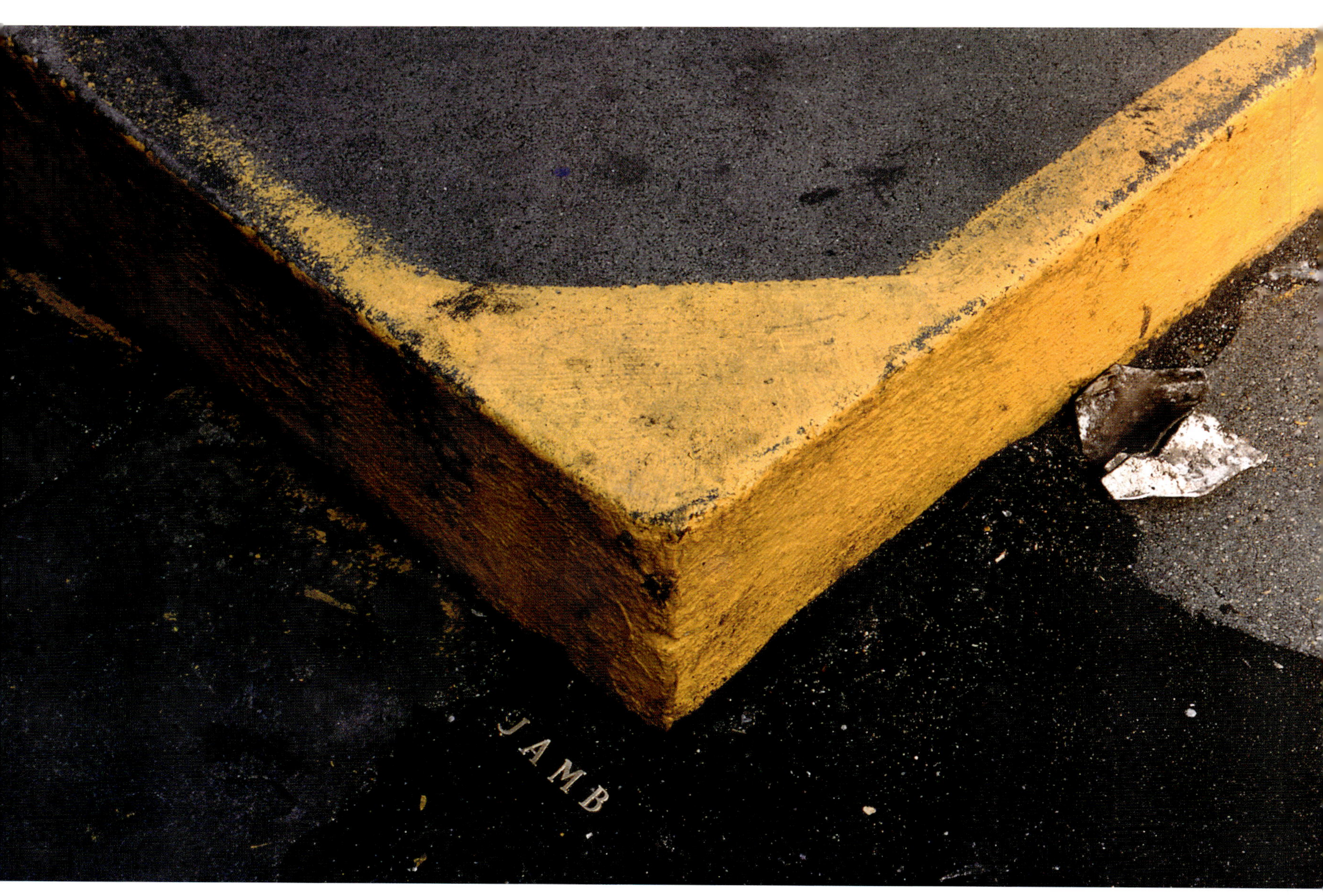

I've always been fascinated how stuff gets fossilized in the soft asphalt in the summer. Over the summer I hammered about 50 words along Broadway from 96th street to the Battery. After a couple of weeks these letters would sink into the pavement and disappear. Sometimes while walking on Broadway I wonder if they're still there.

At the time I was interested in DuChamp and William Burroughs and their experiments with allowing chance to decide the outcome of their work. My idea was that without keeping track, without self-critical intervention, I would inscribe an automatic writing poem down Broadway. Unfortunately the finished poem has been lost, but I do recall it being a lot less interesting to me than the single word images themselves.

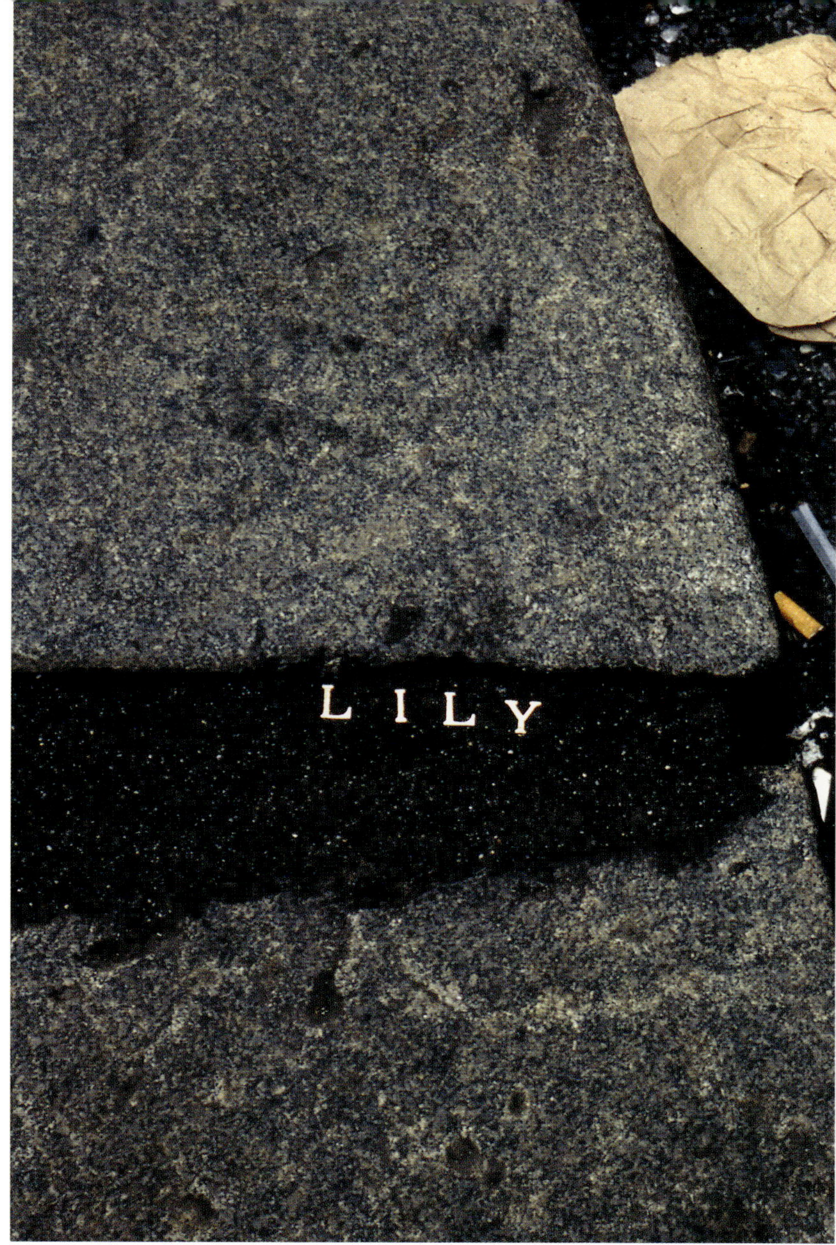

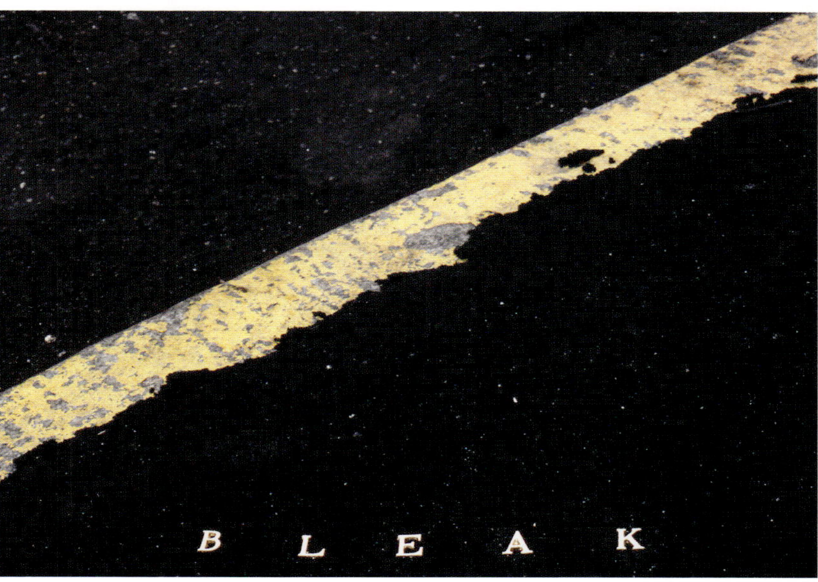

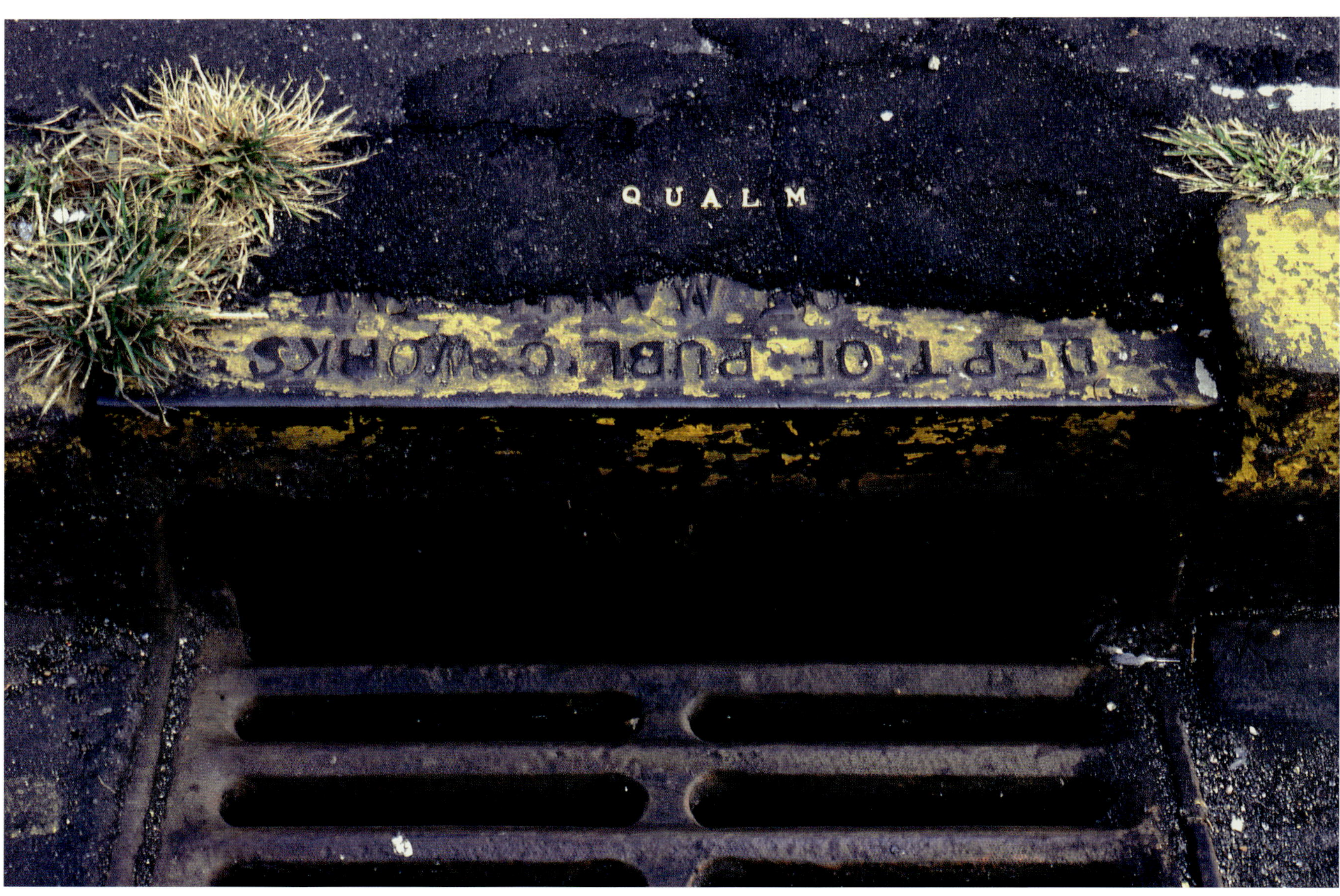
QUALM

SMEAR

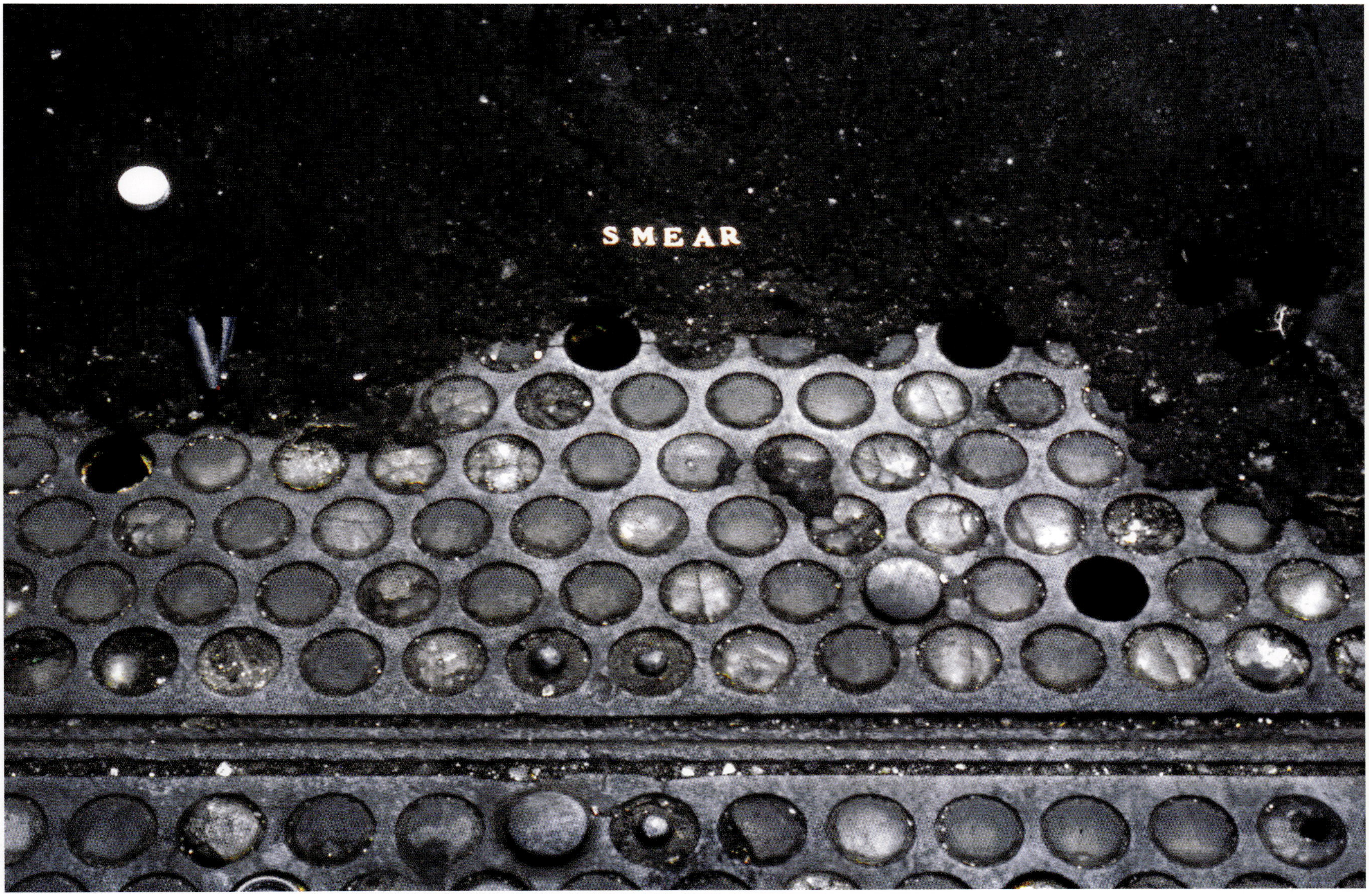

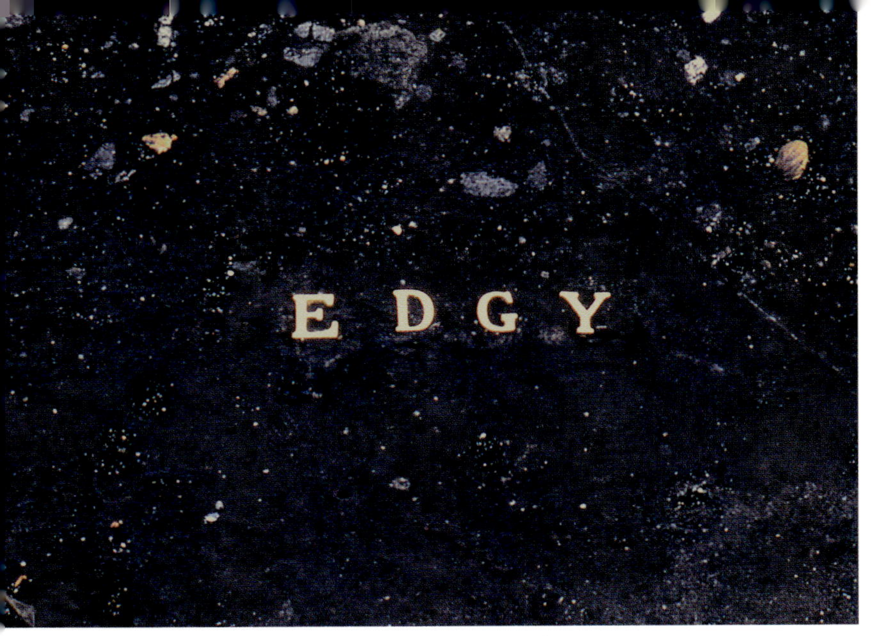
EDGY

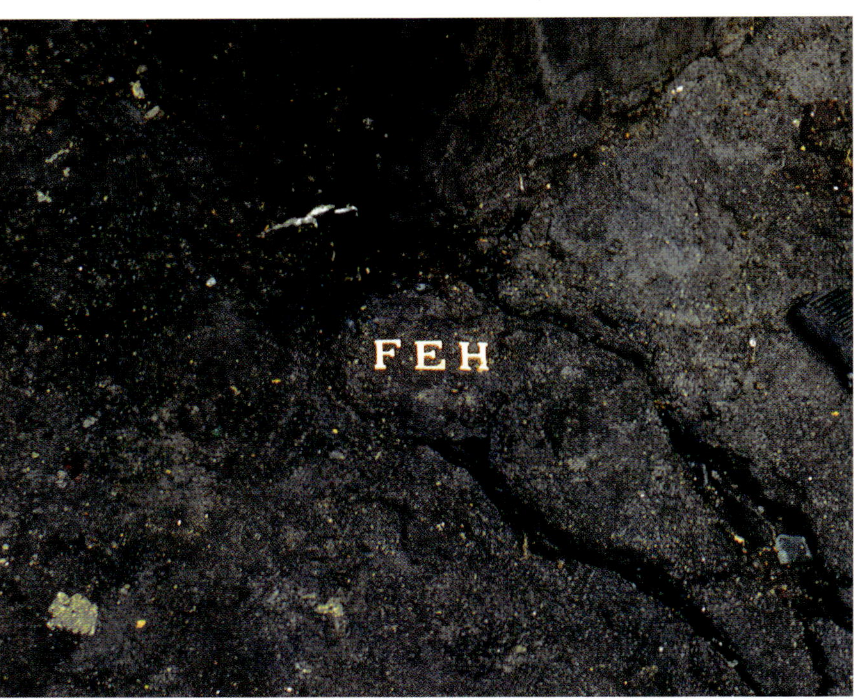
FEH

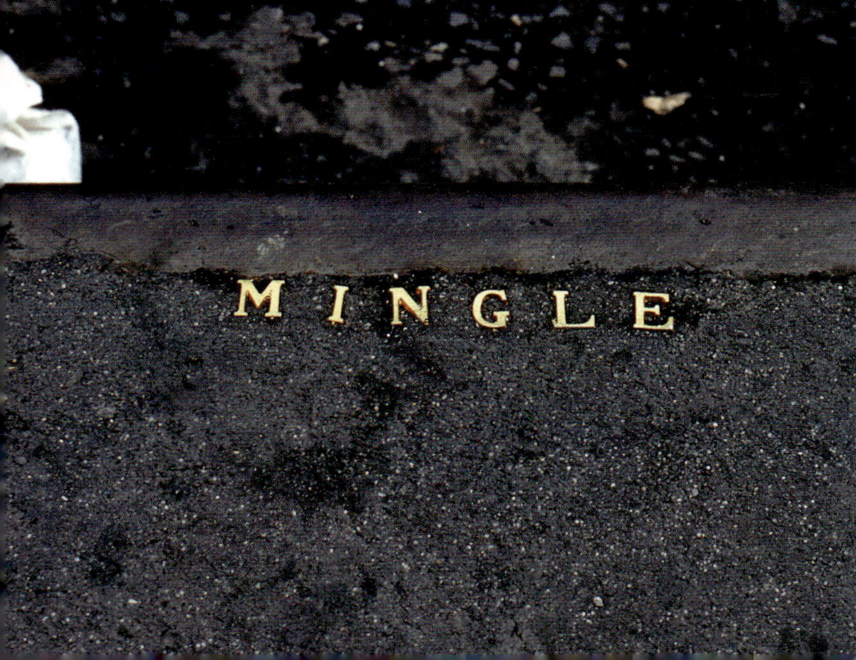
MINGLE

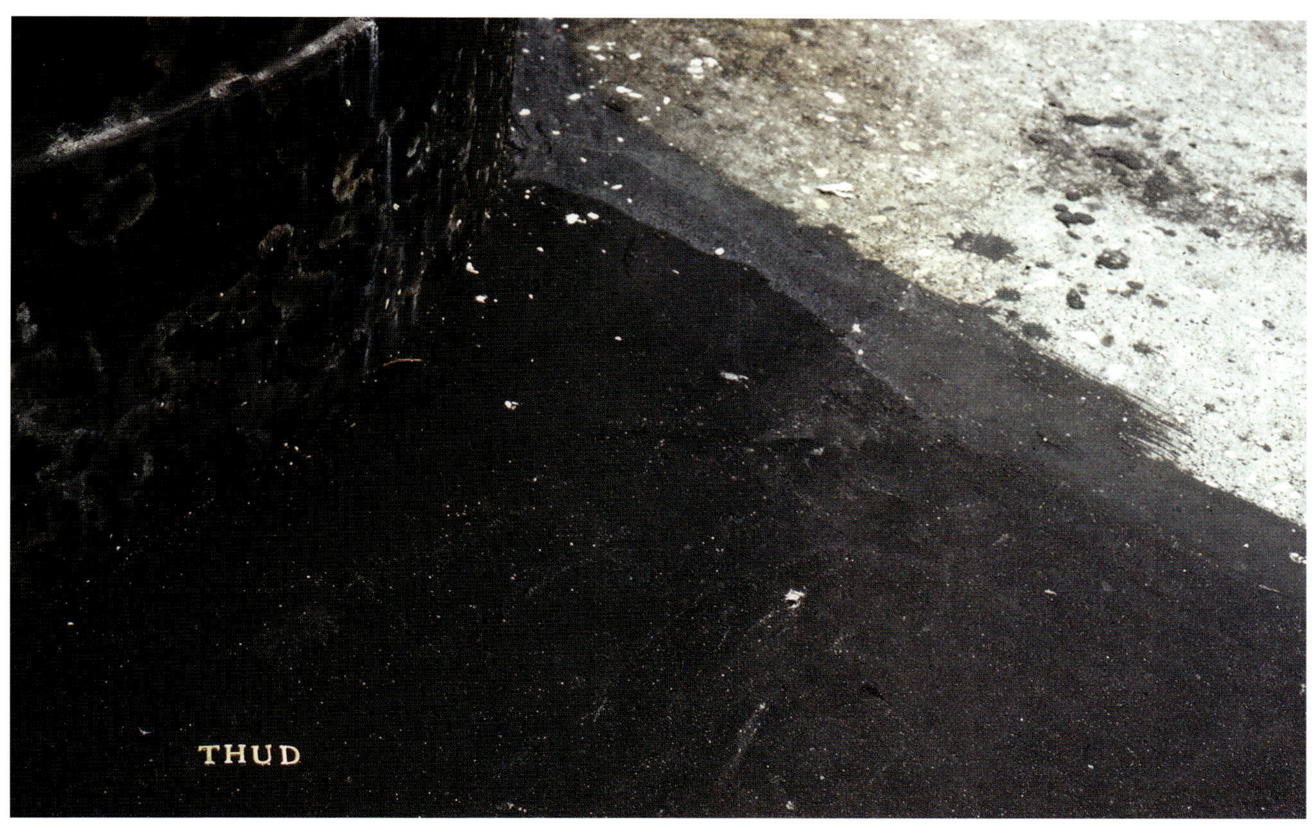
THUD

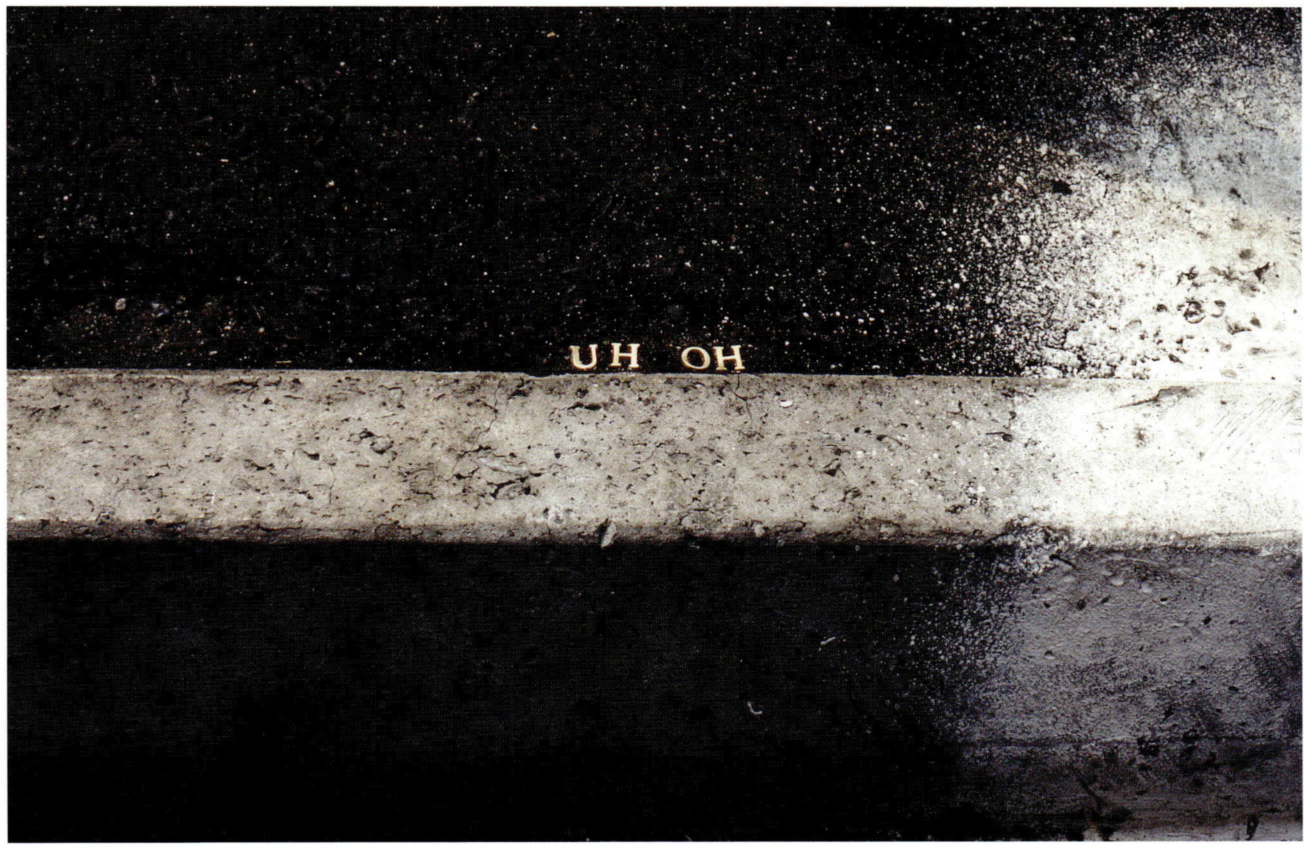
UH OH

PRANK

2004

Usually I work in series. But each year I take some time off to pull a couple of Pranks. Mostly these involve something experimental and out of my comfort zone. Lately I've been saving them for what's become an annual Halloween Prank.

OPPOSITE:

GREENPOINT, BROOKLYN. 2004. // Real weather balloon attached to house front.

BELOW:

PRANK, 2004. // Stills from the film, by Daniela Abke and Christina Vogelsgang.

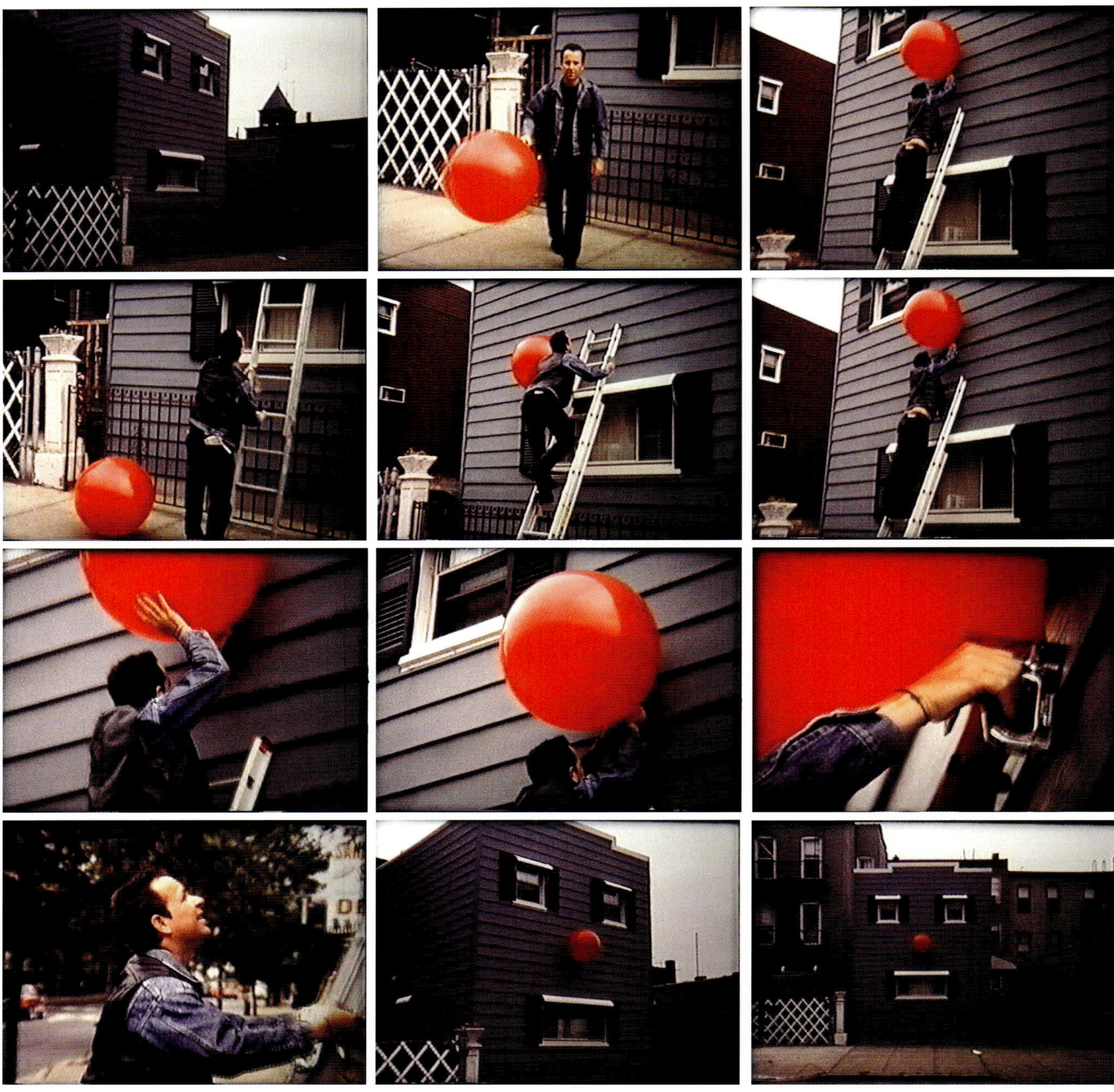

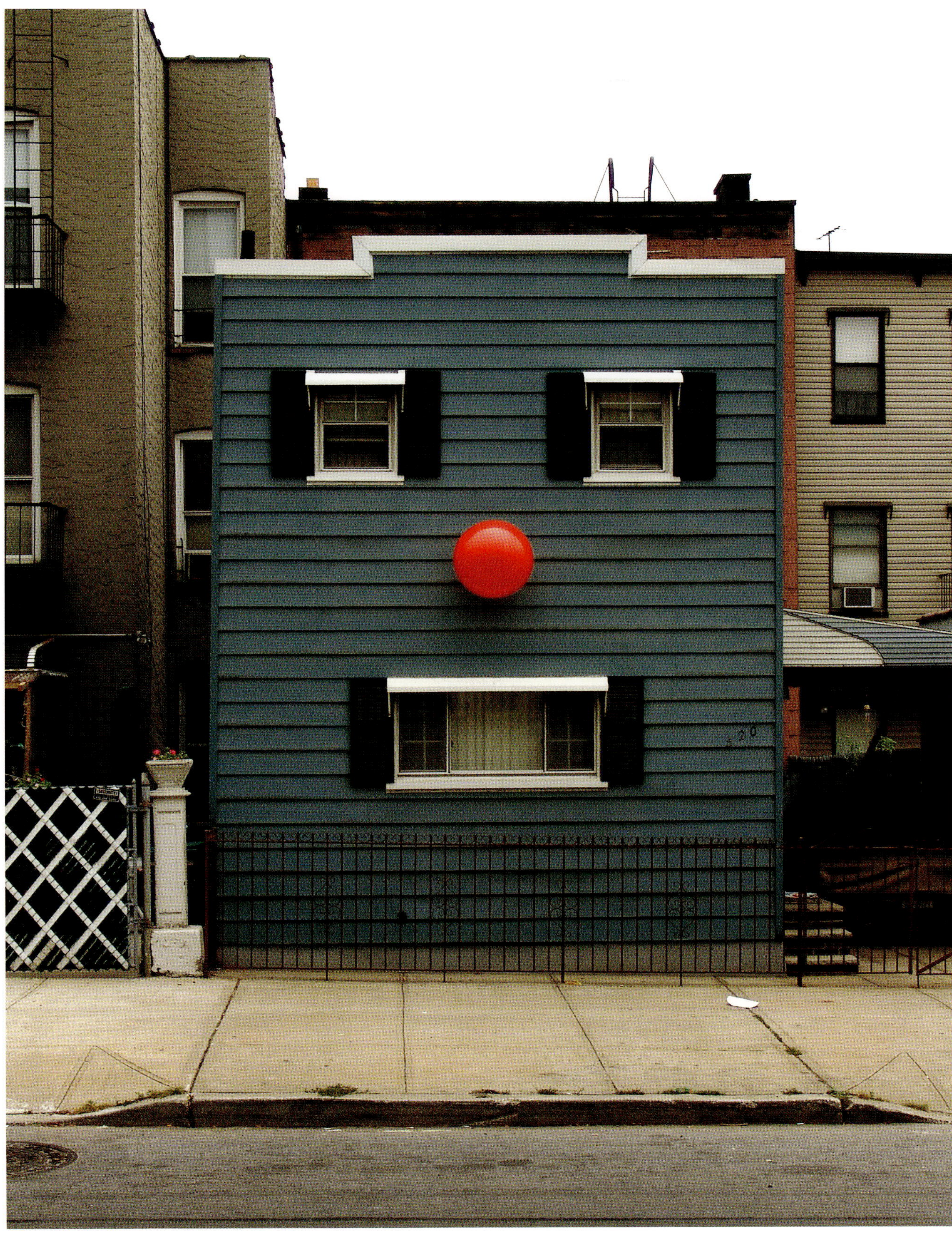
520

HOODYS

1994

By the early nineties my neighborhood was hitting a serious bottom. Drugs, crime, and HIV were taking their toll. Gentrification was forcing people out of their homes. The mood downtown was dismal.

This was one of my most demanding public pieces. Over that summer I wheat pasted about 75 of these figures throughout Manhattan's lower east side. It was a dangerous and strategically complicated piece, involving midnight missions, military precision, and the generous help of many friends.

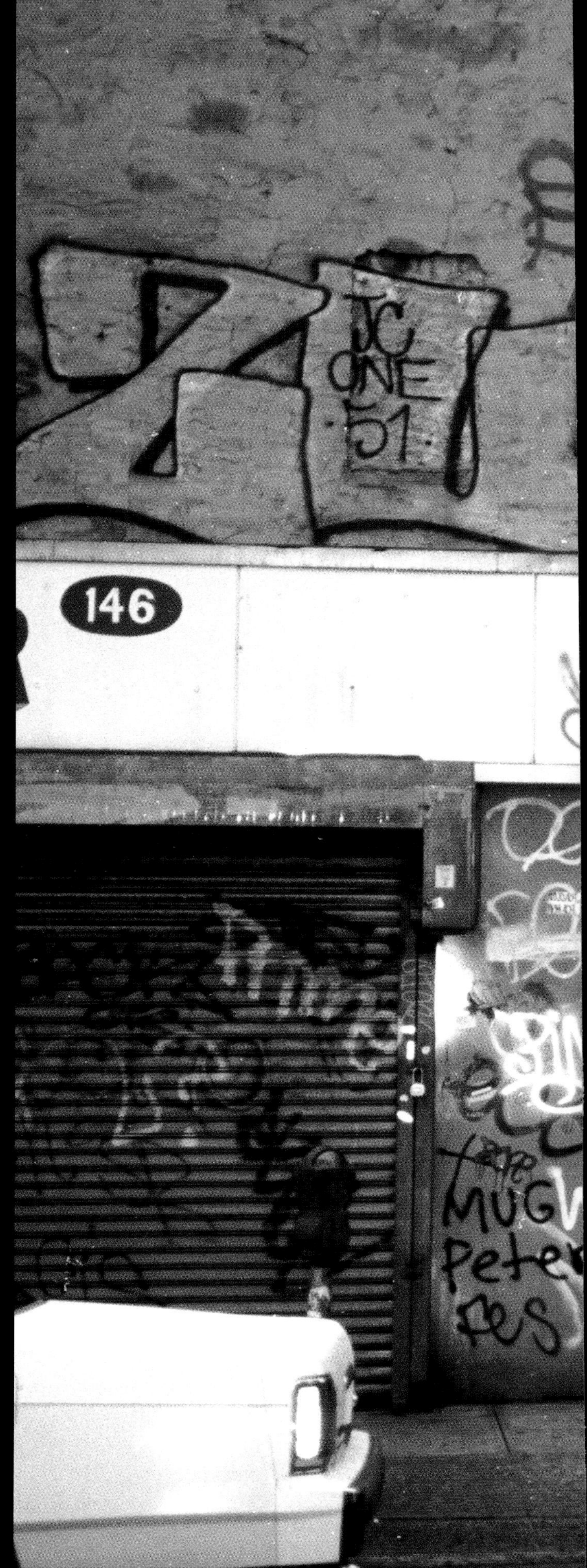

ALLEN ST., NYC., 1994.

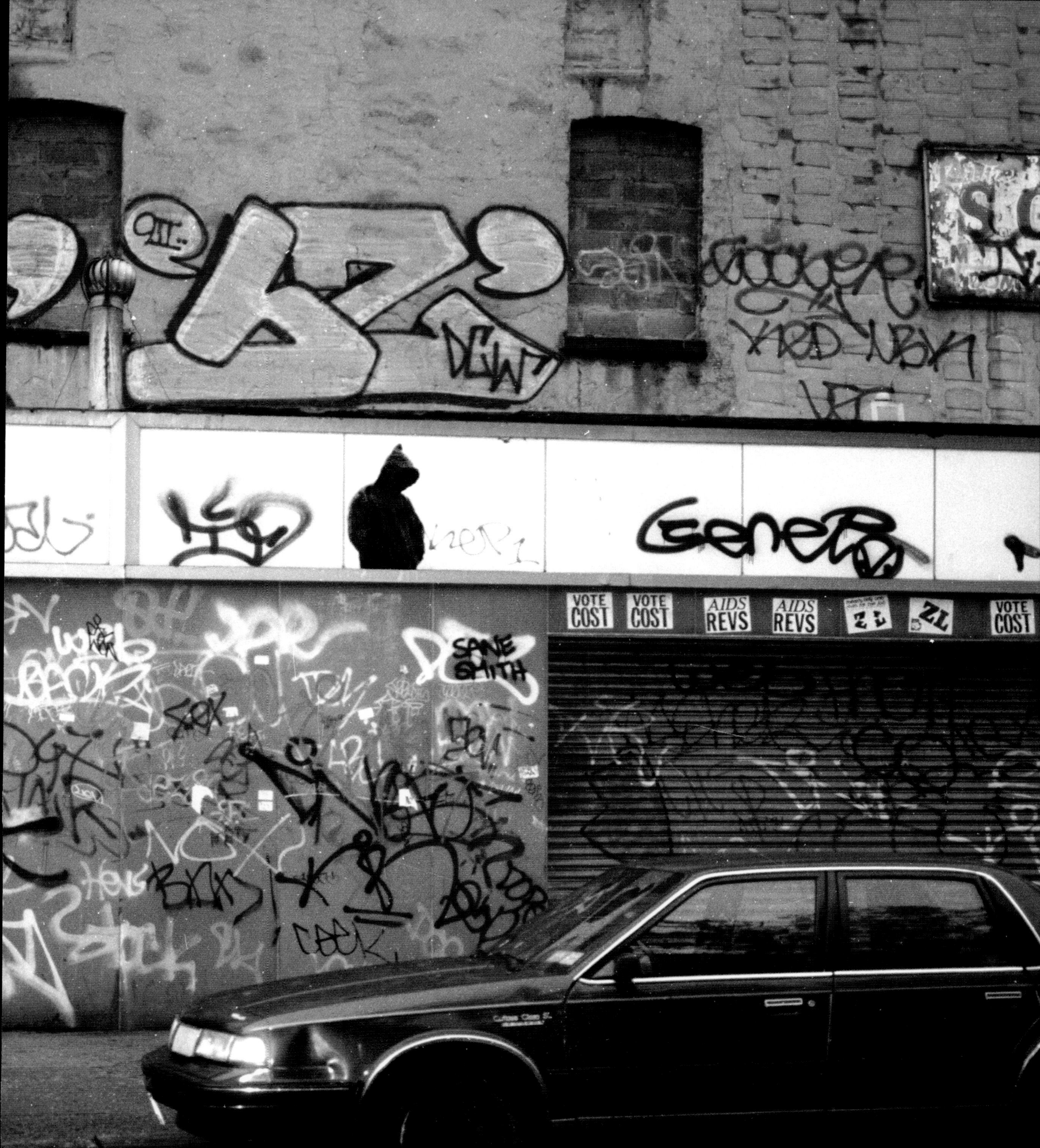

SANE SMITH
VOTE COST
VOTE COST
AIDS REVS
AIDS REVS
ZL
ZL
VOTE COST

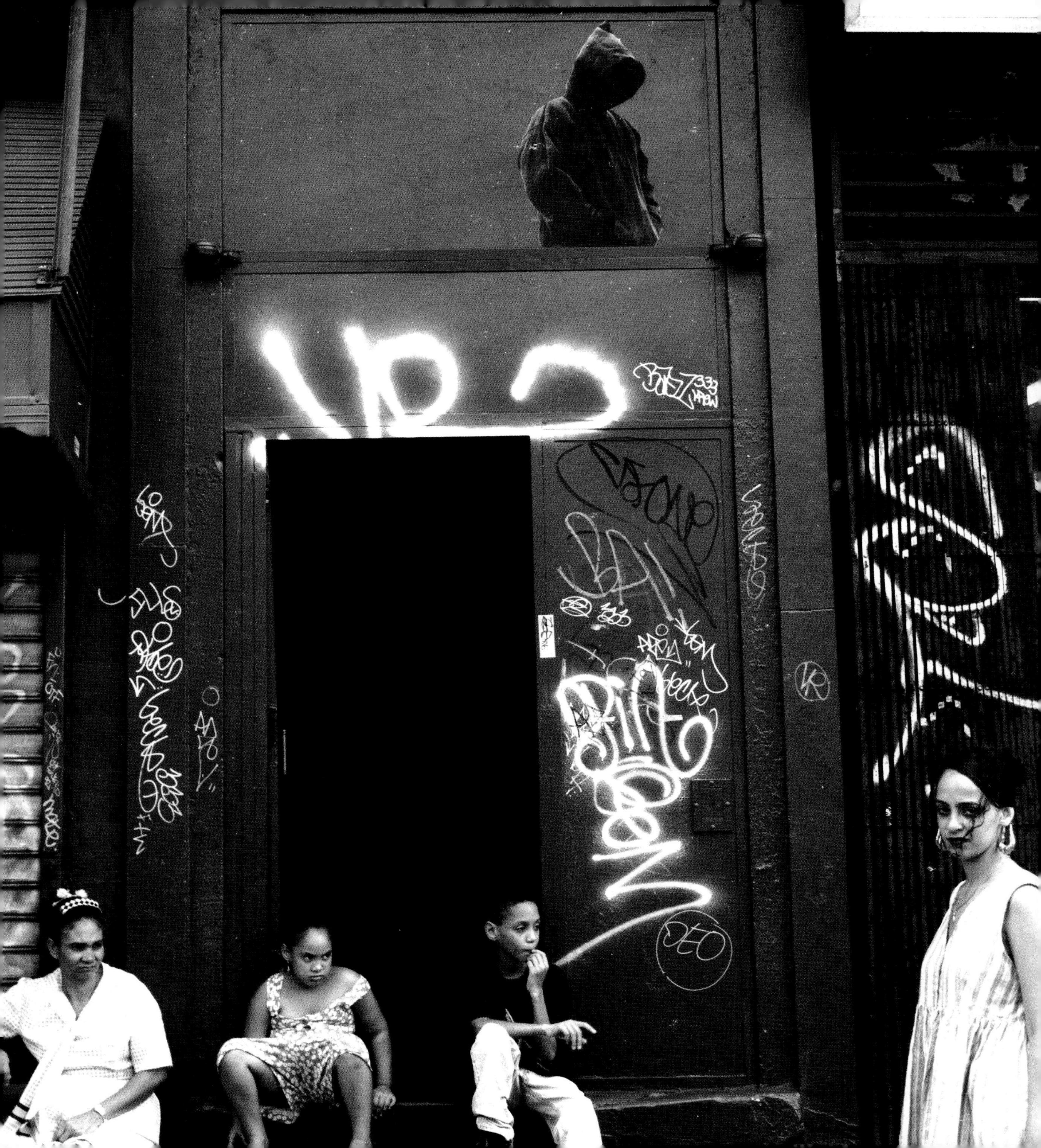

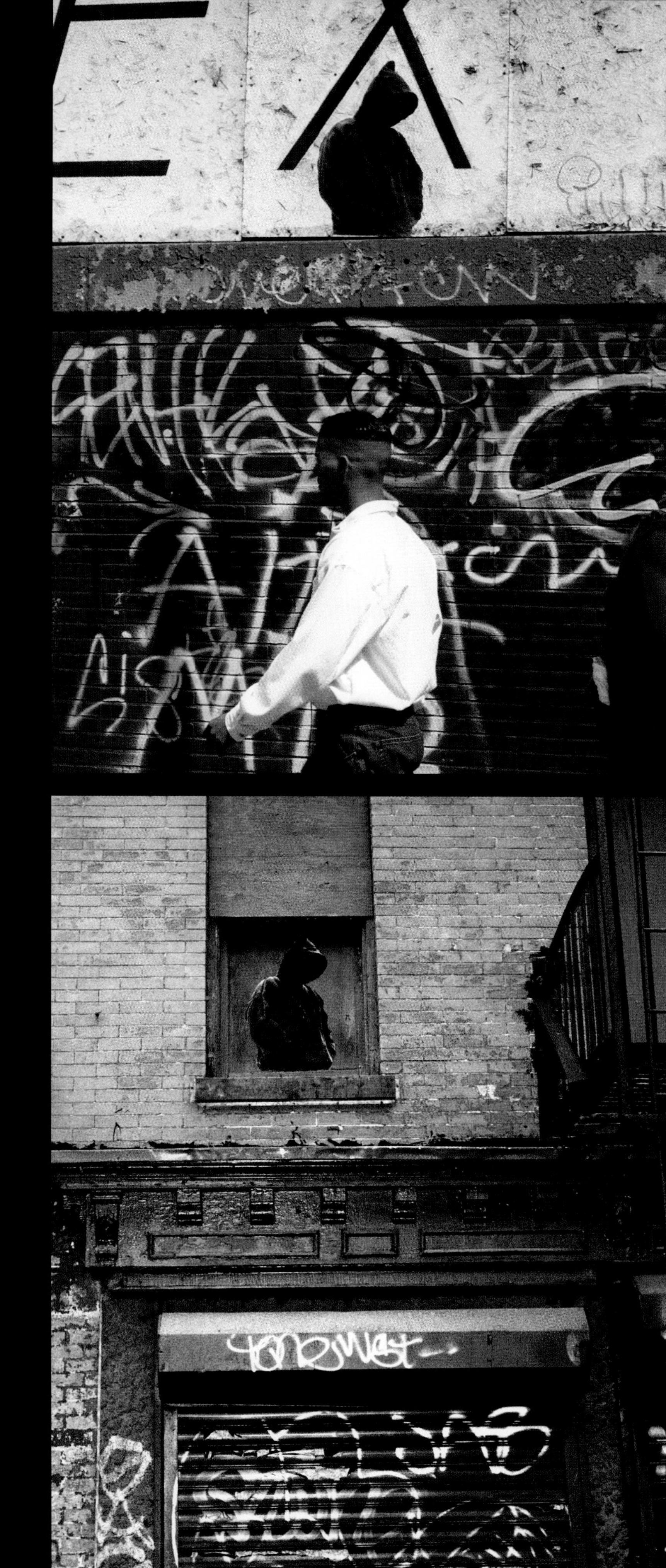

LEFT:

DELANCEY NEAR ALLEN ST., NYC., 1994.

UPPER RIGHT:

ESSEX ST., NYC., 1994.

LOWER RIGHT:

LUDLOW ST., NYC., 1994.

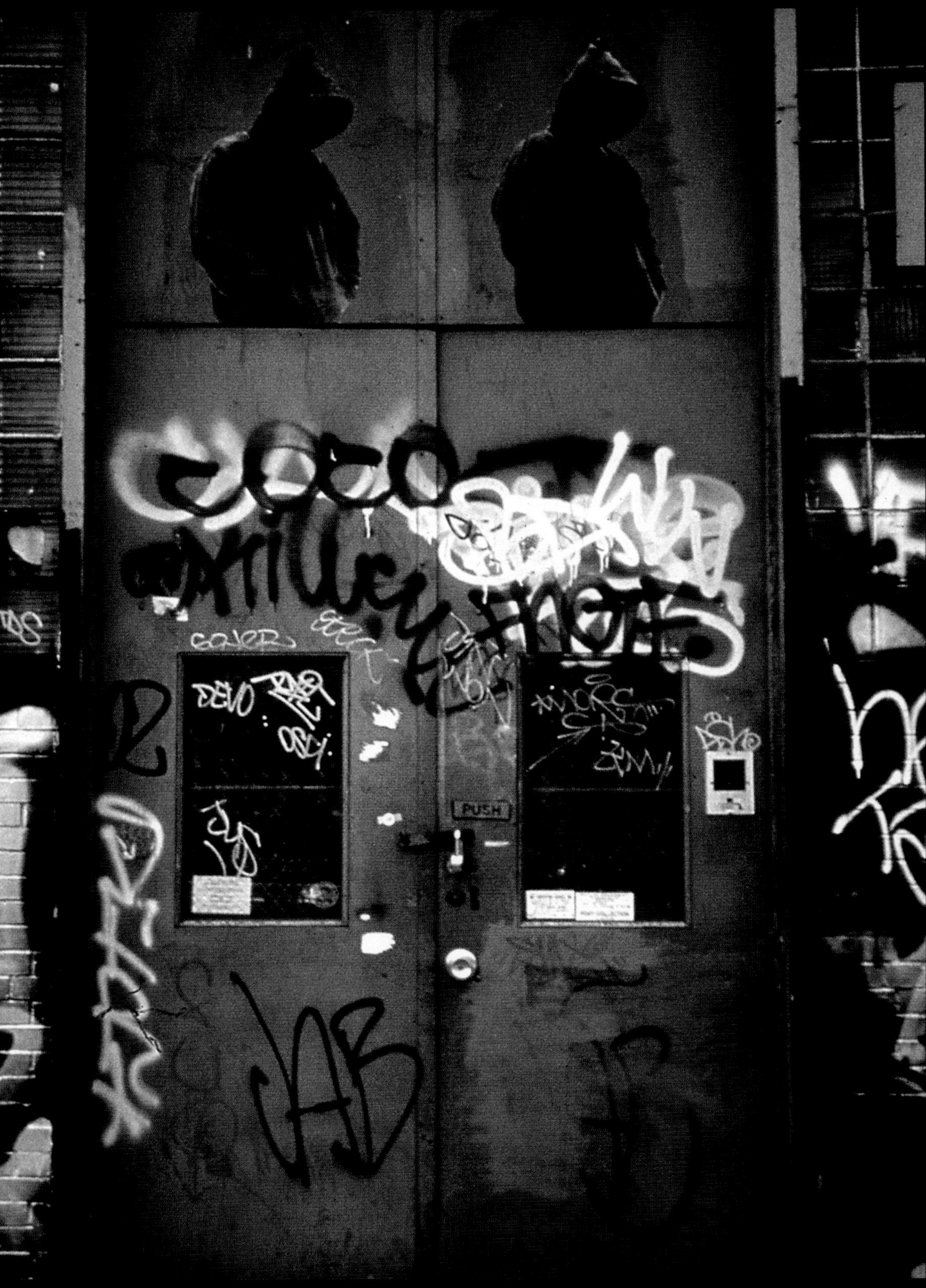

CHRYSTIE ST., NYC., 1994.

9TH ST. NEAR AVE. B, NYC., 1994. (OPPOSITE PAGE)

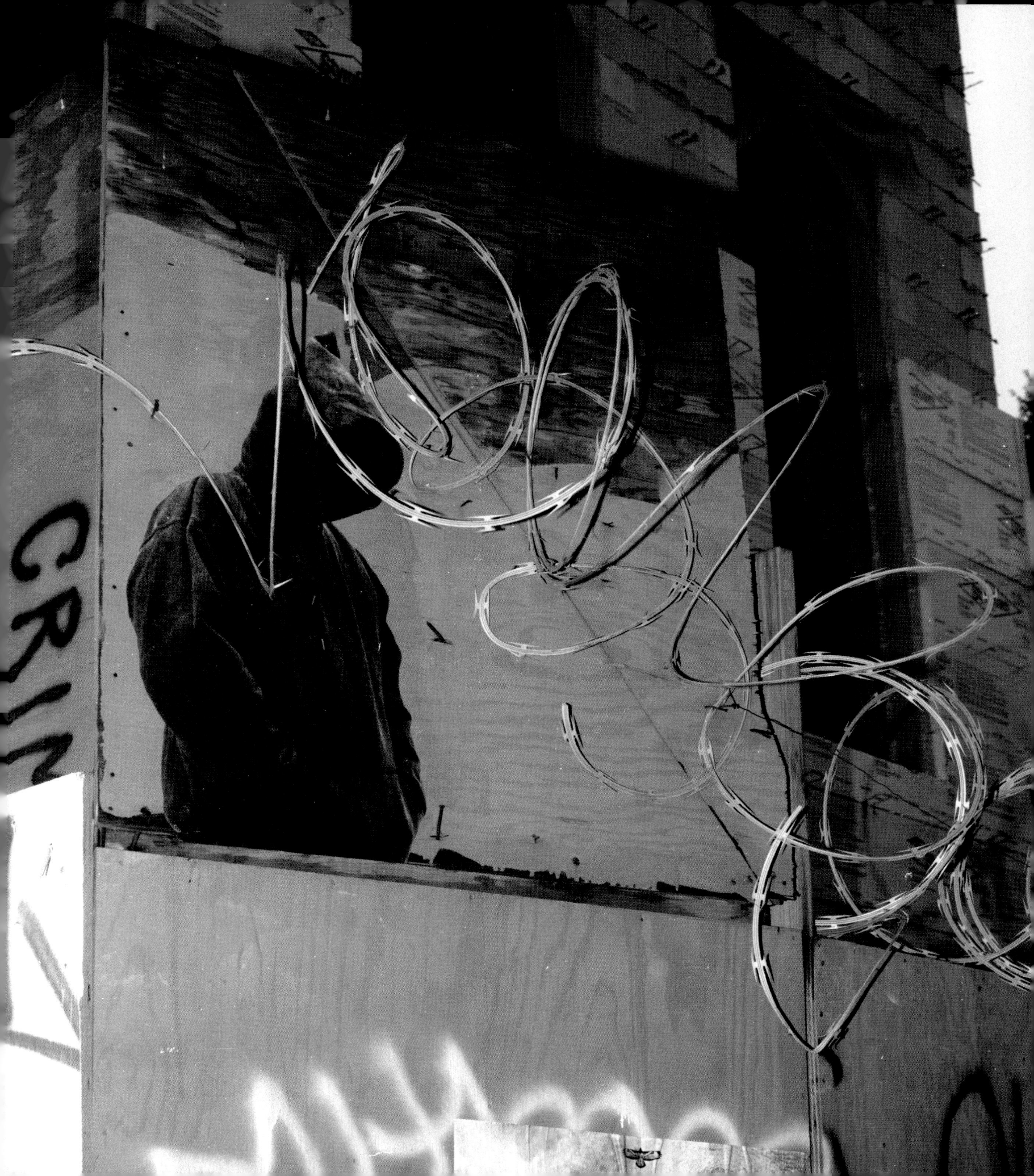

TROMPE L'OEILS

1995 - 1999

Because of the need to avoid getting caught, I began working with sticker modules that I'd prepare at home. I start with a photo printed on vinyl adhesive sticker paper. I paint and draw over the photo to make it more realistic, more three dimensional, then carefully cut it out. For a while I tried hiring someone to cut them out for me but it didn't really work. I realized the cutting was part of the piece, a form of drawing.

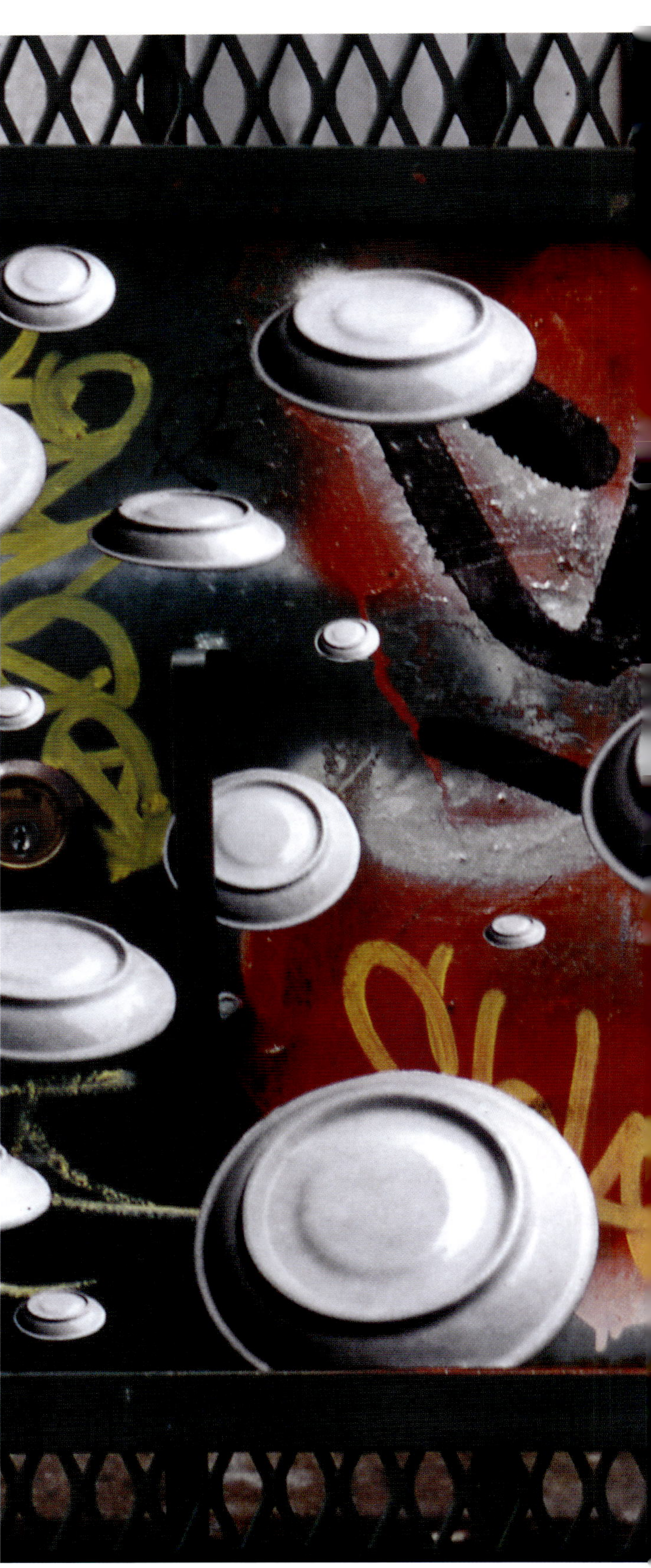

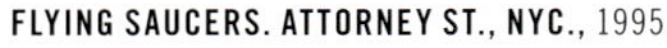

FLYING SAUCERS. ATTORNEY ST., NYC., 1995.

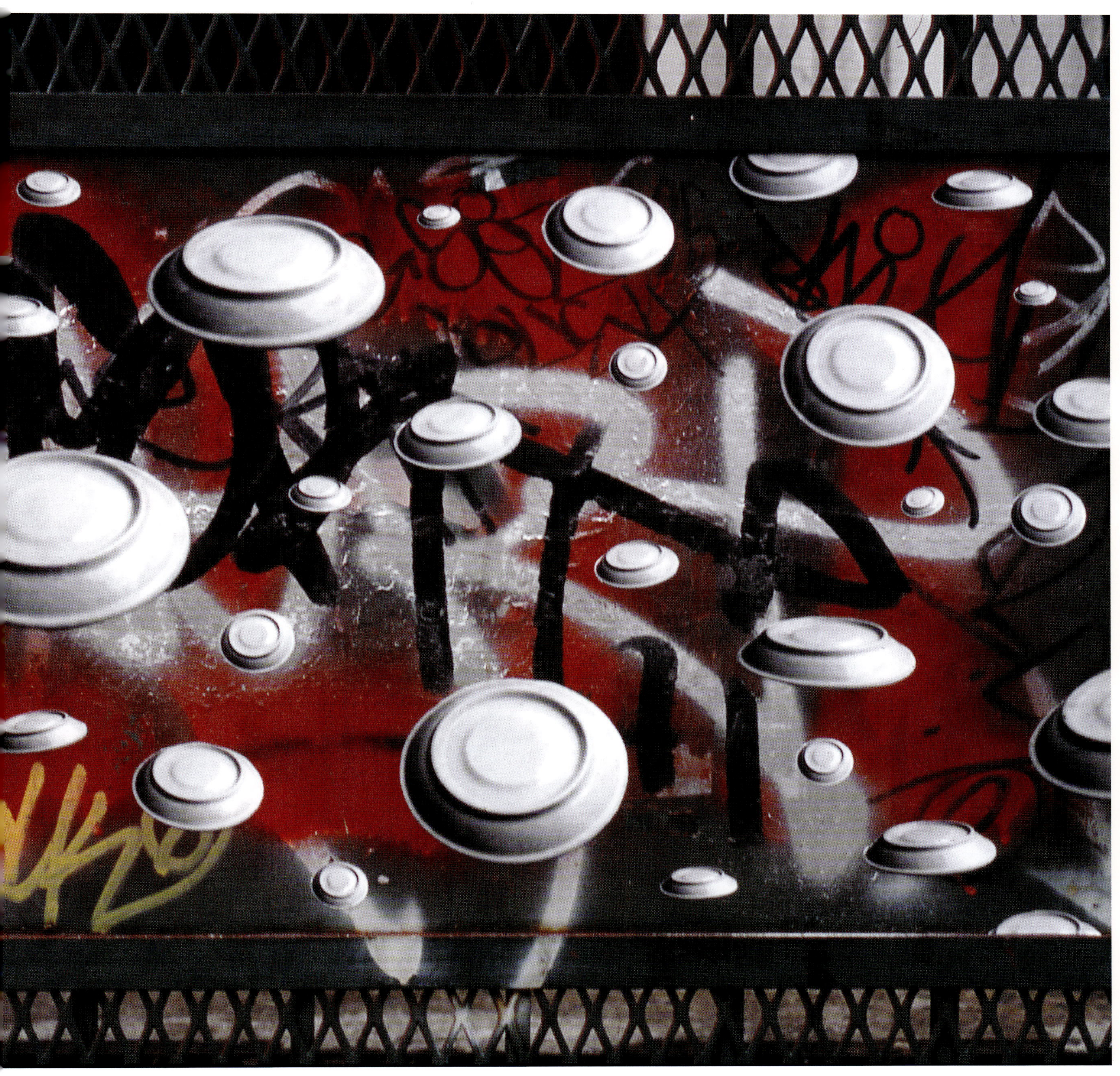

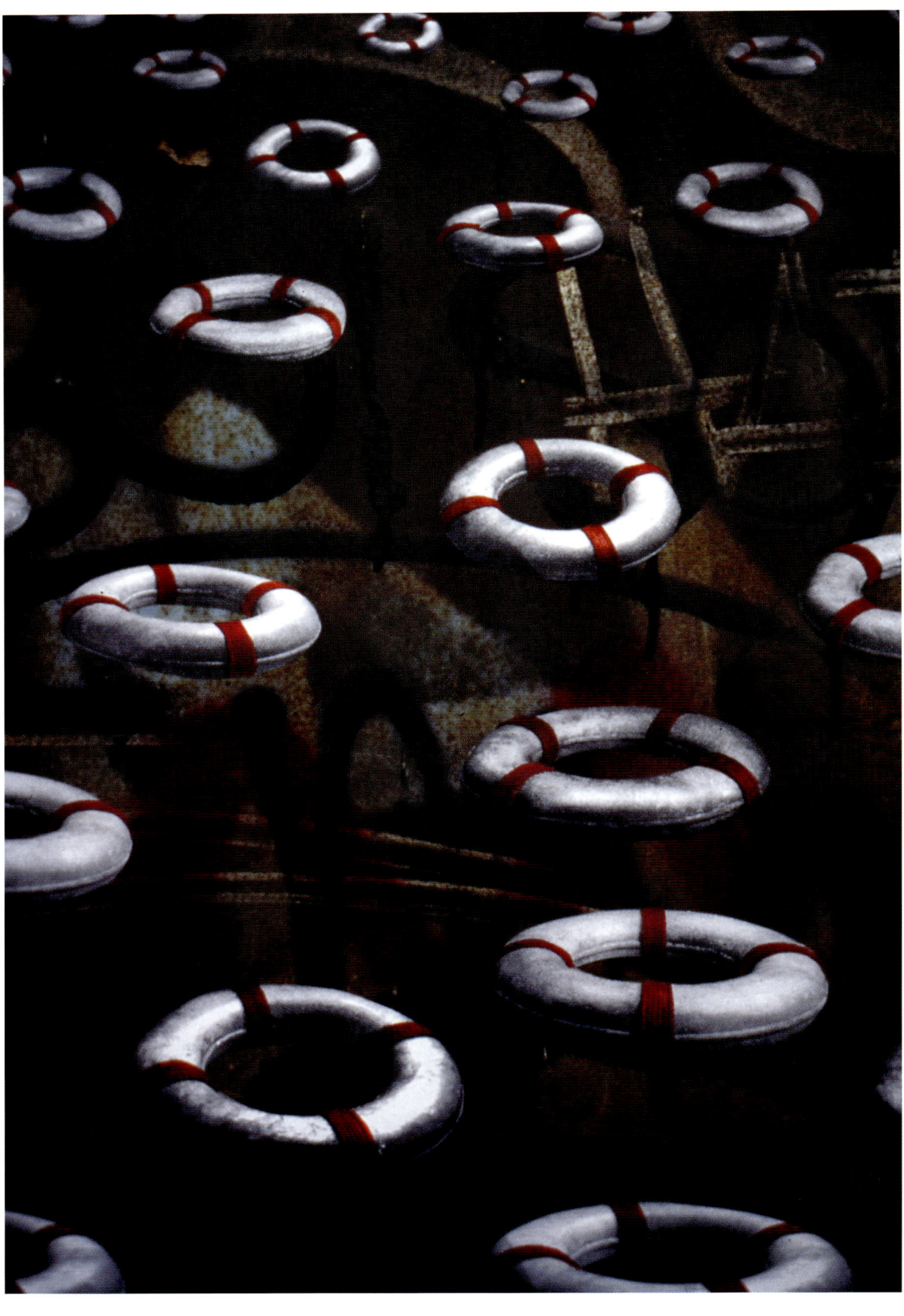

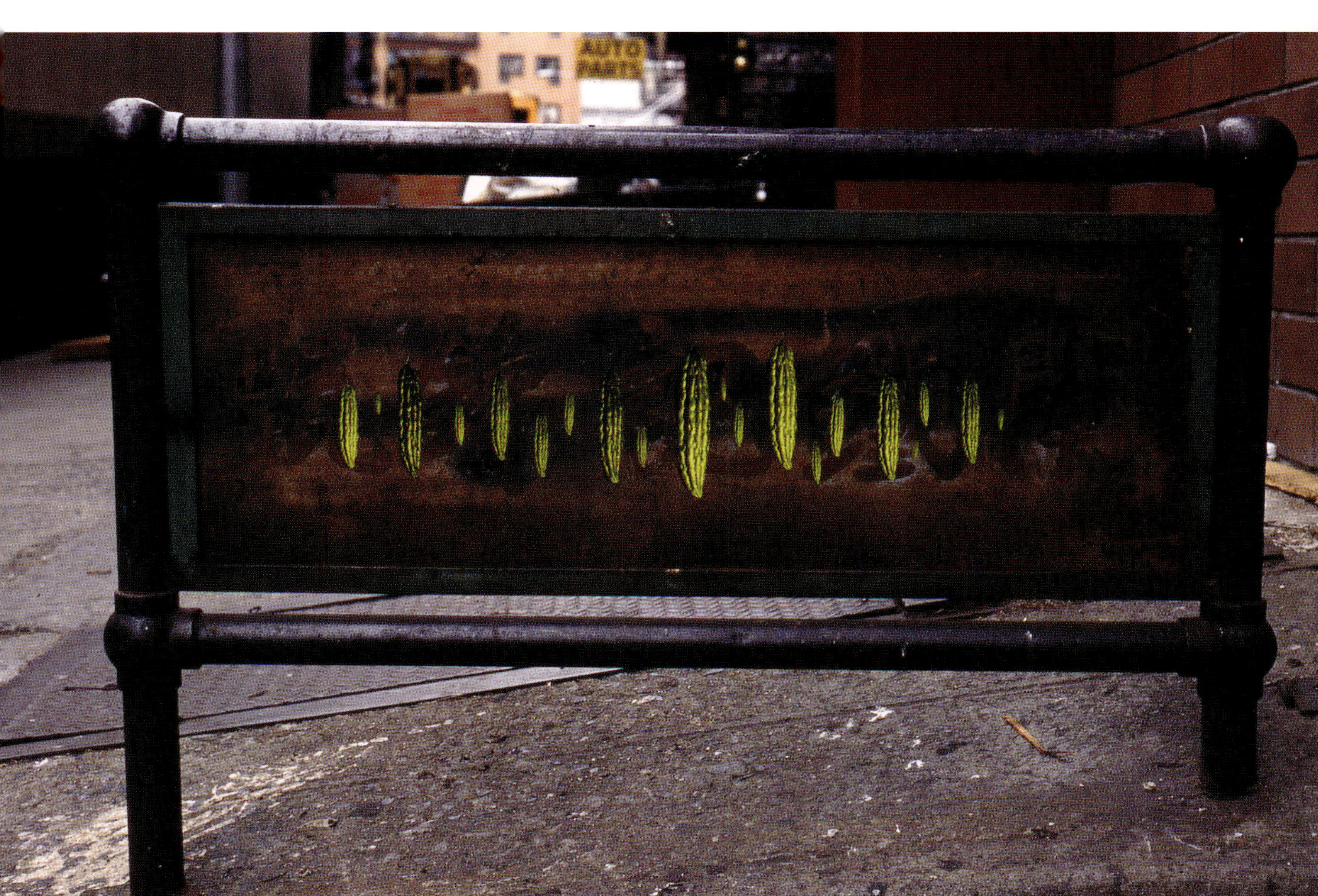

LEFT:

ORCHARD ST., NYC., 1995.

ABOVE:

LUDLOW ST., NYC., 1995.

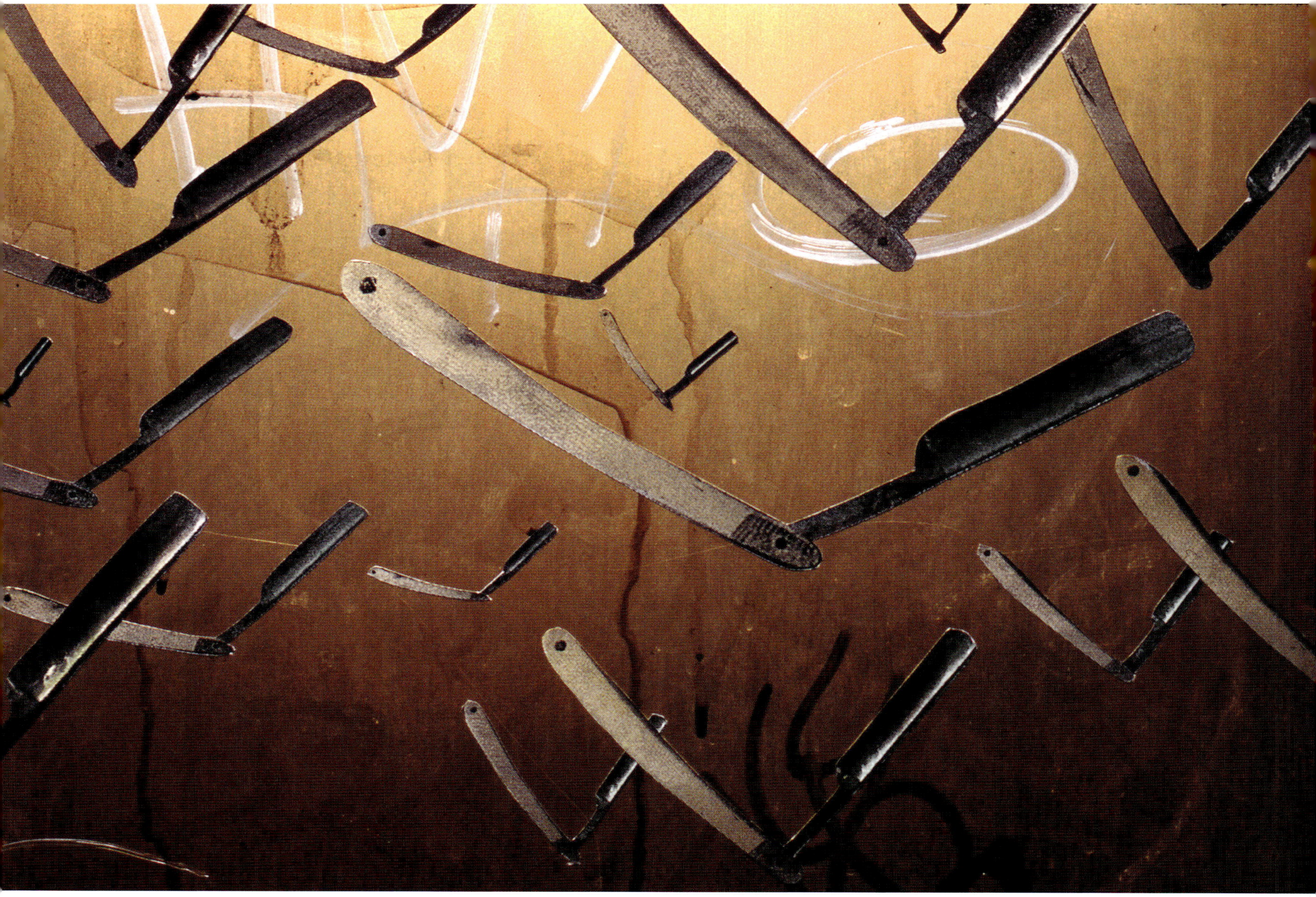

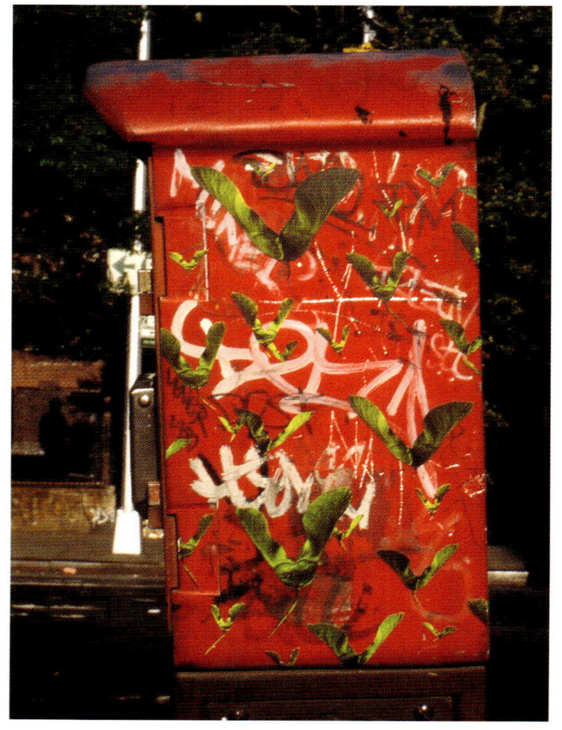

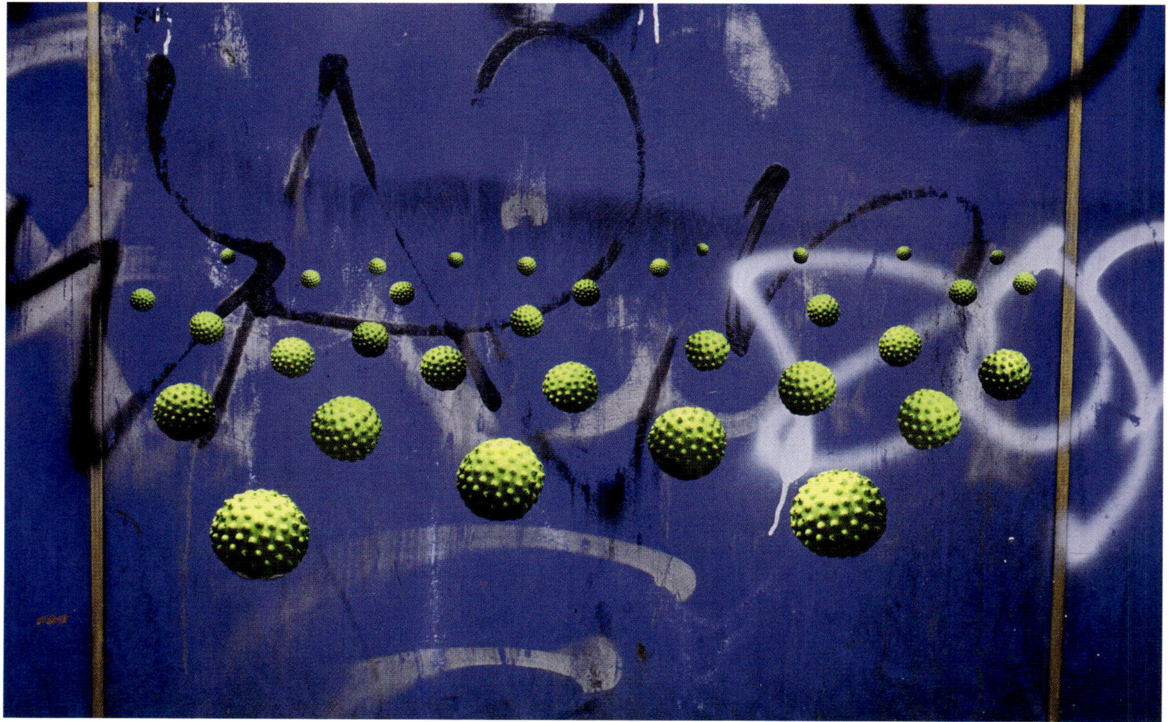

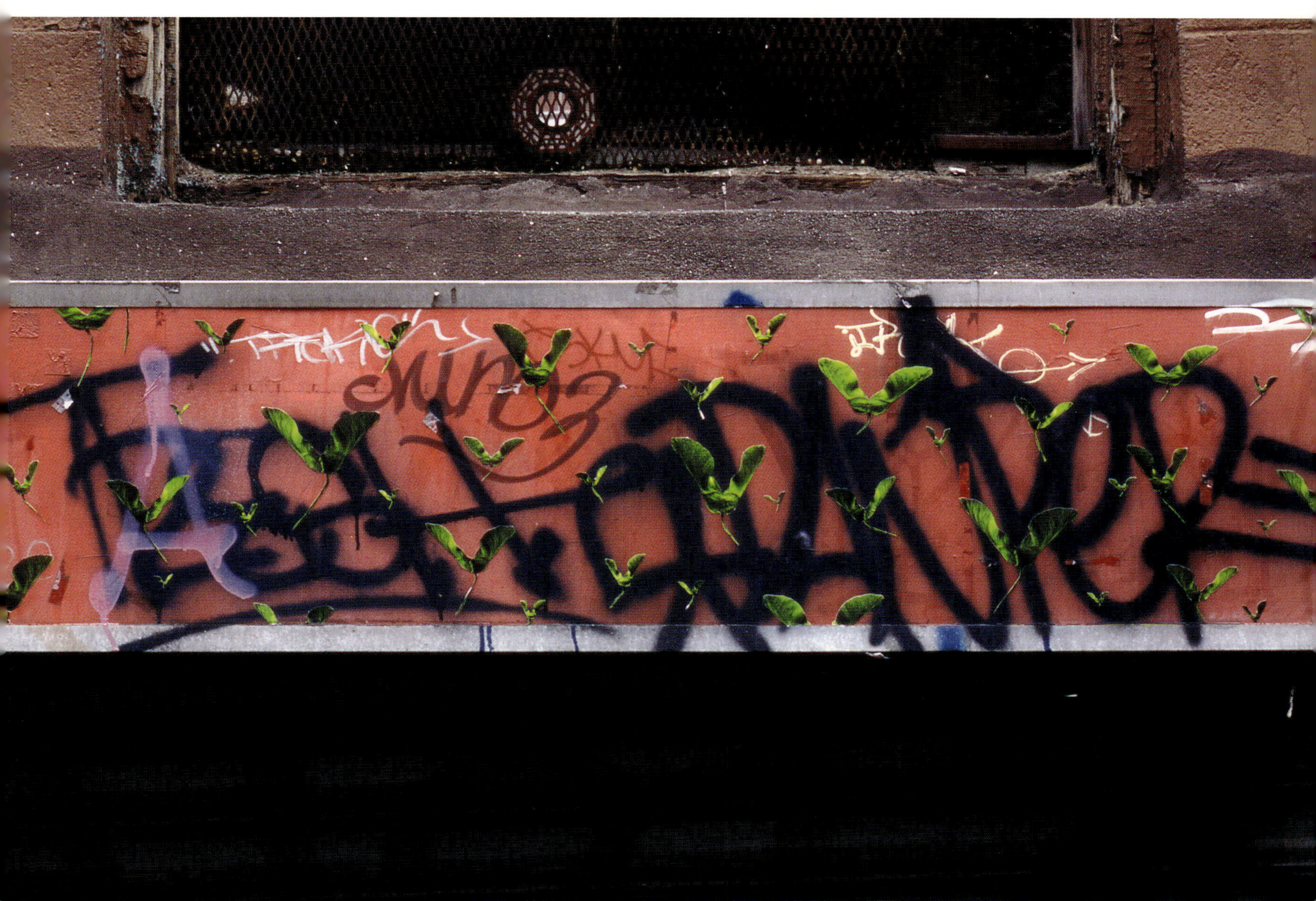

Thanks to the new digital technology, over the next few summers, my work really took off. Where previously I'd work three days to paint one sticker, now I could produce fifty.

OPPOSITE PAGE, TOP:

CUTTHROATS, HESTER BETWEEN CHRYSTIE AND ELDRIDGE, NYC., 1995.

OPPOSITE PAGE, LOWER LEFT:

SEED PODS, HESTER AND ESSEX ST., NYC., 1995.

OPPOSITE, LOWER RIGHT:

VAUGHAN'S TOY. ALLEN ST., NEAR STANTON., 1995.

ABOVE:

SEED PODS. HESTER BETWEEN ELDRIDGE AND FORSYTH, NYC., 1995.
Painted vinyl stickers on metal sign.

NEXT PAGE:

ORCHARD ST. BETWEEN HESTER AND BROOME, NYC., 1995.

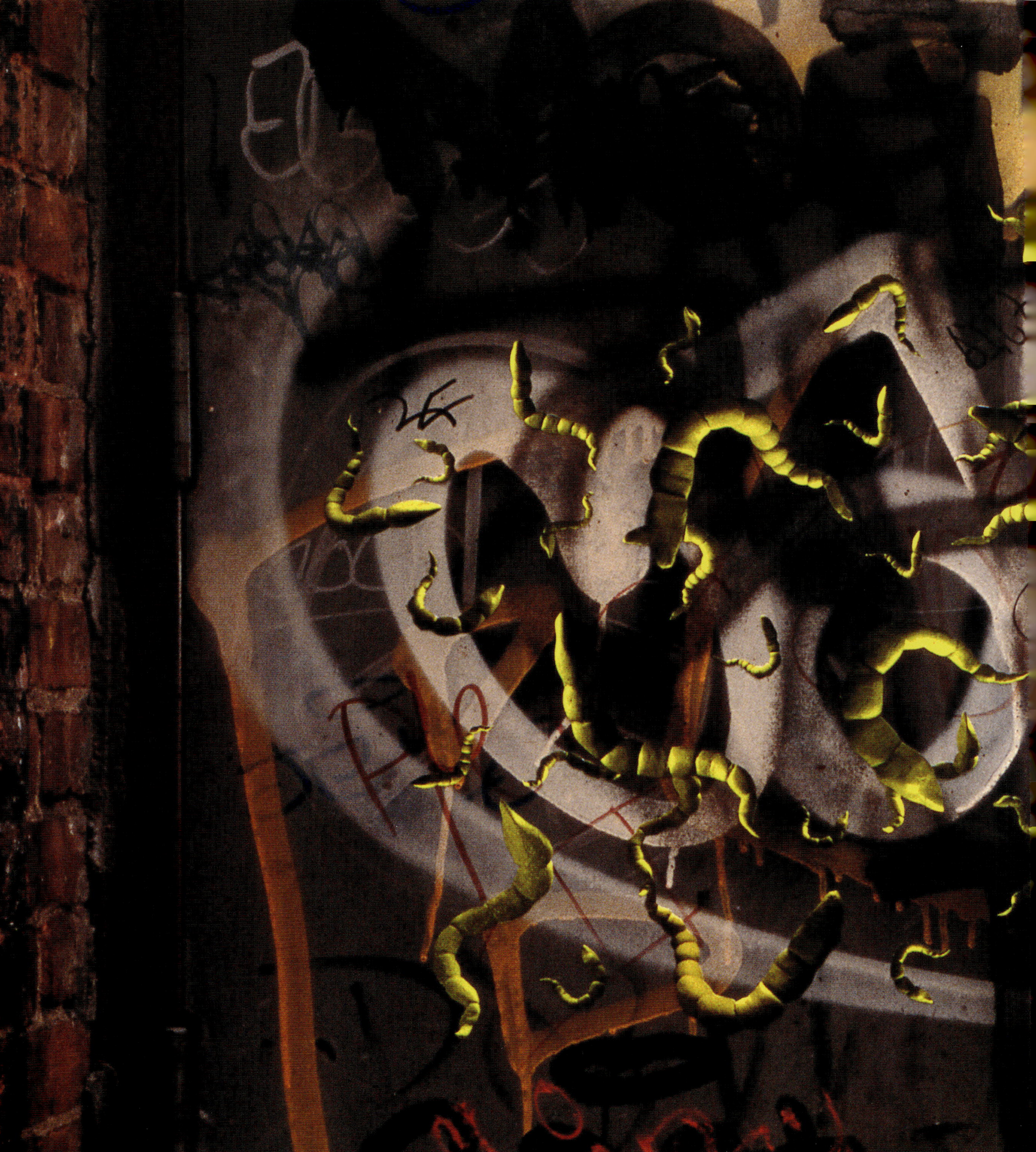

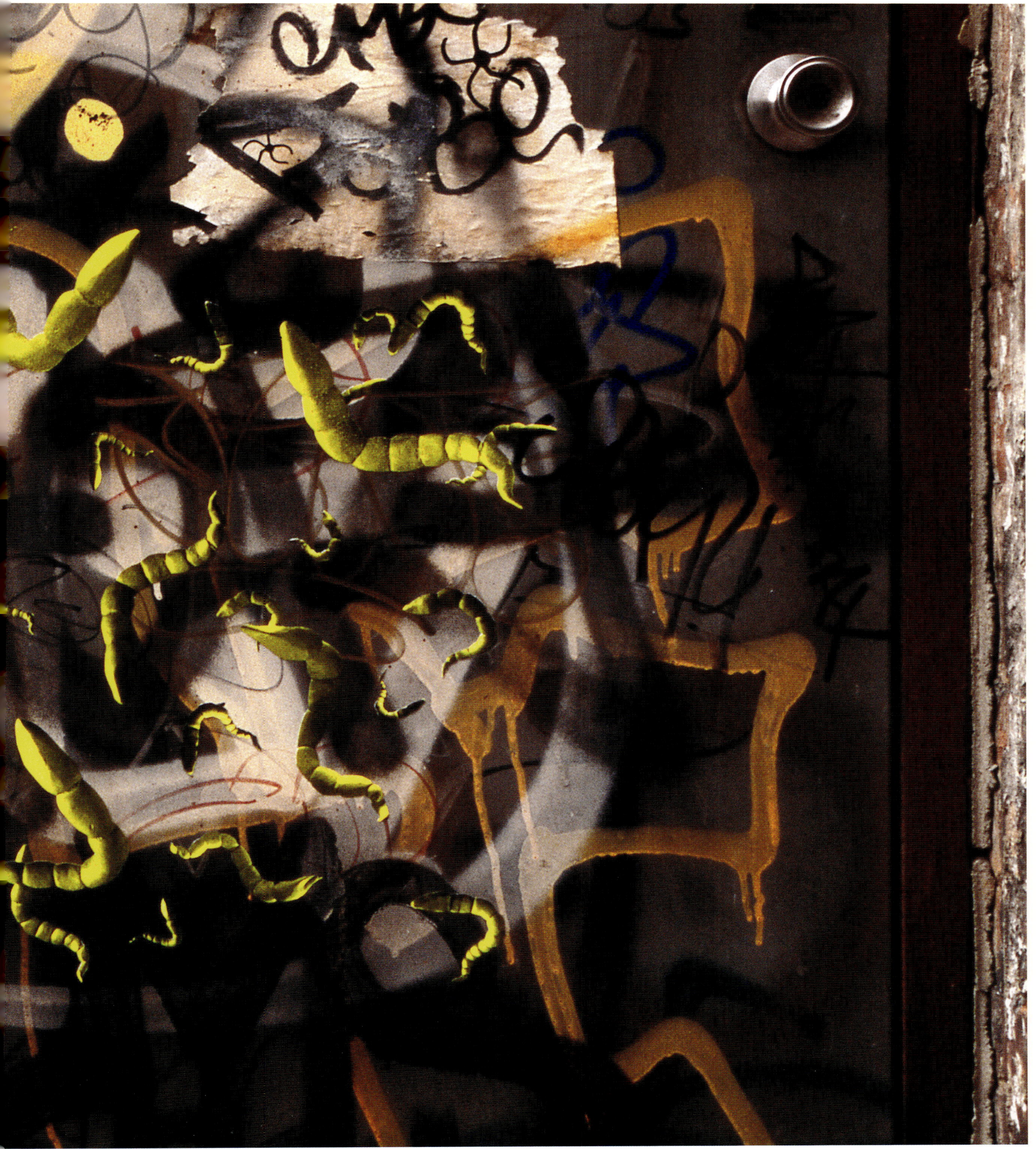

1996

Growing up I'd always been fascinated by various so called low-brow painting techniques like hot rod pinstriping, tattooing, and custom van airbrushing. One day, after I'd been doing the stickers for about a year, I was looking at an abstract illusionist painting my dermatologist had up in her waiting room. This one was the usual thing: cheesy squiggles of paint floating very convincingly over airbrush shadows; I didn't really like it but suddenly it was as if a light bulb went off. Seriously. A revelation. I went straight from her office and bought an airbrush and started putting shadows under all my stickers. 1996 was probably my most productive year ever.

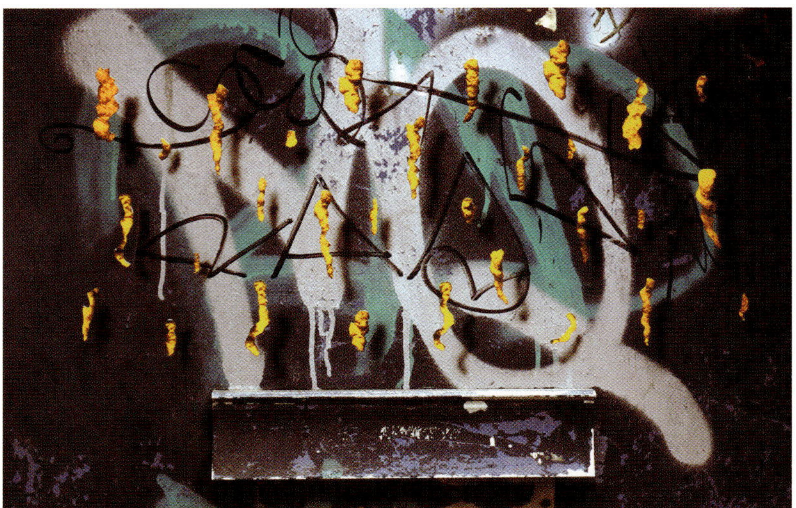

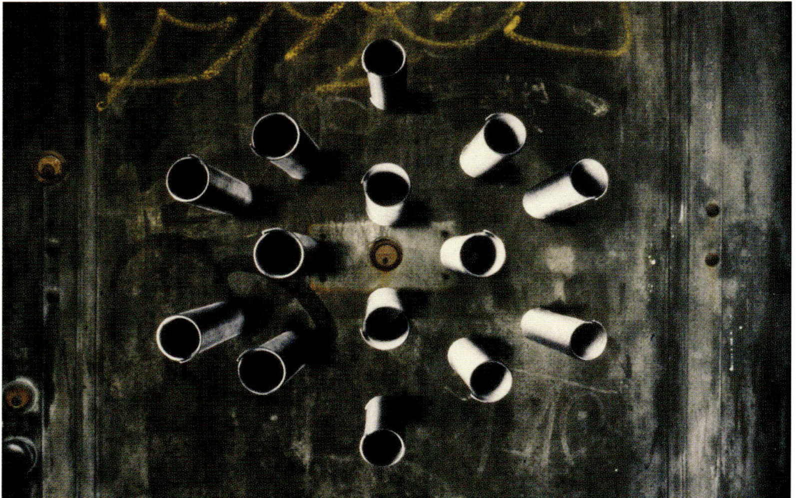

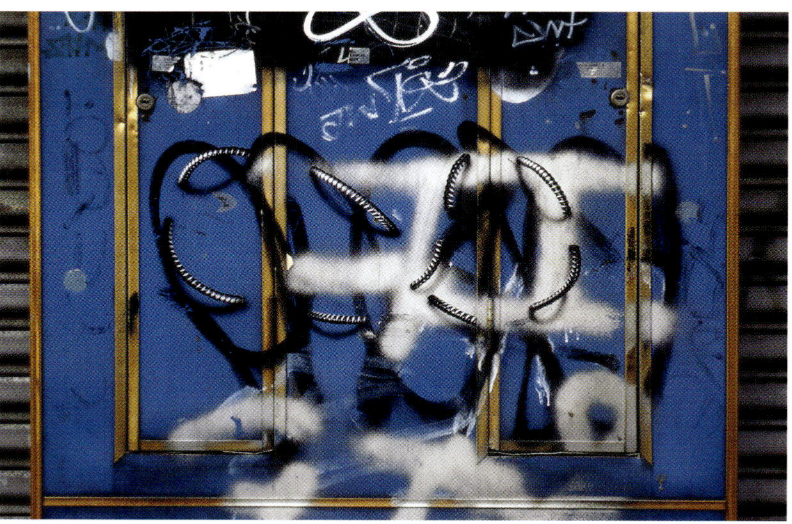

TOP:

MULBERRY ST. NEAR HESTER, NYC., 1996.

MIDDLE:

FRANKLIN ST. NEAR WASHINGTON, NYC., 1996.

BOTTOM:

ALLEN ST. NEAR STANTON, NYC., 1996.

OPPOSITE PAGE:

BEEKMAN ST. NEAR WILLIAM, NYC., 1996.

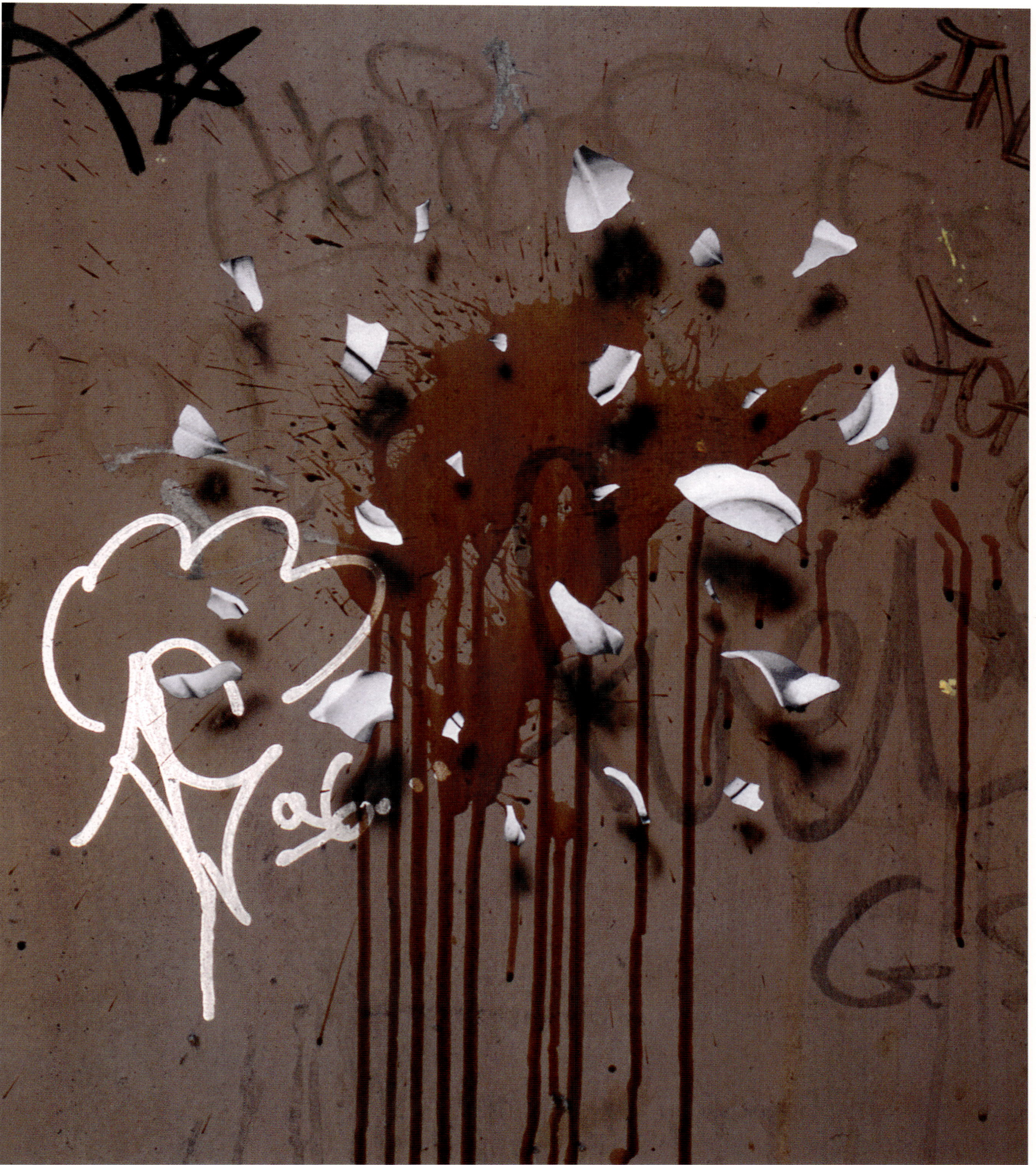

HARRISON NEAR MIDDLETON, WILLIAMSBURG, BROOKLYN, 1997.

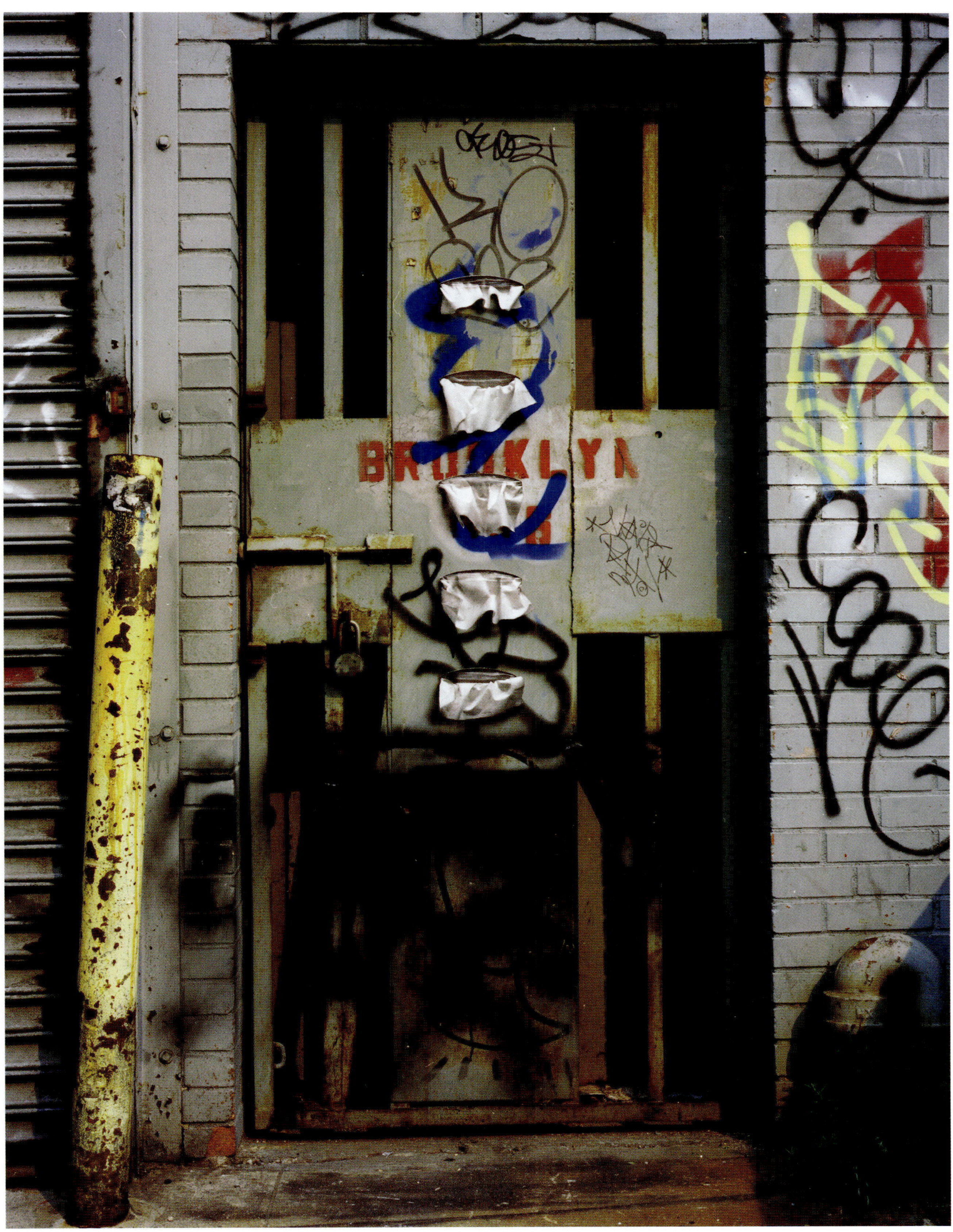

RODNEY BETWEEN METROPOLITAN AND AINSLIE, WILLIAMSBURG, BROOKLYN, 1997.

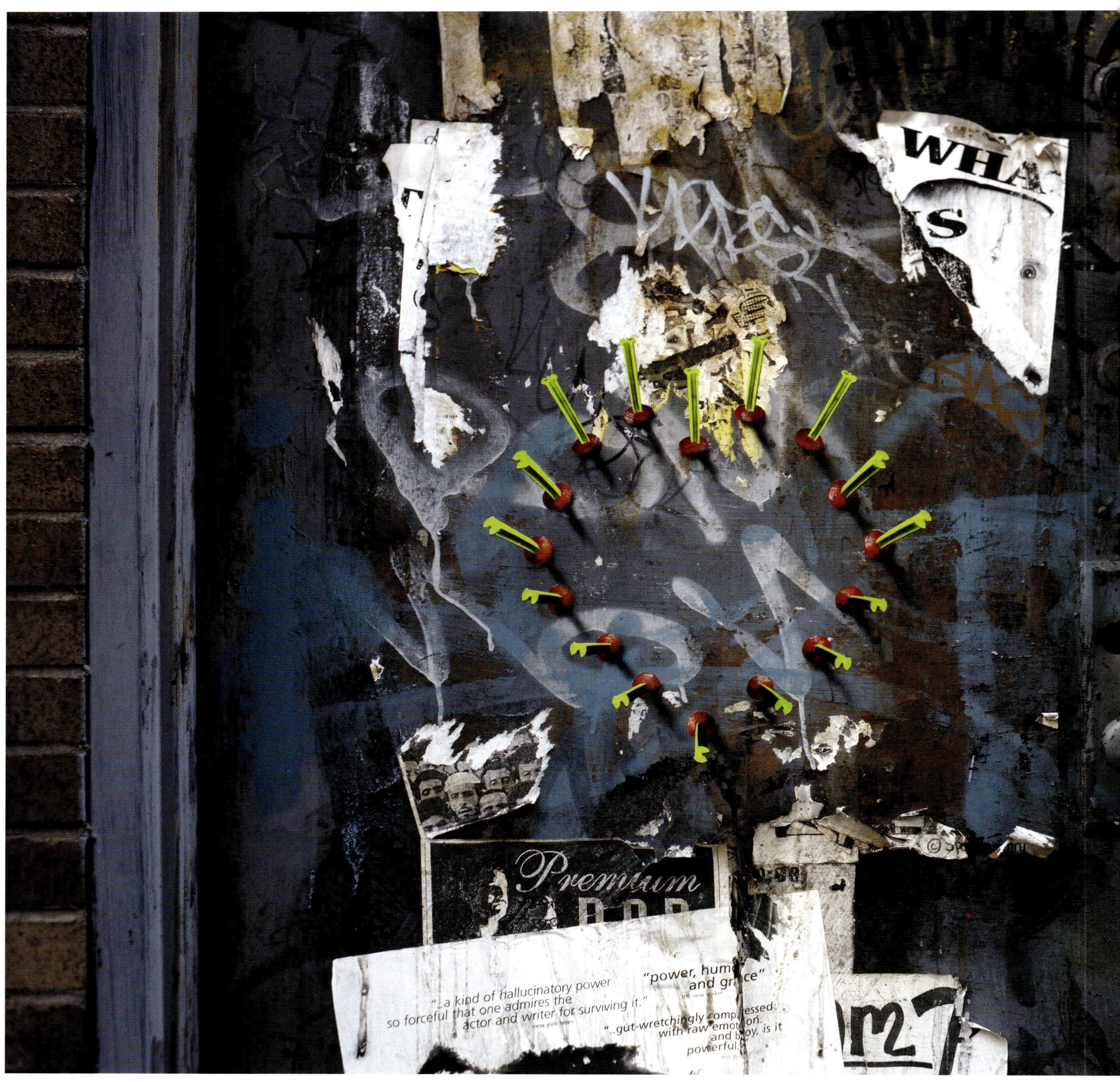
Premium
"...a kind of hallucinatory power
so forceful that one admires the
actor and writer for surviving it."

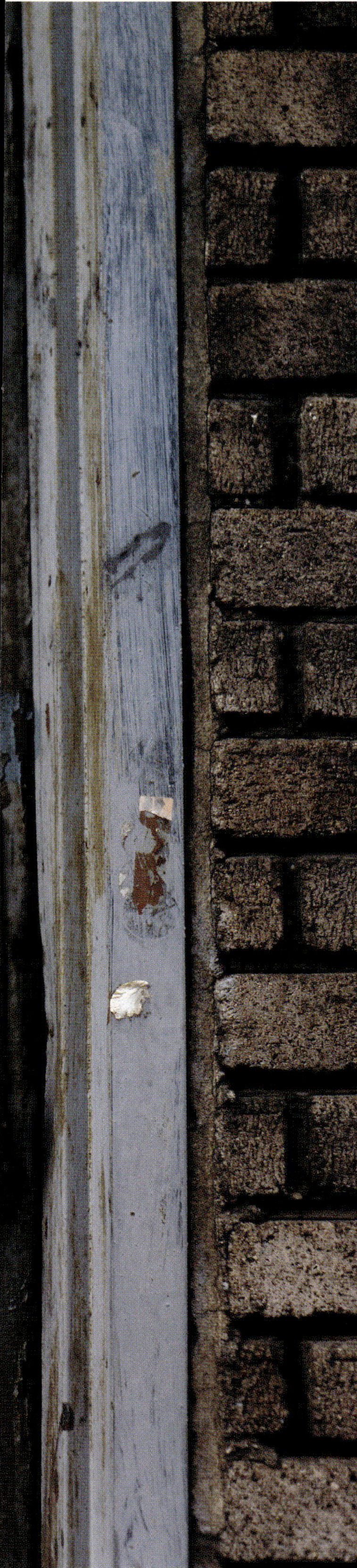

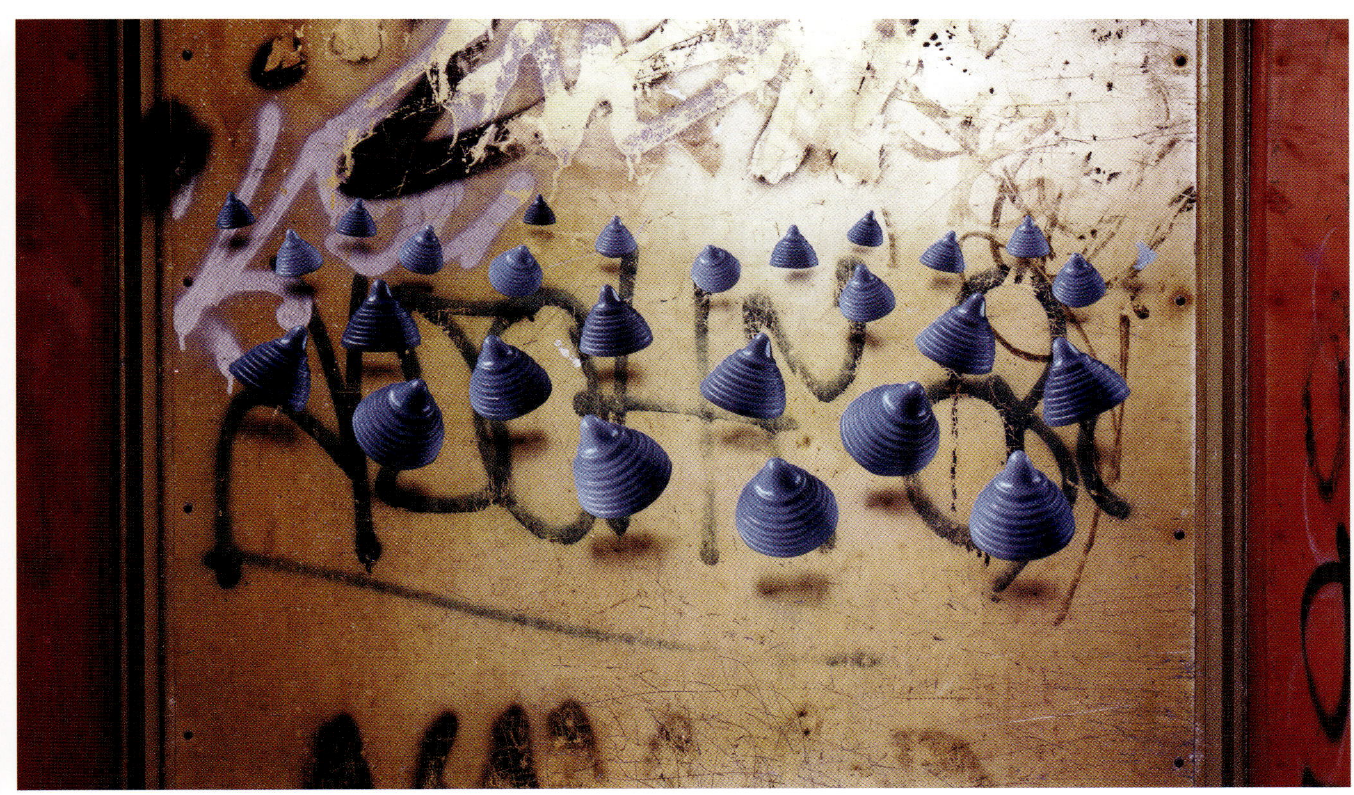

LEFT:

BROOME BETWEEN THOMPSON AND SULLIVAN, NYC., 1996.

ABOVE:

ORCHARD BETWEEN CANAL AND HESTER, NYC., 1996.

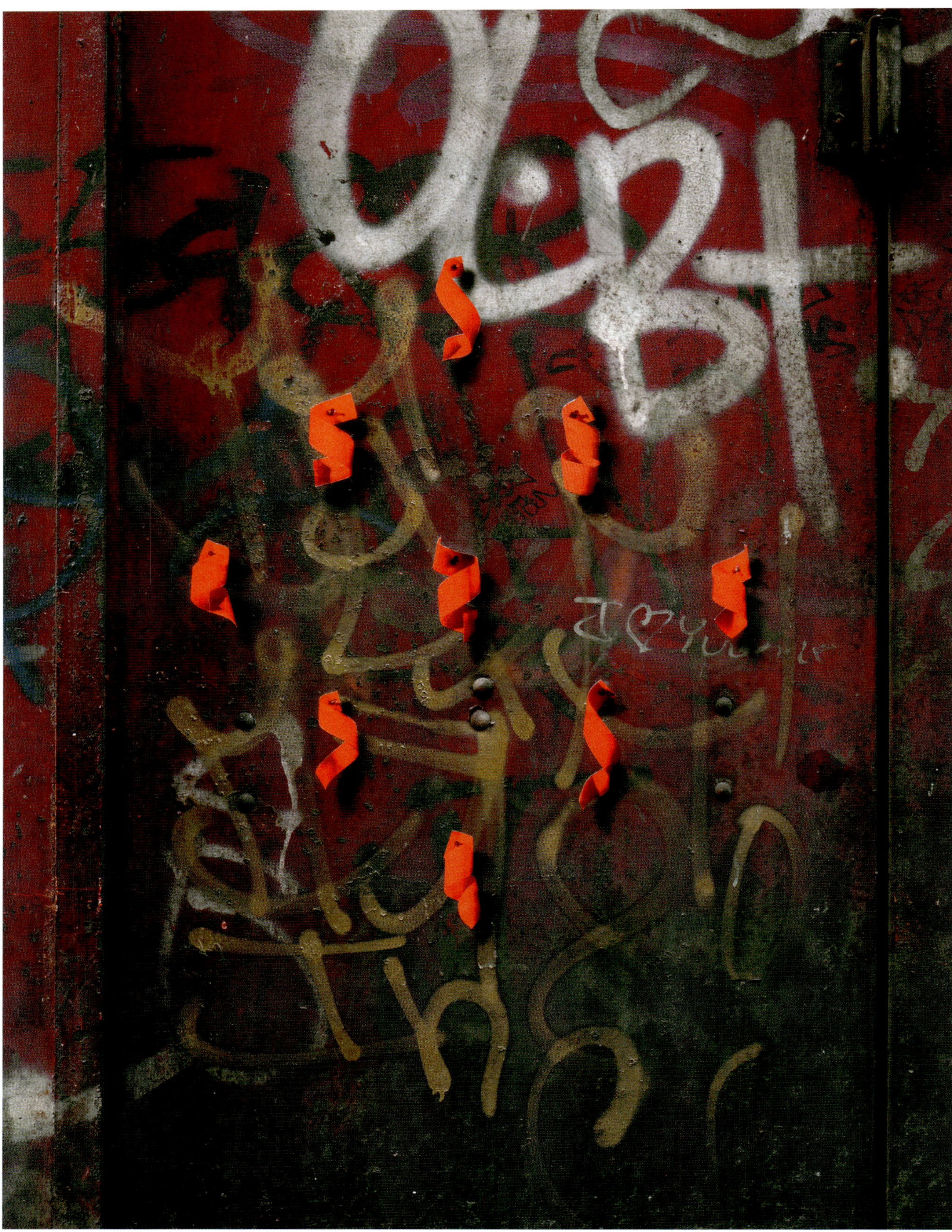

FORSYTH NEAR E. BROADWAY, NYC., 1996.

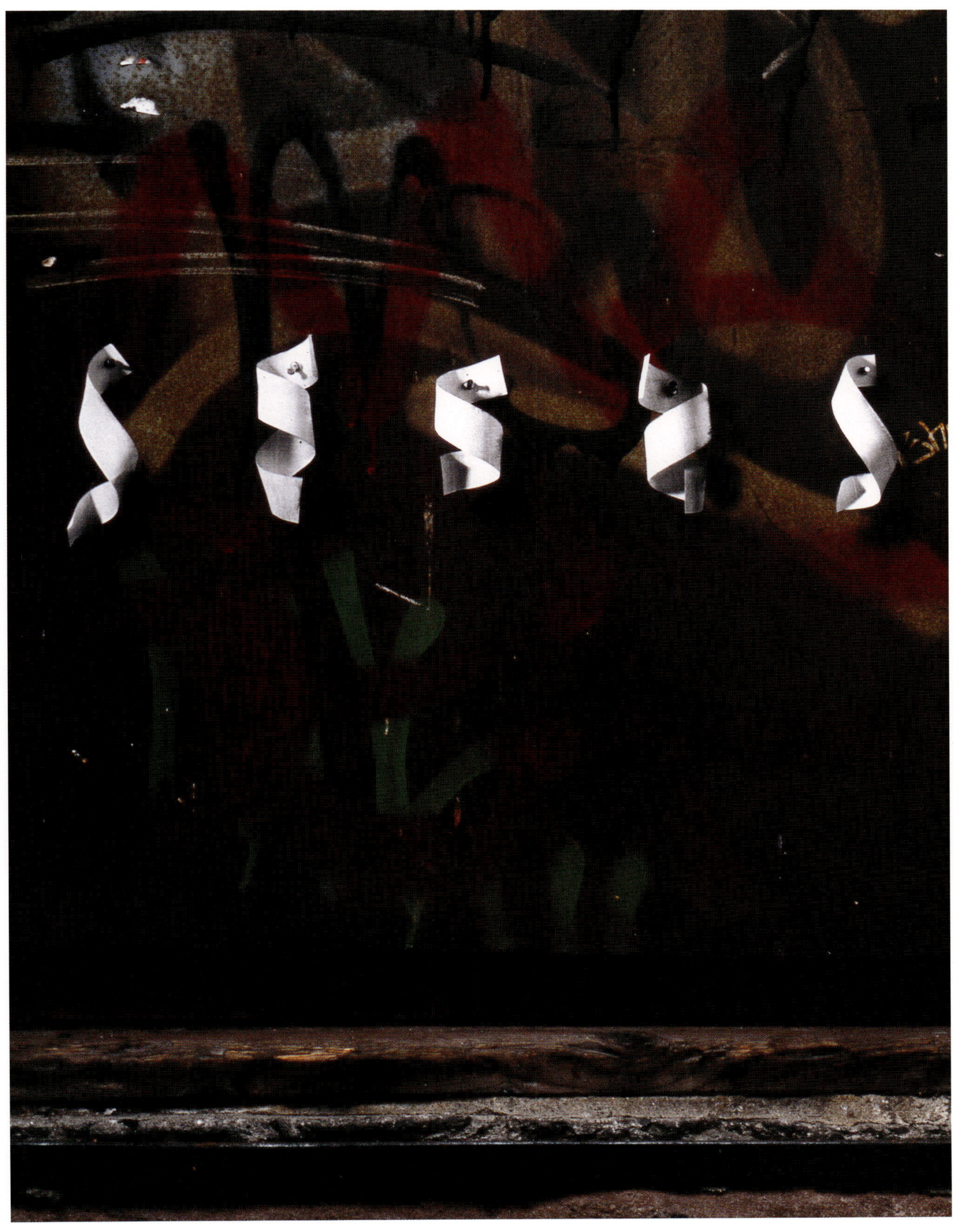

ORCHARD NEAR RIVINGTON, NYC., 1996.

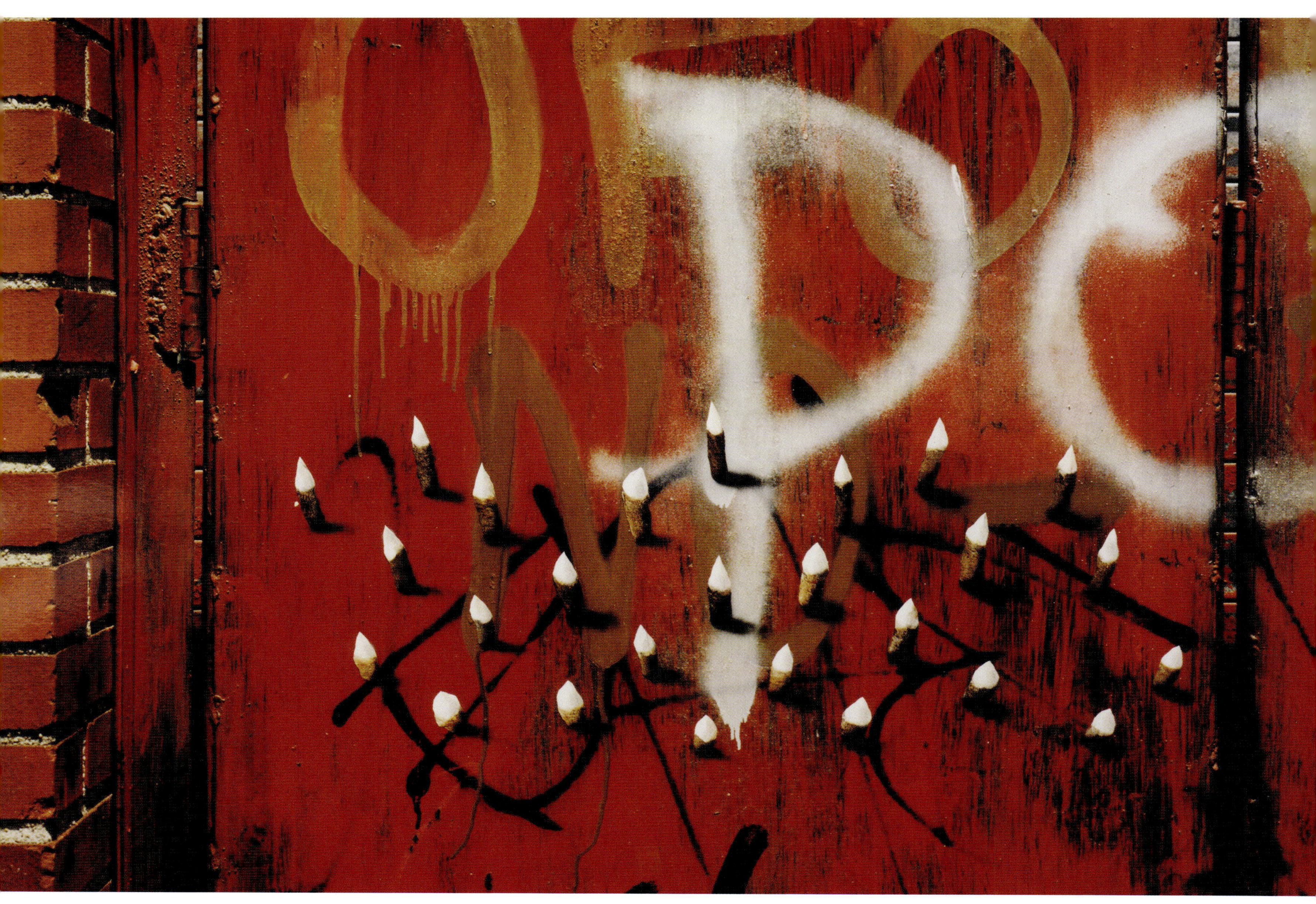

N.6TH ST. BETWEEN WYTHE AND KENT, WILLIAMSBURG, BROOKLYN, 1997.

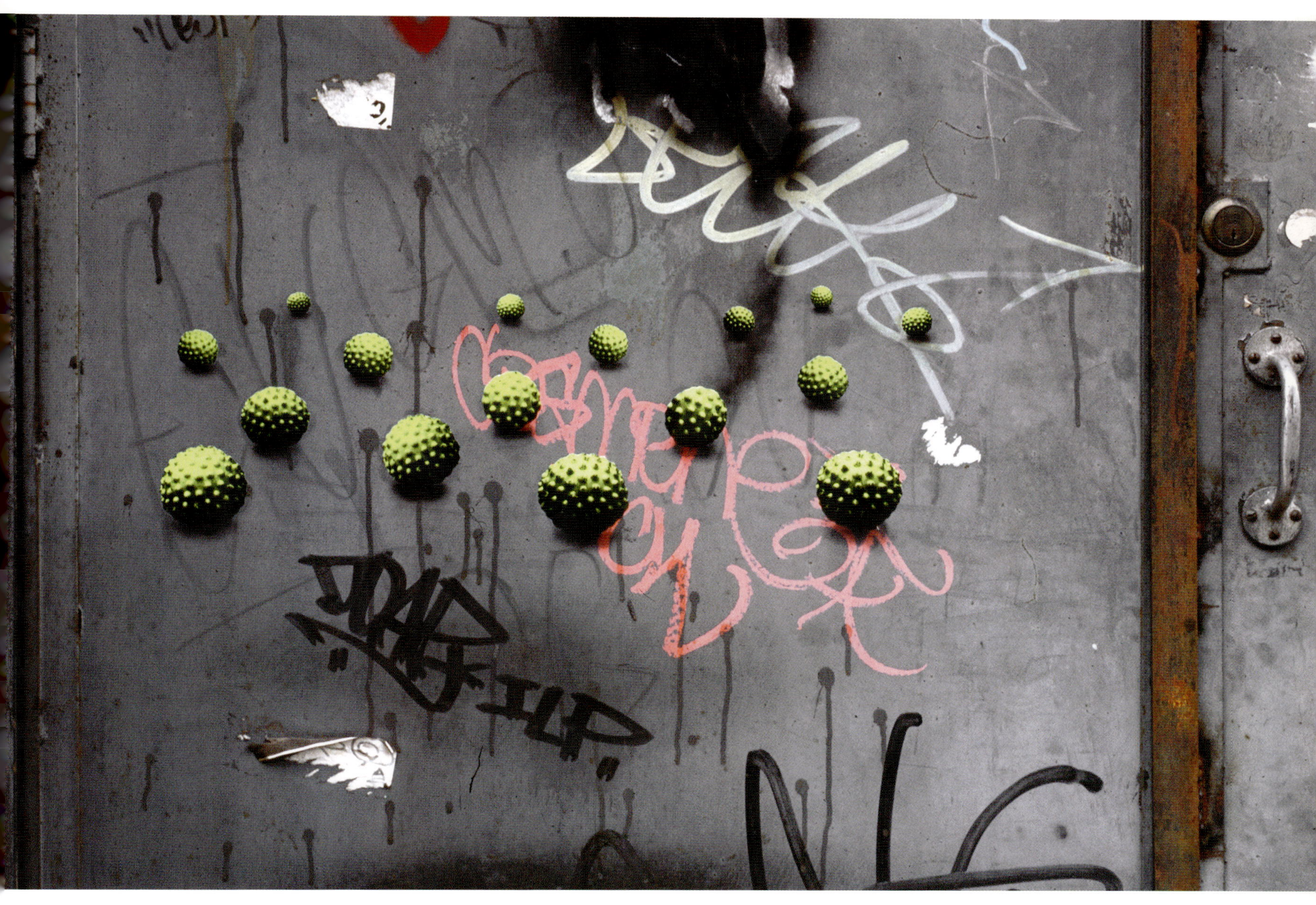

BROOME BETWEEN CENTRE AND LAFAYETTE, NYC., 1996.

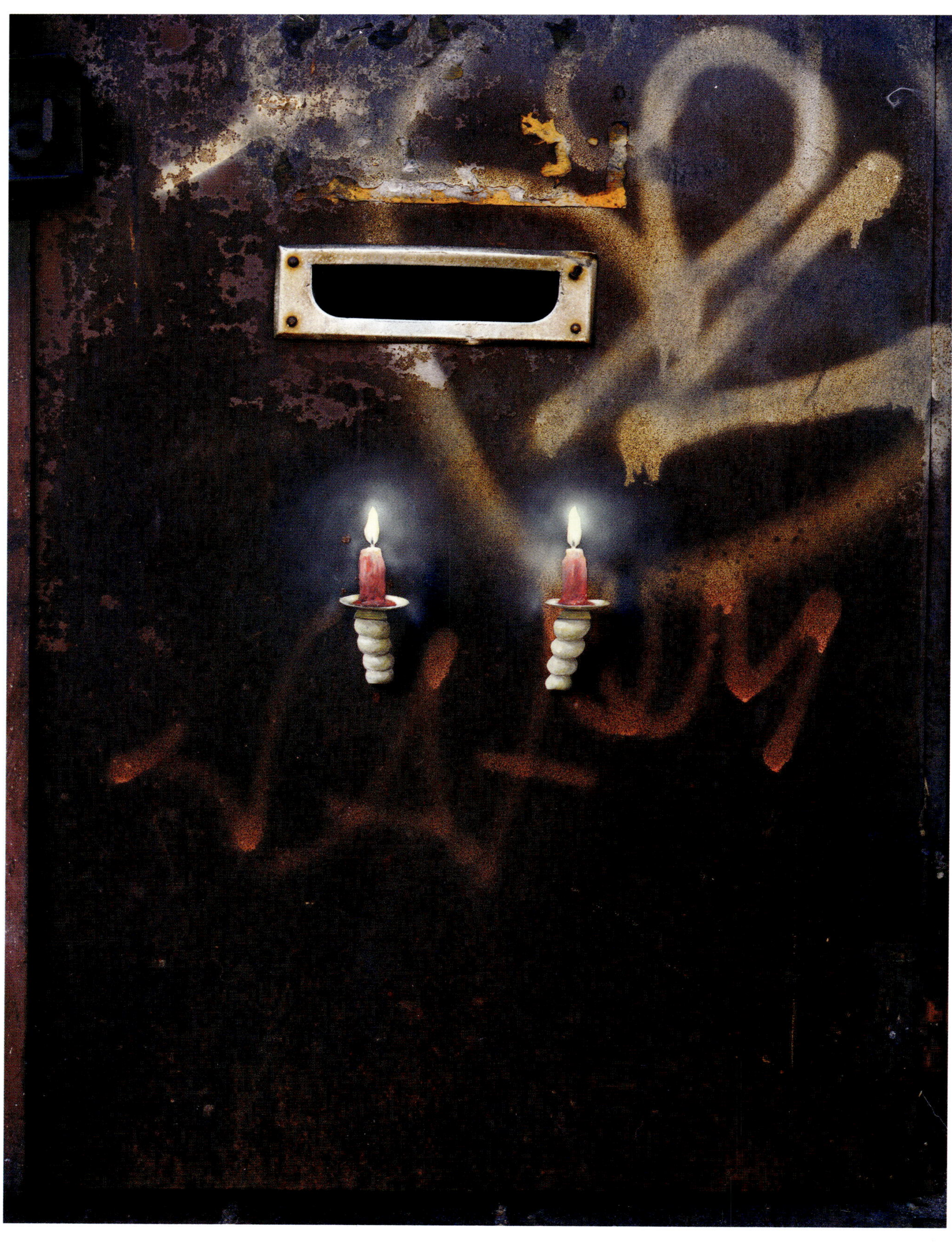

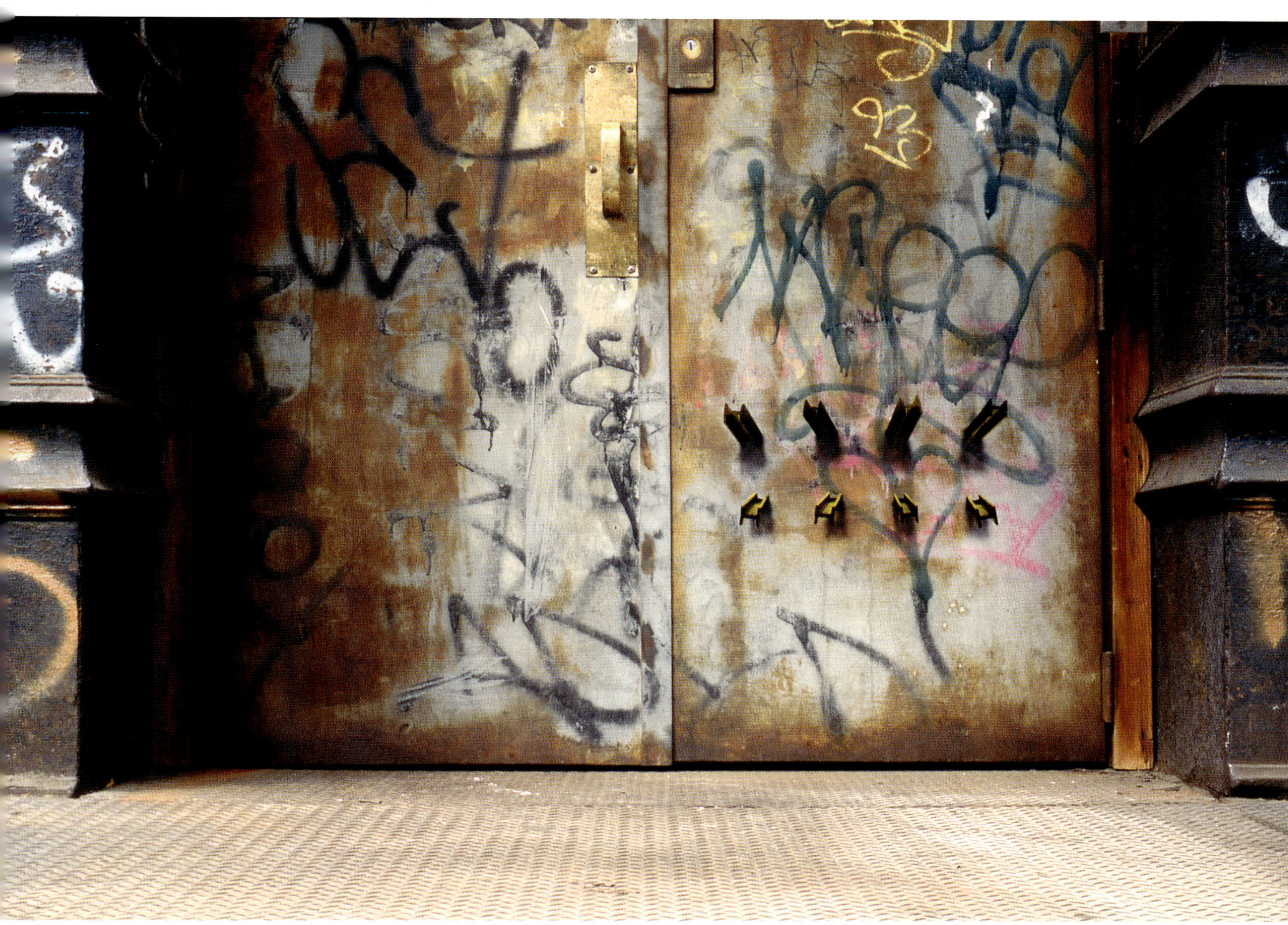

LEFT:

BROADWAY BETWEEN BEDFORD AND DRIGGS. WILLIAMSBURG, BROOKLYN, 1997.

ABOVE:

FRANKLIN BETWEEN CHURCH AND W. BROADWAY. NYC., 1996.

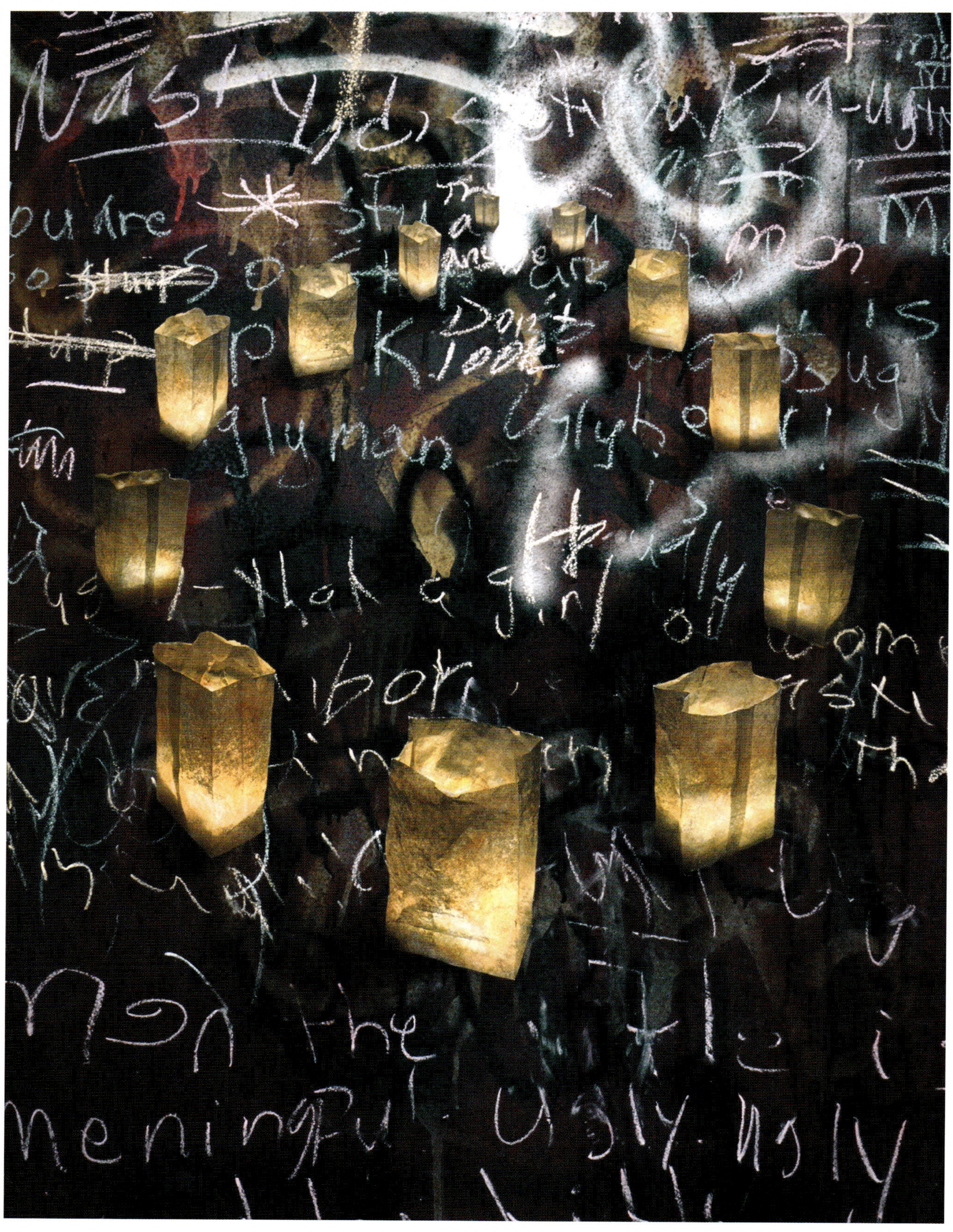

HARRISON NEAR MORGAN, WILLIAMSBURG, BROOKLYN, NYC., 1997.

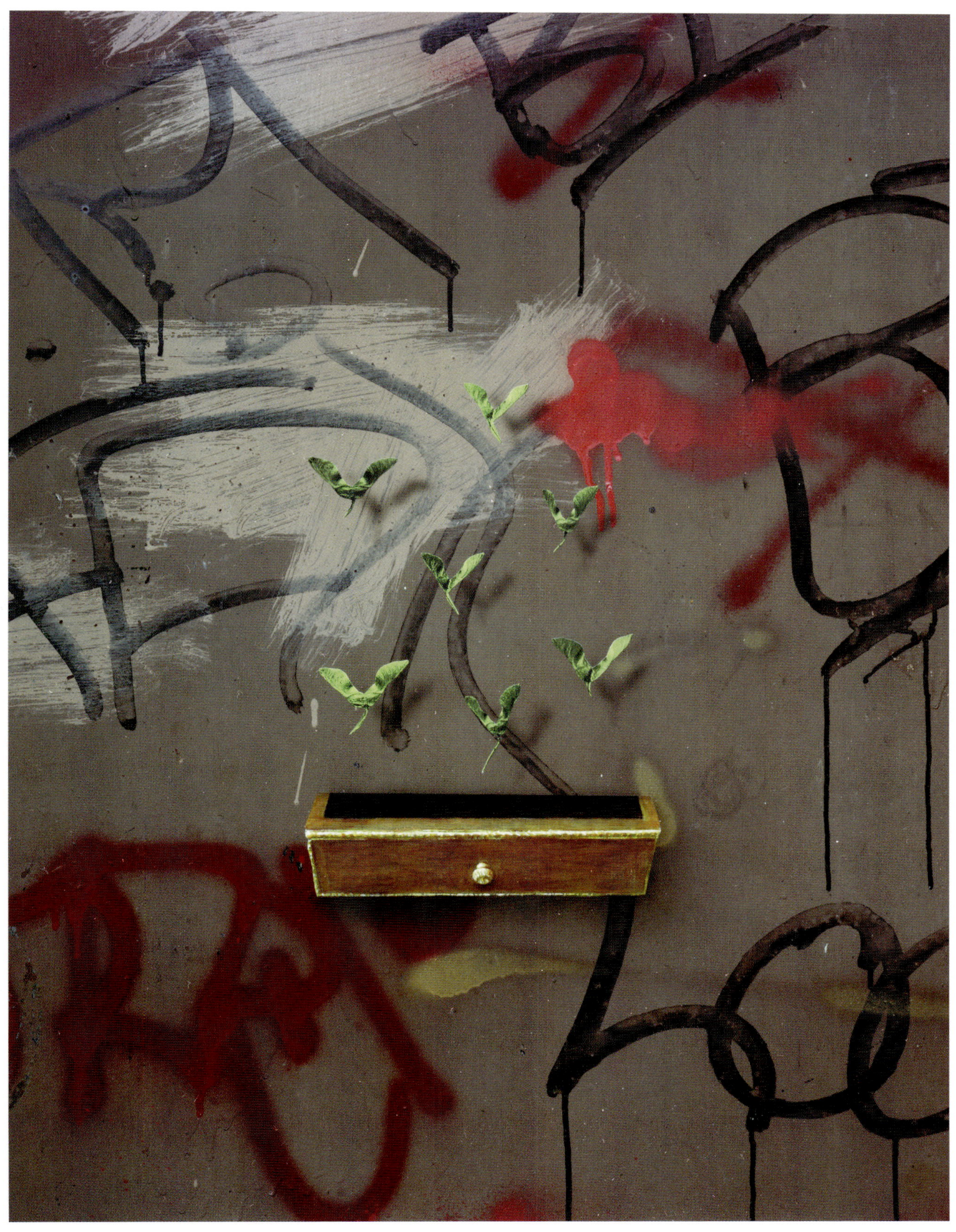

BERRY BETWEEN S.8TH AND S.9TH., WILLIAMSBURG, BROOKLYN, 1997.

HOLES

1996 - 1999

BROOKLYN AND NYC. I must have done dozens of hole pieces. The illusions were so convincing that the pieces were practically invisible. After enjoying that for a while I broke down and started adding elements that would let people know it was art.

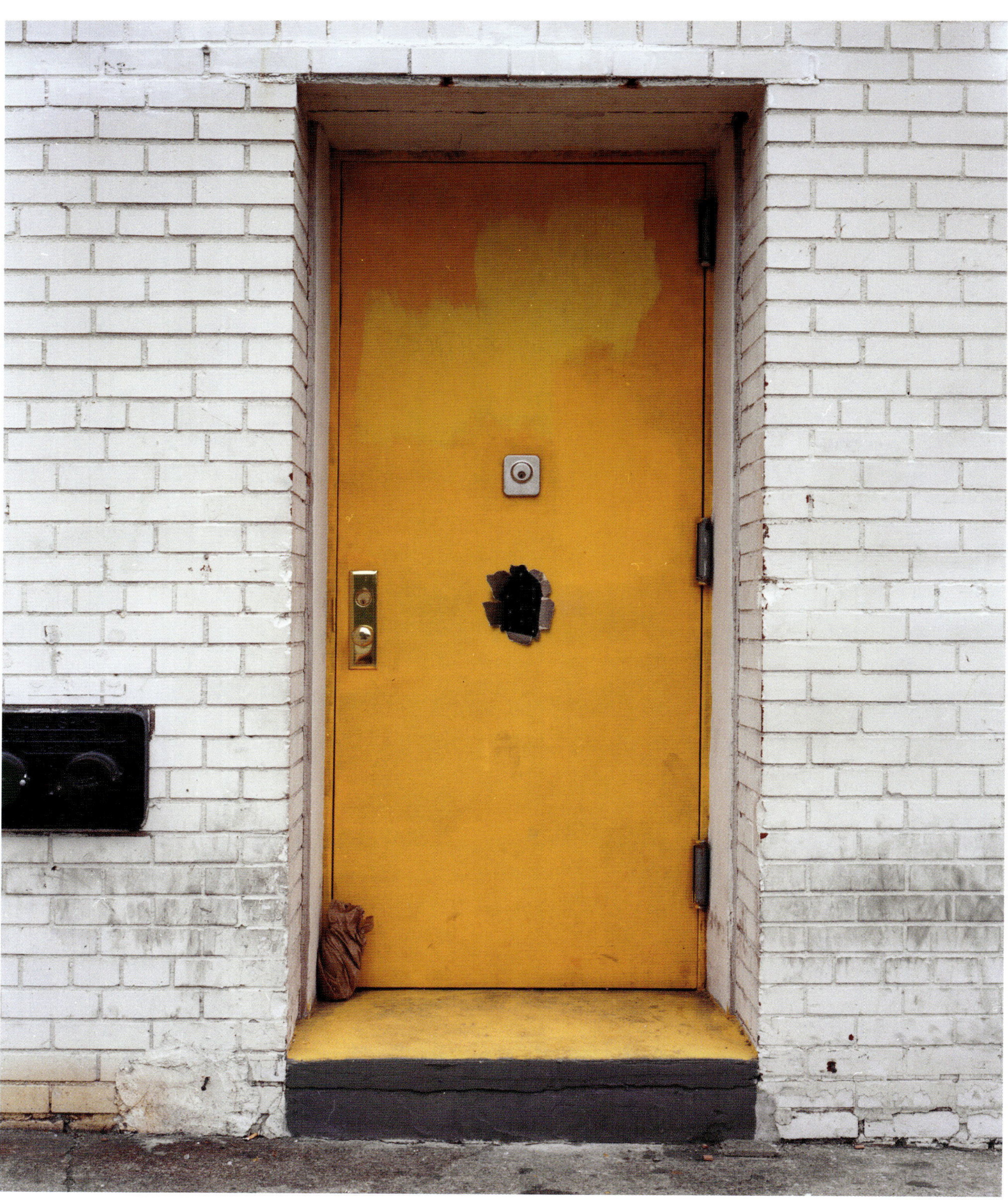

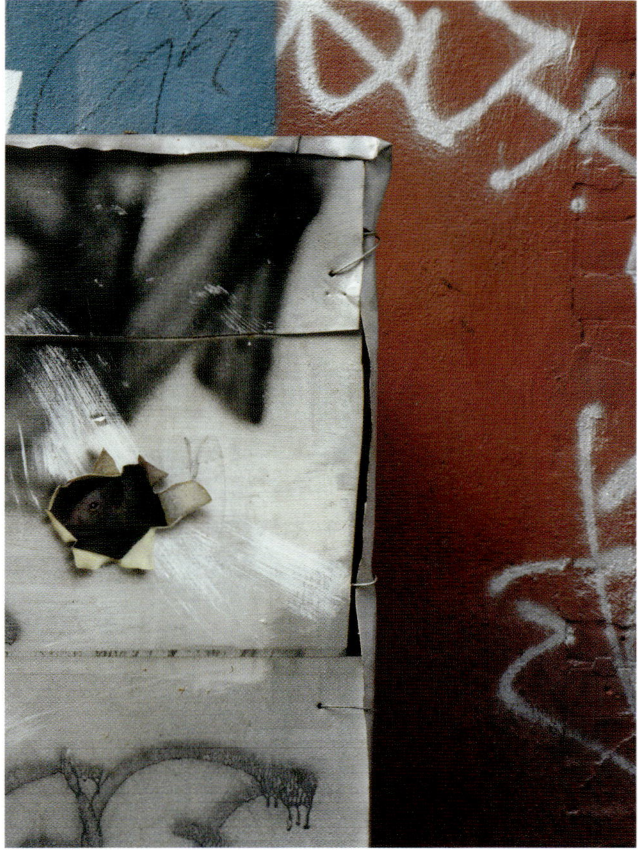

OPPOSITE PAGE:

N.14TH NEAR KENT, WILLIAMSBURG, BROOKLYN, 1997.

RIGHT:

LONG ISLAND CITY, QUEENS, NY., 1999.

BOTTOM RIGHT:

N. 9TH NEAR BEDFORD, WILLIAMSBURG, BROOKLYN, 1997.

ABOVE:

MERCER NEAR BROOME ST., NYC., 1998.

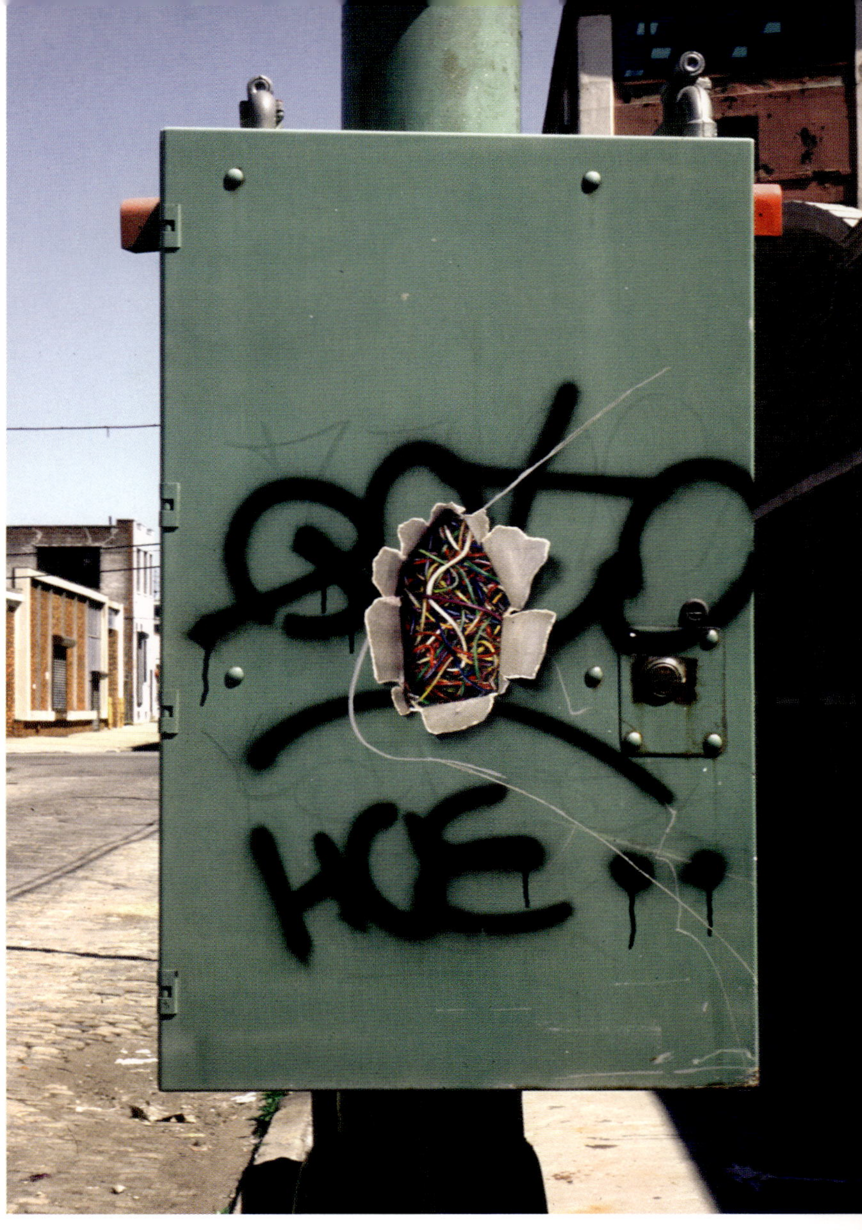

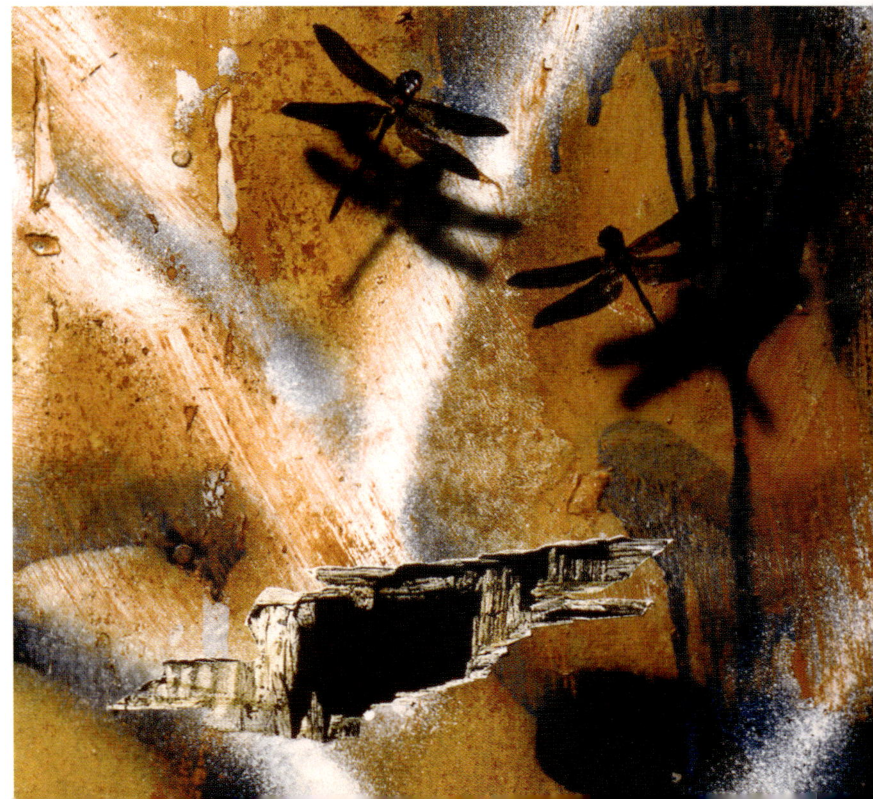

LOS ANGELES

1997

After the revelation of the airbrush and all the progress of my summer of 96's work, I couldn't wait for warm weather to get back at it. I went to L.A., rented a motorcycle (Harley), packed the saddlebags and did about 30 pieces in 3 days. I concentrated on the downtown manufacturing area and tried to get all my locations to be in sunlight. For the piece at right I thought it would be a nice gift to bring some fall foliage to a place that never had it.

WASHINGTON BETWEEN MAIN AND LOS ANGELES AVE., LOS ANGELES, 1997.

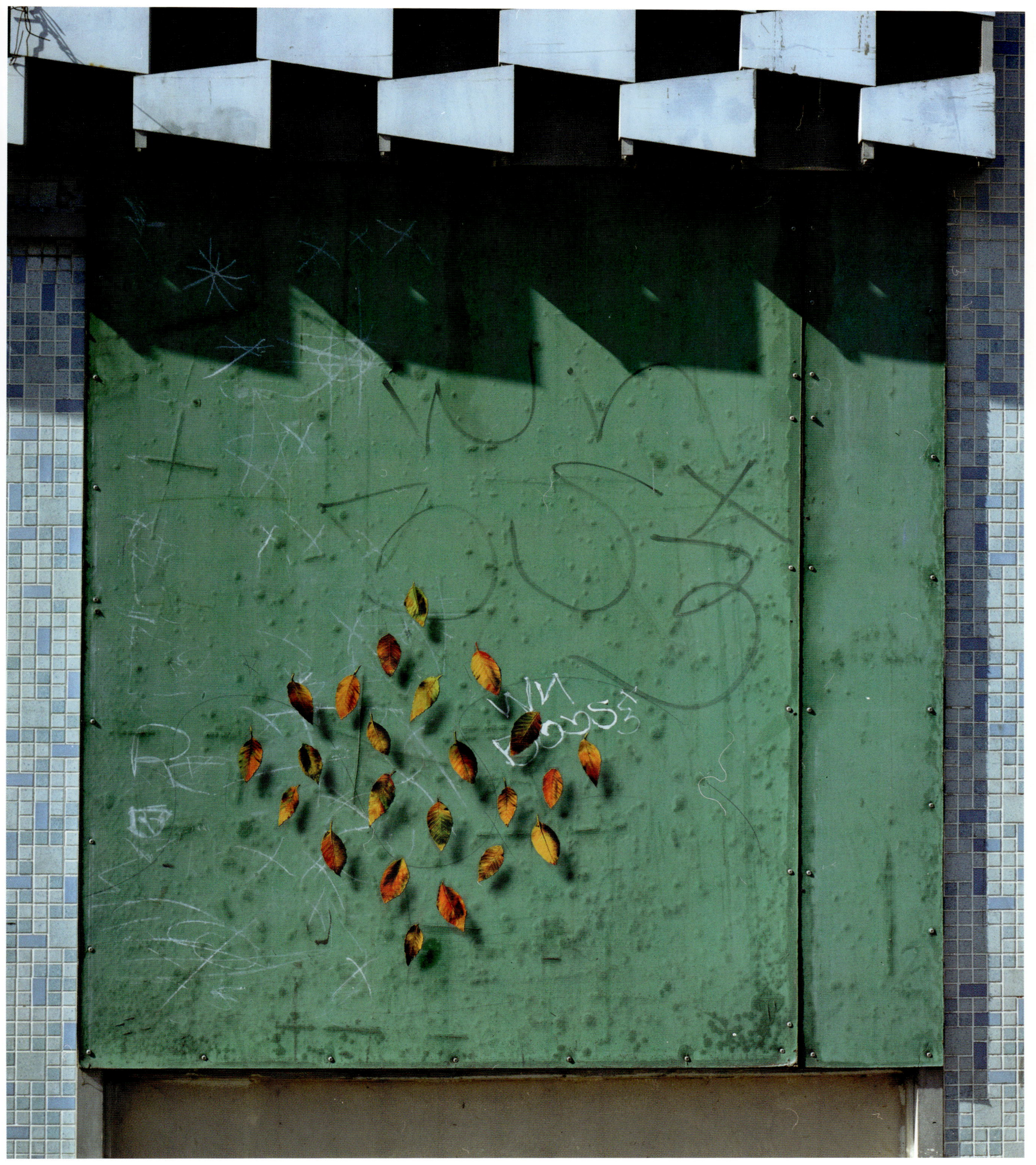

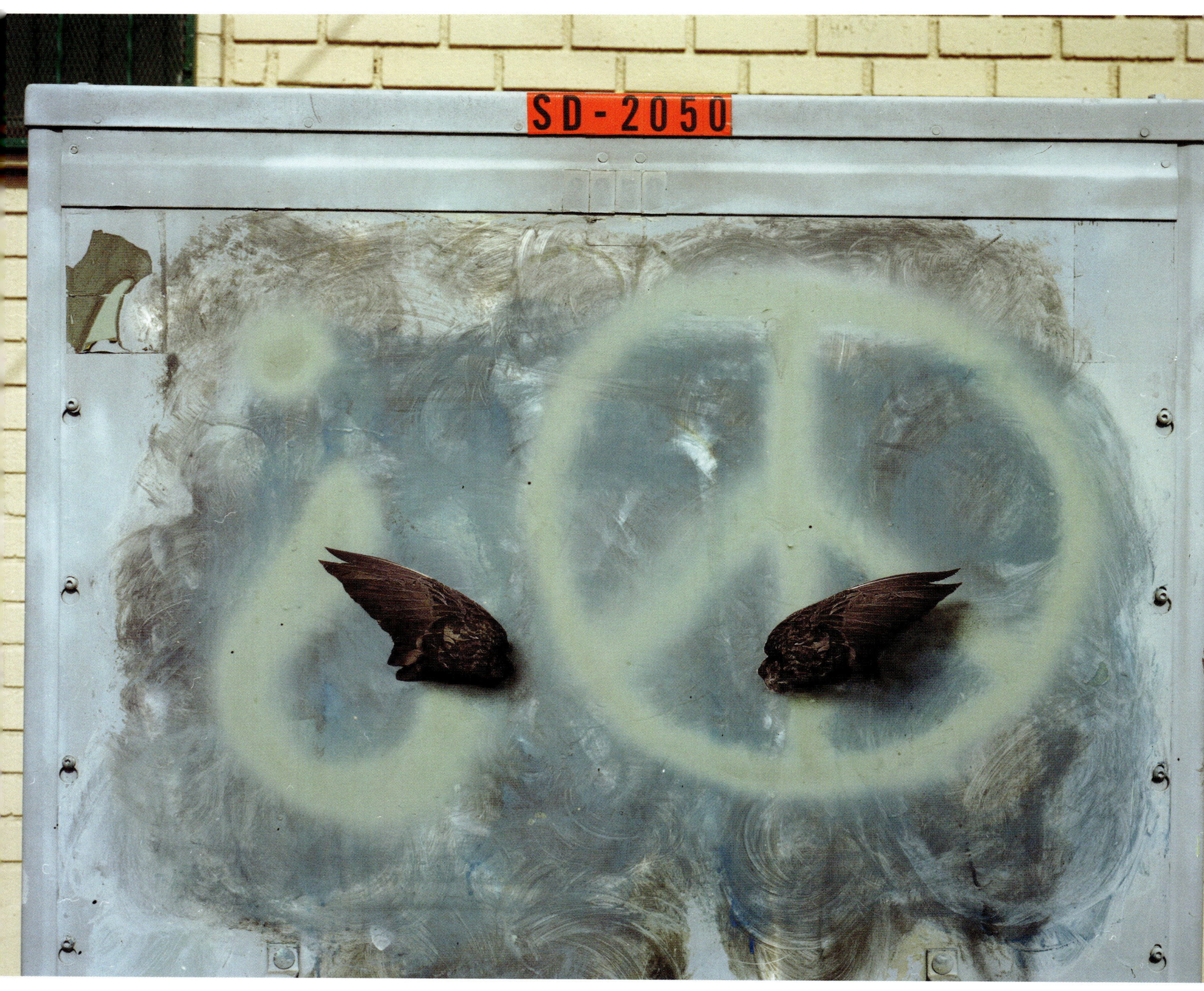
SD-2050

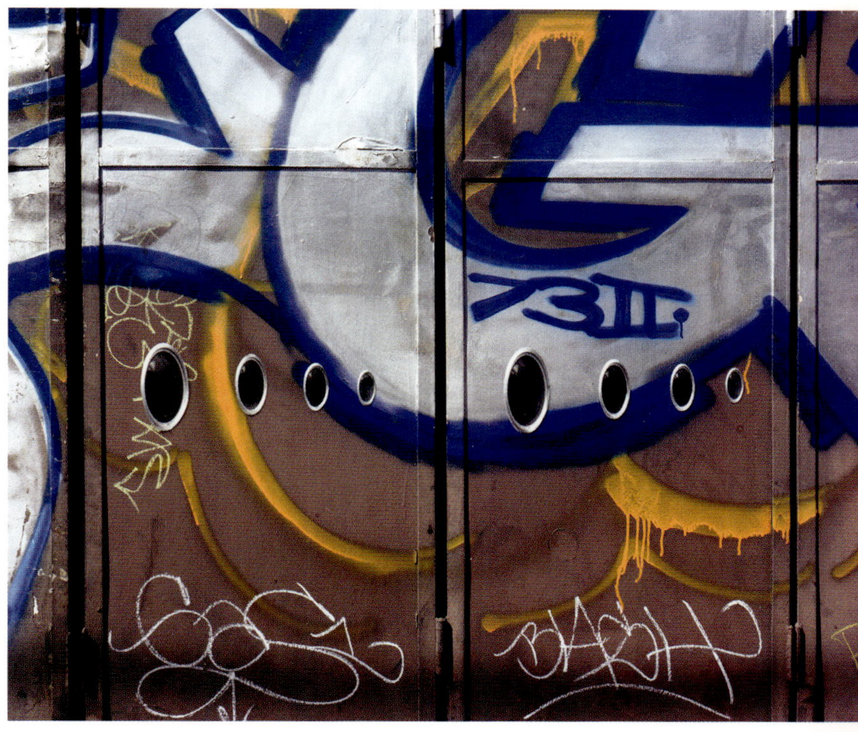

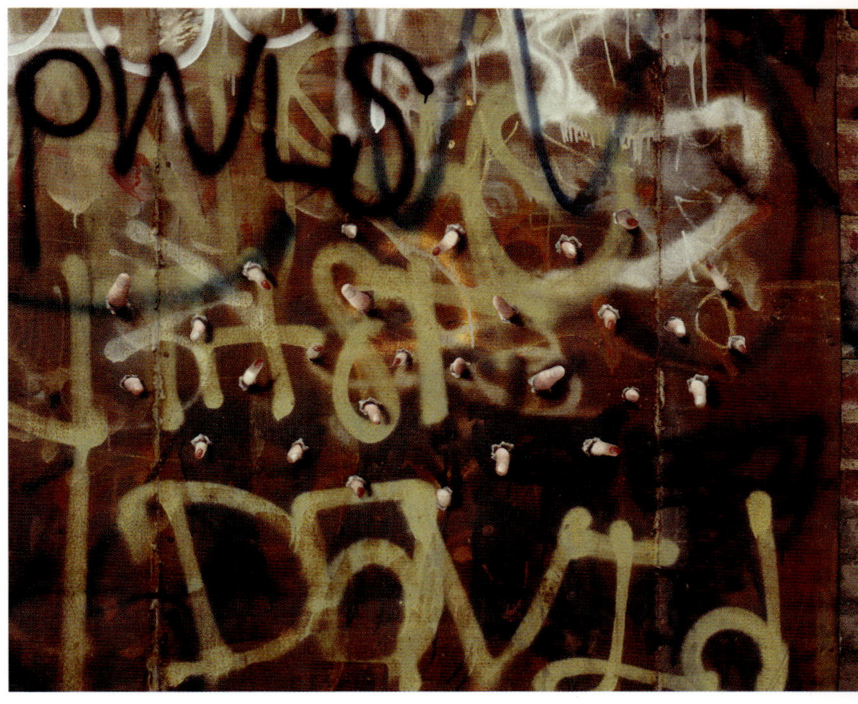

OPPOSITE:

S.SOTO NEAR E.4TH ST., LOS ANGELES, 1997.

UPPER RIGHT:

BAY ST. BETWEEN MATEO AND WILSON, LOS ANGELES, 1997.

LOWER RIGHT:

SACRAMENTO NEAR WILSON, LOS ANGELES, 1997.

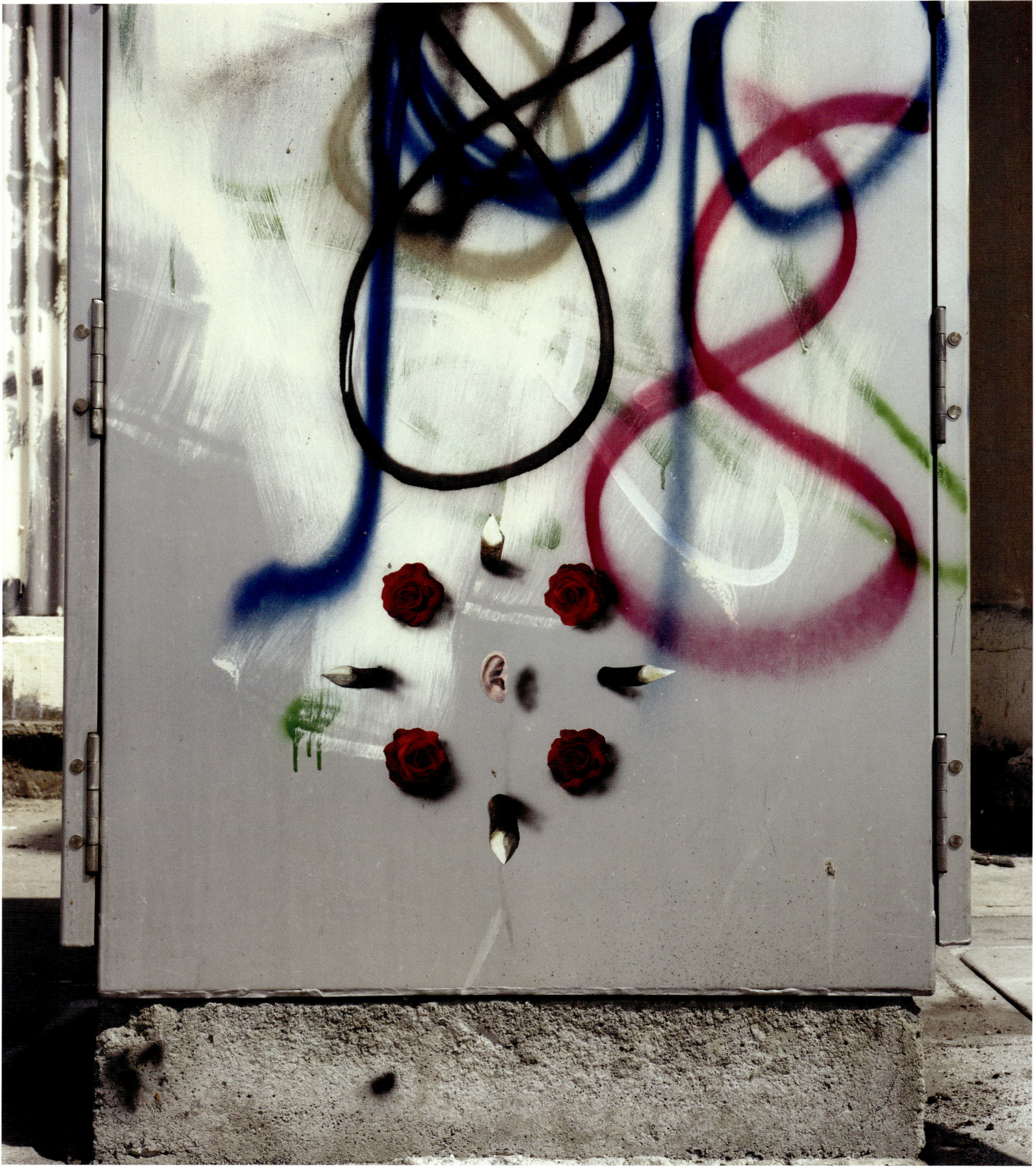

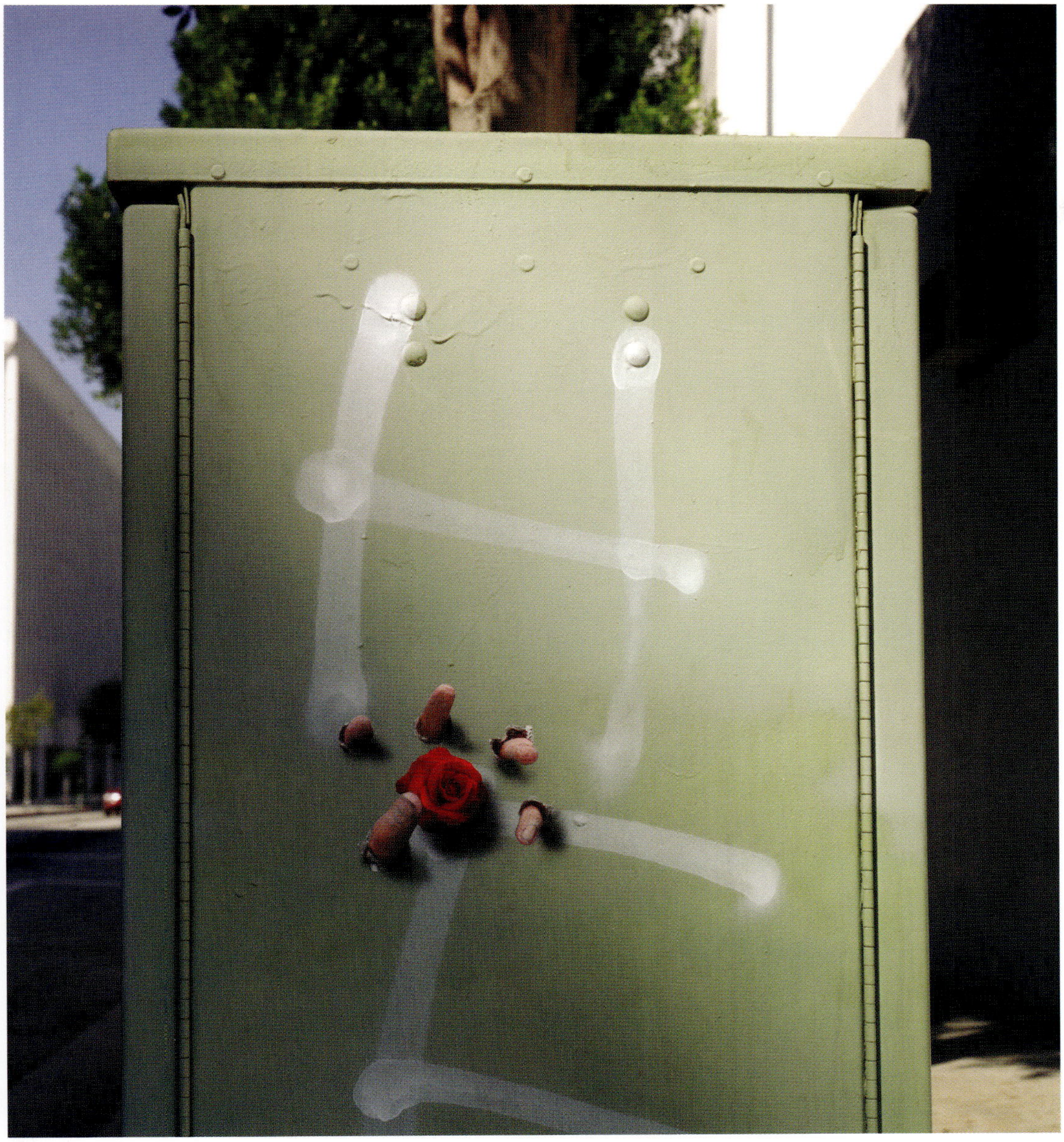

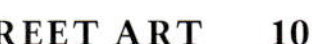

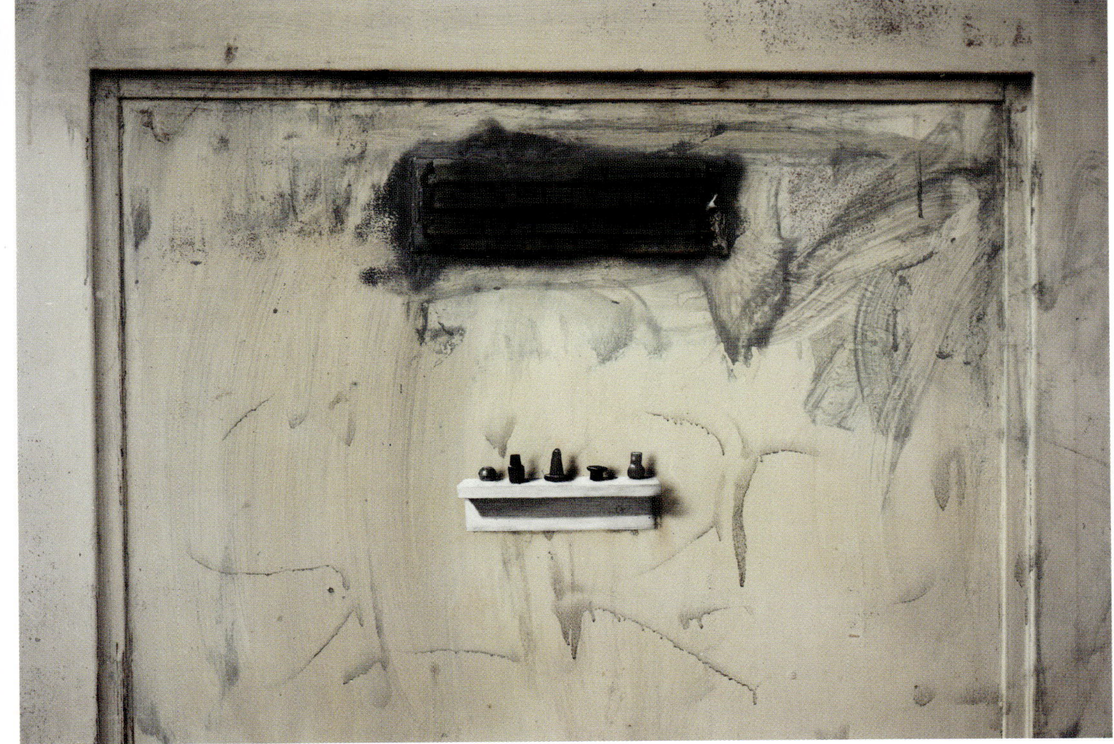

OPPOSITE:

LONG BEACH AVE. BETWEEN 21ST AND COMPTON, LOS ANGELES, 1997.

TOP LEFT:

PICO BETWEEN HOPE AND GRAND, LOS ANGELES, 1997.

LOWER LEFT:

GRAND BETWEEN 25TH AND 26TH STREETS, LOS ANGELES, 1997.

RING AROUND BROOKLYN

1999

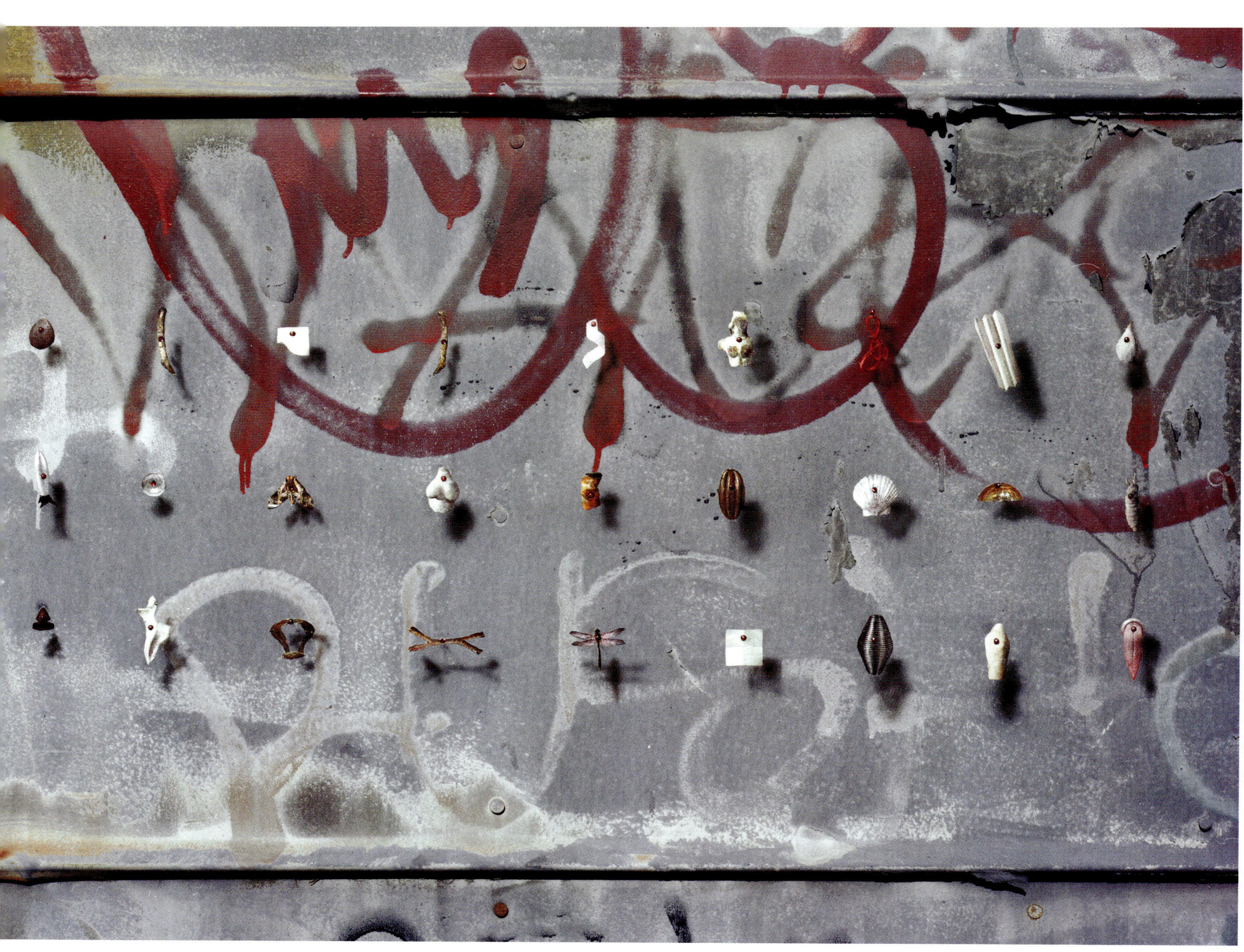

For the summer of 1999's project I made a complete ring around the perimeter of Brooklyn. My idea was to encounter and respond to as many diverse neighborhoods (and surfaces) as I could.

OPPOSITE PAGE:

RUSSELL ST. GREENPOINT BROOKLYN, 1998.

BELOW:

CONEY ISLAND, BROOKLYN, 1999.

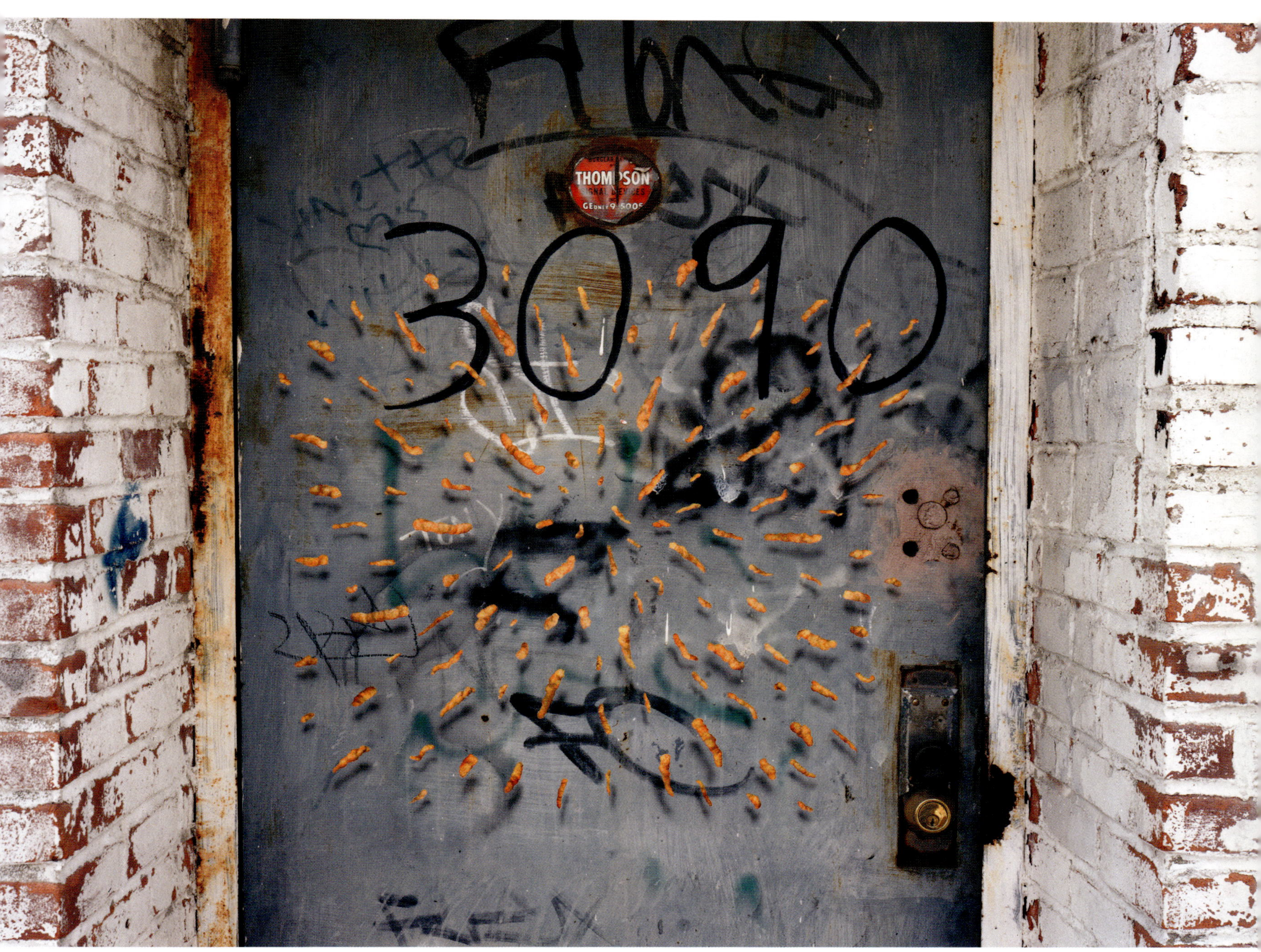

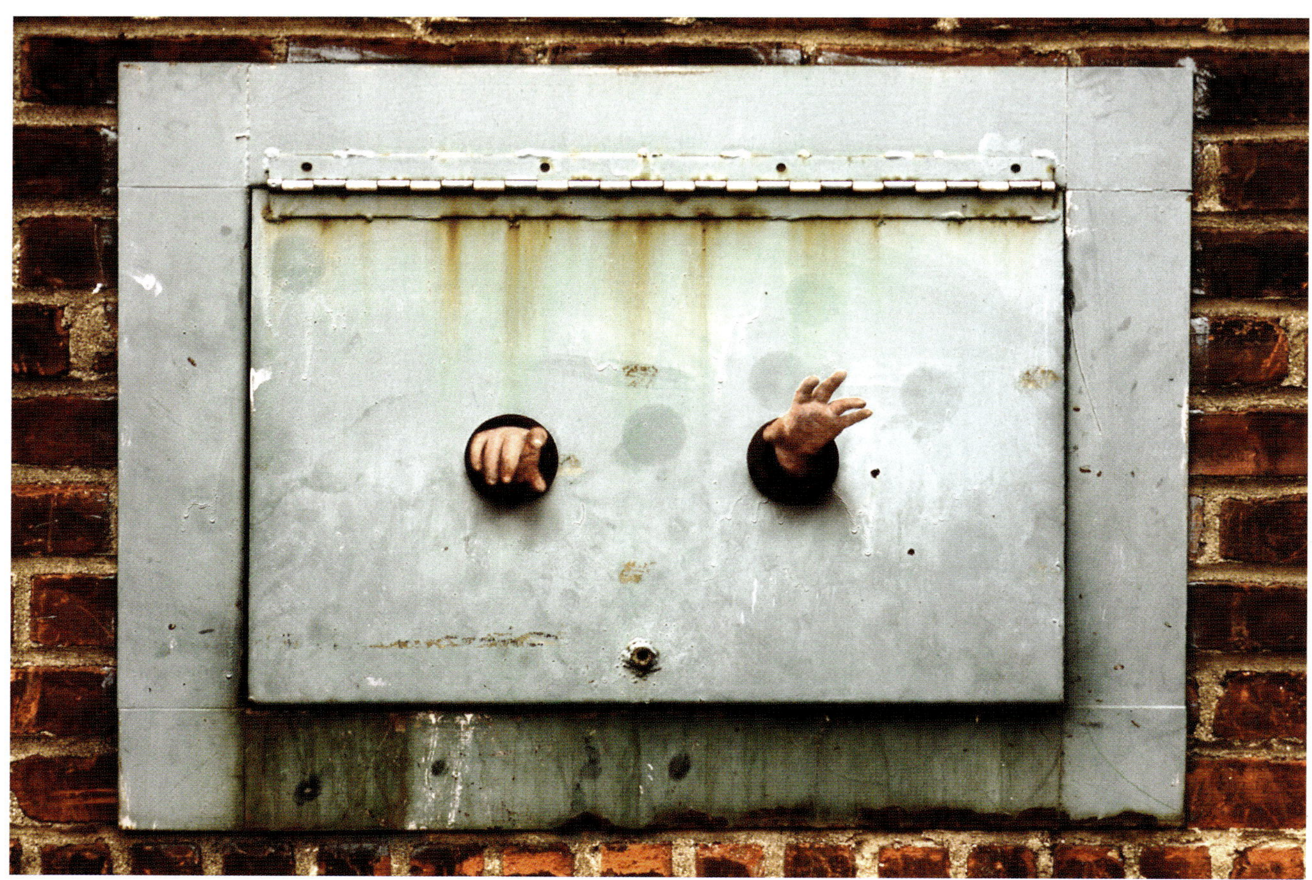

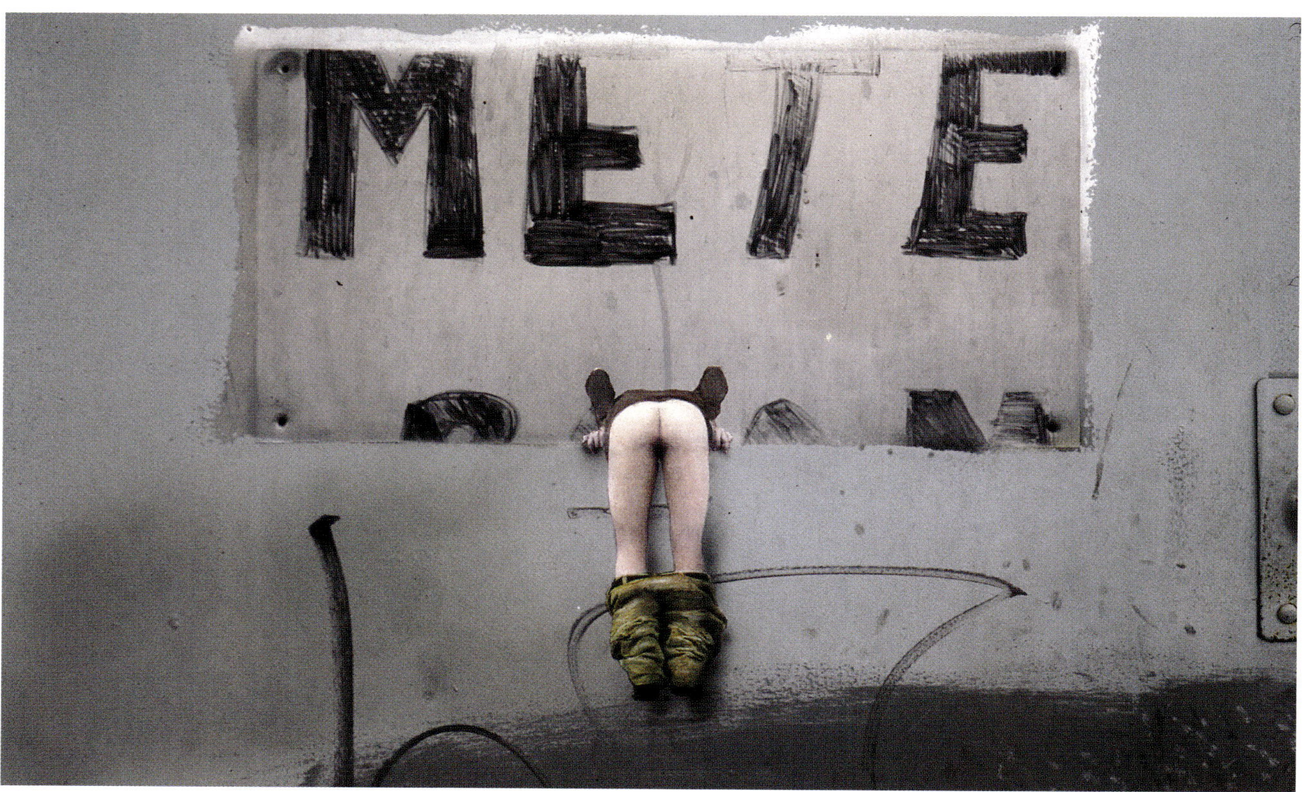
METE

LEFT:

DUMBO, BROOKLYN, 1999.

LOWER LEFT:

EAST NEW YORK, BROOKLYN, 1999.

RIGHT:

KEAP ST. WILLIAMSBURG, BROOKLYN, 1997.

CENTER RIGHT:

RUTLEDGE ST. WILLIAMSBURG, BROOKLYN, 1997.
In the window is my friend Lisa Gregersen.

BOTTOM RIGHT:

WEST ST. NEAR OAK, GREENPOINT, BROOKLYN, 1997.

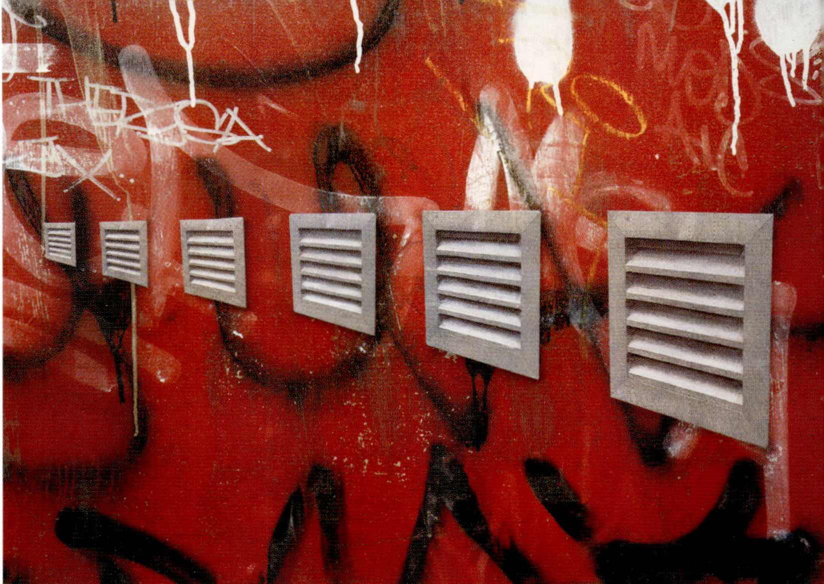

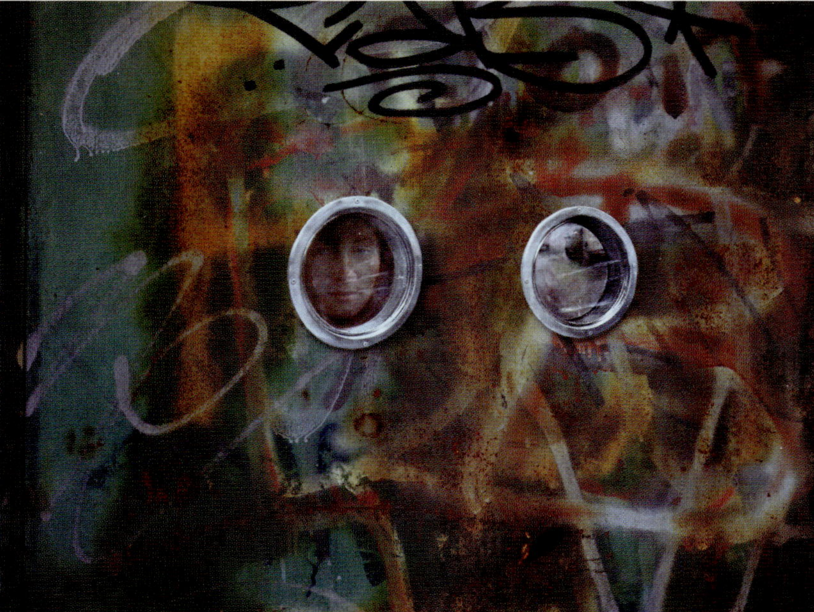

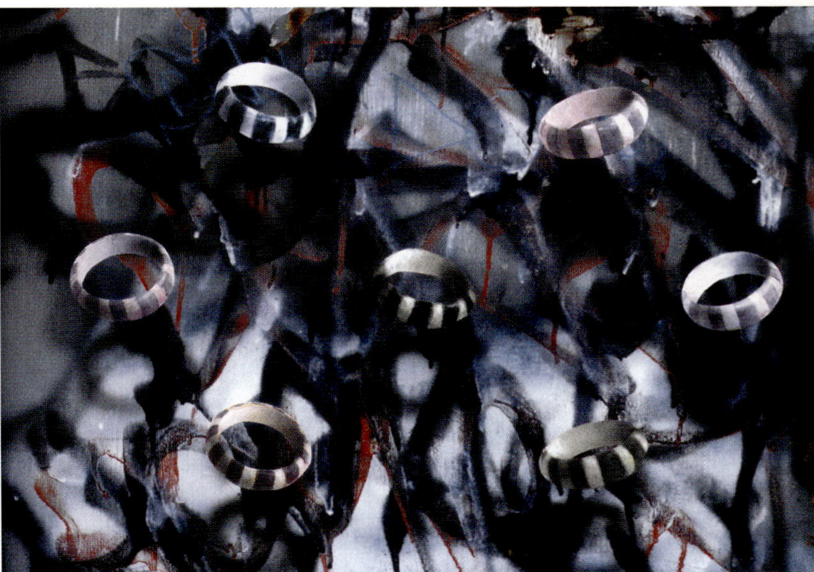

NEXT PAGE, UPPER LEFT:

BAY BRIDGE, BROOKLYN, 1999.

NEXT PAGE, LOWER LEFT:

RED HOOK, BROOKLYN, 1999.

NEXT PAGE, CENTER RIGHT:

LOWER EAST SIDE, NYC., 1998.

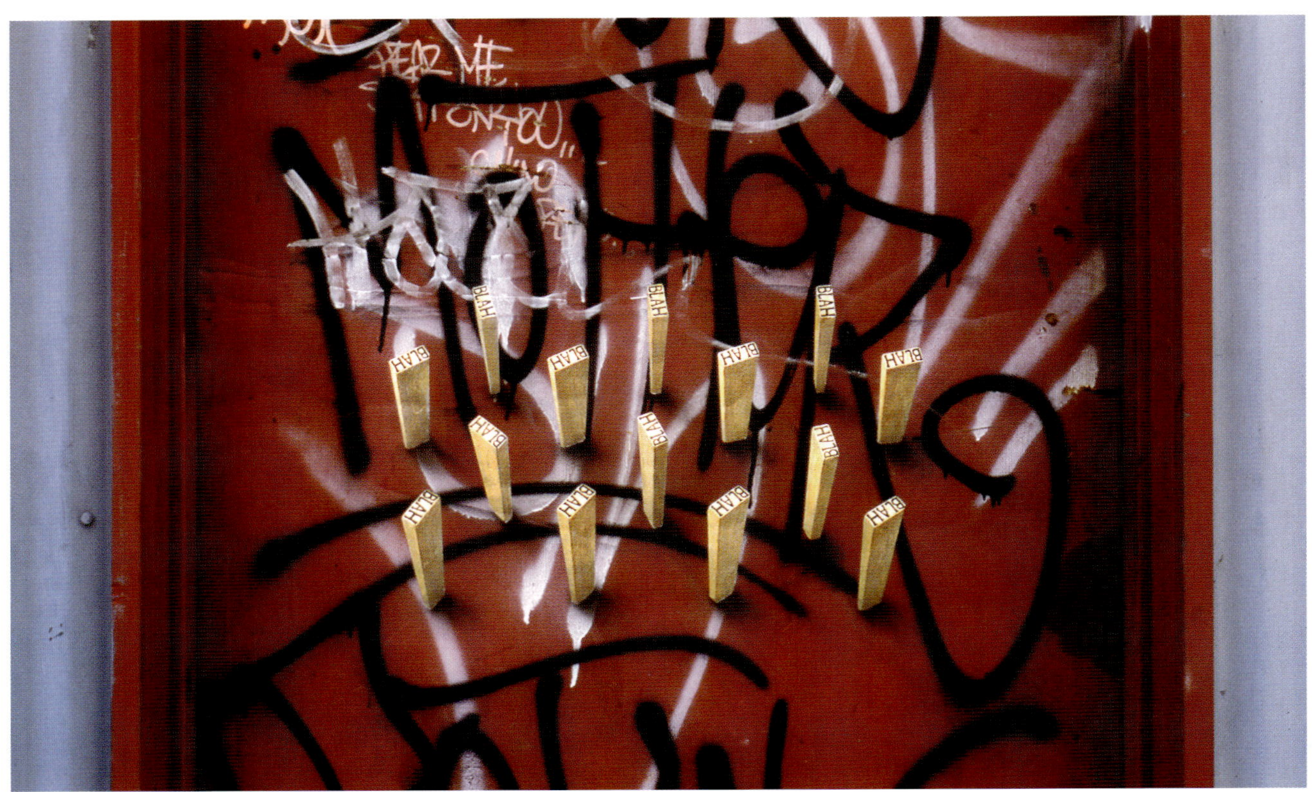
BLAH

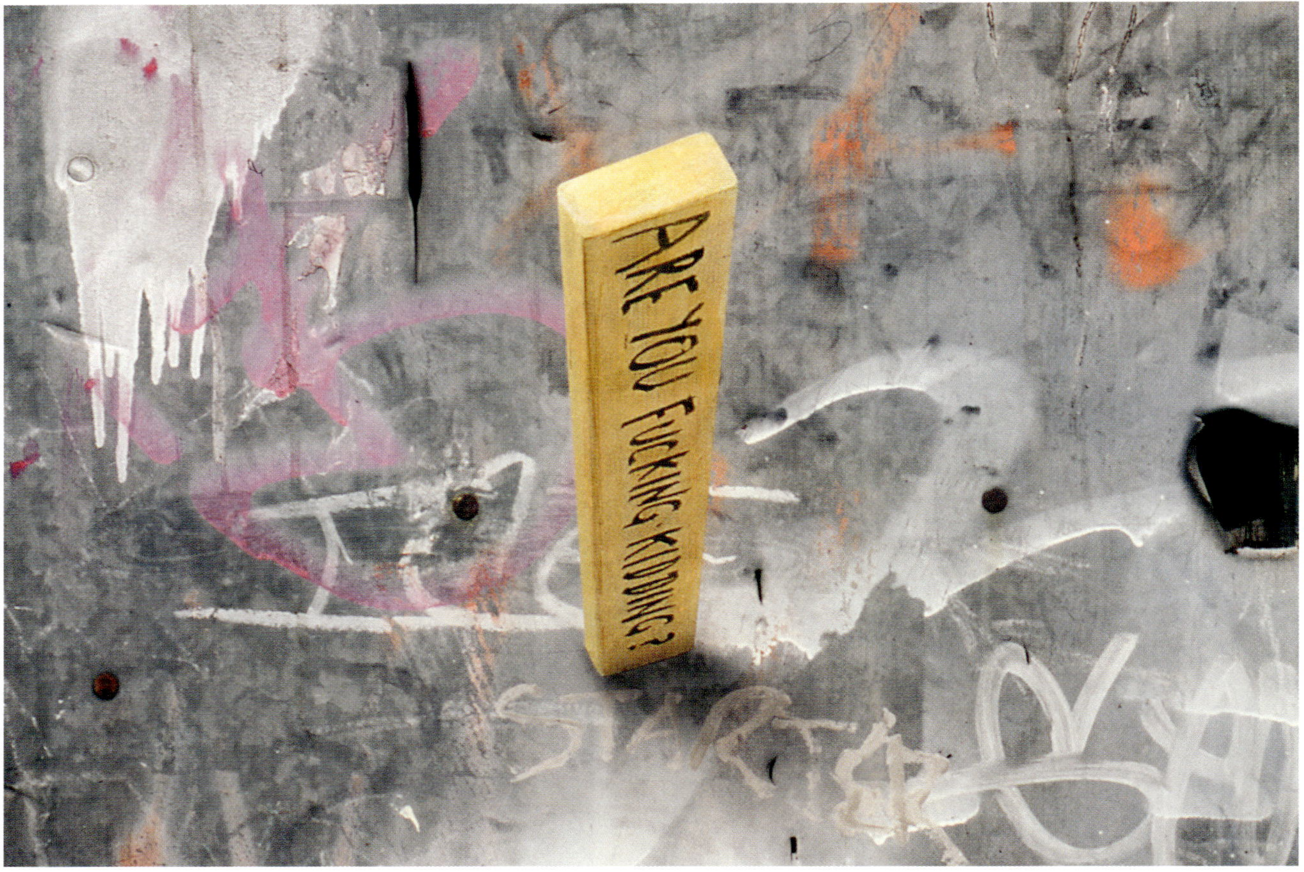
ARE YOU FUCKING KIDDING?

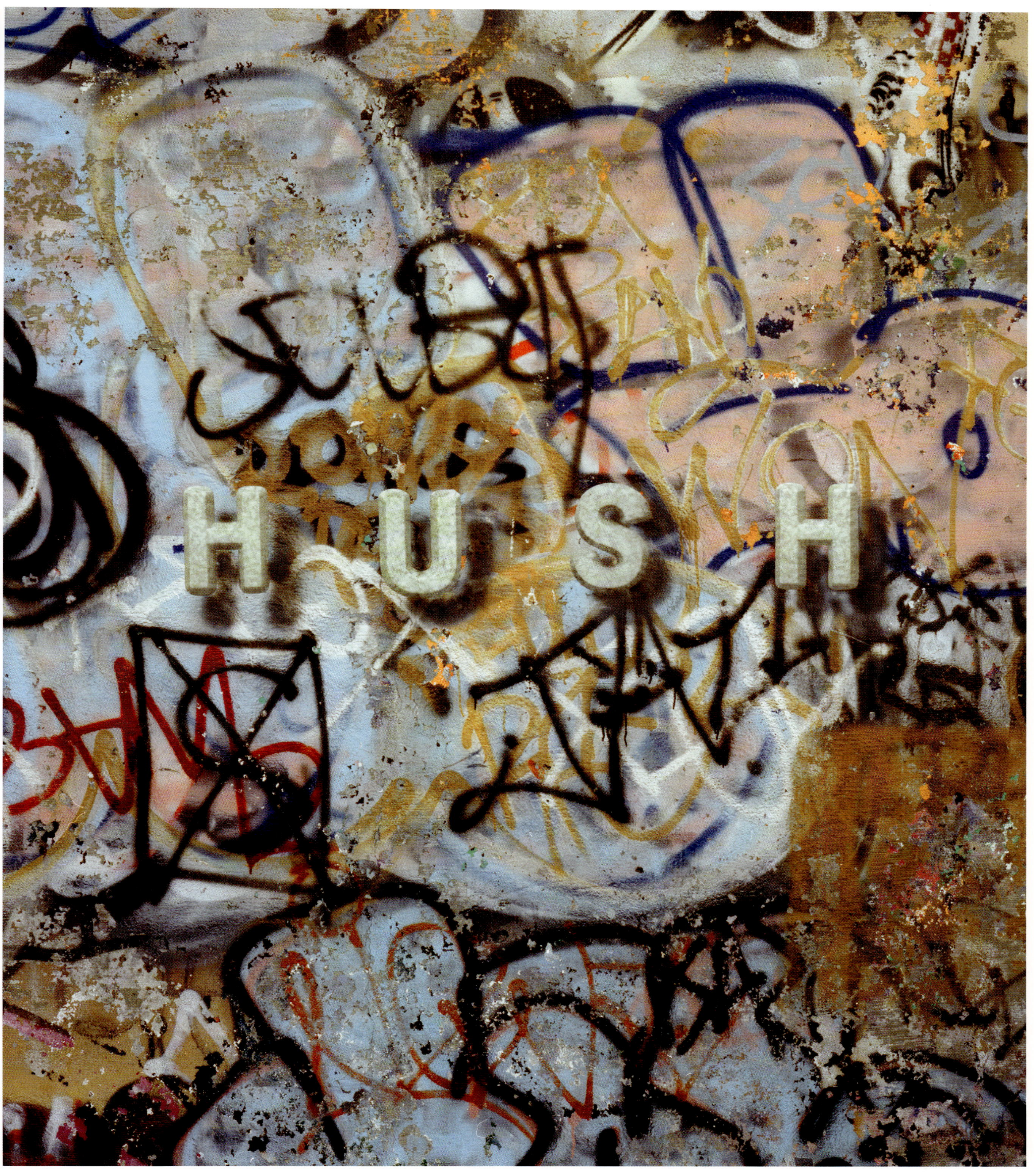
HUSH

HENRY ST. SETTLEMENT HOUSE

1998 - 1999

Commissioned by the Public Art Fund. Inspired by corporate vandalism. I was responding to the vinyl banner billboards that were just starting to crop up in the city. The Henry St. Settlement House invited me back the next year. There was even some suggestion about making it a yearly thing, but I let it go. The trees were taking over and frankly, being up on the cherry picker frightened me.

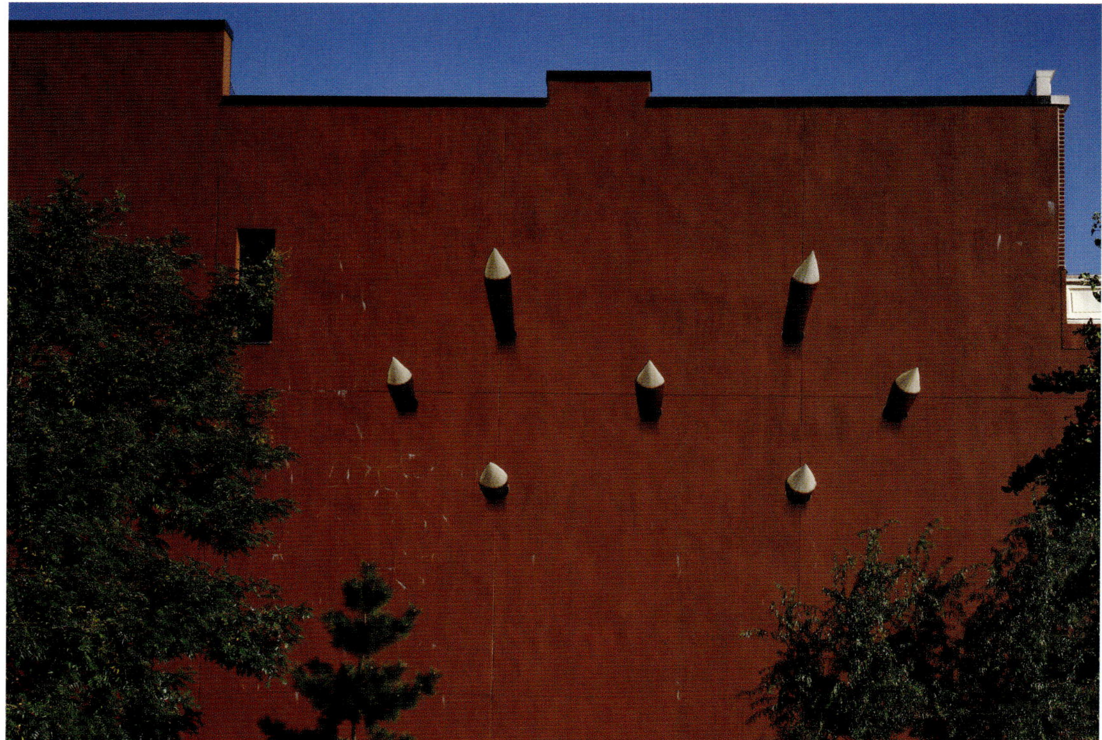

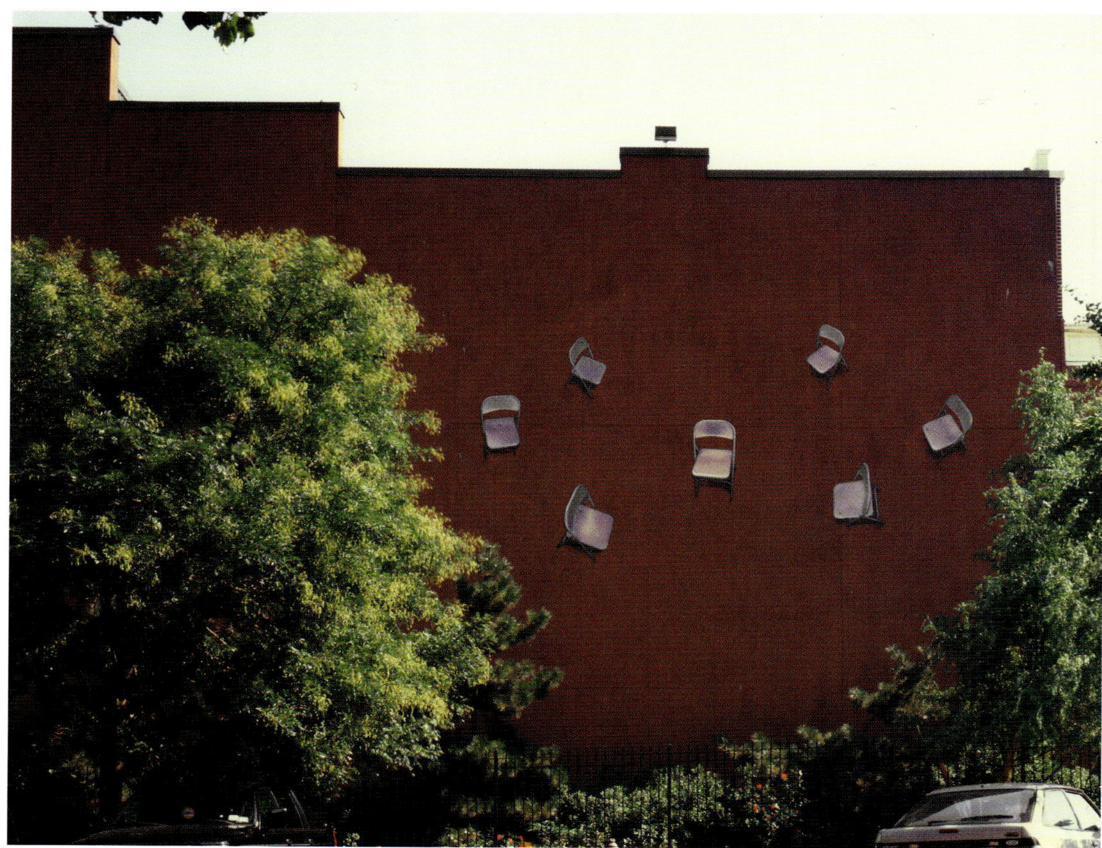

THIS PAGE, TOP:

STICKS, HENRY ST. SETTLEMENT HOUSE ABRONS ART CENTER, GRAND ST., NYC., 1998.

THIS PAGE, BOTTOM:

CHAIRS, HENRY ST. SETTLEMENT HOUSE ABRONS ART CENTER, GRAND ST., NYC., 1999.

OPPOSITE PAGE:

CAT. // Thanks to the Henry St. commissions I got a chance to develop a technique for doing larger pieces. Unfortunately it was too expensive for me at the time so I couldn't do much with it. But the technical knowledge was to come in handy later.

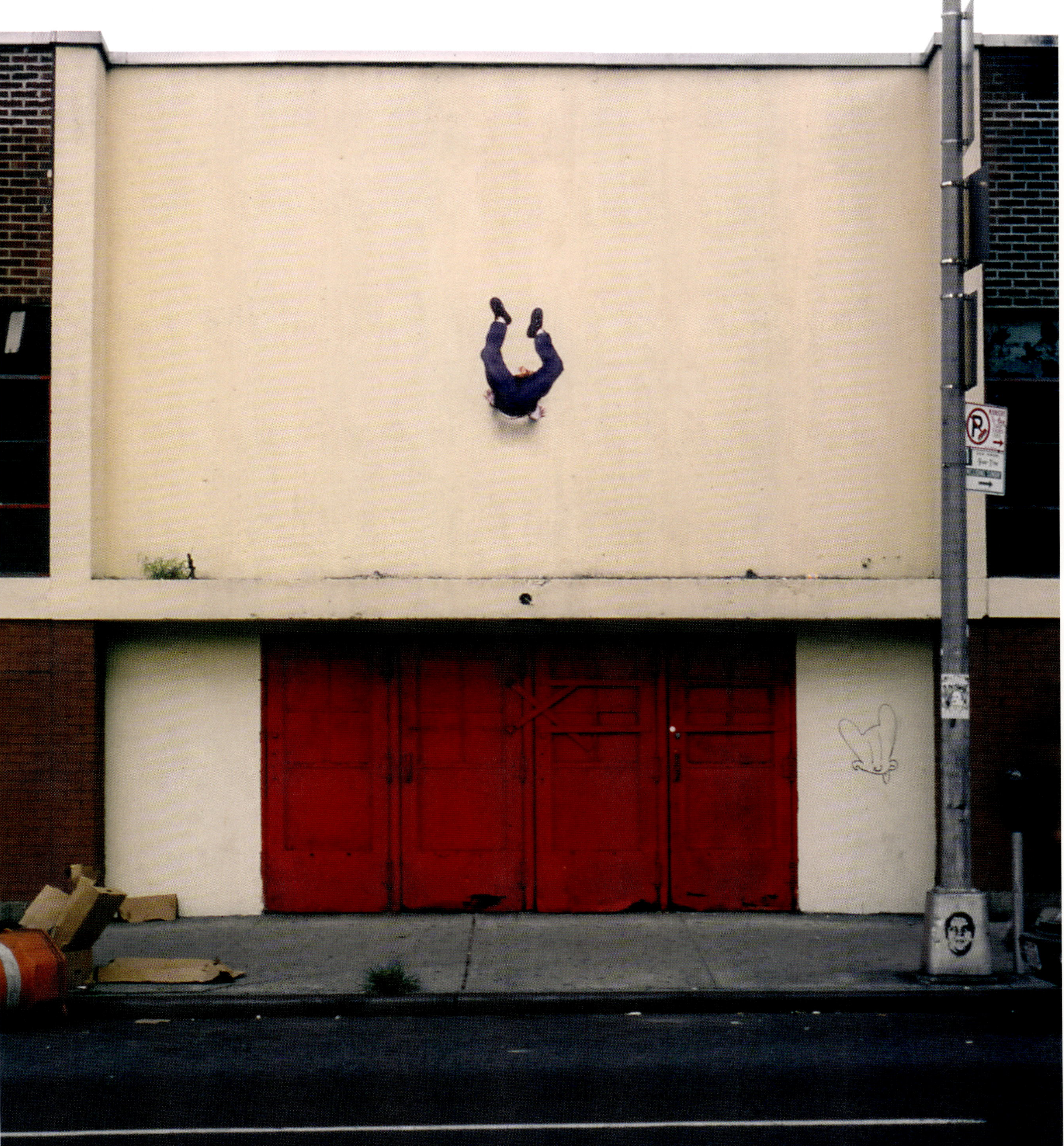

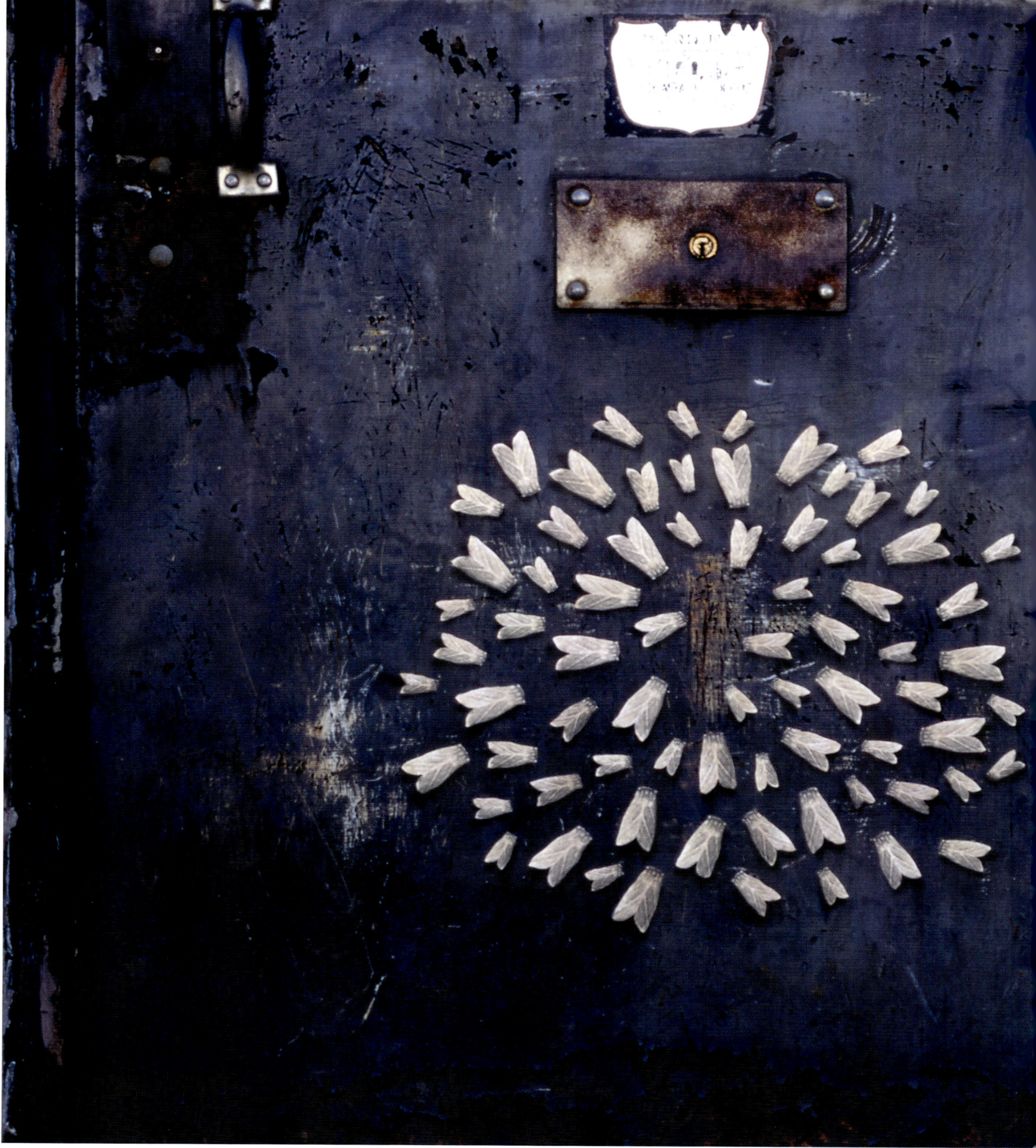

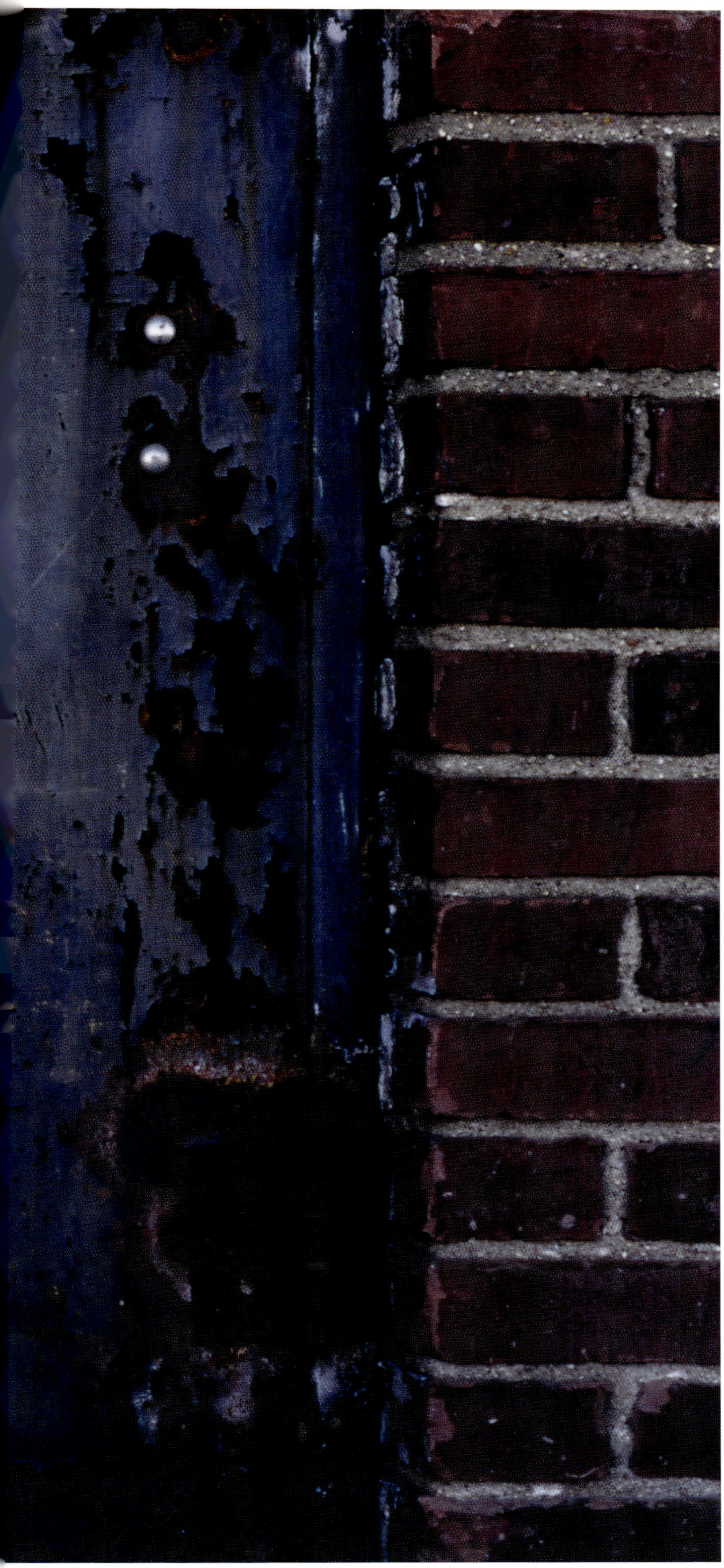

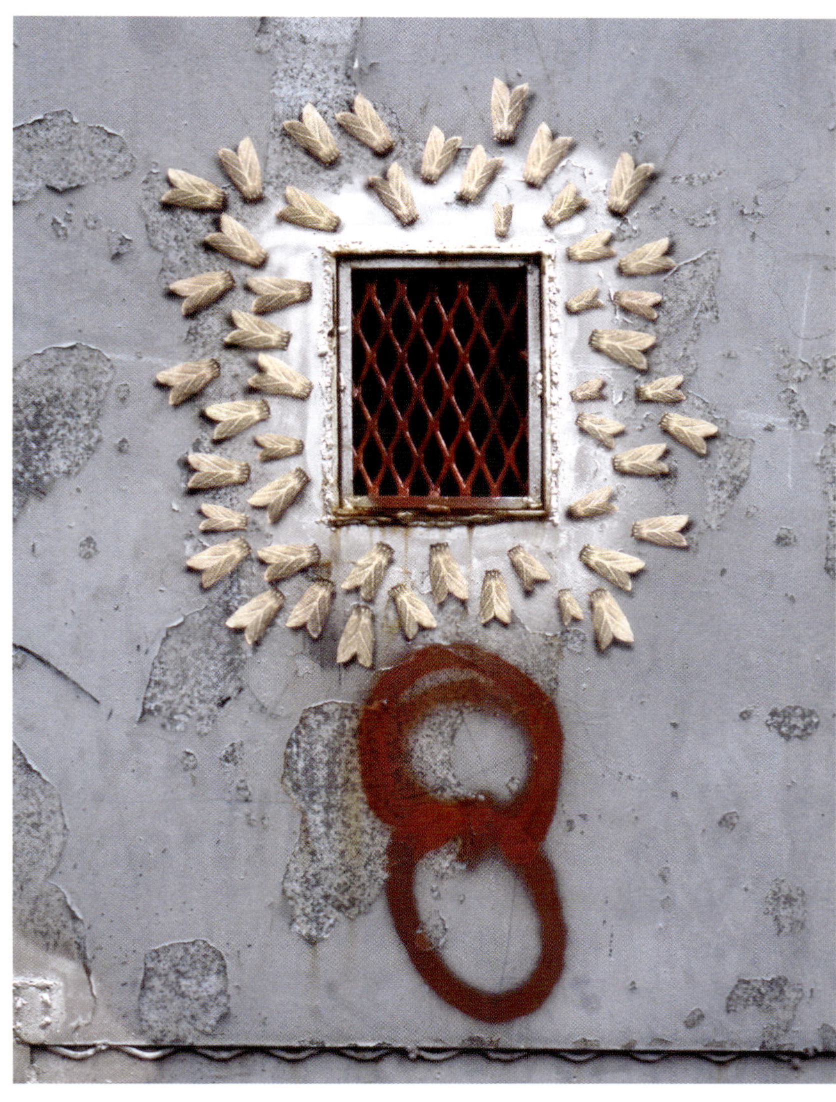

BEDFORD STUYVESANT, BROOKLYN, 1999.

BROOKLYN NAVY YARD, 1999.

BIRDS

2000

After decades of being chased out of live/work spaces by gentrification, it was becoming clear that my days in Manhattan were numbered. Housing court had me: I was facing eviction from my beloved loft on the lower east side. To close the curtain on my Manhattan career I decided to go out the way I started: painting hummingbirds.

RIGHT:

LUDLOW ST, NYC., 2000. // On my front door. Acrylic on vinyl applied to metal door. The '5' is a sticker also.

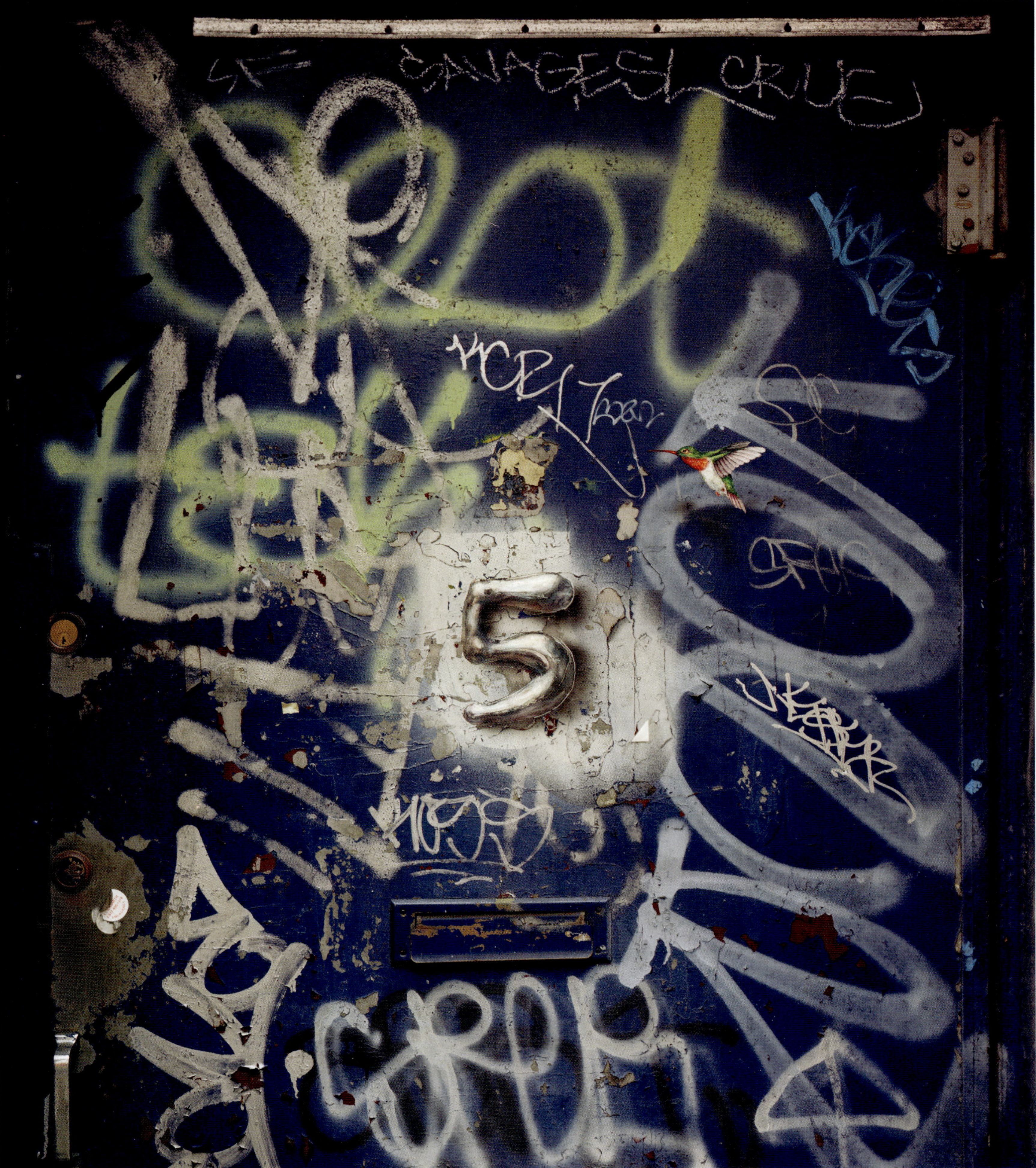
5

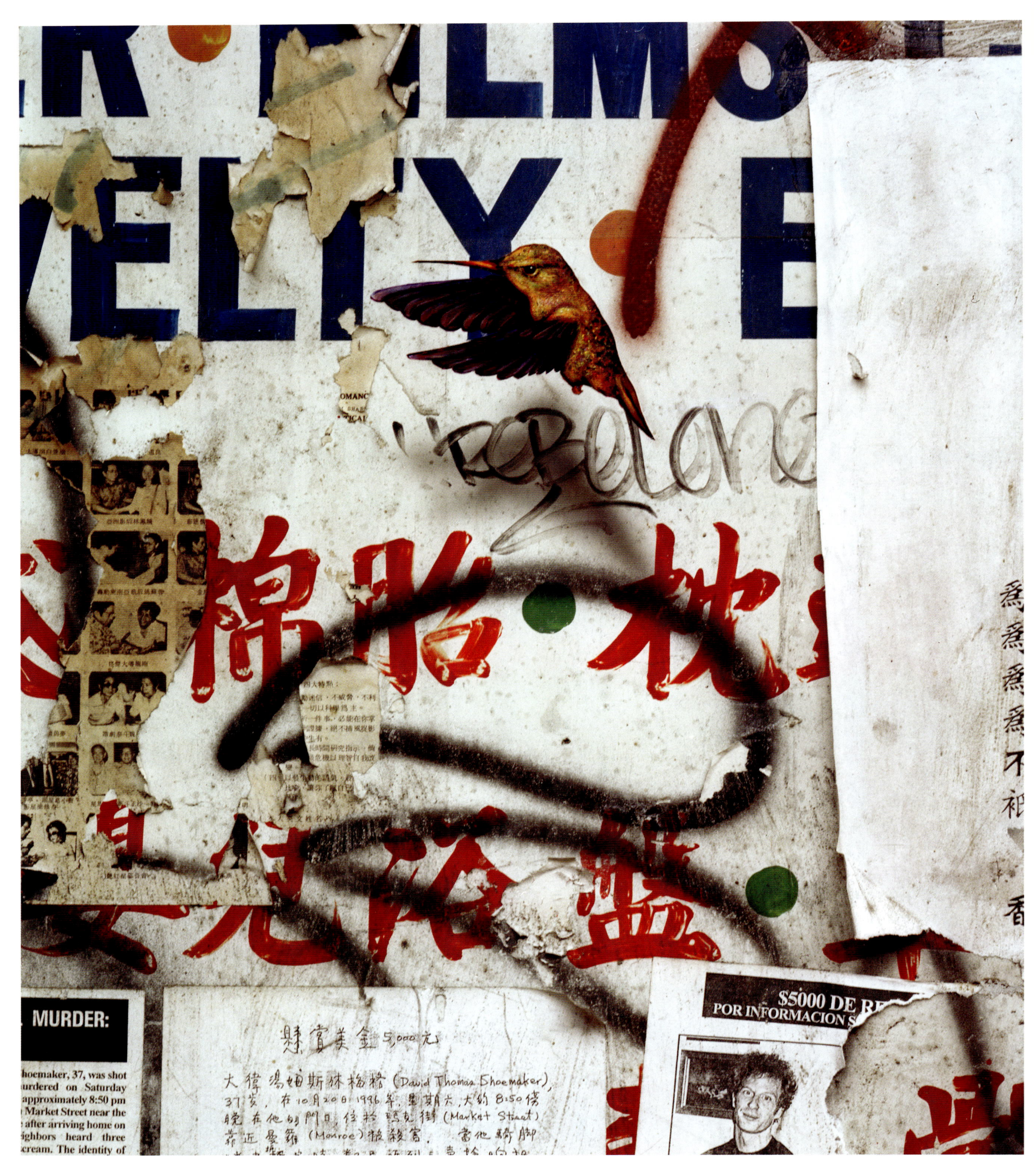

MURDER:
hoemaker, 37, was shot
urdered on Saturday
approximately 8:50 pm
Market Street near the
after arriving home on
ighbors heard three
cream. The identity of
懸賞美金5,000元
(David Thomas Shoemaker),
(Market Street)
(Monroe)
$5000 DE RE
POR INFORMACION S

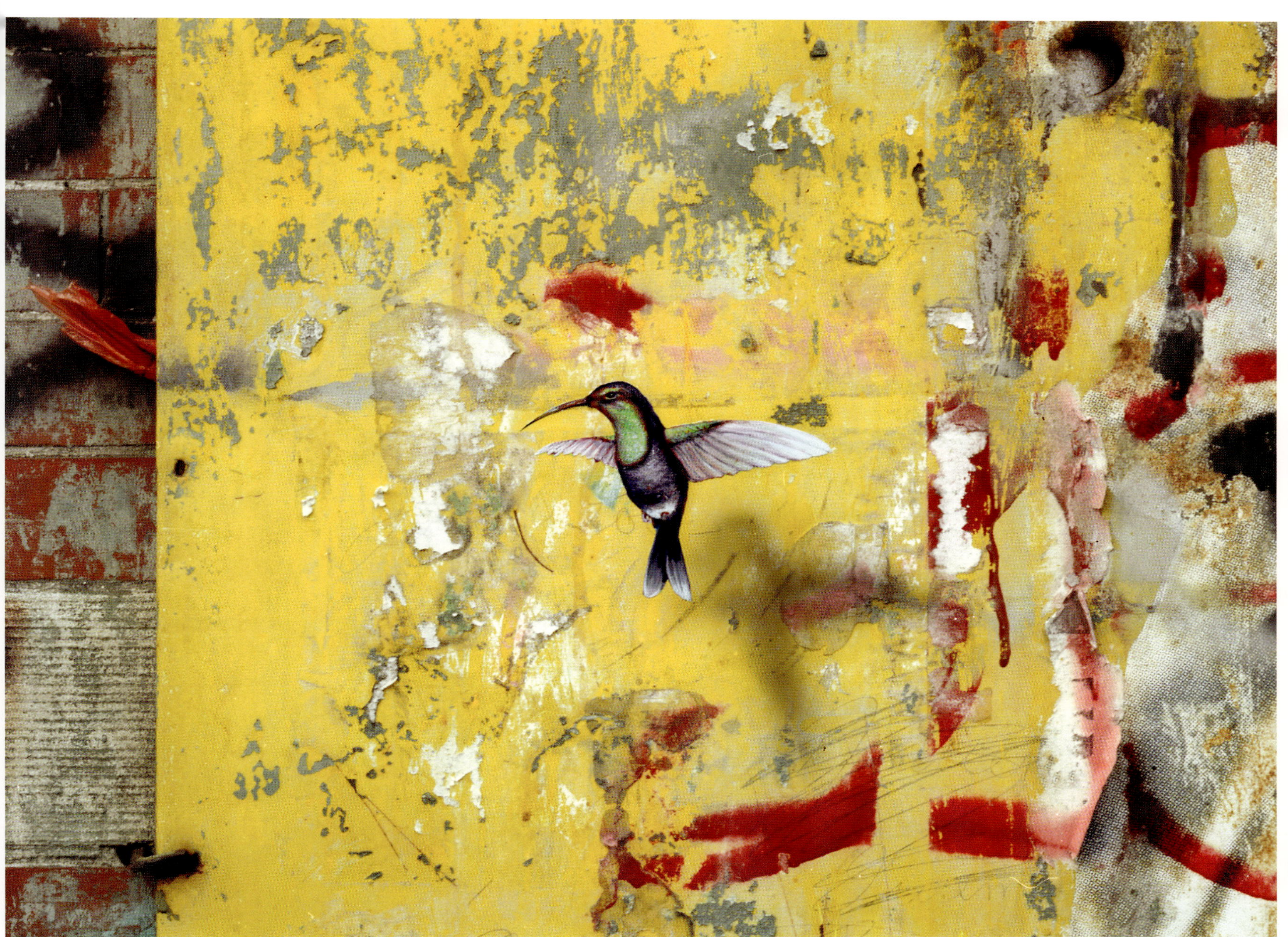

OPPOSITE PAGE:

OLIVER NEAR PEARL ST, NYC., 2000. // Acrylic on vinyl applied to metal wall.

THIS PAGE:

HENRY NEAR PIKE ST, NYC., 2000. // Acrylic on vinyl applied to metal wall.

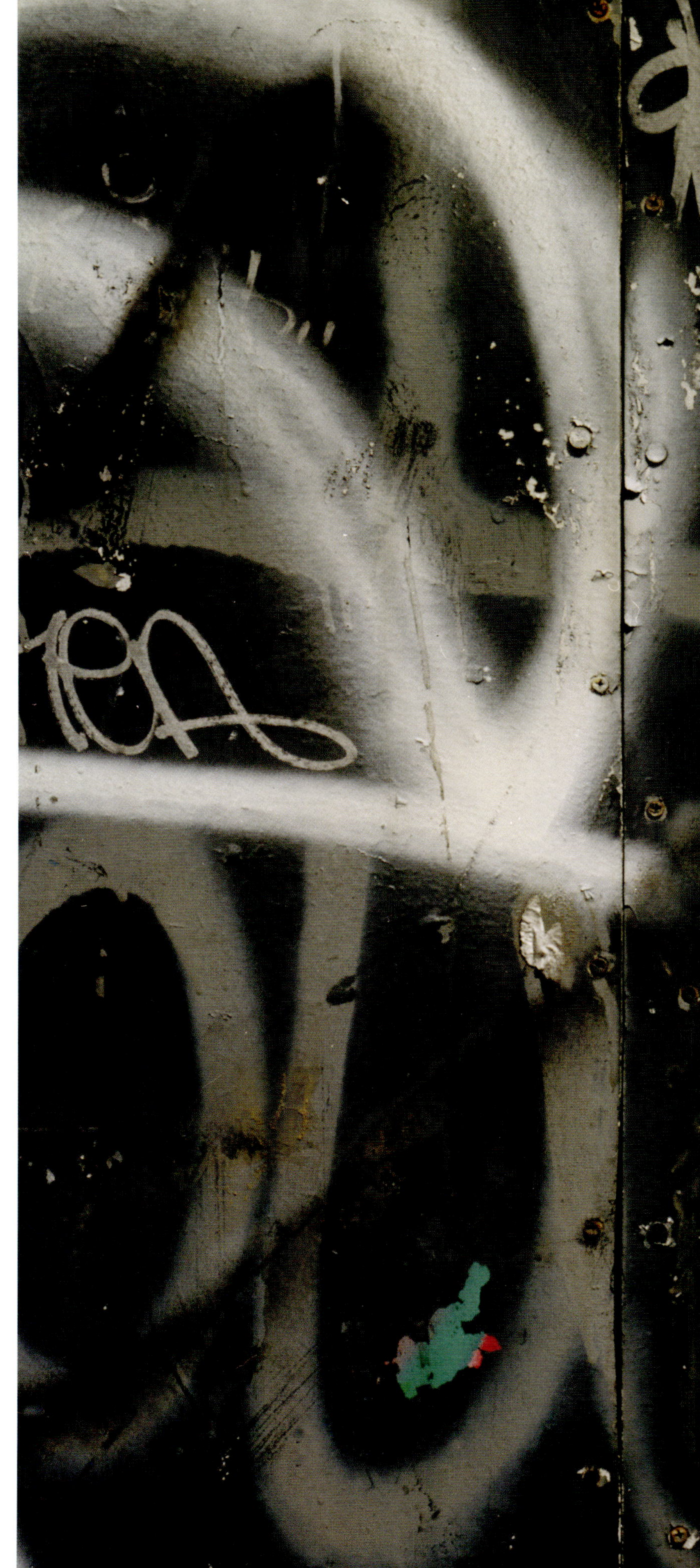

NORFOLK ST, NEAR RIVINGTON, NYC., 2000.
Acrylic on vinyl applied to metal wall.

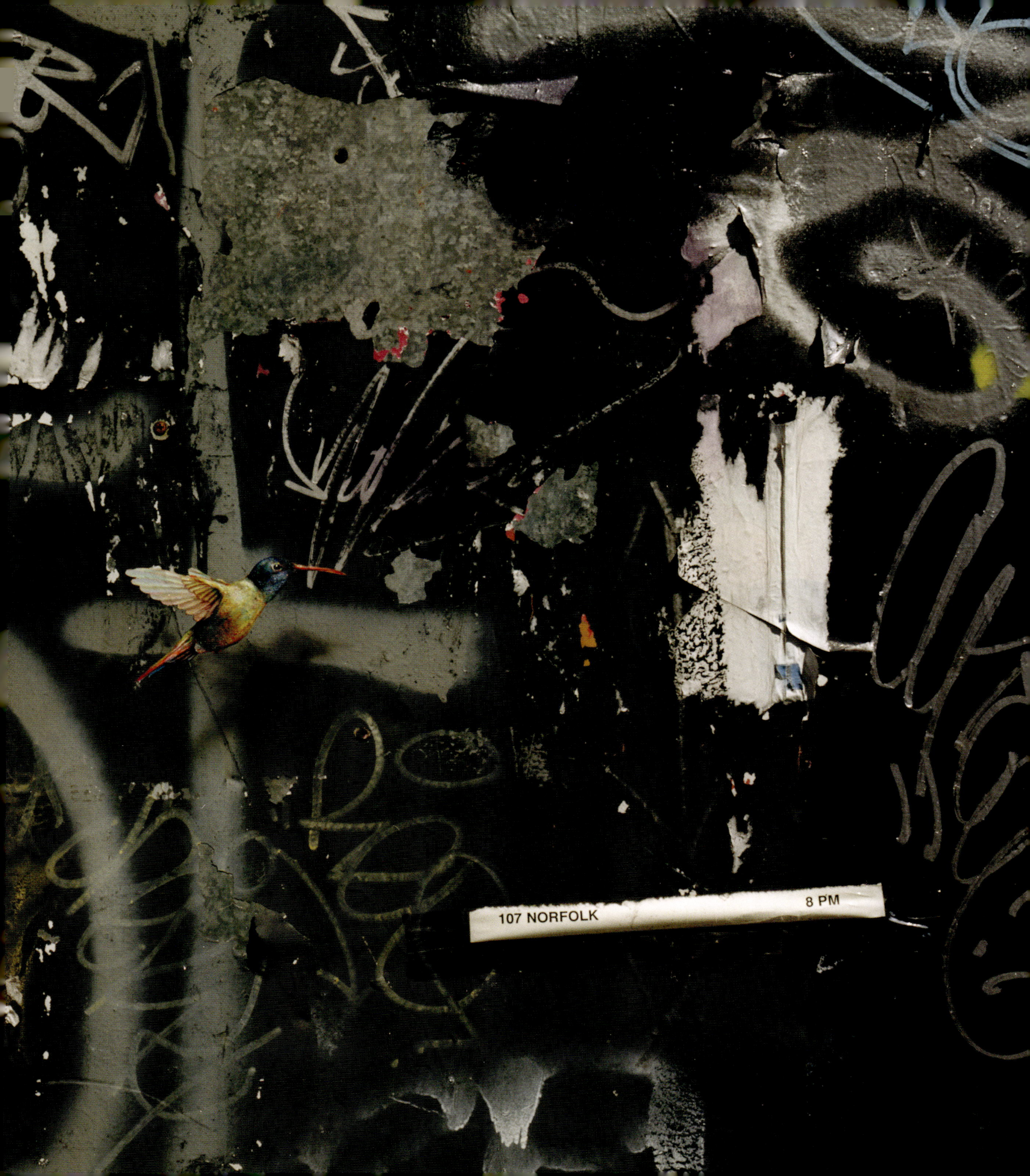
107 NORFOLK
8 PM

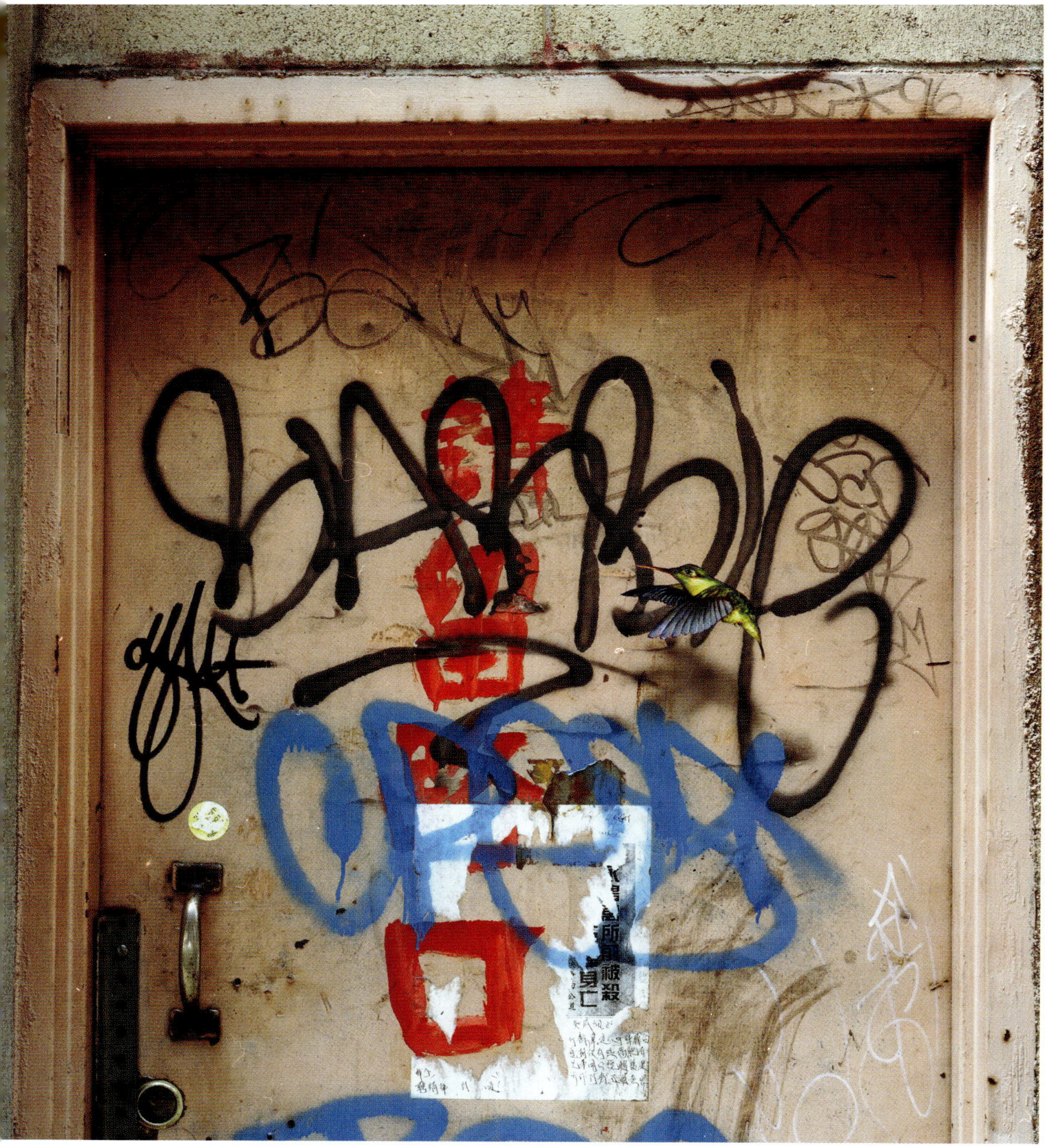

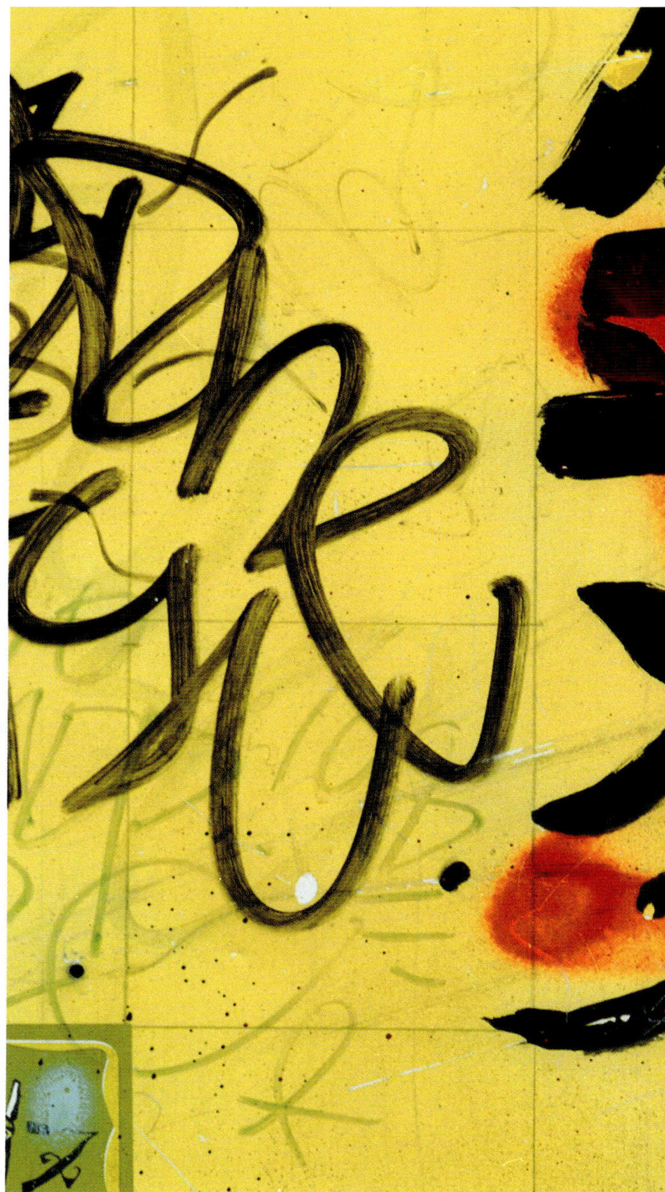

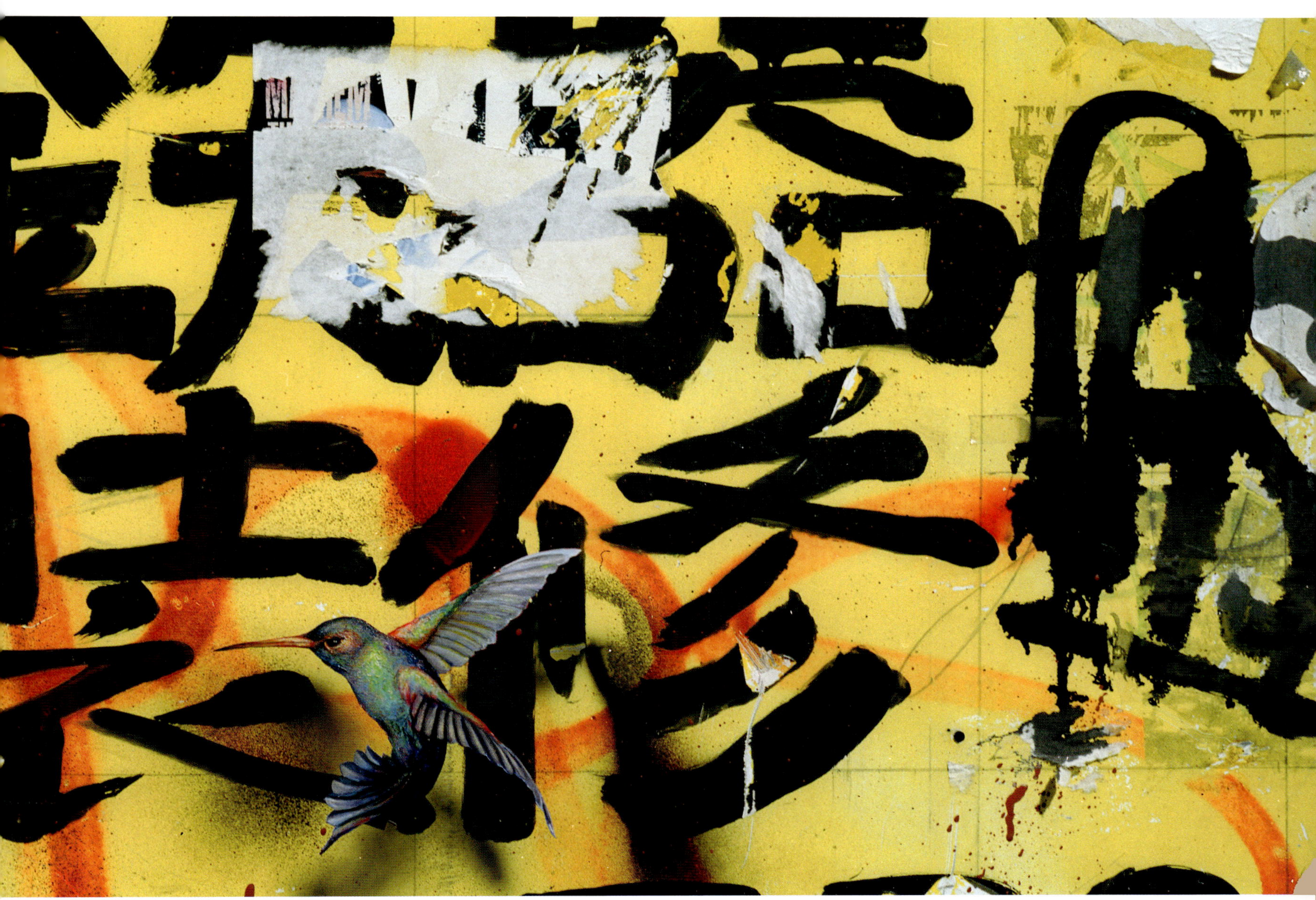

I painted these at home with acrylic paint on vinyl bumper sticker paper then airbrushed the shadow onto the actual wall. Probably the least challenging of all my pieces. And one of my favorites.

OPPOSITE PAGE:

HESTER ST. BETWEEN RUTGERS AND JEFFERSON, NYC., 2000. Acrylic on vinyl applied to metal wall.

THIS PAGE:

DELANCEY BETWEEN ATTORNEY AND SUFFOLK, NYC., 2000. Acrylic on vinyl applied to metal wall.

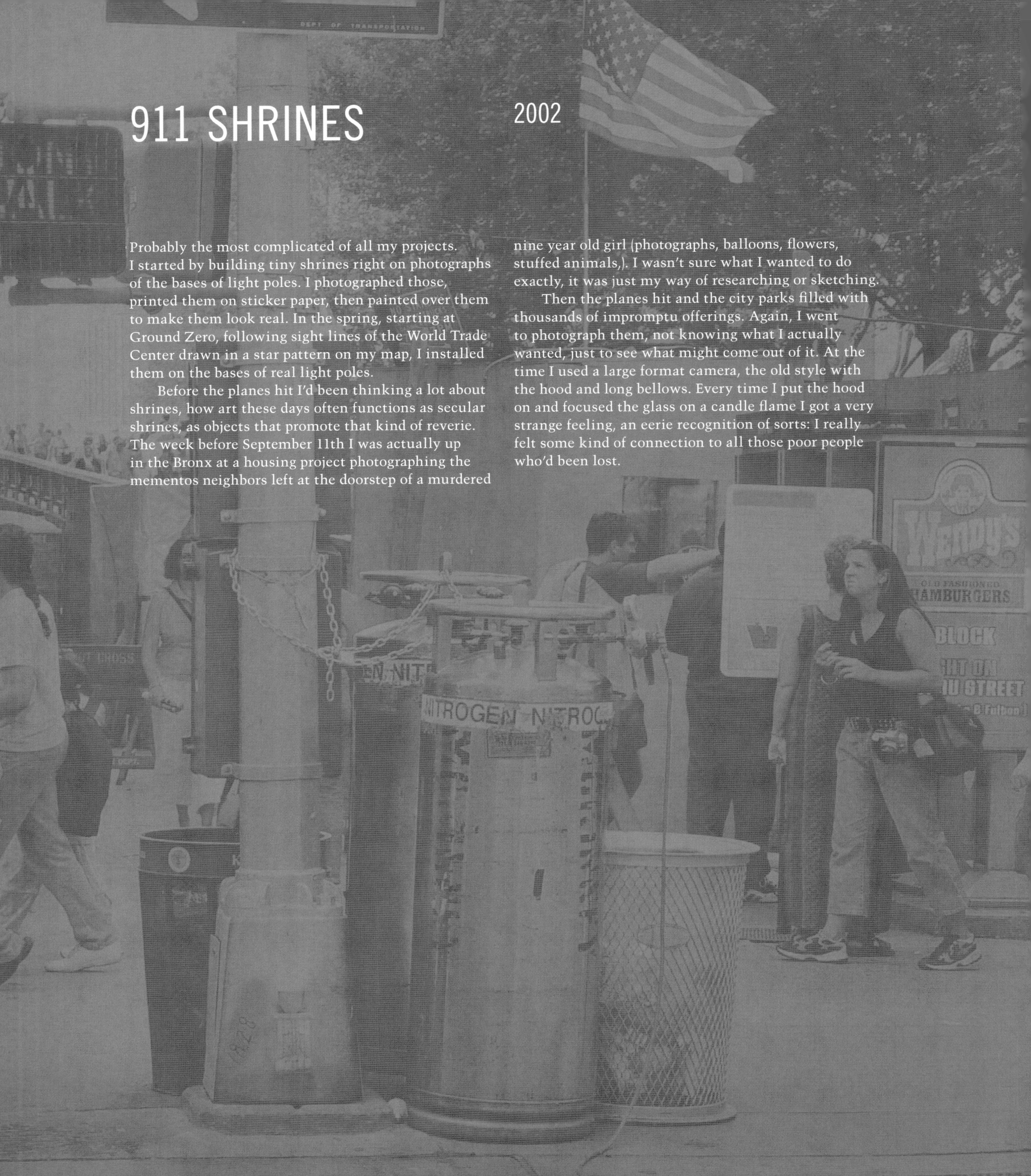

911 SHRINES

2002

Probably the most complicated of all my projects. I started by building tiny shrines right on photographs of the bases of light poles. I photographed those, printed them on sticker paper, then painted over them to make them look real. In the spring, starting at Ground Zero, following sight lines of the World Trade Center drawn in a star pattern on my map, I installed them on the bases of real light poles.

Before the planes hit I'd been thinking a lot about shrines, how art these days often functions as secular shrines, as objects that promote that kind of reverie. The week before September 11th I was actually up in the Bronx at a housing project photographing the mementos neighbors left at the doorstep of a murdered nine year old girl (photographs, balloons, flowers, stuffed animals,). I wasn't sure what I wanted to do exactly, it was just my way of researching or sketching.

Then the planes hit and the city parks filled with thousands of impromptu offerings. Again, I went to photograph them, not knowing what I actually wanted, just to see what might come out of it. At the time I used a large format camera, the old style with the hood and long bellows. Every time I put the hood on and focused the glass on a candle flame I got a very strange feeling, an eerie recognition of sorts: I really felt some kind of connection to all those poor people who'd been lost.

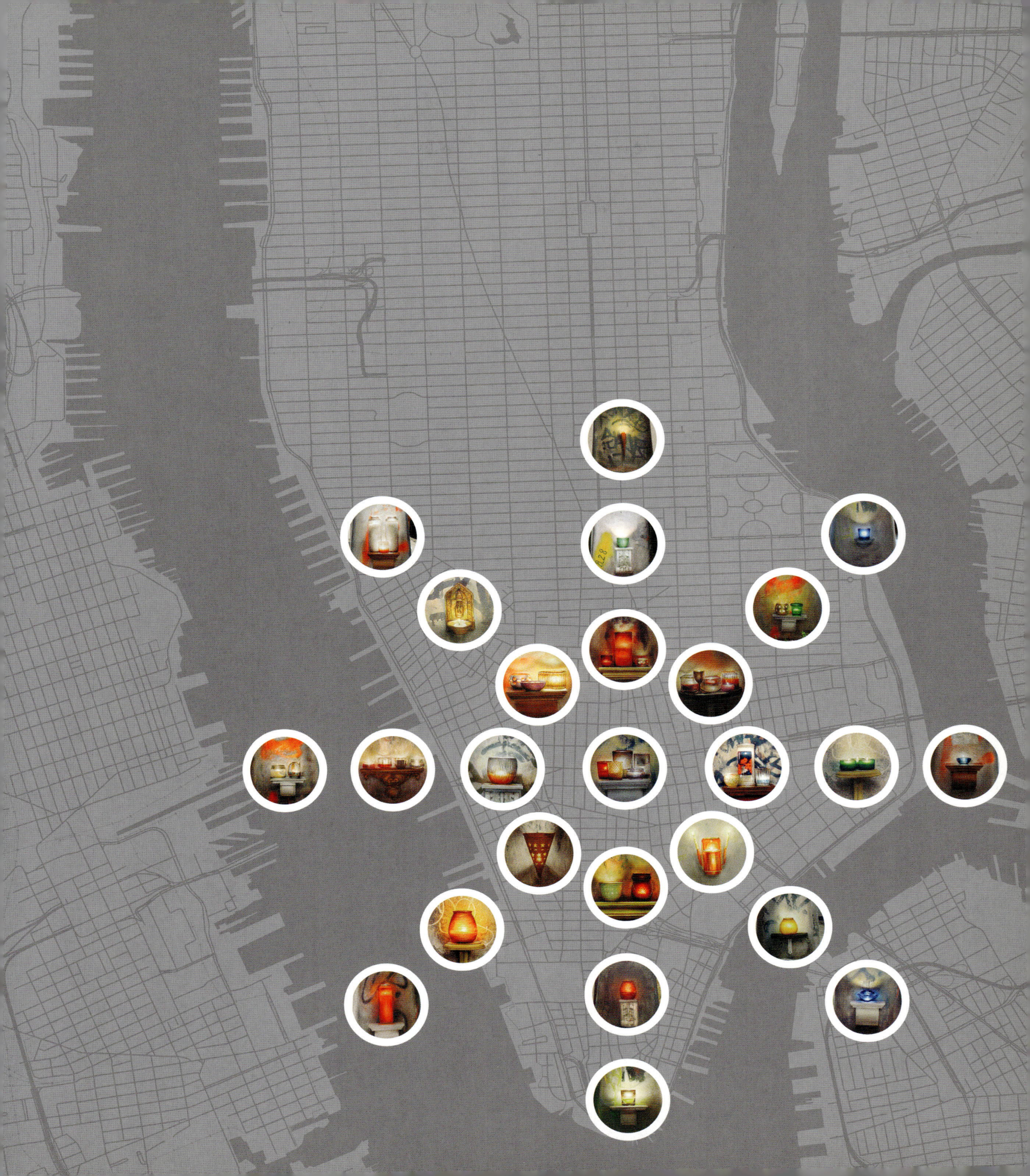

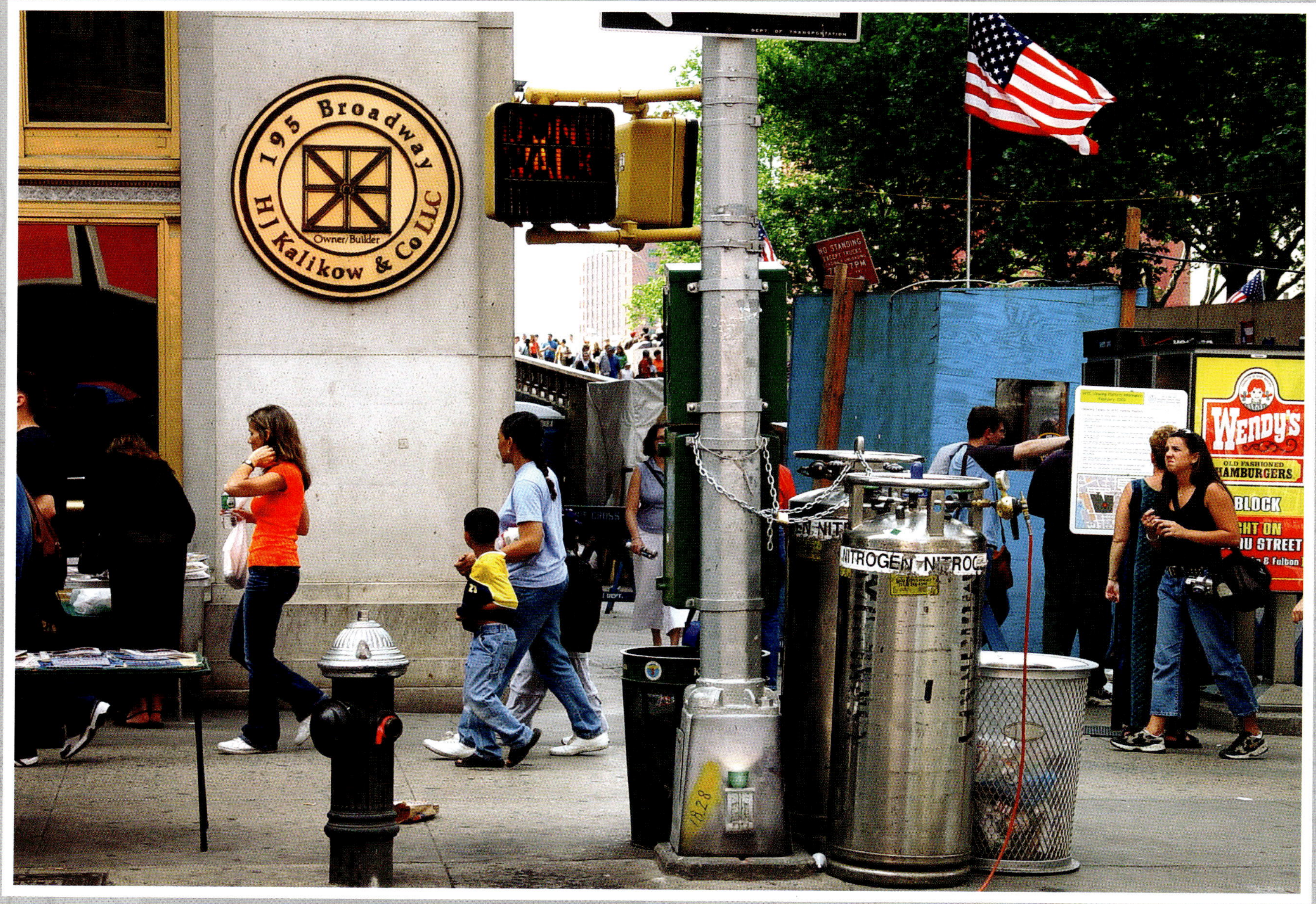
195 Broadway
HJ Kalikow & Co LLC
Owner/Builder
NITROGEN
WENDY'S
OLD FASHIONED
HAMBURGERS

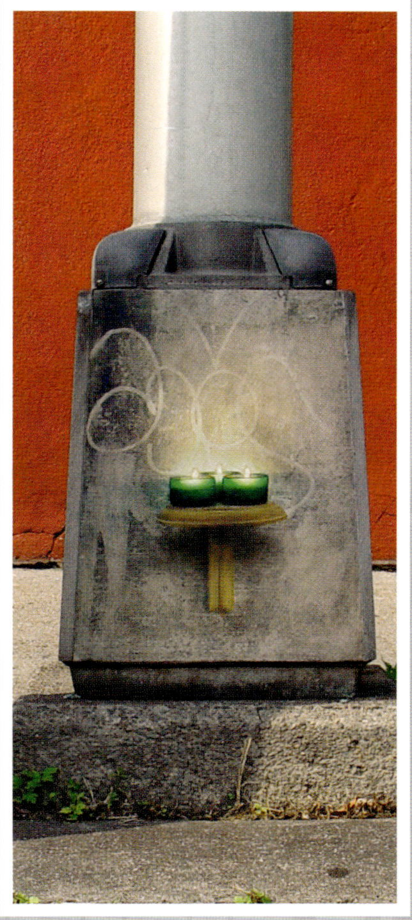

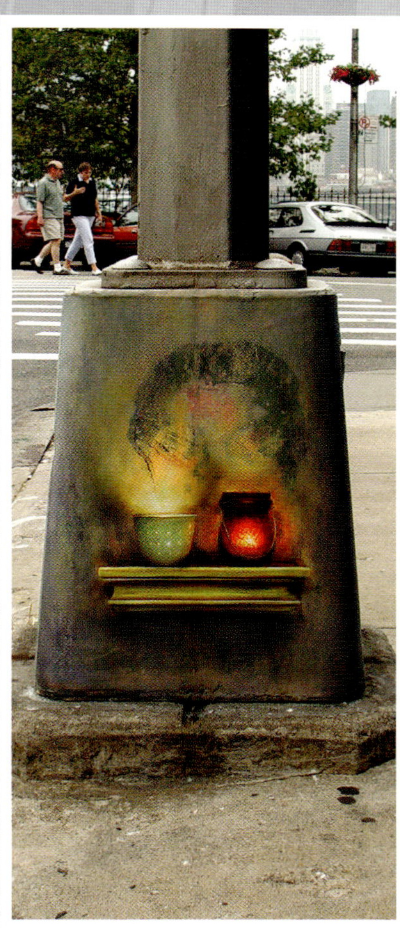

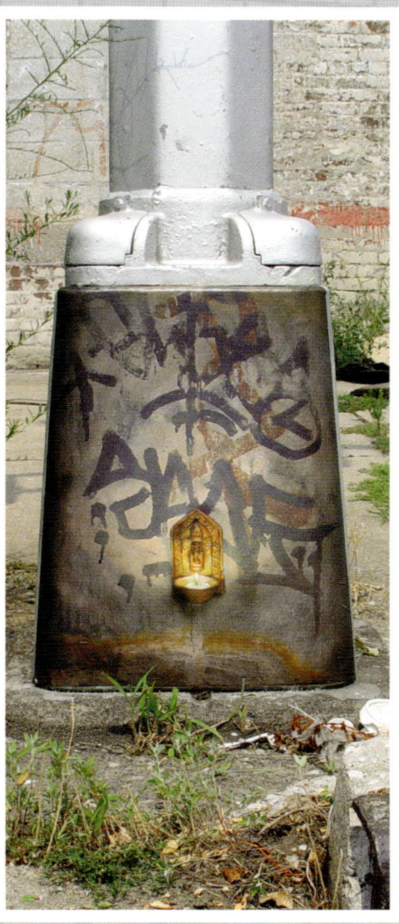

ABOVE LEFT:

WEEHAWKEN, NEW JERSEY, 2002.

ABOVE CENTER:

BROOKLYN BRIDGE, BROOKLYN, 2002.

ABOVE RIGHT:

WILLIAMSBURG, BROOKLYN, 2002.

OPPOSITE PAGE:

FULTON ST AND BROADWAY, NYC., 2002.

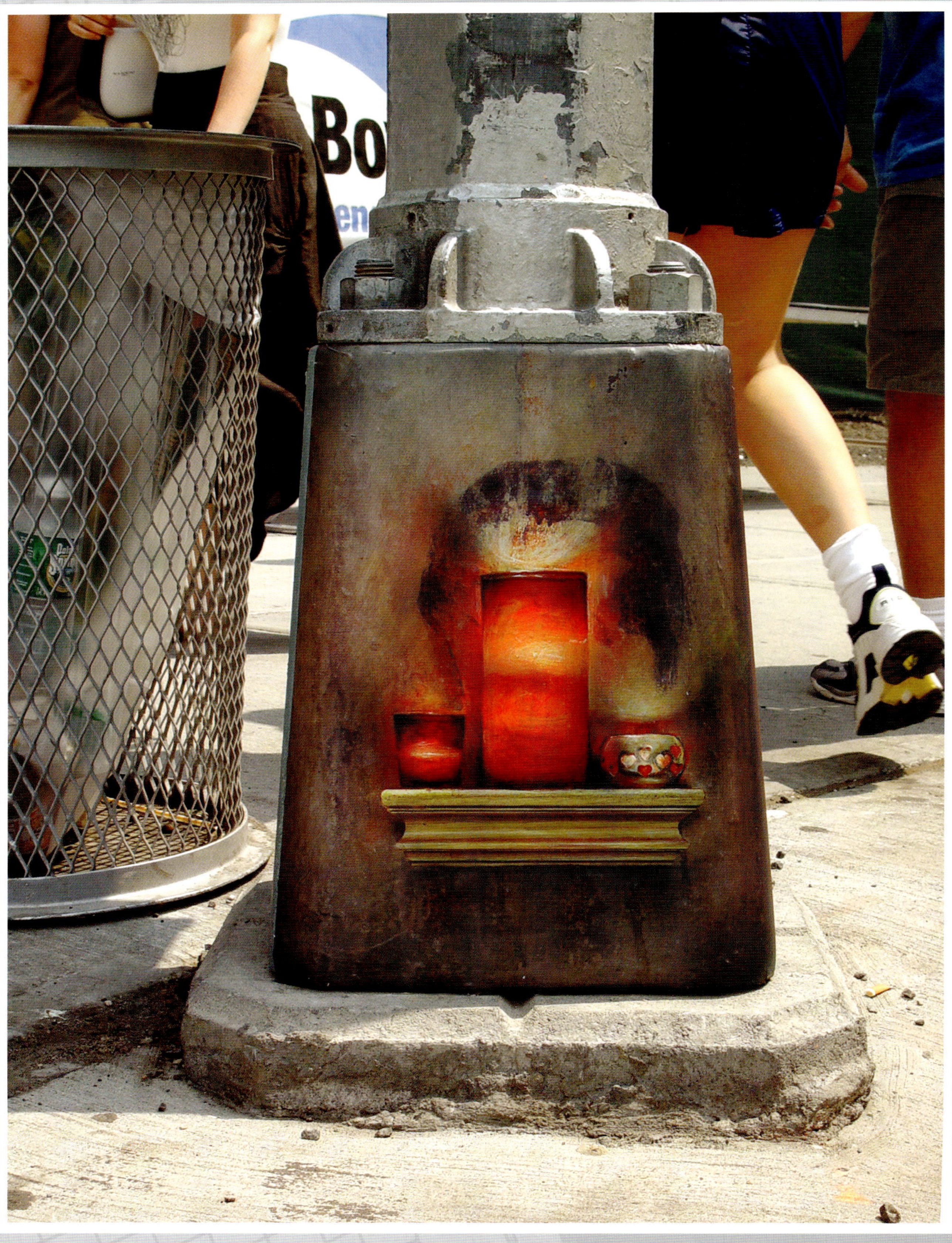

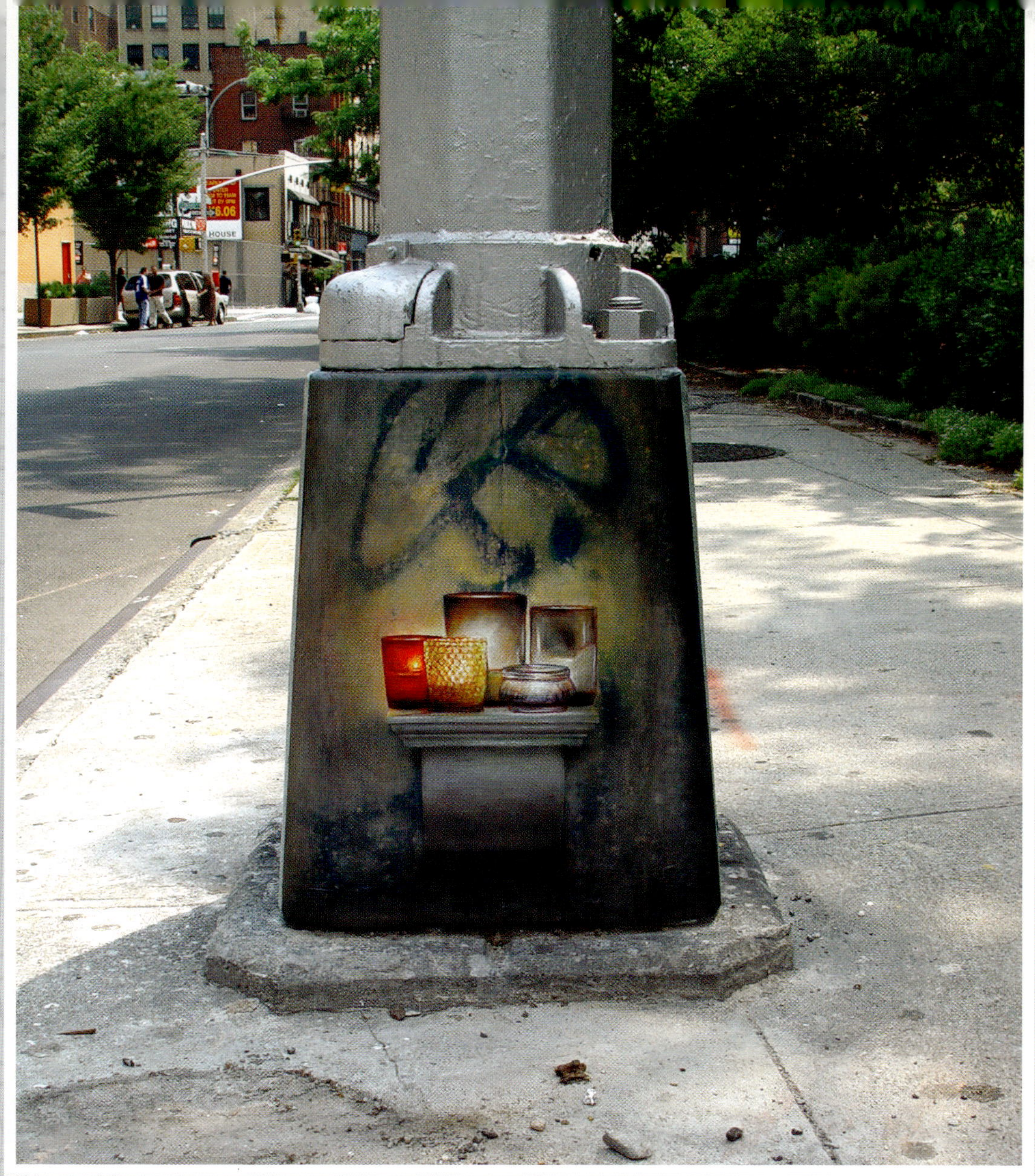

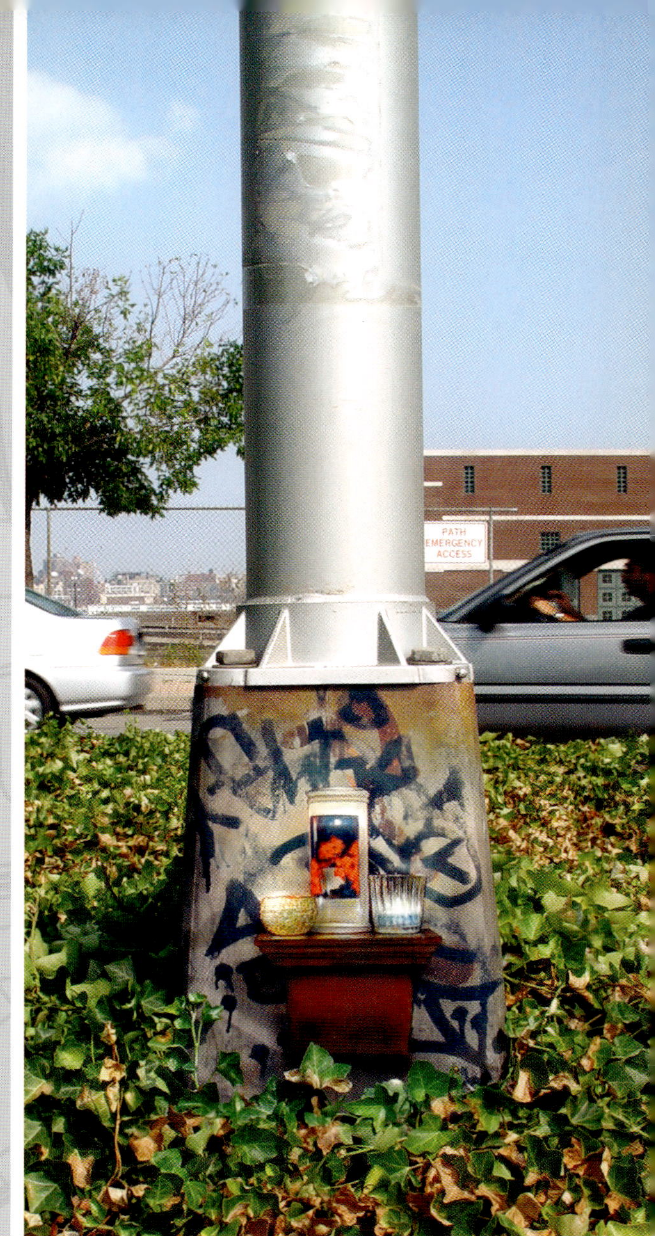

ABOVE RIGHT:

JERSEY CITY, 2002.

ABOVE LEFT:

TRIBECA, 2002.

OPPOSITE PAGE:

GROUND ZERO, NYC., 2002.

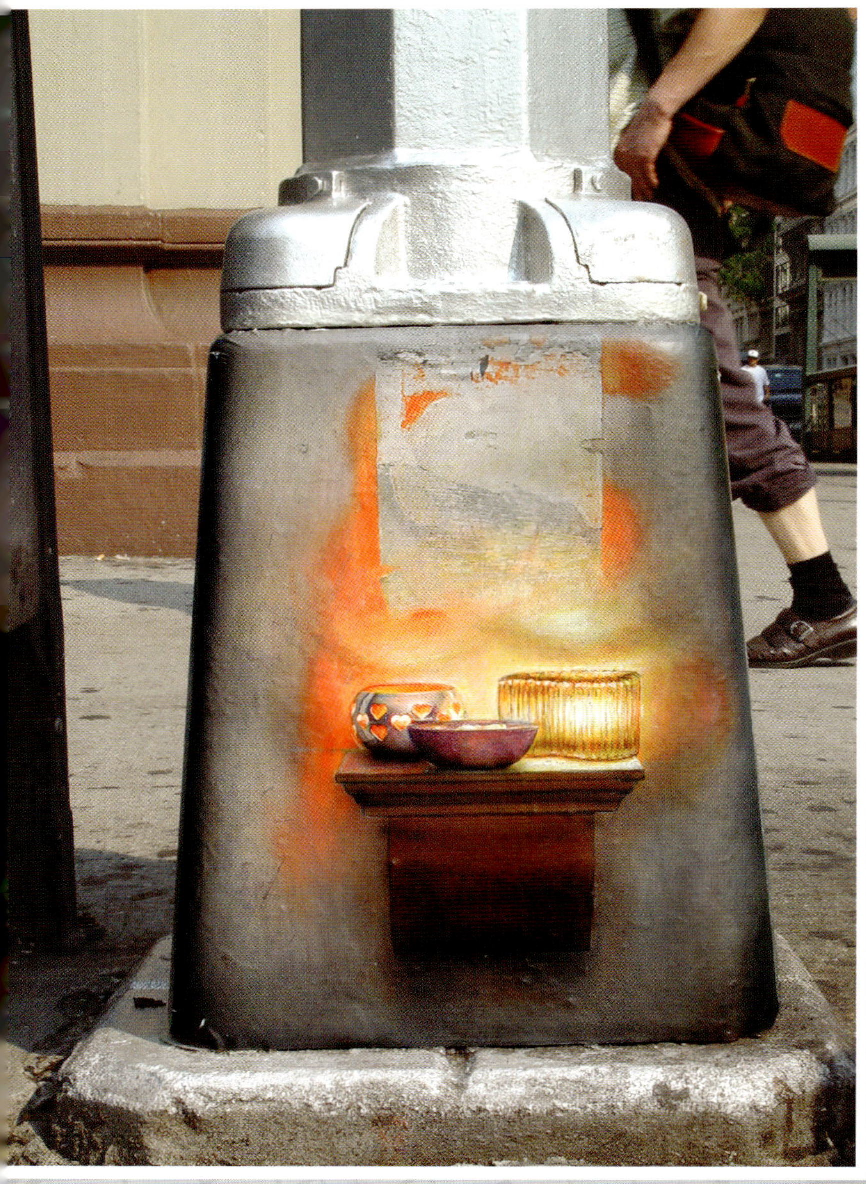

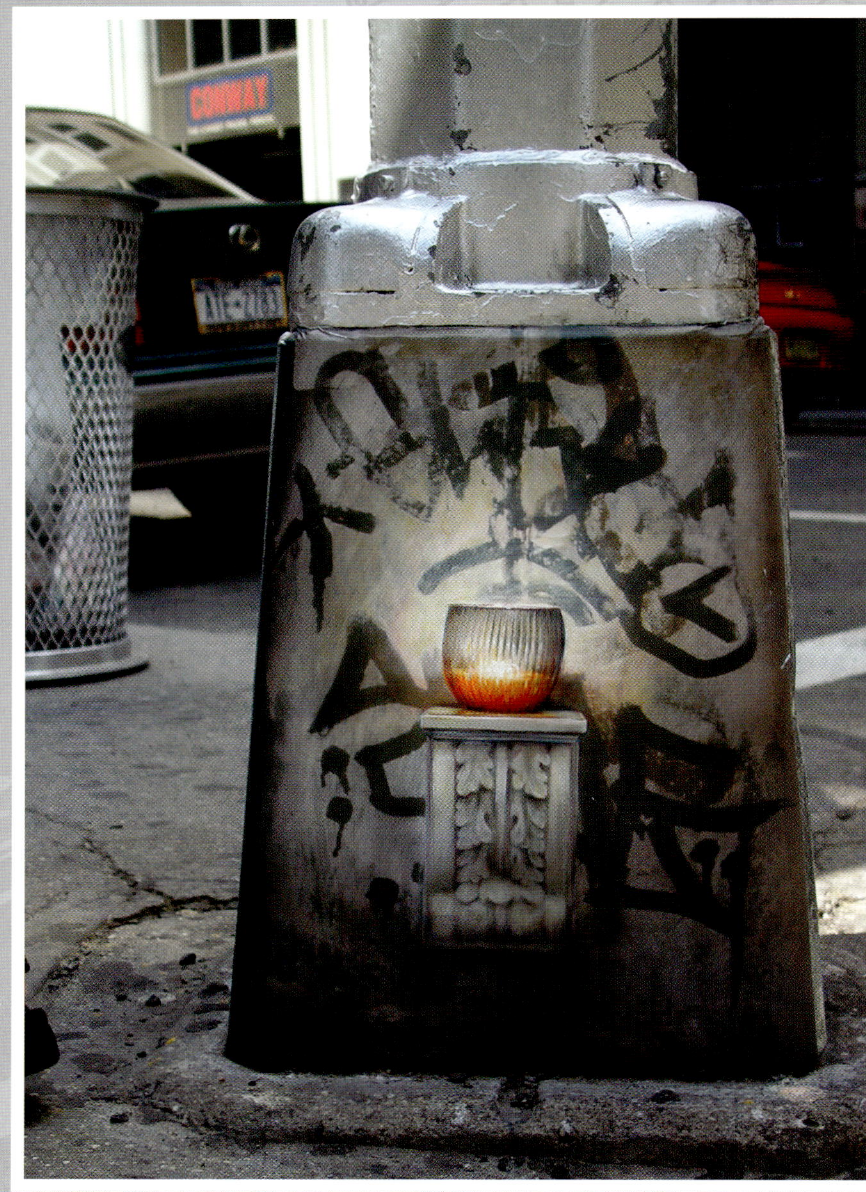

23RD ST. AND 6TH AVE., NYC., 2002.

FINANCIAL DISTRICT, NYC., 2002.

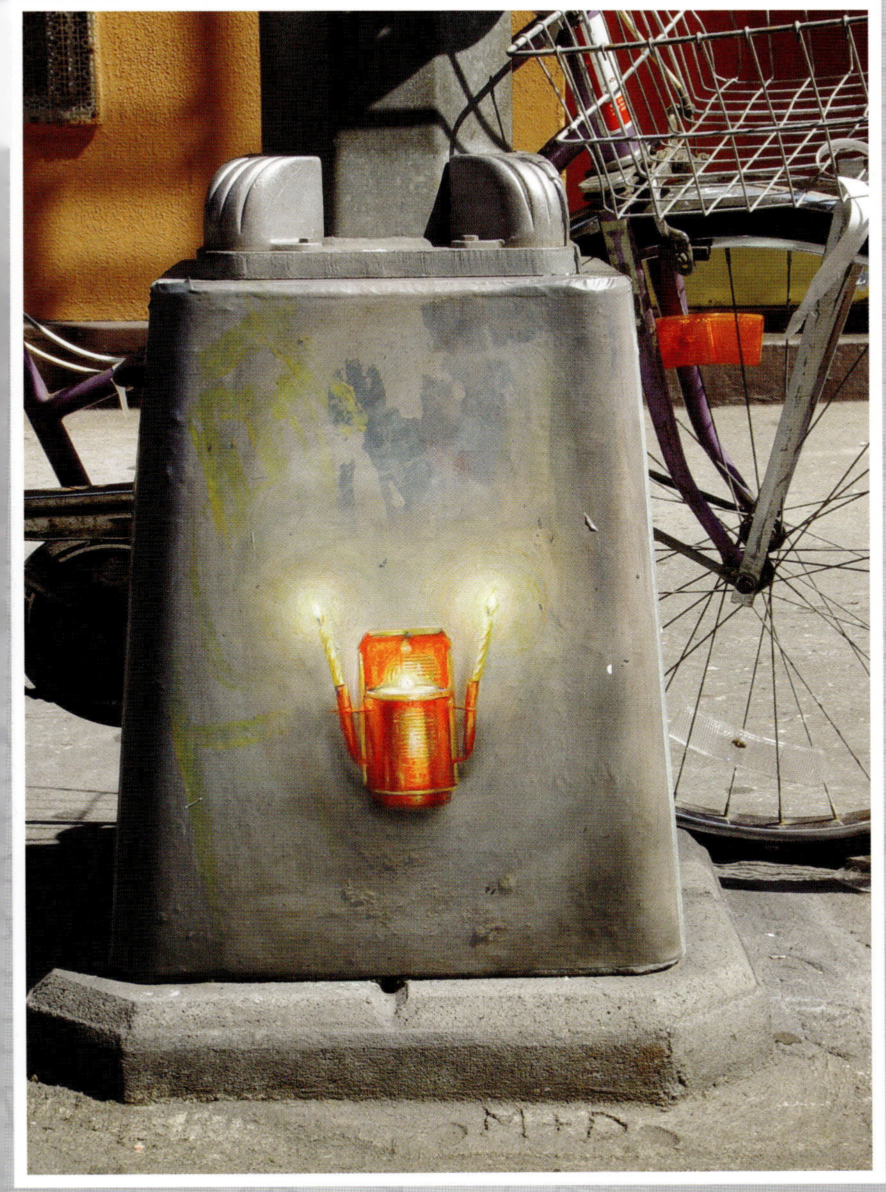

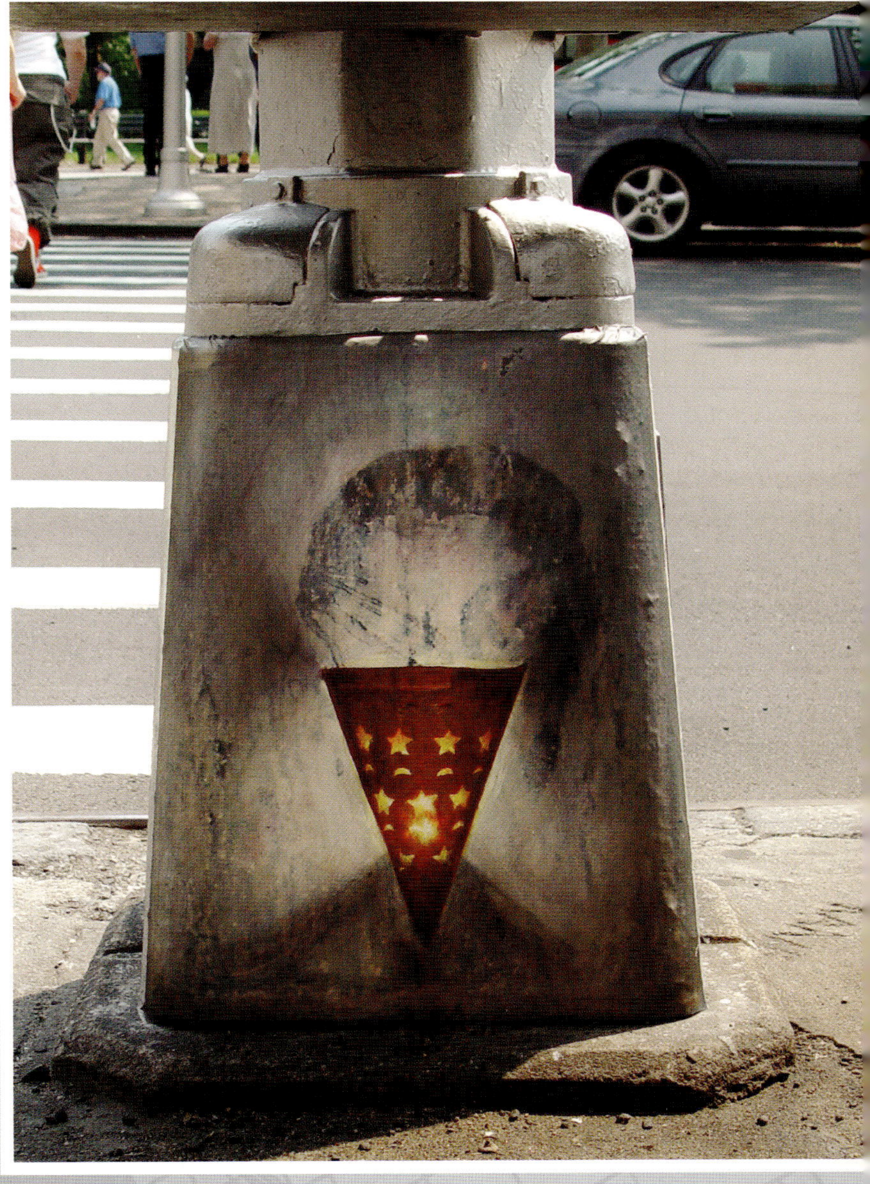

SOHO, NYC., 2002.

BATTERY PARK, NYC., 2002.

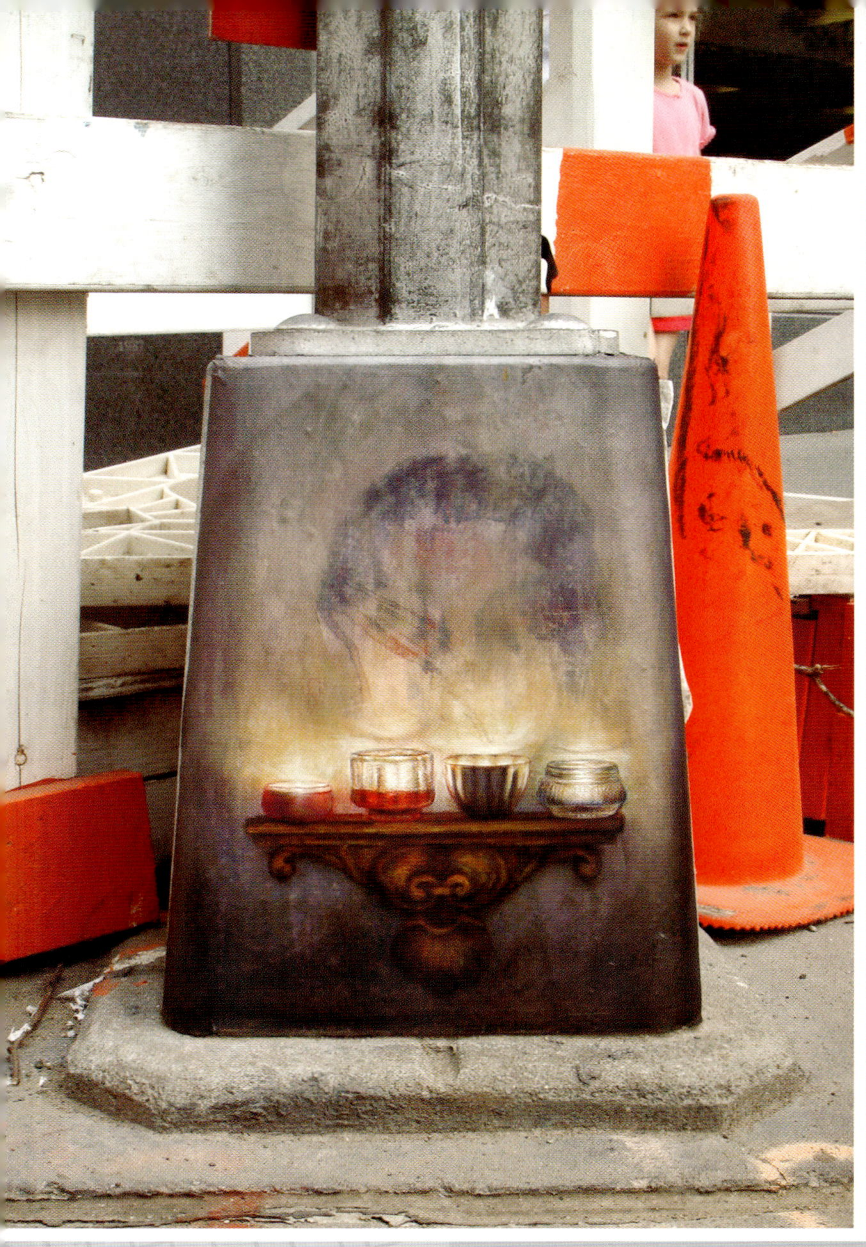

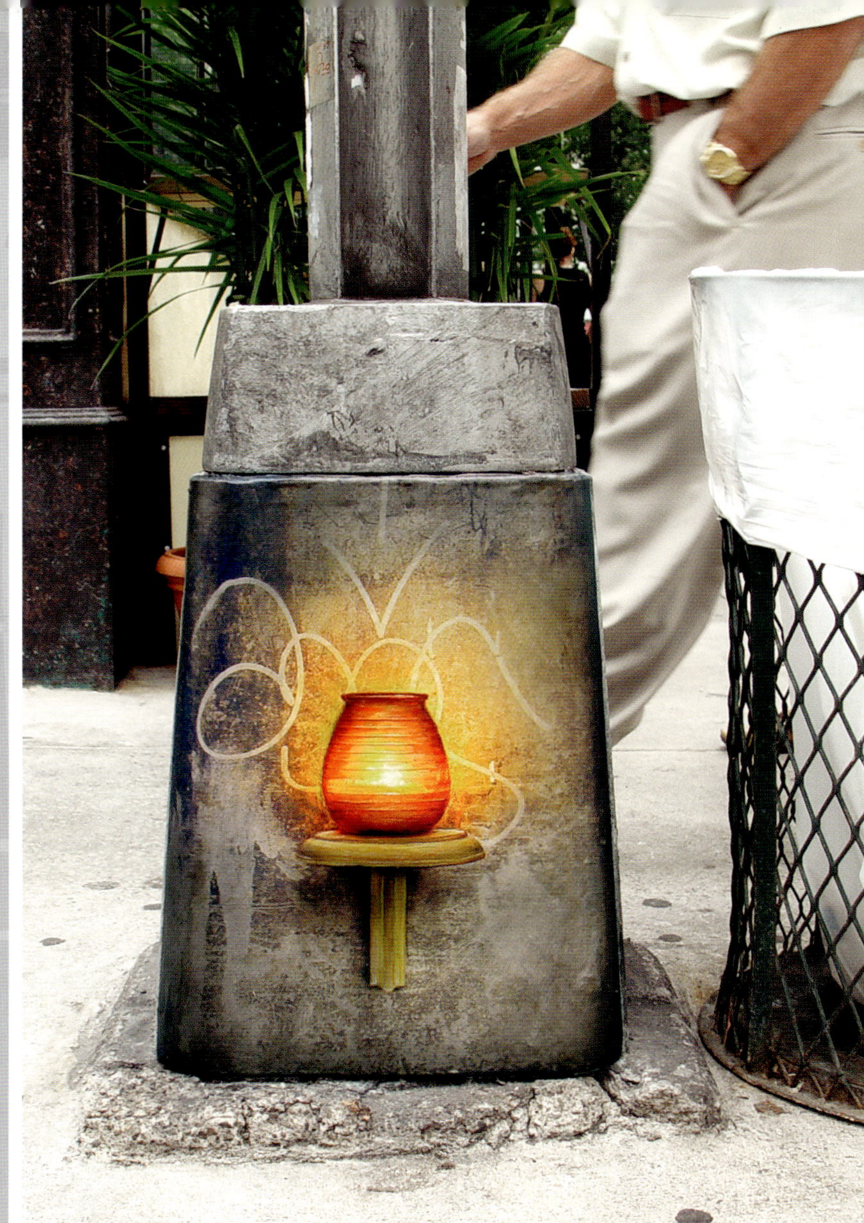

ABOVE LEFT:

LOWER WEST SIDE, NYC., 2002.

ABOVE RIGHT:

THOMPSON ST., NYC., 2002.

OPPOSITE PAGE:

WATER ST., NYC., 2002.

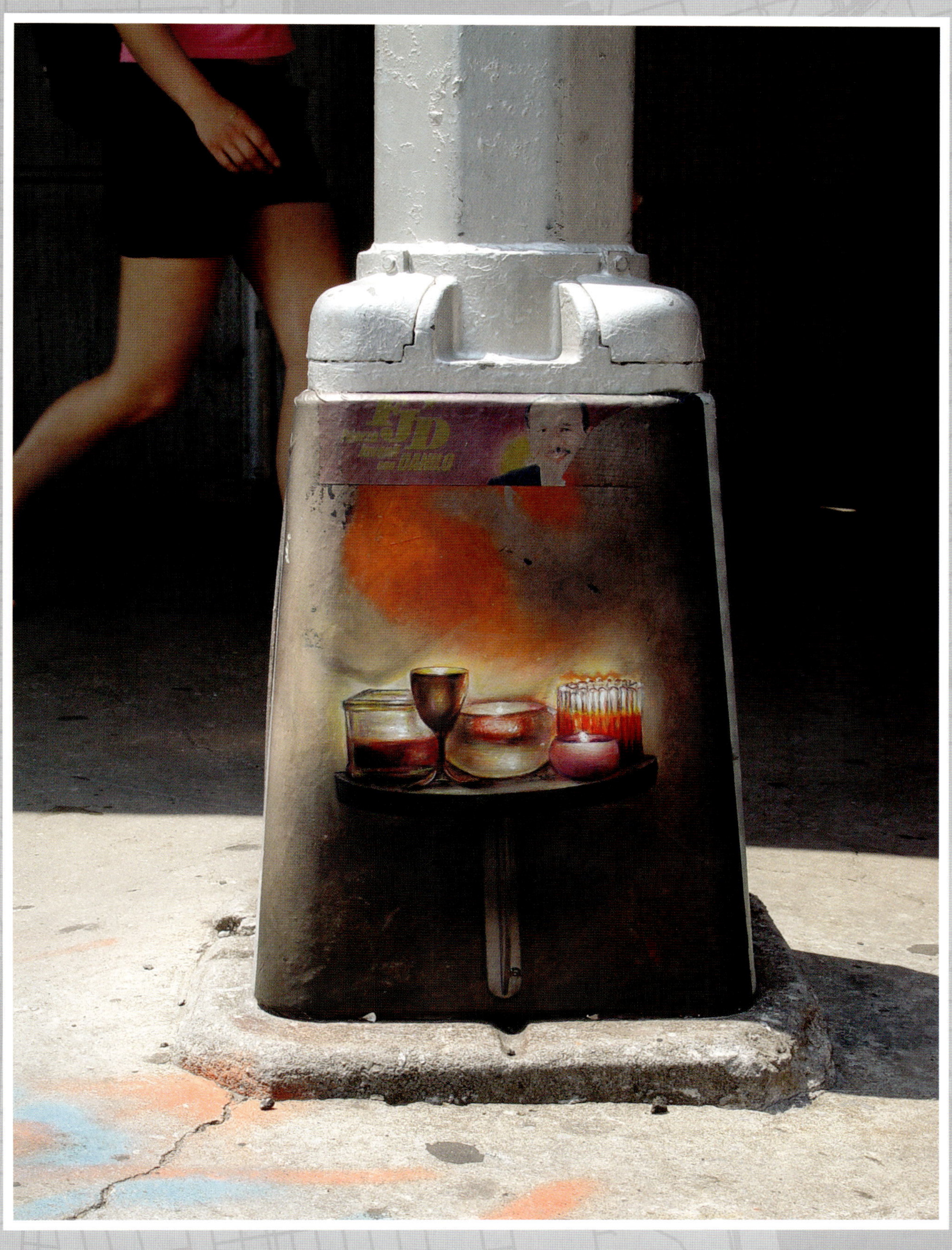

SKATEBOARDERS ARE GRAFFITI

2003 - 2005

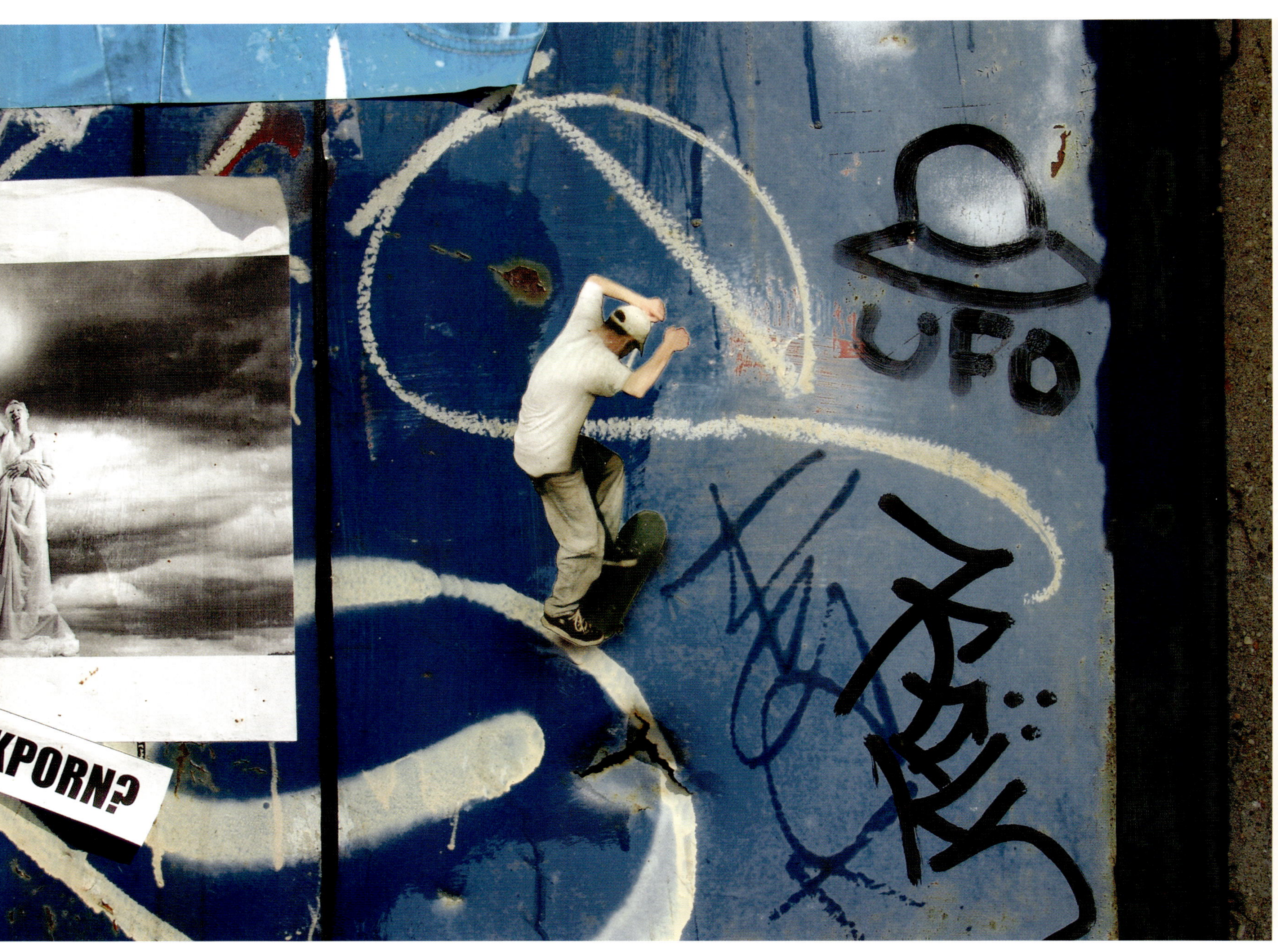

To me, skateboarders and graffiti express similar world views. Dissonant, curvilinear, in your face... I did about 30 of these in Williamsburg and Greenpoint, Brooklyn.

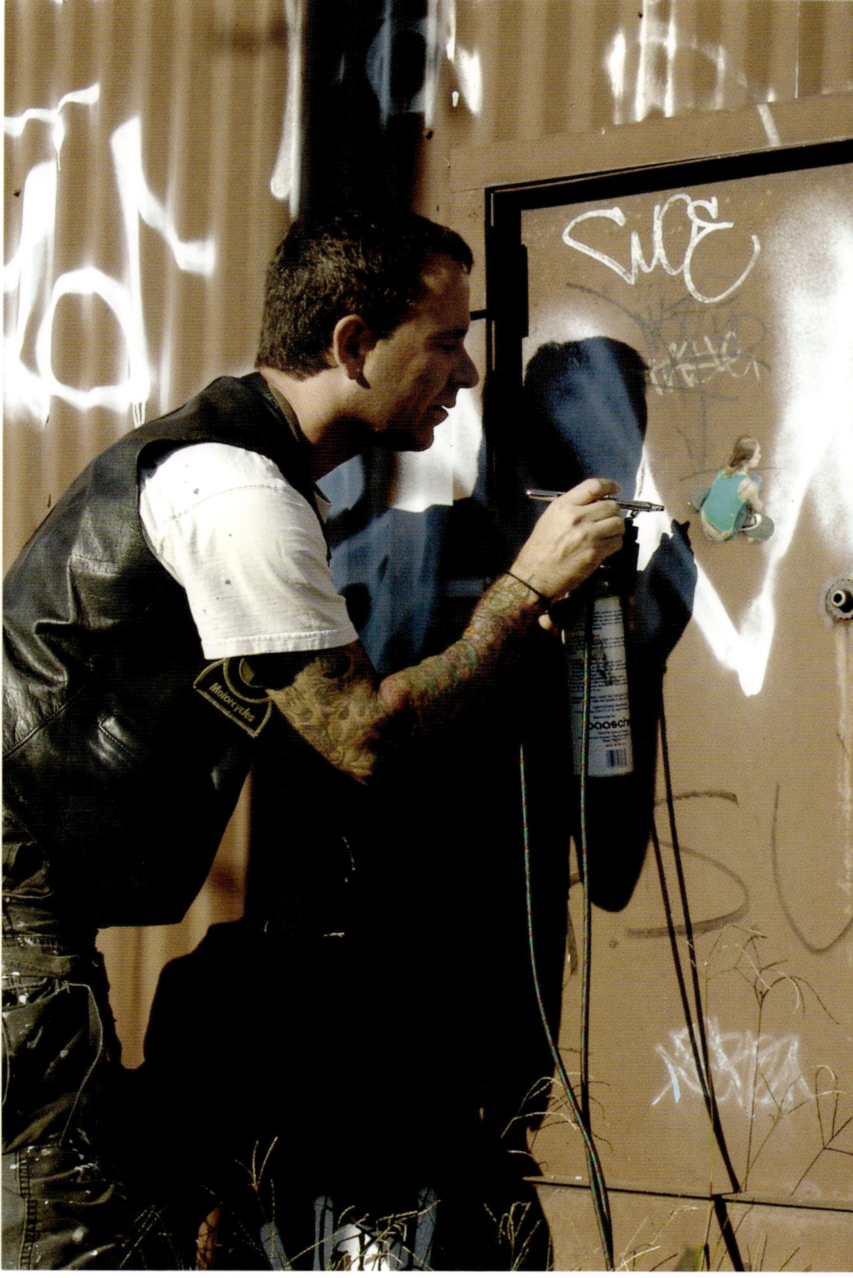

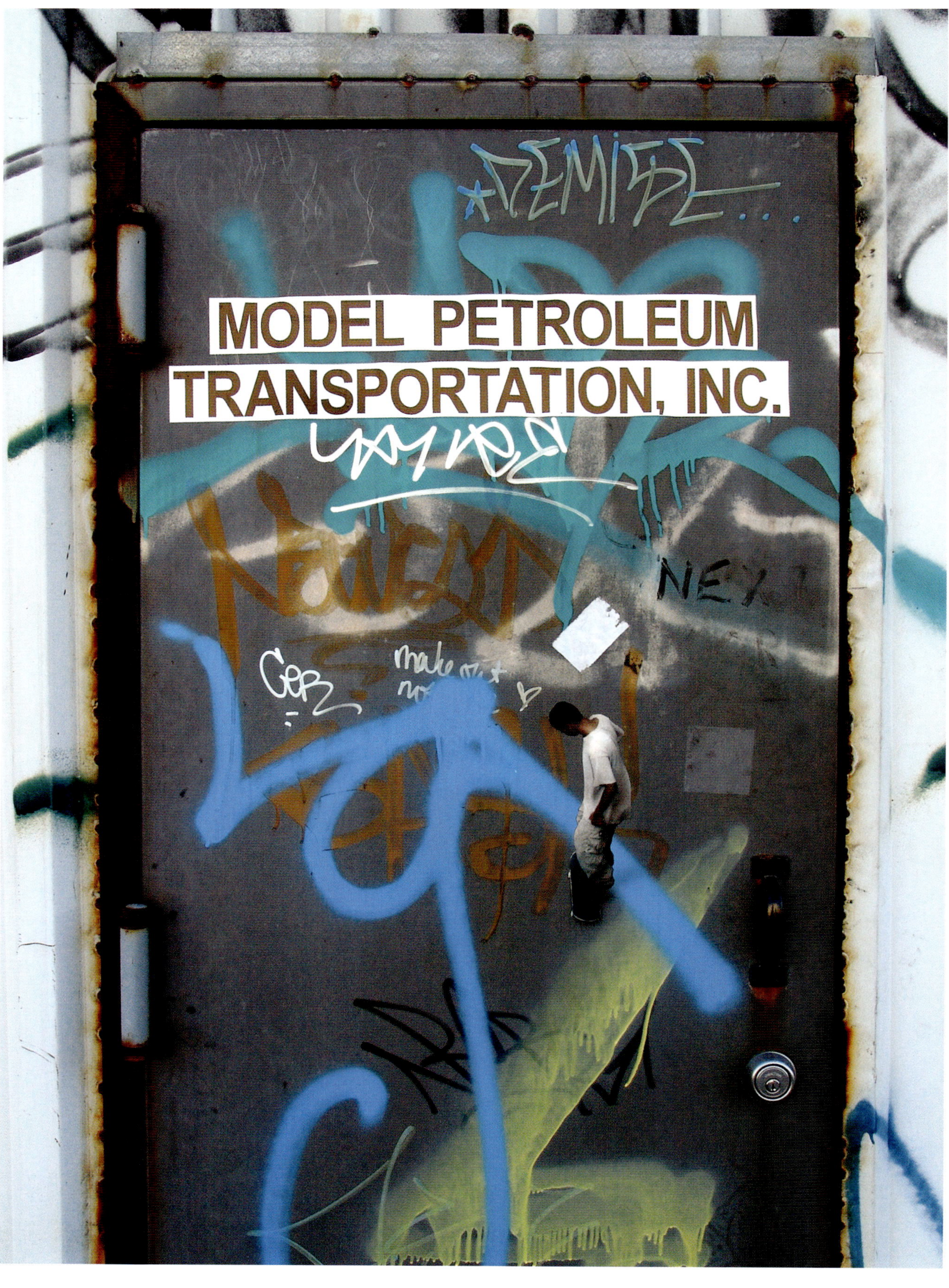
MODEL PETROLEUM
TRANSPORTATION, INC.

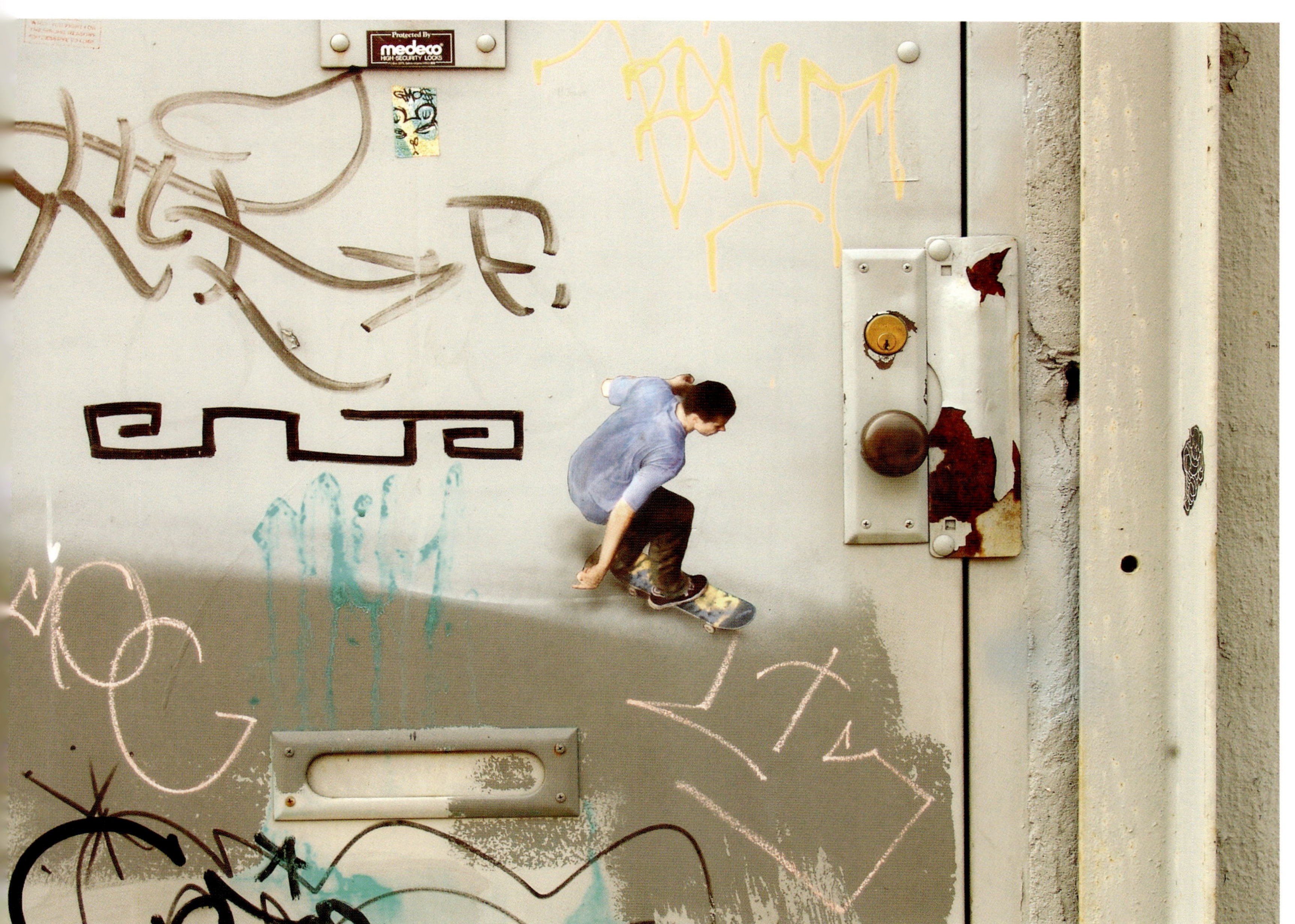
Protected By
medeco
HIGH-SECURITY LOCKS

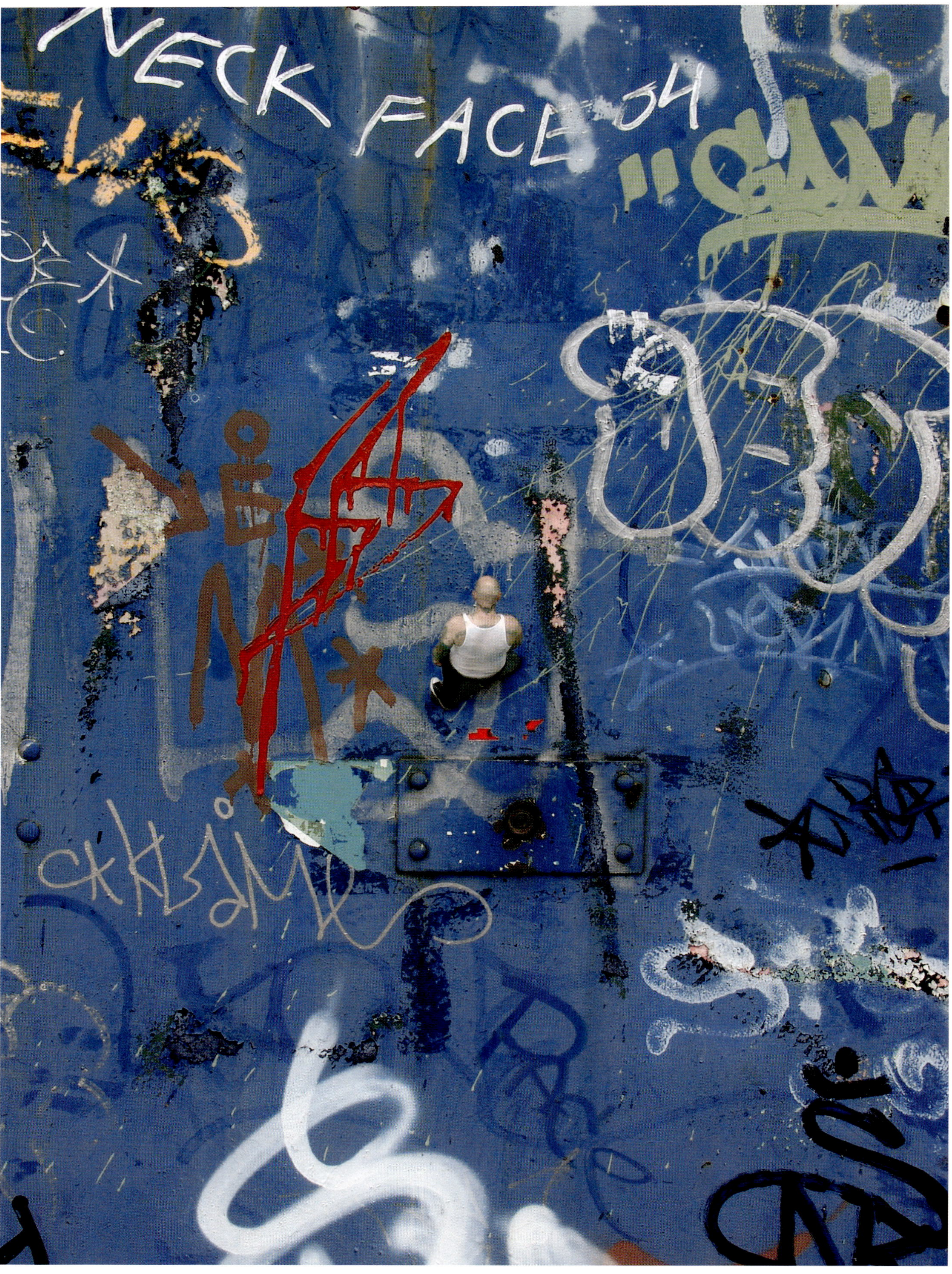
NECK FACE 04

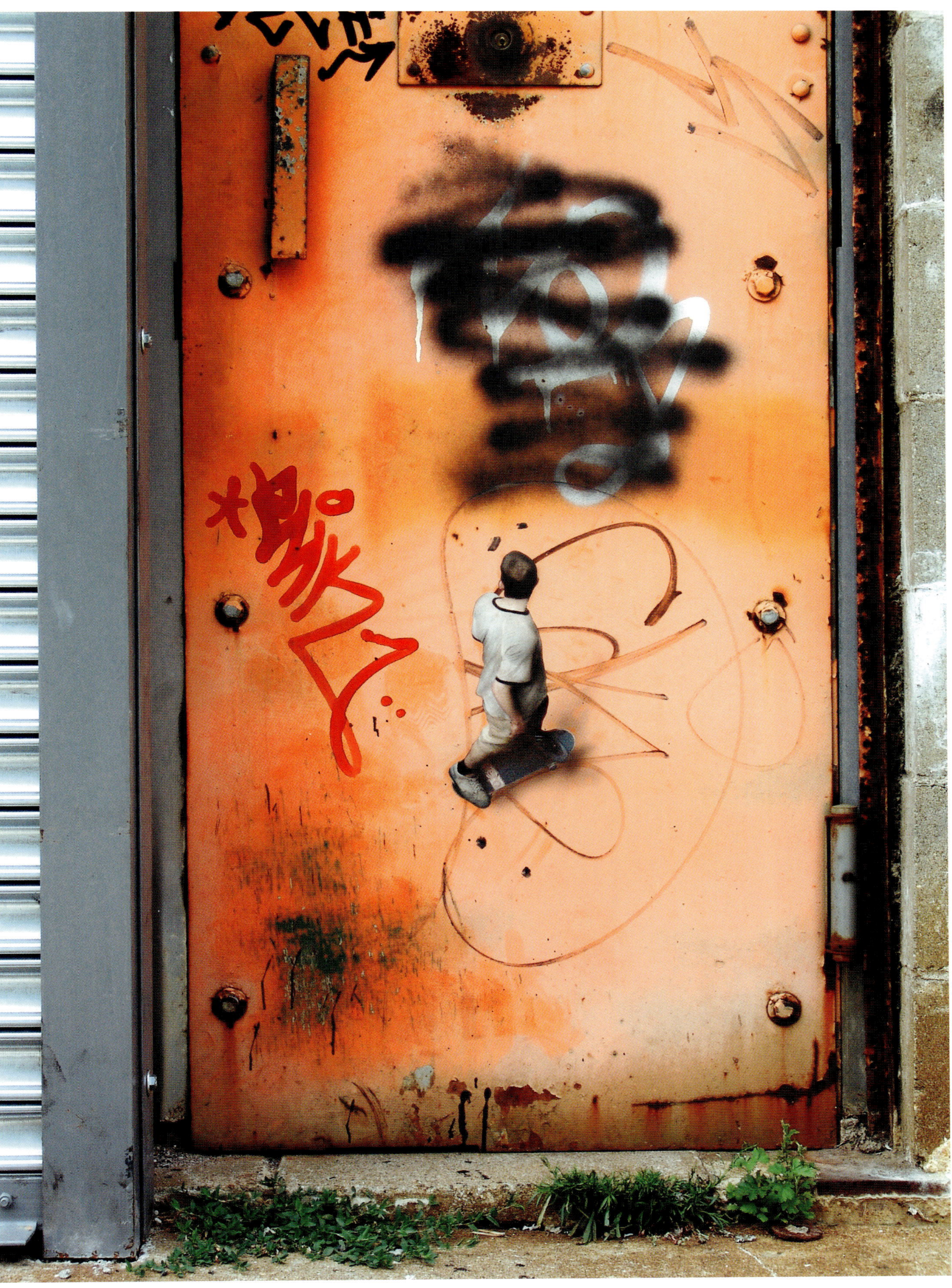

FRAMES

2005

Found Collages in Greenpoint and Williamsburg, Brooklyn. Mixed Media on vinyl adhesive paper on various walls.

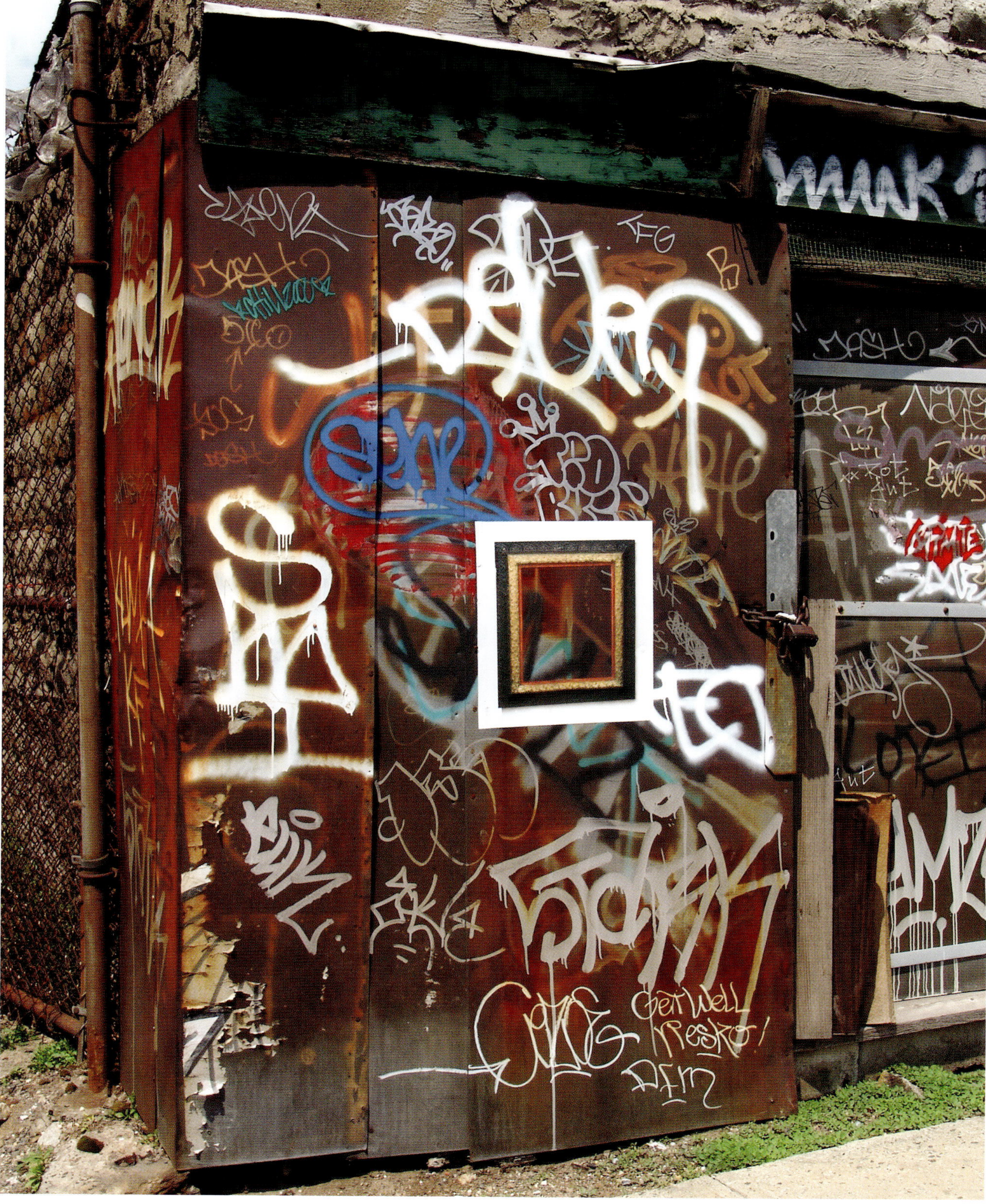

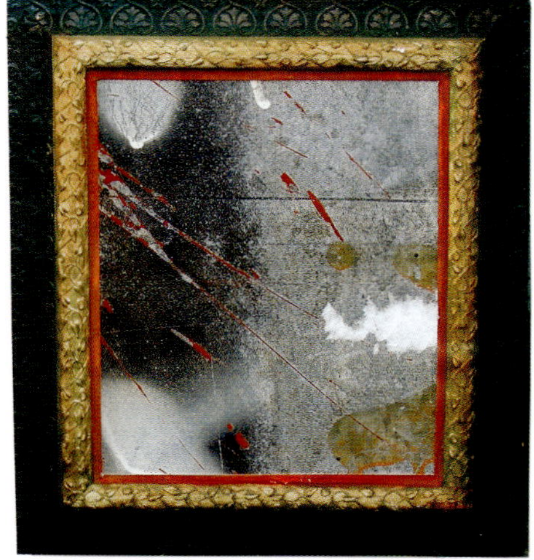

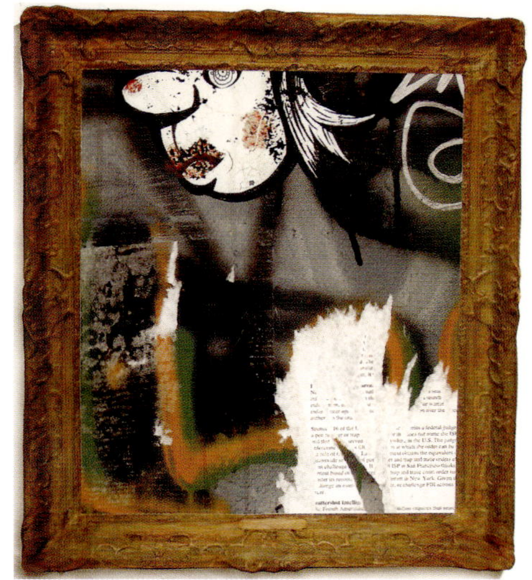

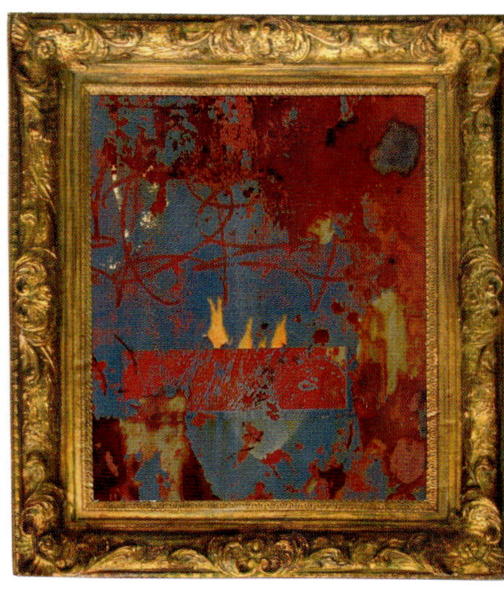

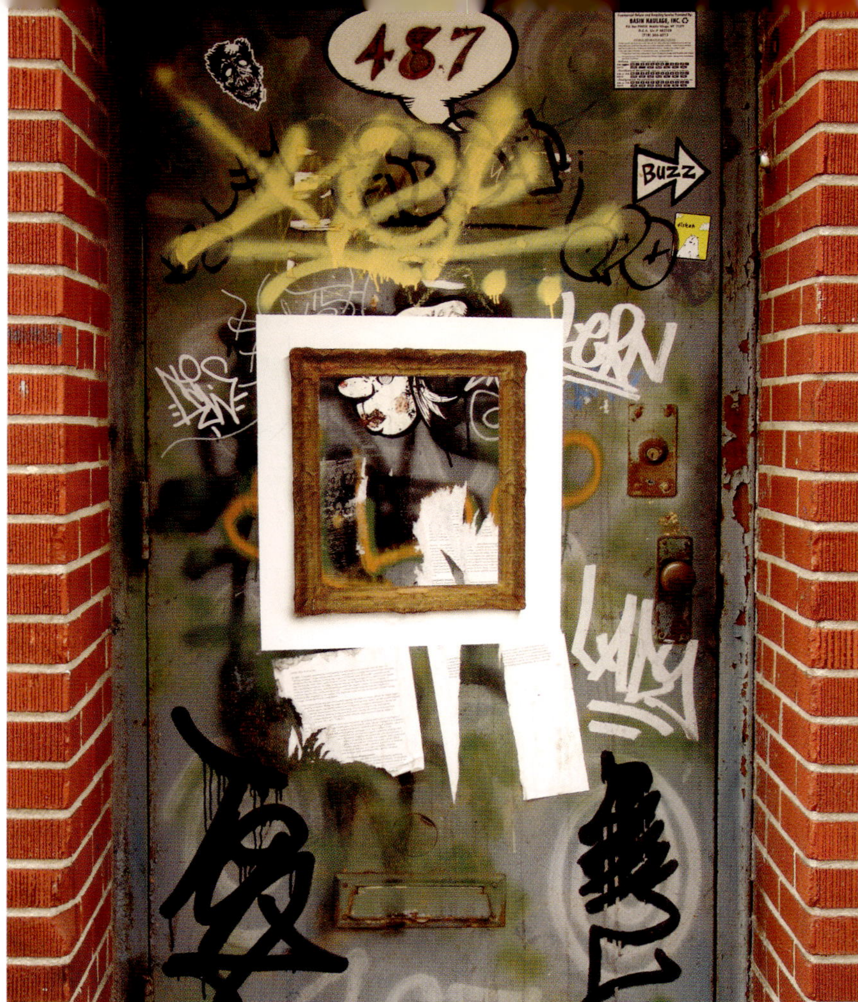
487
BUZZ

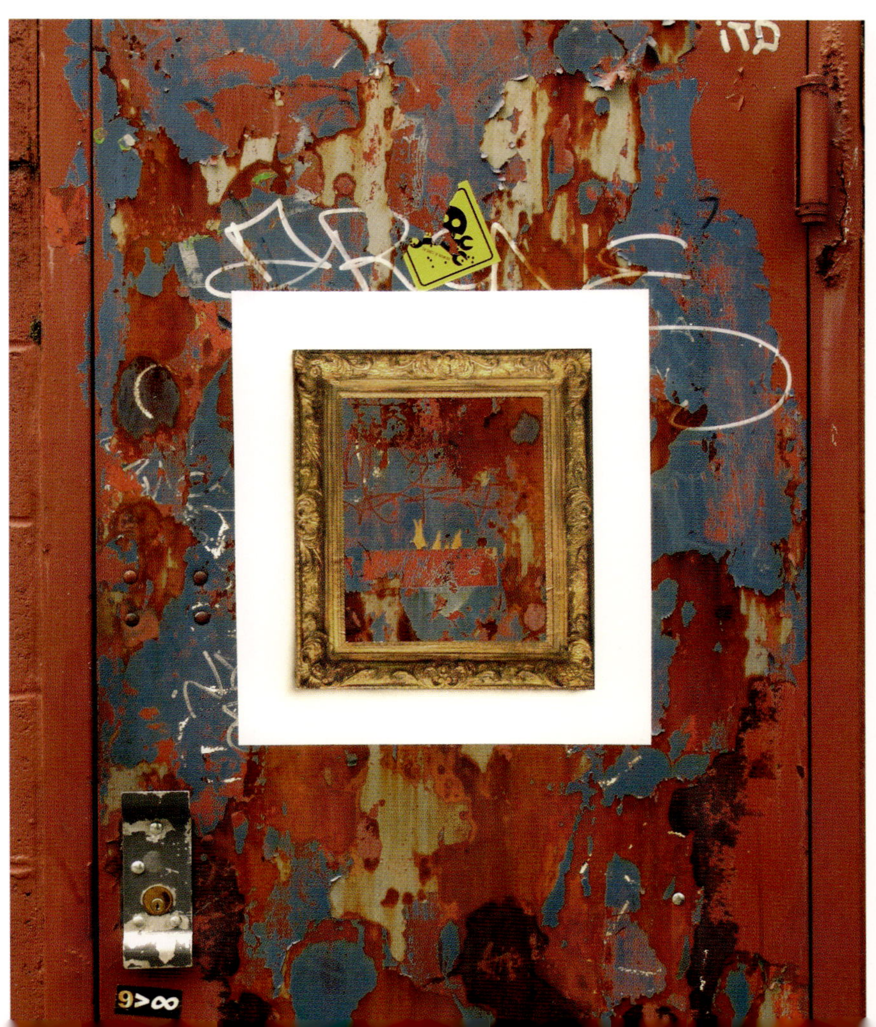
9>∞

LONESOME BOATS

2005

Around this time Street Art was beginning to get a lot of attention in the media. To avoid getting too self conscious, which always has a negative effect on my work, I decided to detach, to literally let my pieces go. I hit dumpsters, freight trains, tractor trailers, bulldozers – anything that would be moving out into the world beyond my control. Of all the surfaces I've worked on, these have been my favorite.

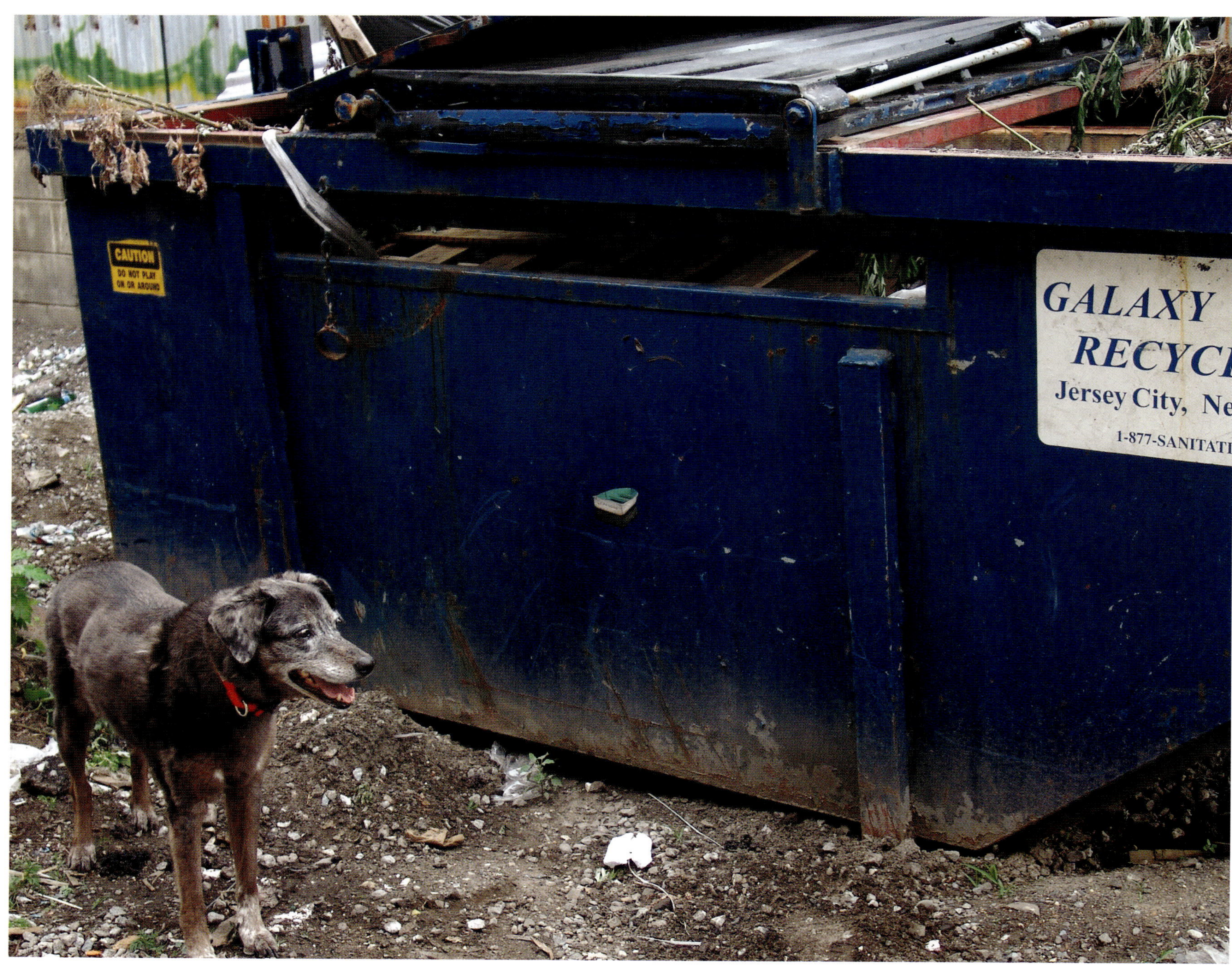

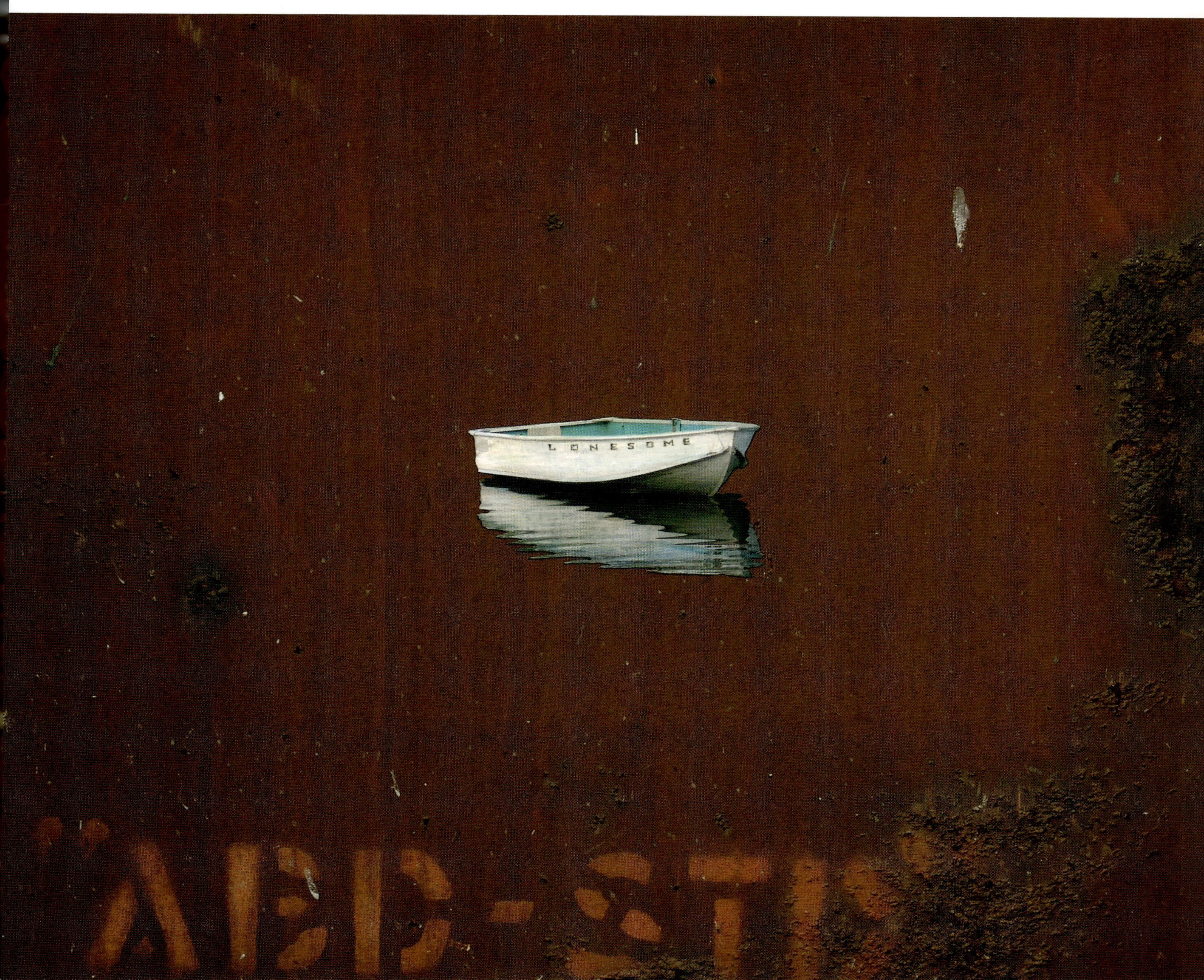
LONESOME

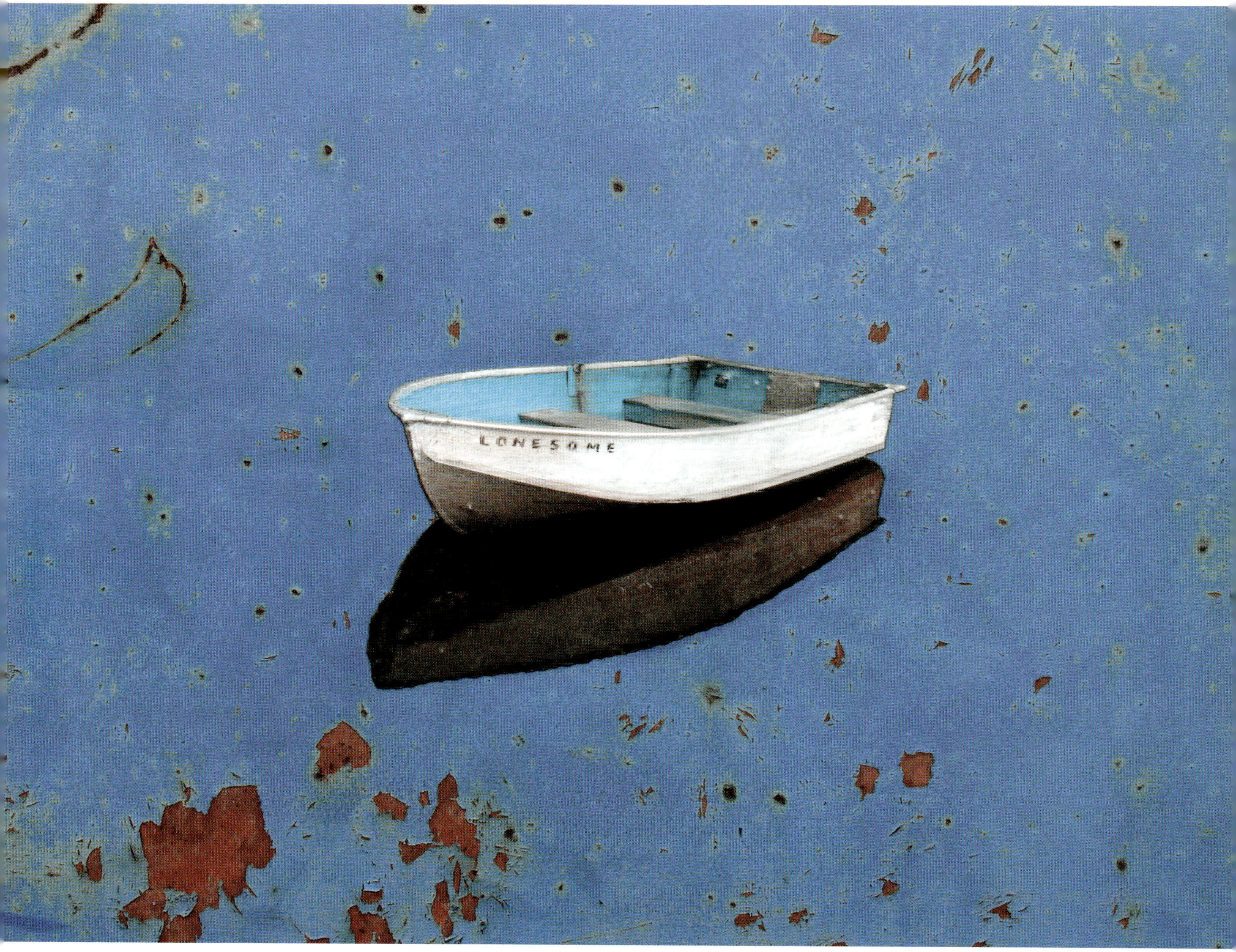

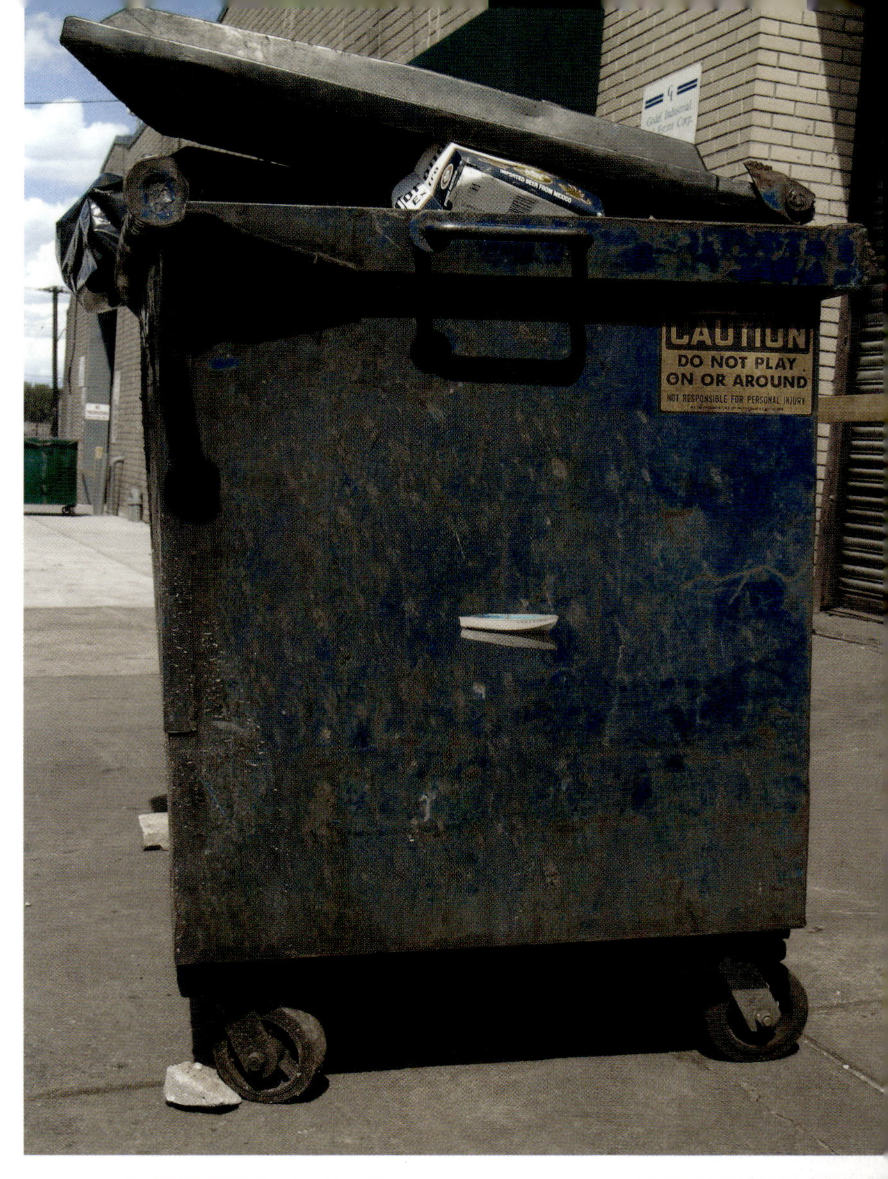
CAUTION
DO NOT PLAY
ON OR AROUND
NOT RESPONSIBLE FOR PERSONAL INJURY

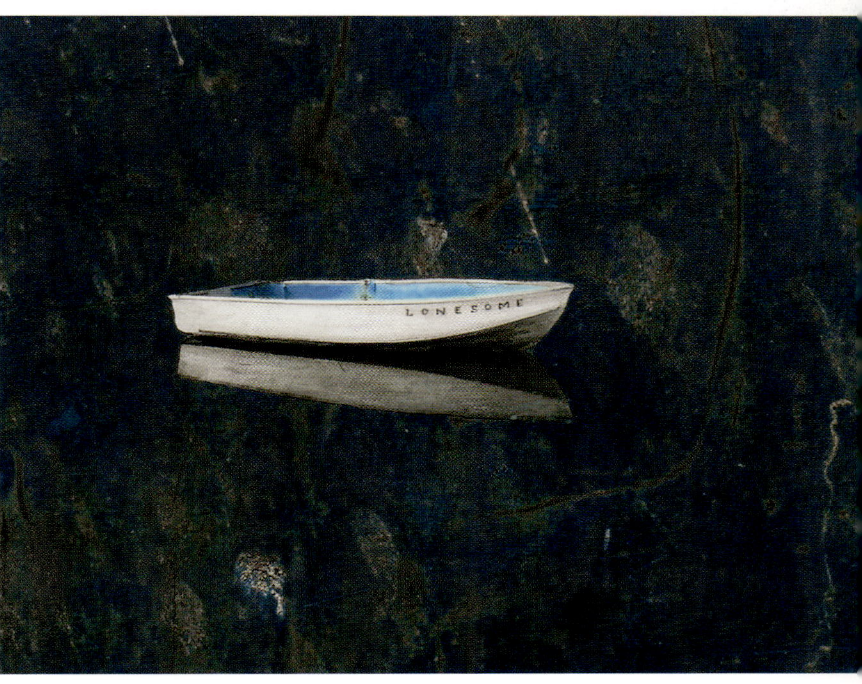
LONESOME

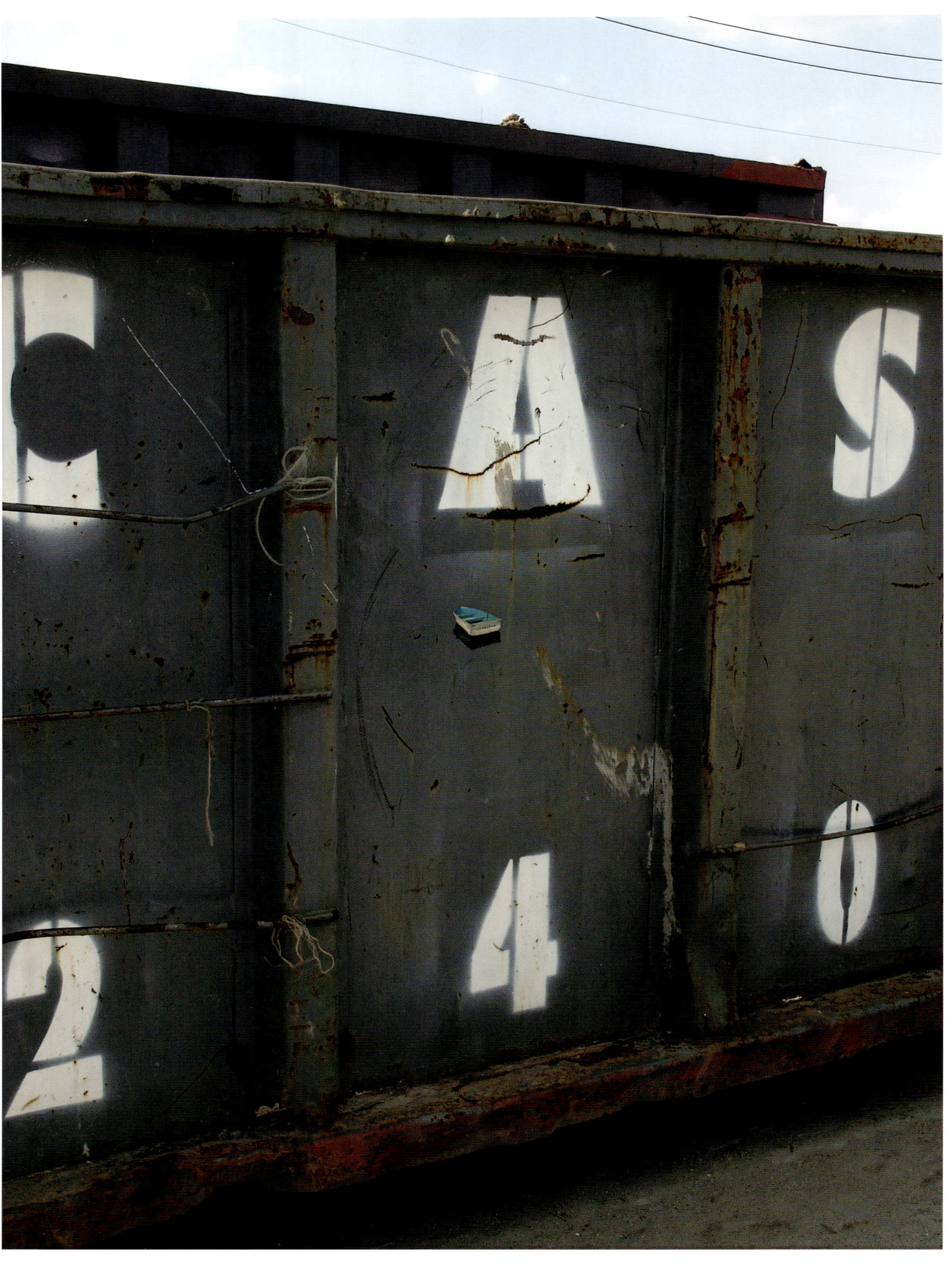
A S
4 0

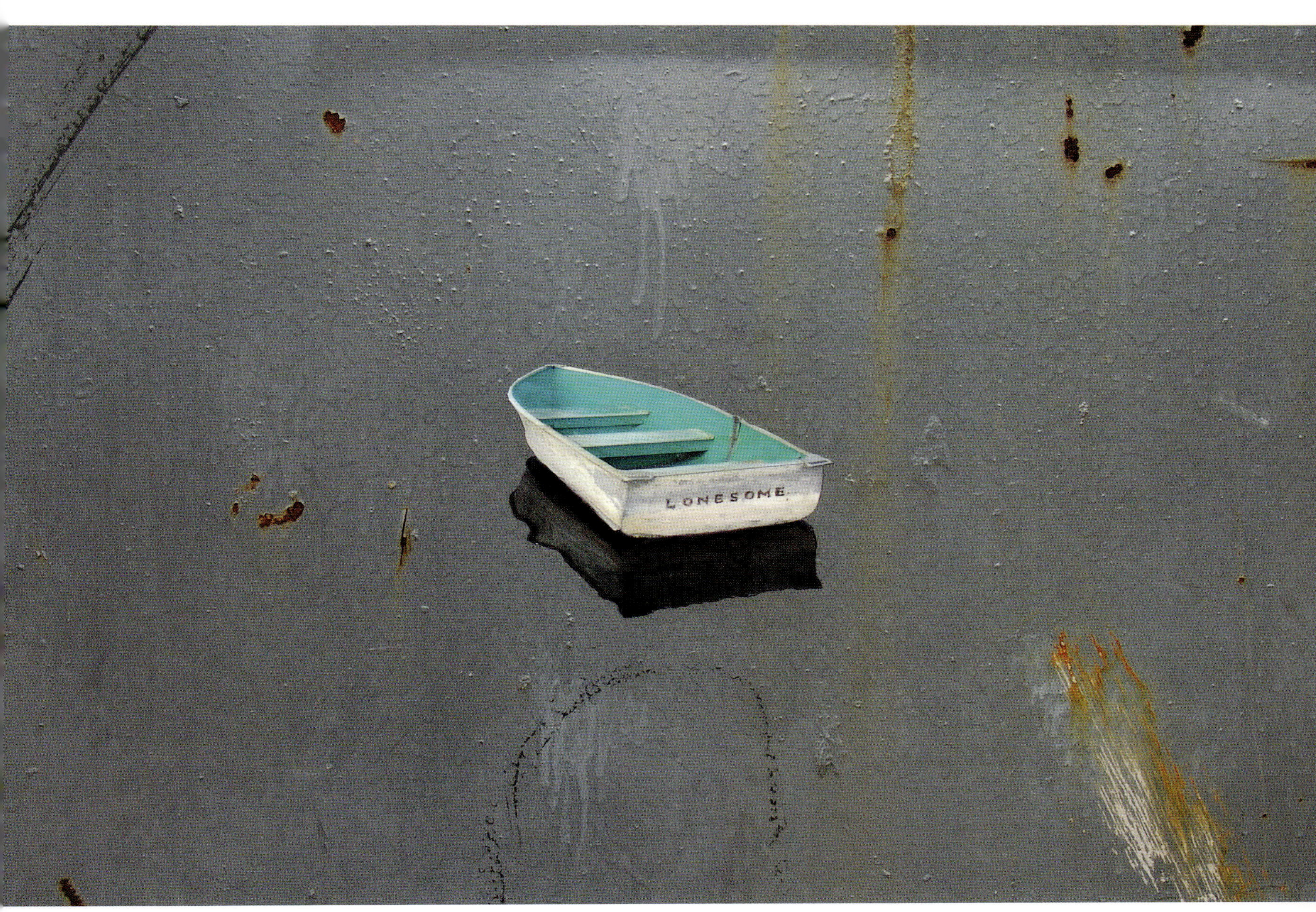
LONESOME

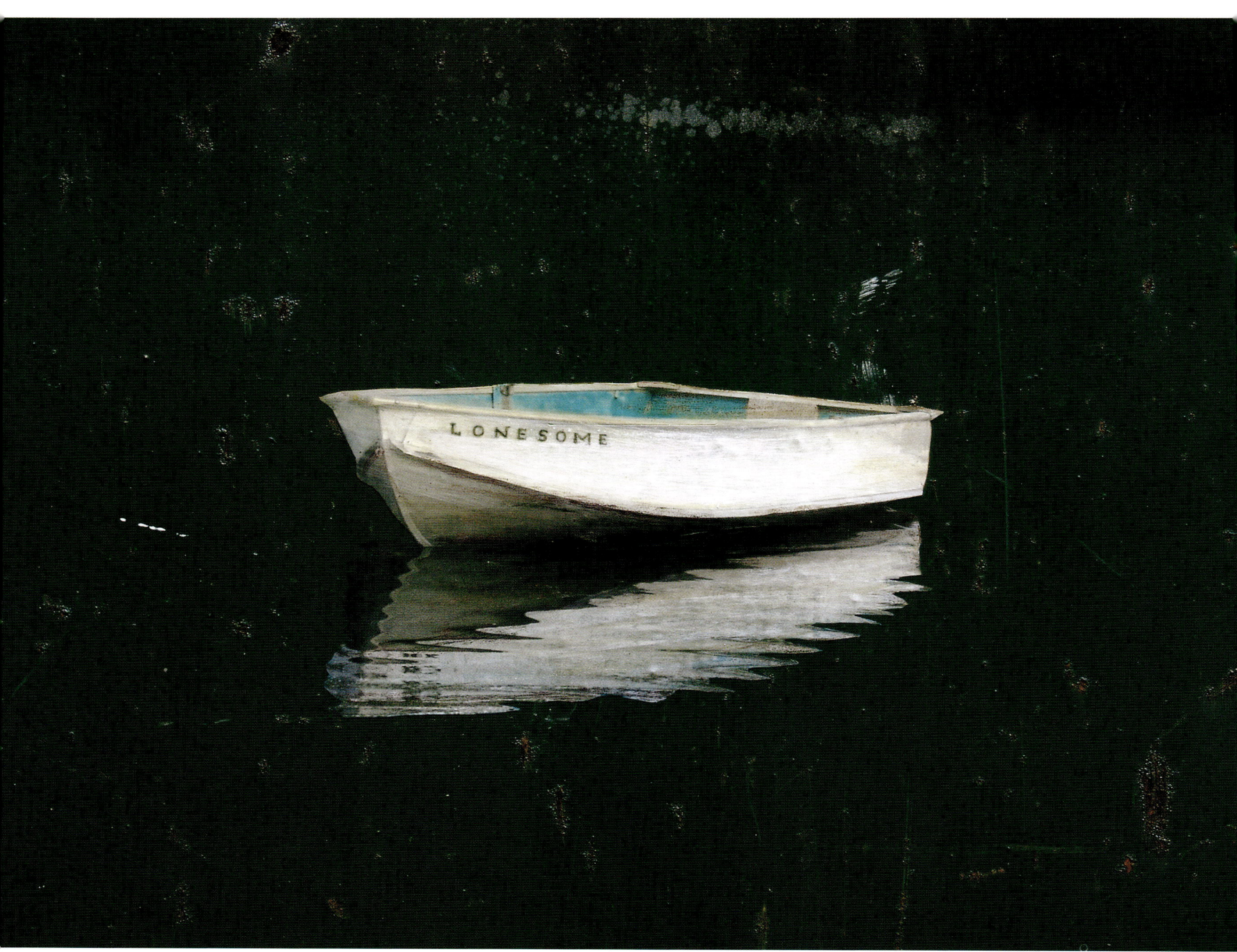
LONESOME

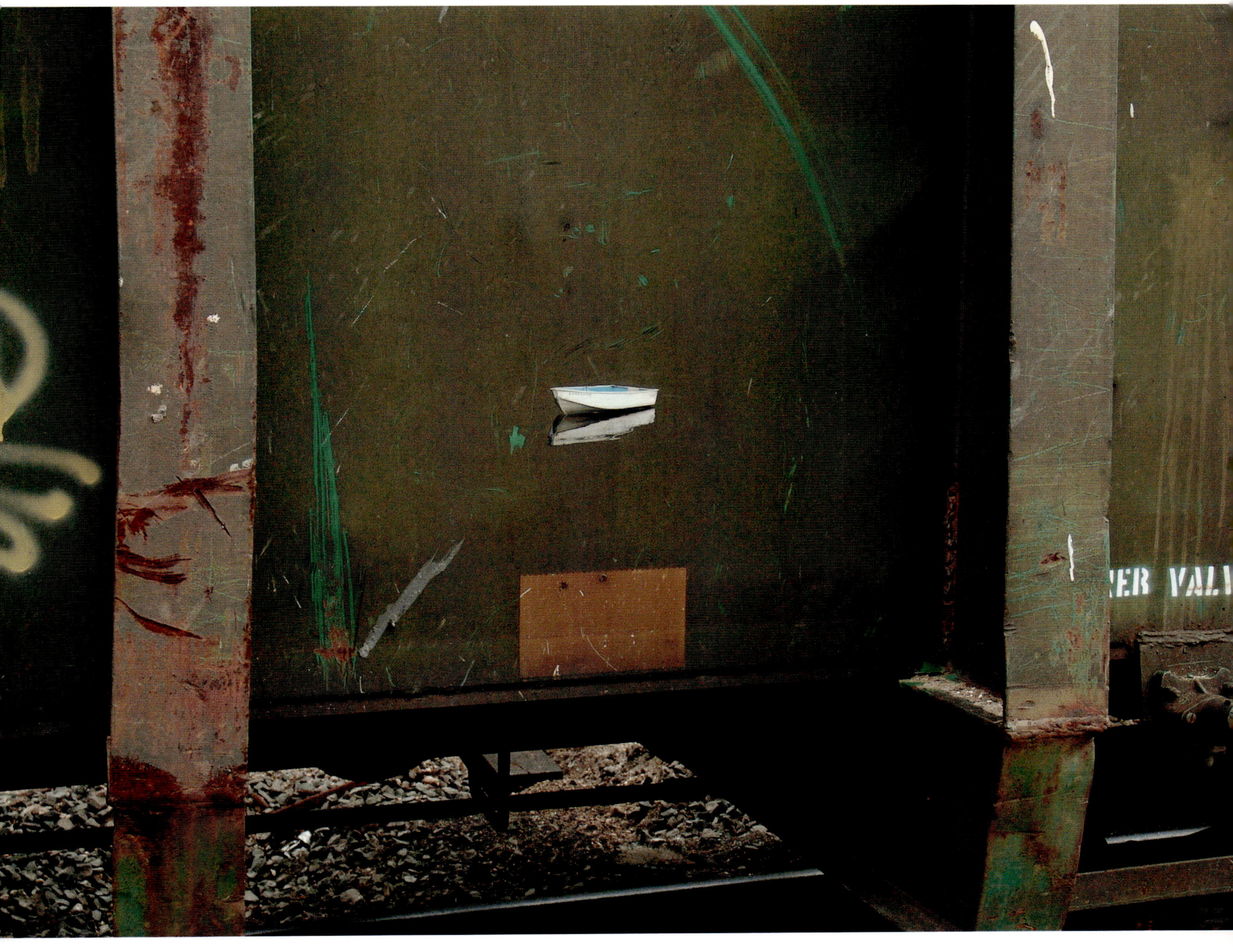

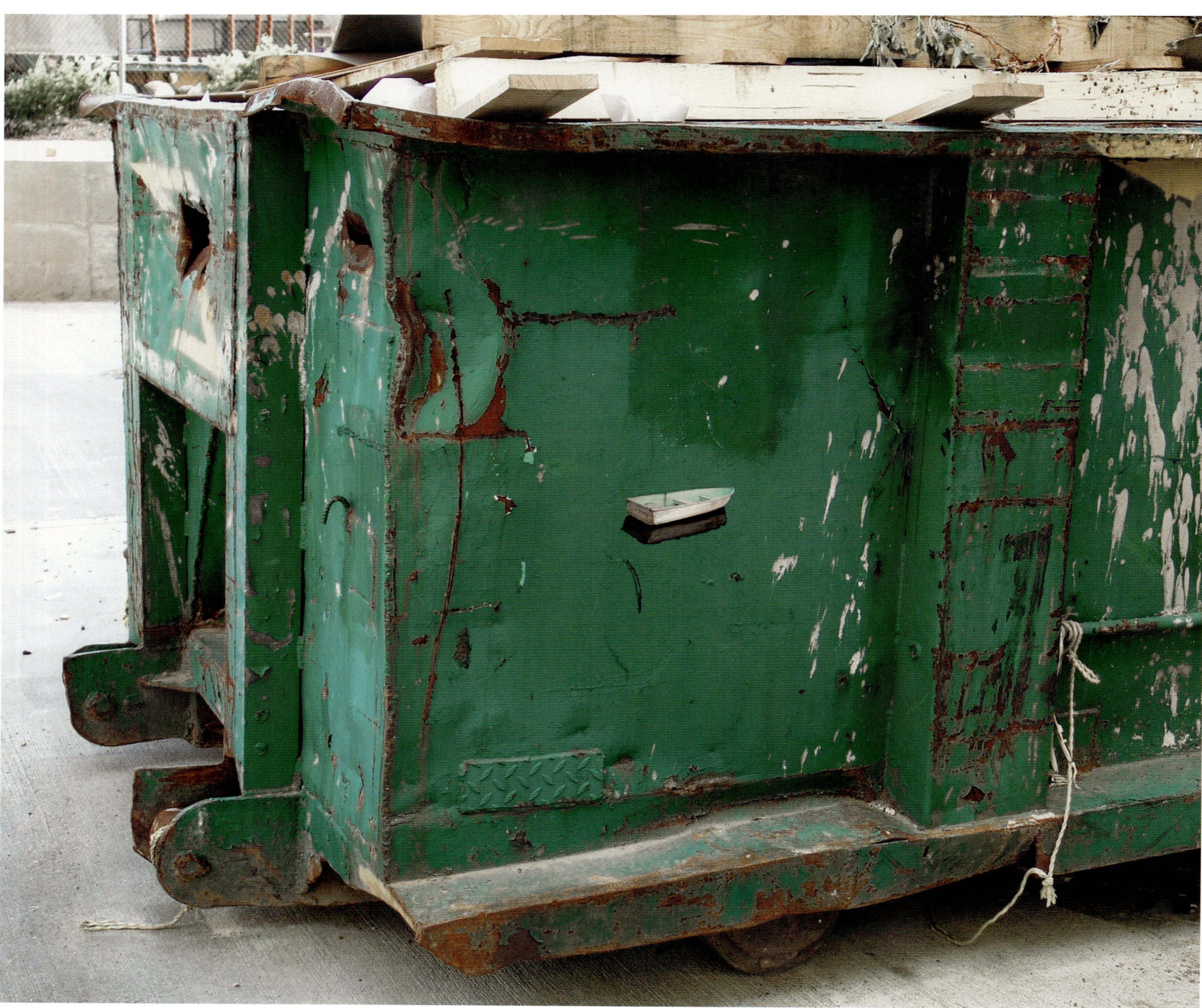

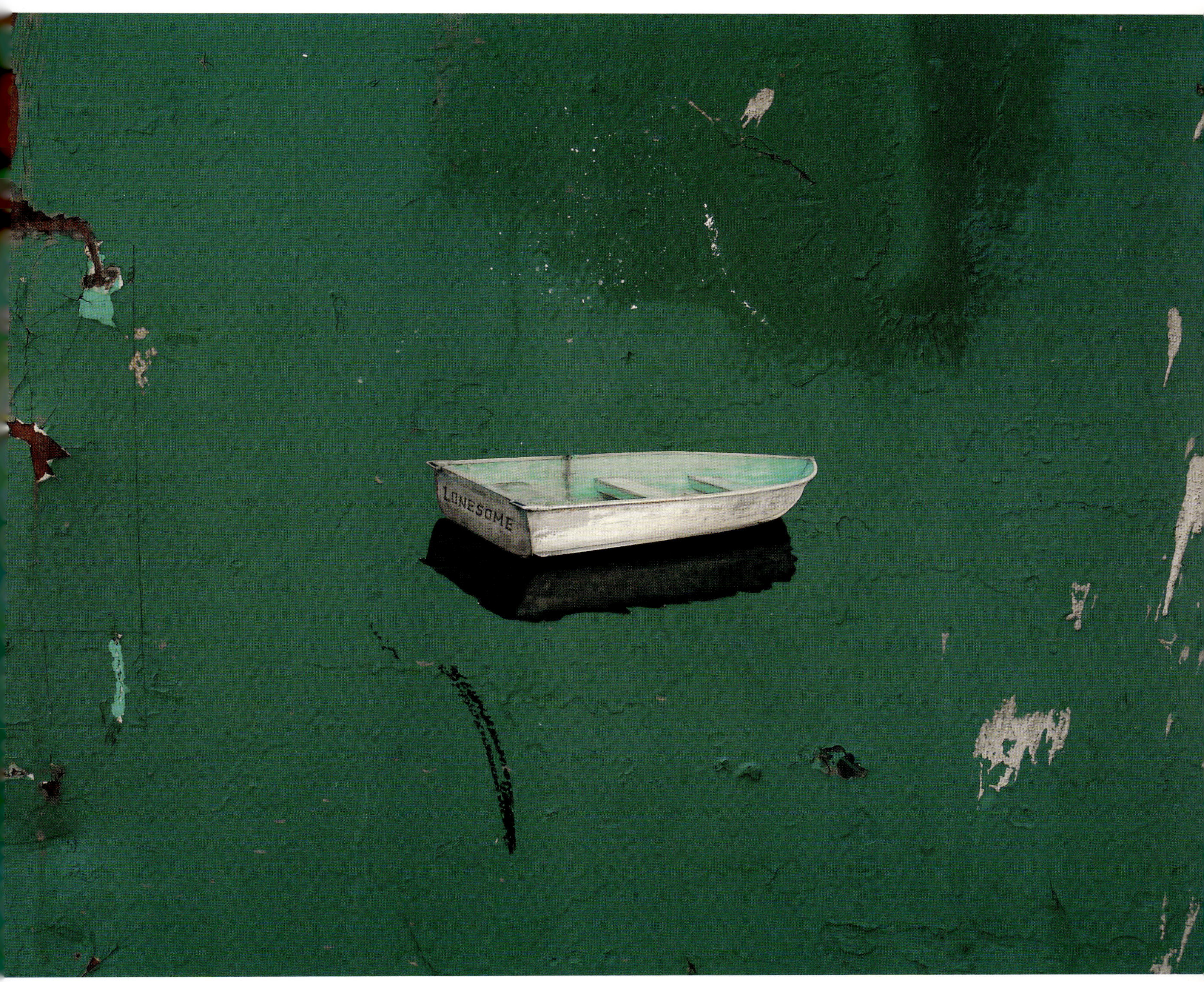
LONESOME

KILROY VARIATIONS

2007

Beginning in World War II, following movements of the American military, the "Kilroy Was Here" expression and its accompanying cartoon character became representative of America's far-flung presence. This was the first graffiti I remember being aware of as a kid. To this day I don't think I've ever gotten over my youthful amazement at how a simple line can be magically transformed into the top of a wall. Starting in 2006, I spent 3 years riffing on this idea in several full scale projects.

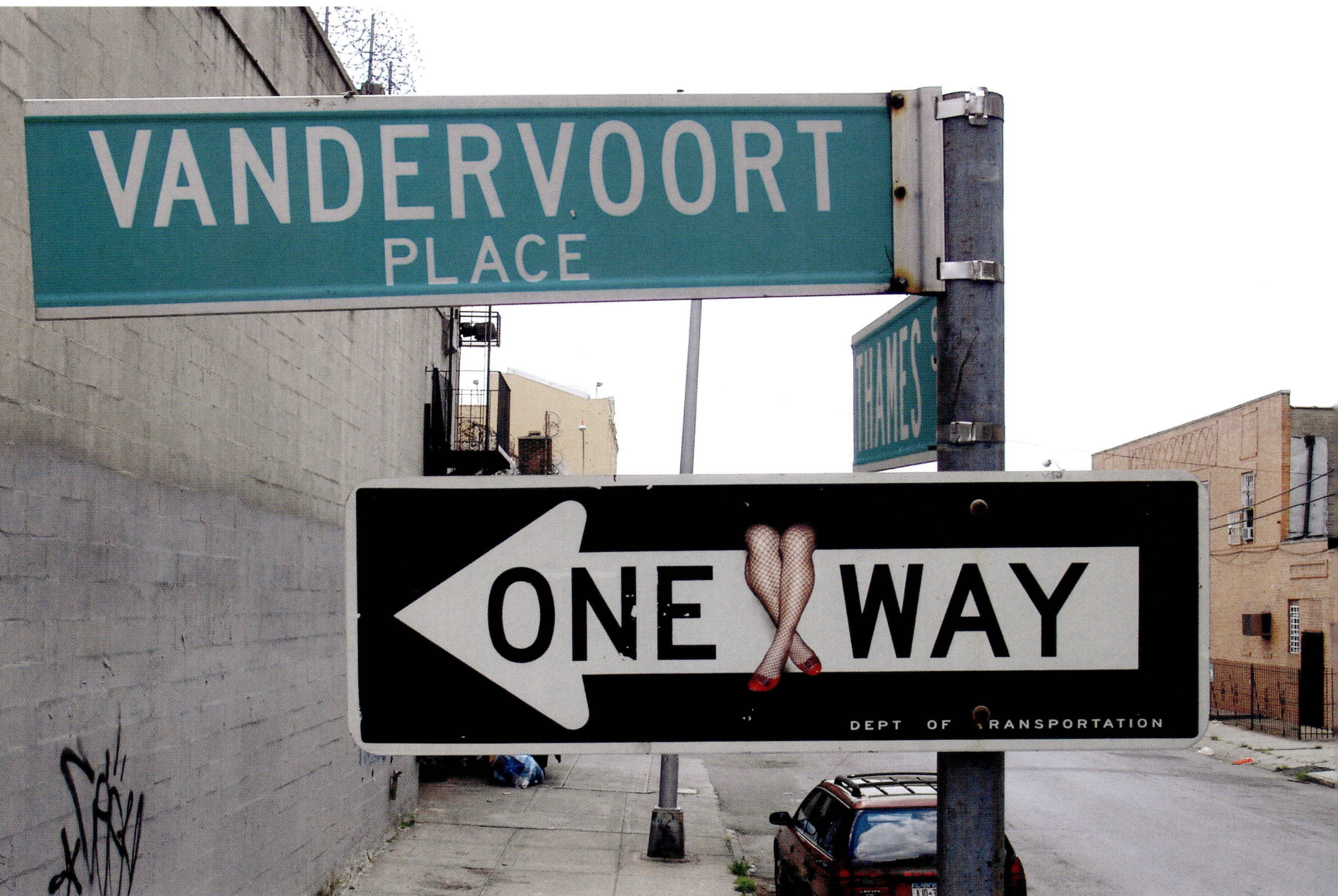

THIS PAGE:

BUSHWICK, BROOKLYN, 2006.

PAGE RIGHT:

SELF PORTRAIT, GREENPOINT, BROOKLYN, 2008. // From the Do Not Enter Series.

DO NOT

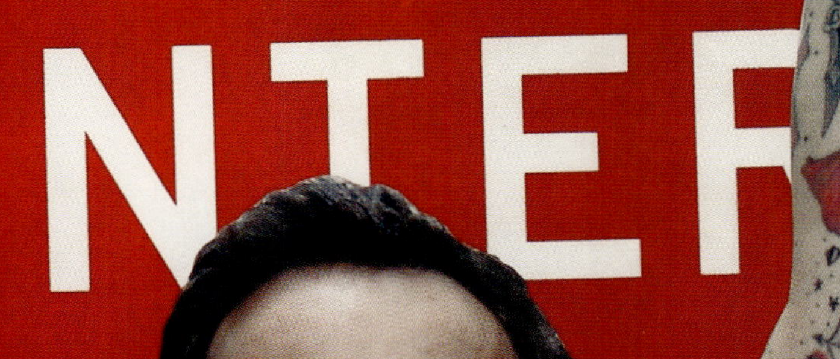

MAN OF SORROWS

2006 - 2007

A collaboration with the Butoh artist Ian Caskey. We created this trickster/clown/martyr dynamic, a man of sorrows who suffers for our sins. This was at the time when the extent of the Bush administration's war crimes in Iraq were just beginning to be revealed. Acrylic and digital media on vinyl and on various exterior surfaces. This and the next page's installations are in San Francisco. The following pages are in NYC in "undisclosed" locations.

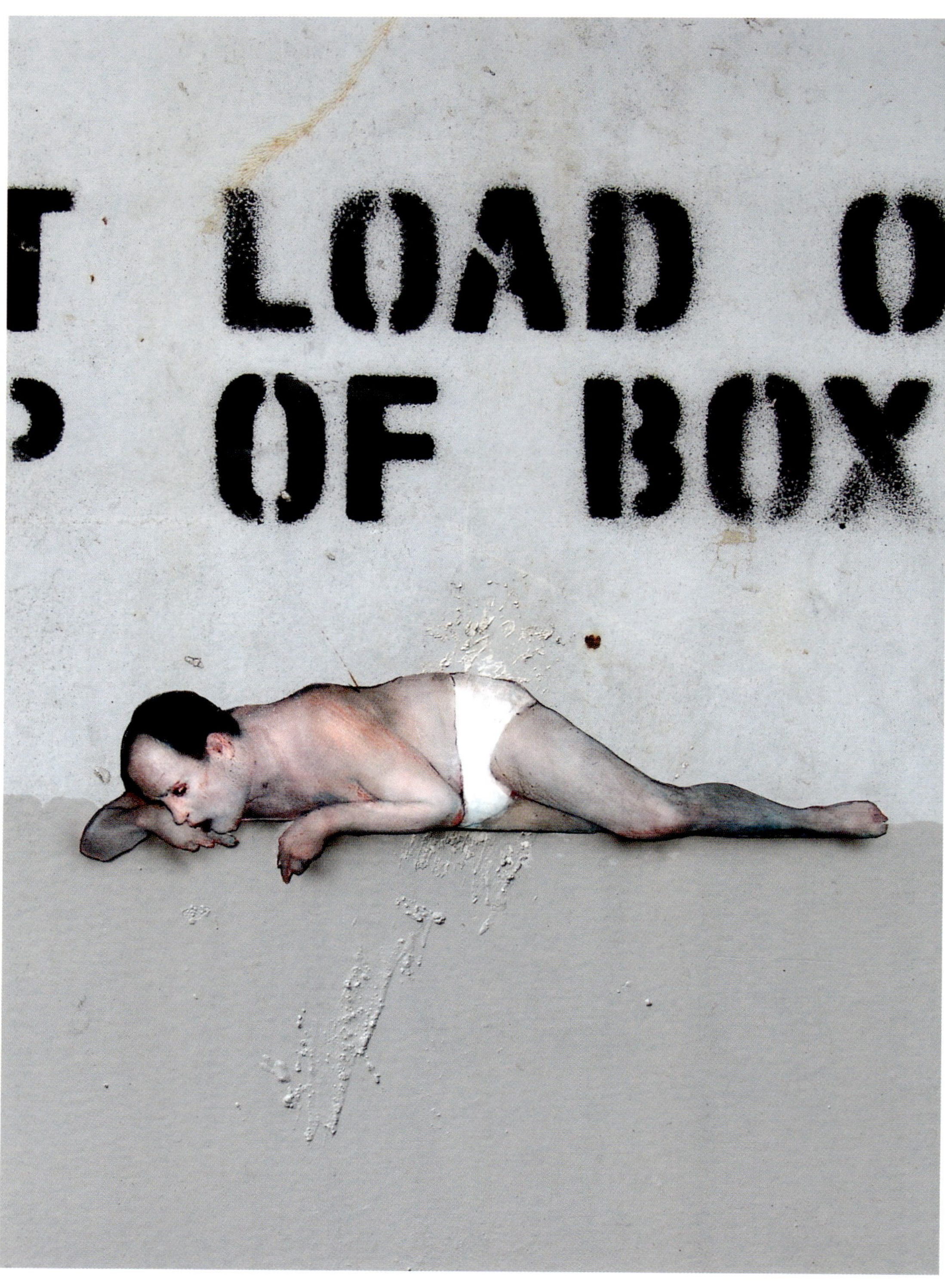

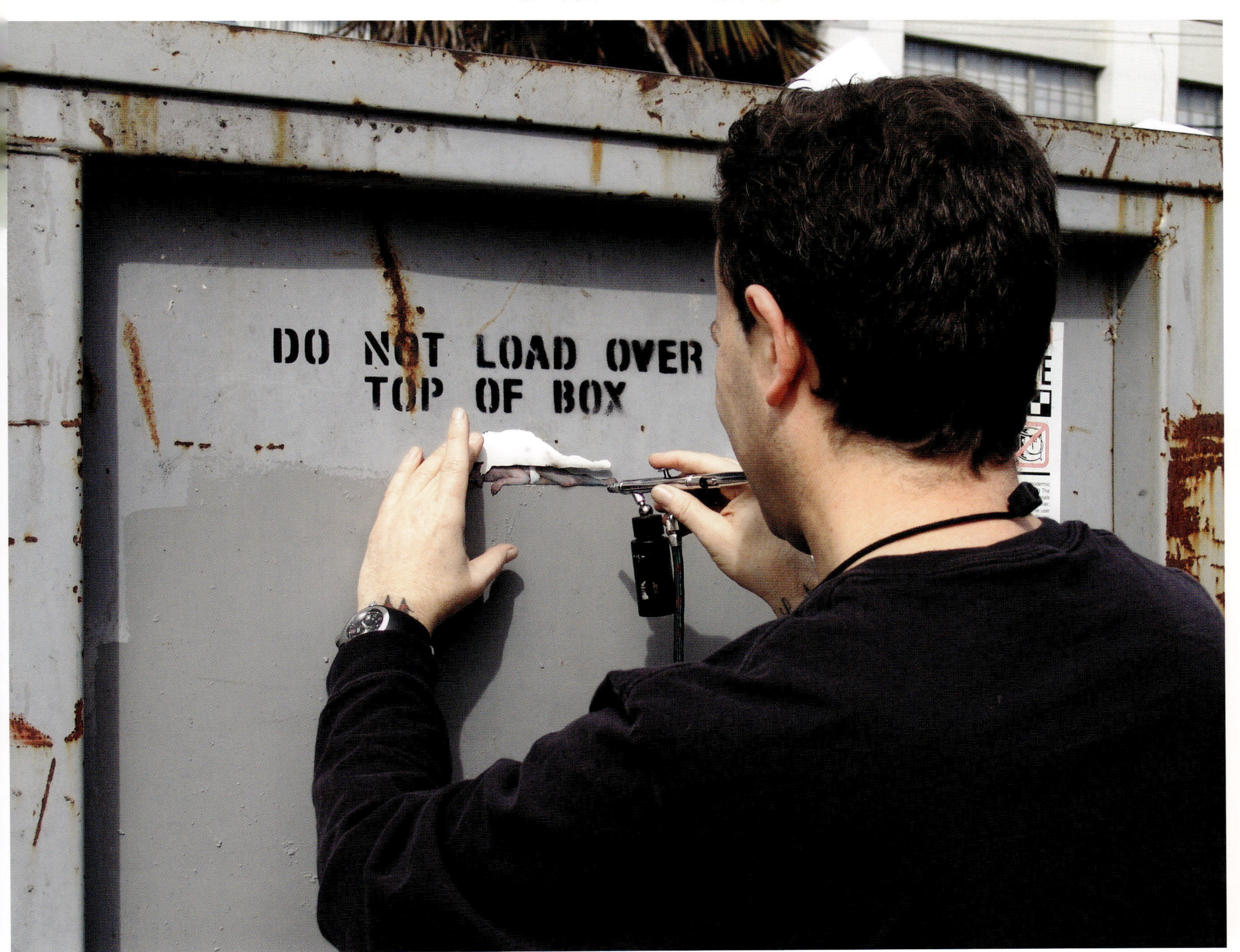

ALABAMA & 17TH, SAN FRANCISCO, CA, 2006. // Photo by Ali Norad.

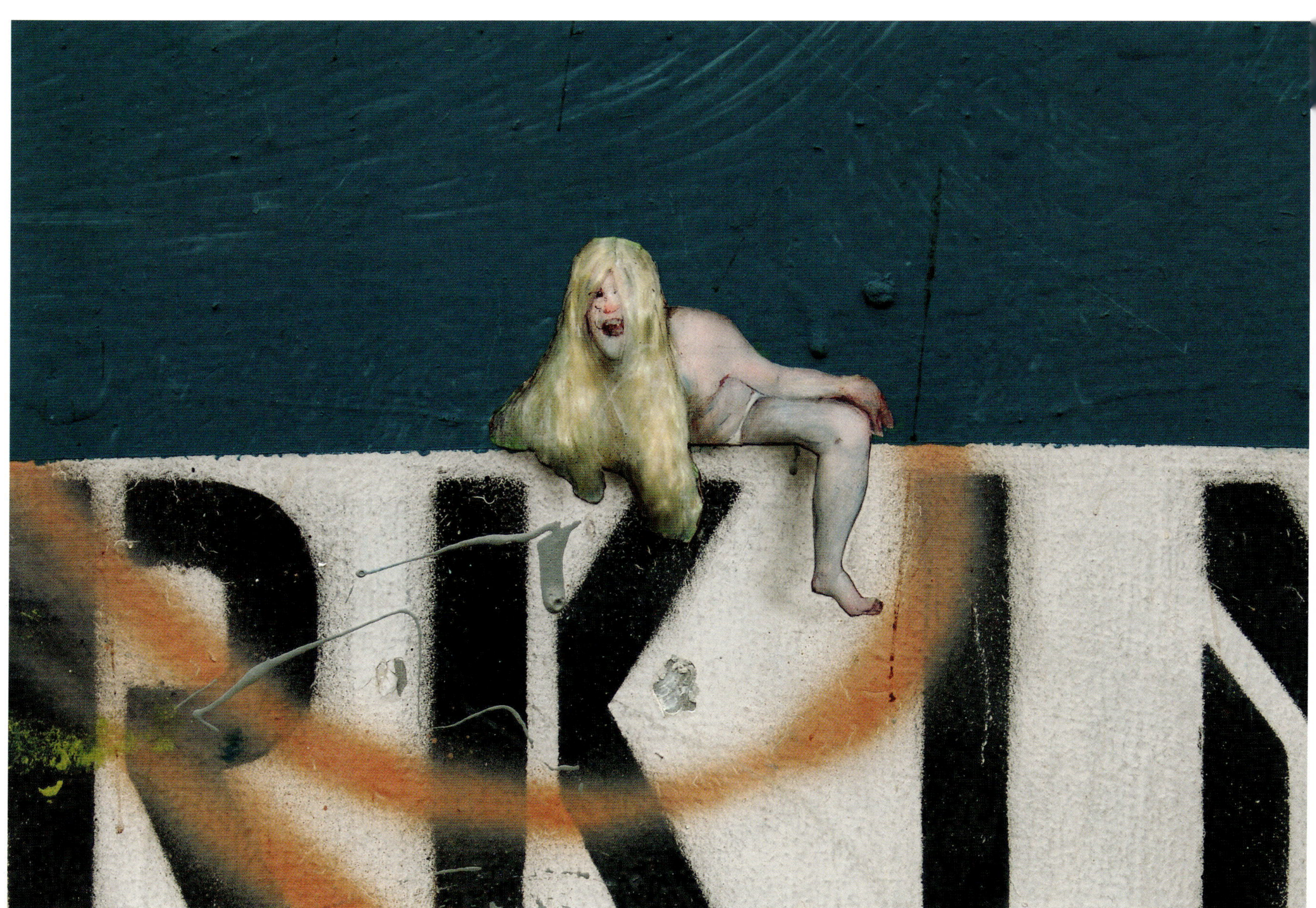

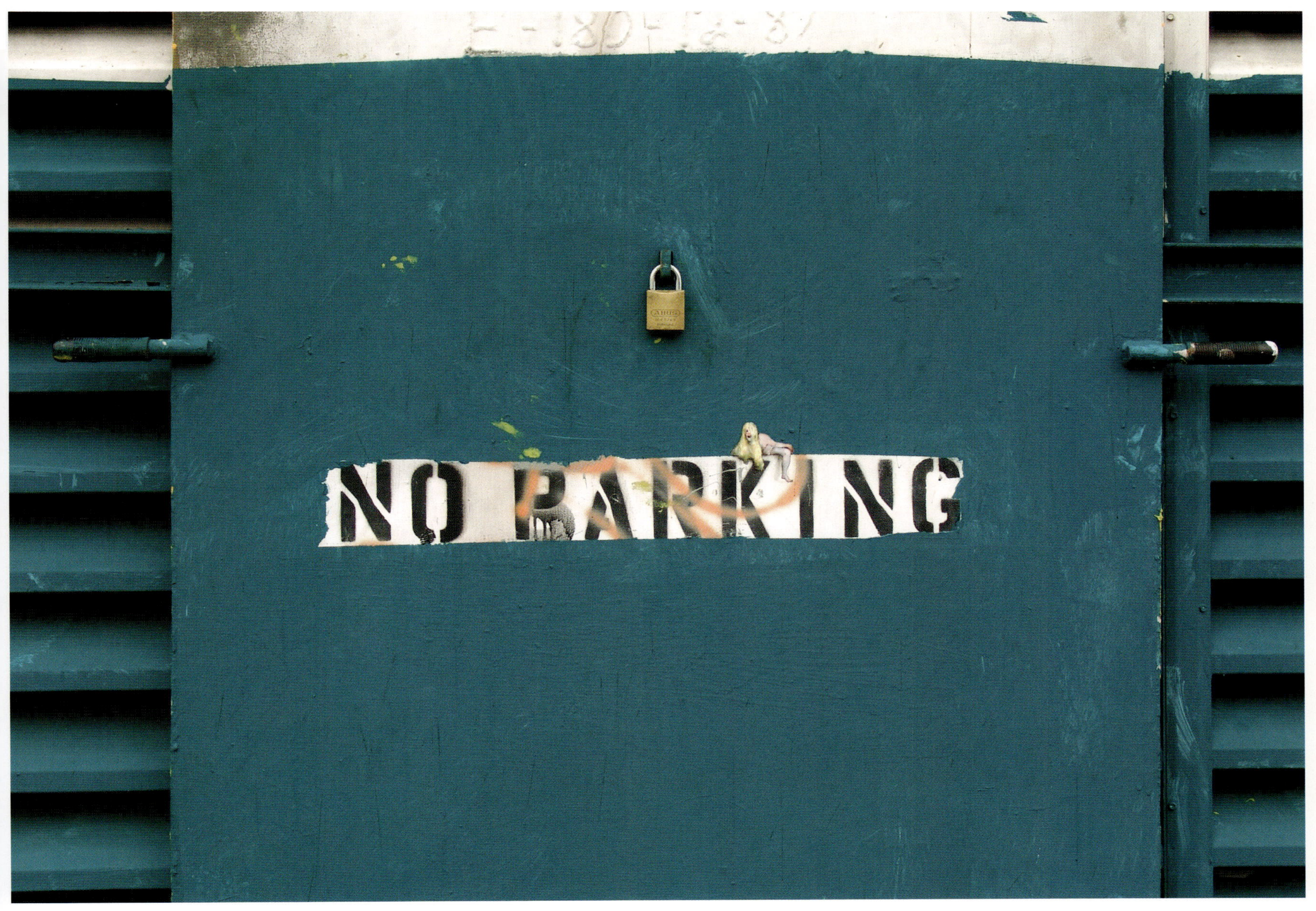

MARIPOSA & 17TH, SAN FRANCISCO, CA., 2006.

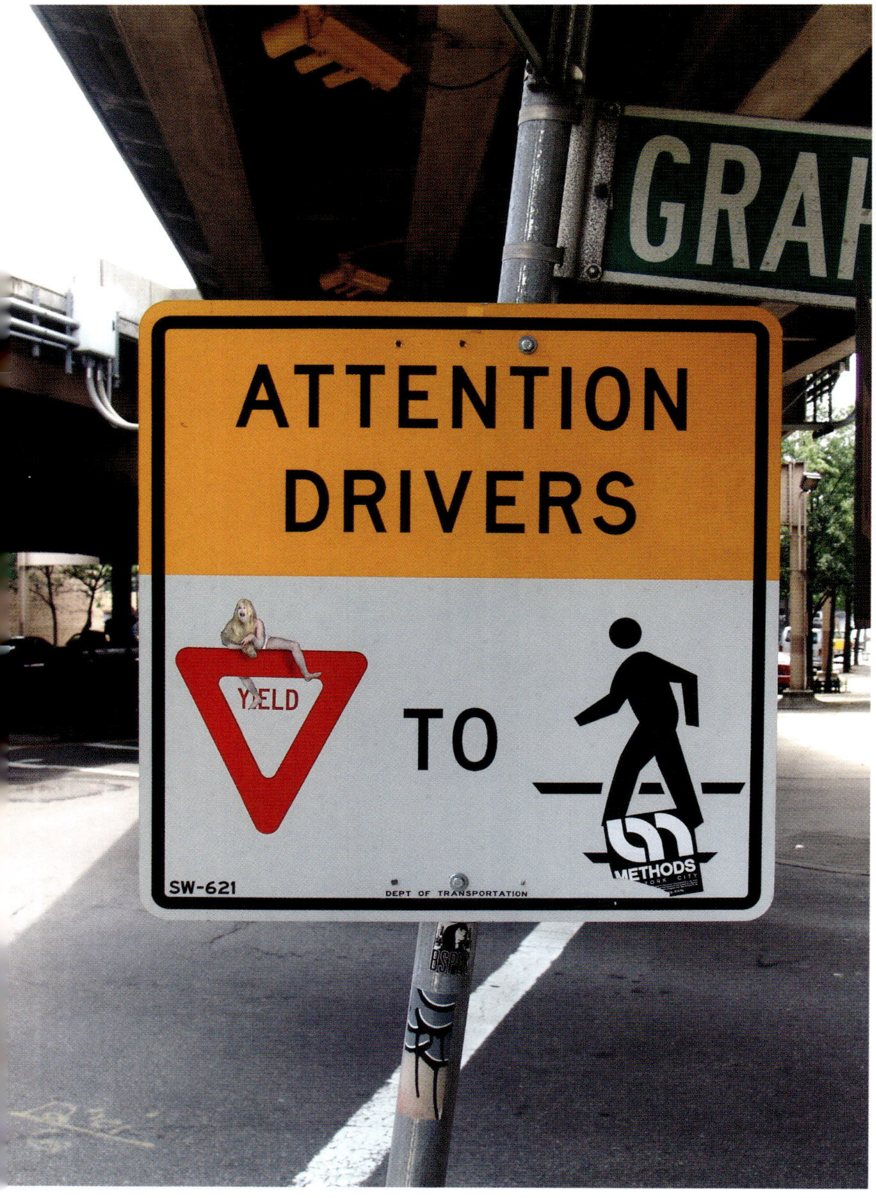

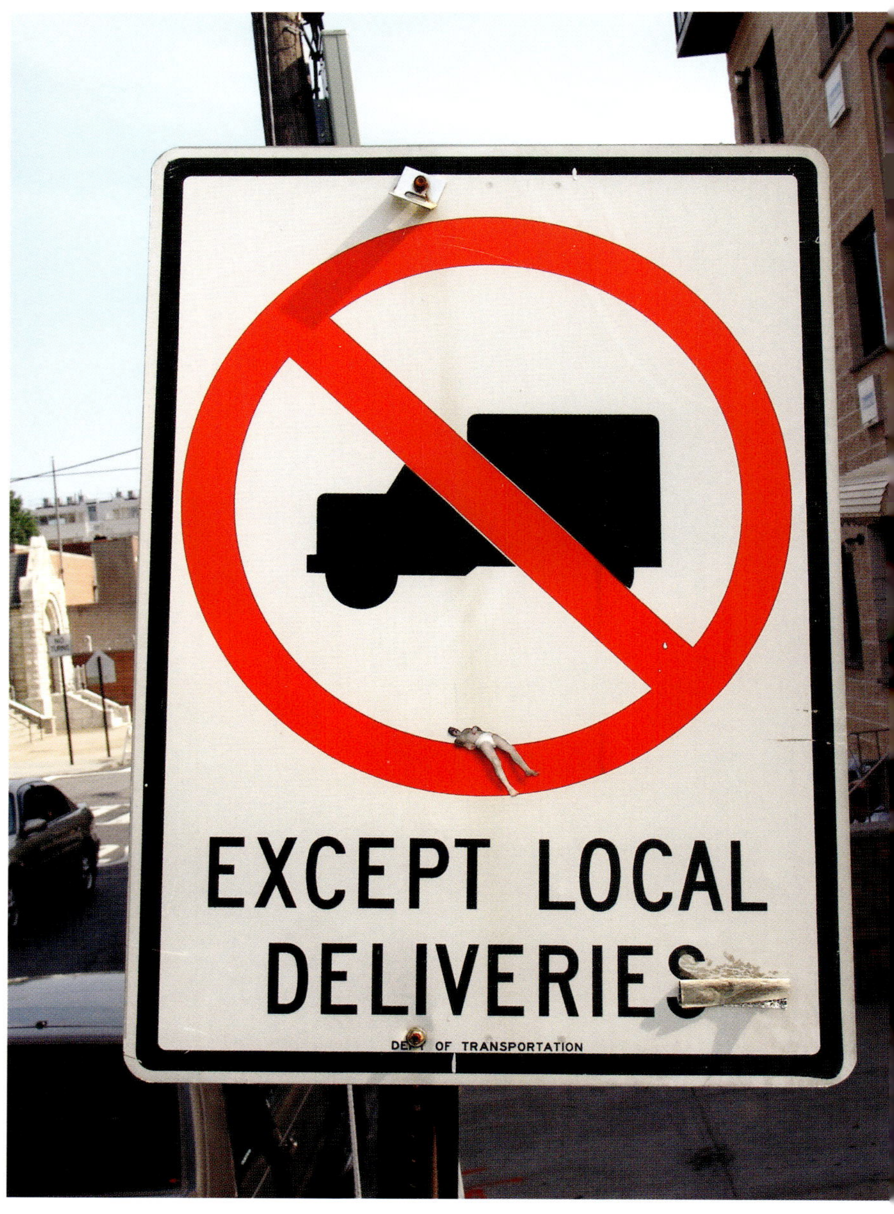

THIS PAGE LEFT:

Brooklyn, New York, 2006.

THIS PAGE RIGHT:

Brooklyn, New York, 2006.

PAGE RIGHT:

Brooklyn, New York, 2006.

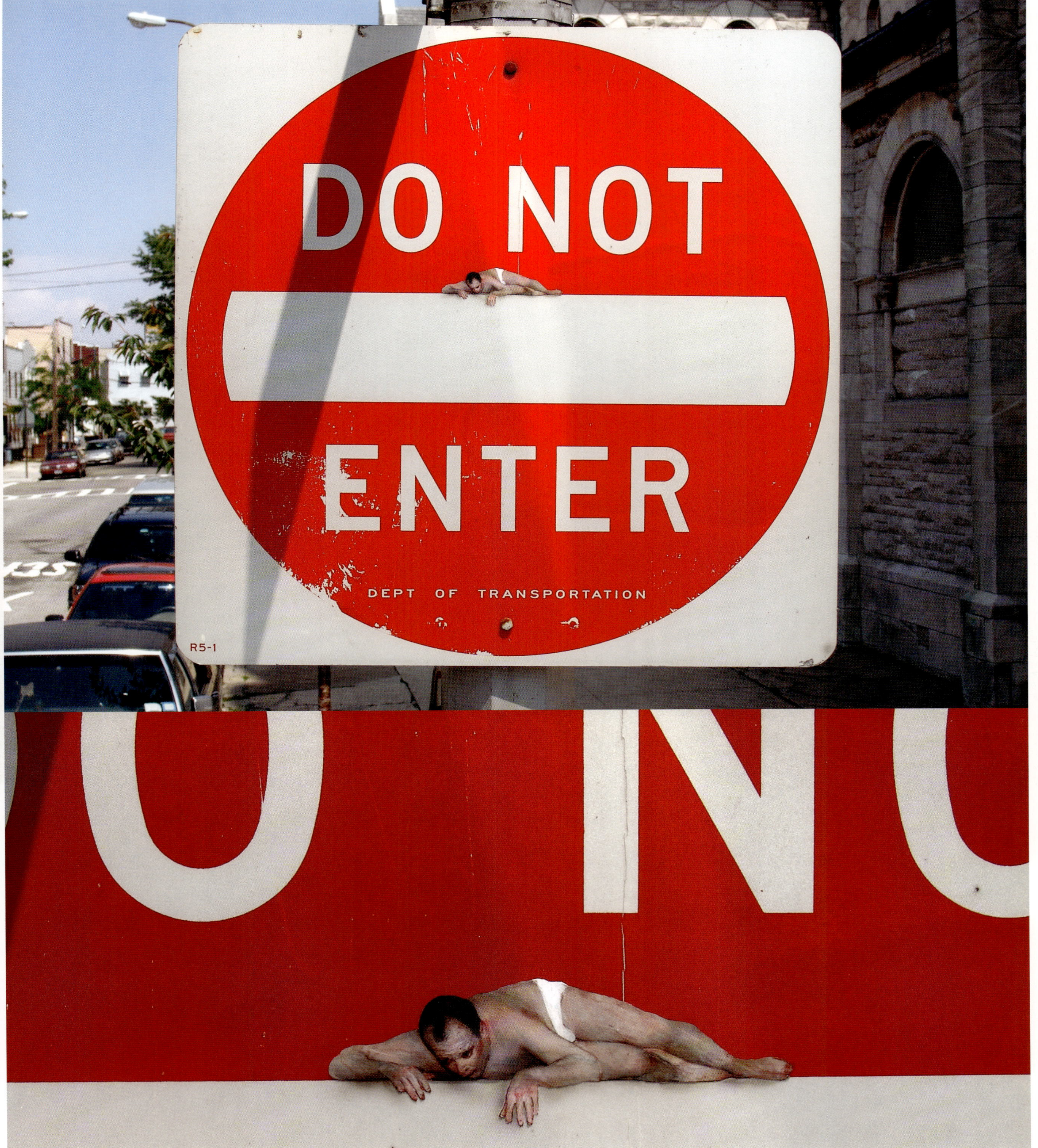
DO NOT
ENTER
DEPT OF TRANSPORTATION
R5-1

DO NOT ENTER PROJECT

2006 - 2007

New York, London, Copenhagen.

BELOW:

COPENHAGEN, DENMARK, 2007.
Mixed media on plastic affixed to street sign.

PAGE RIGHT:

LONG ISLAND CITY, QUEENS, 2007.
Mixed media on plastic affixed to street sign.

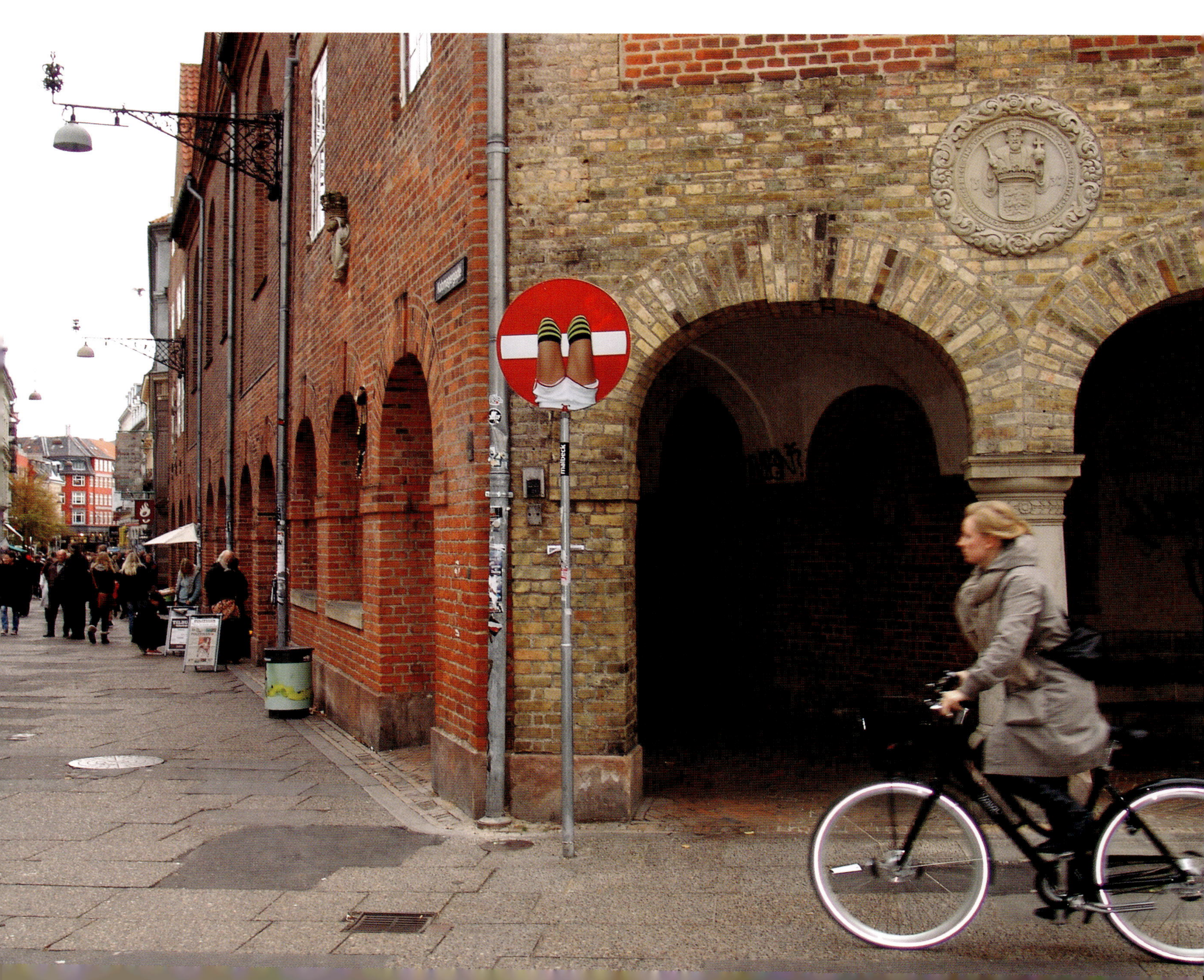

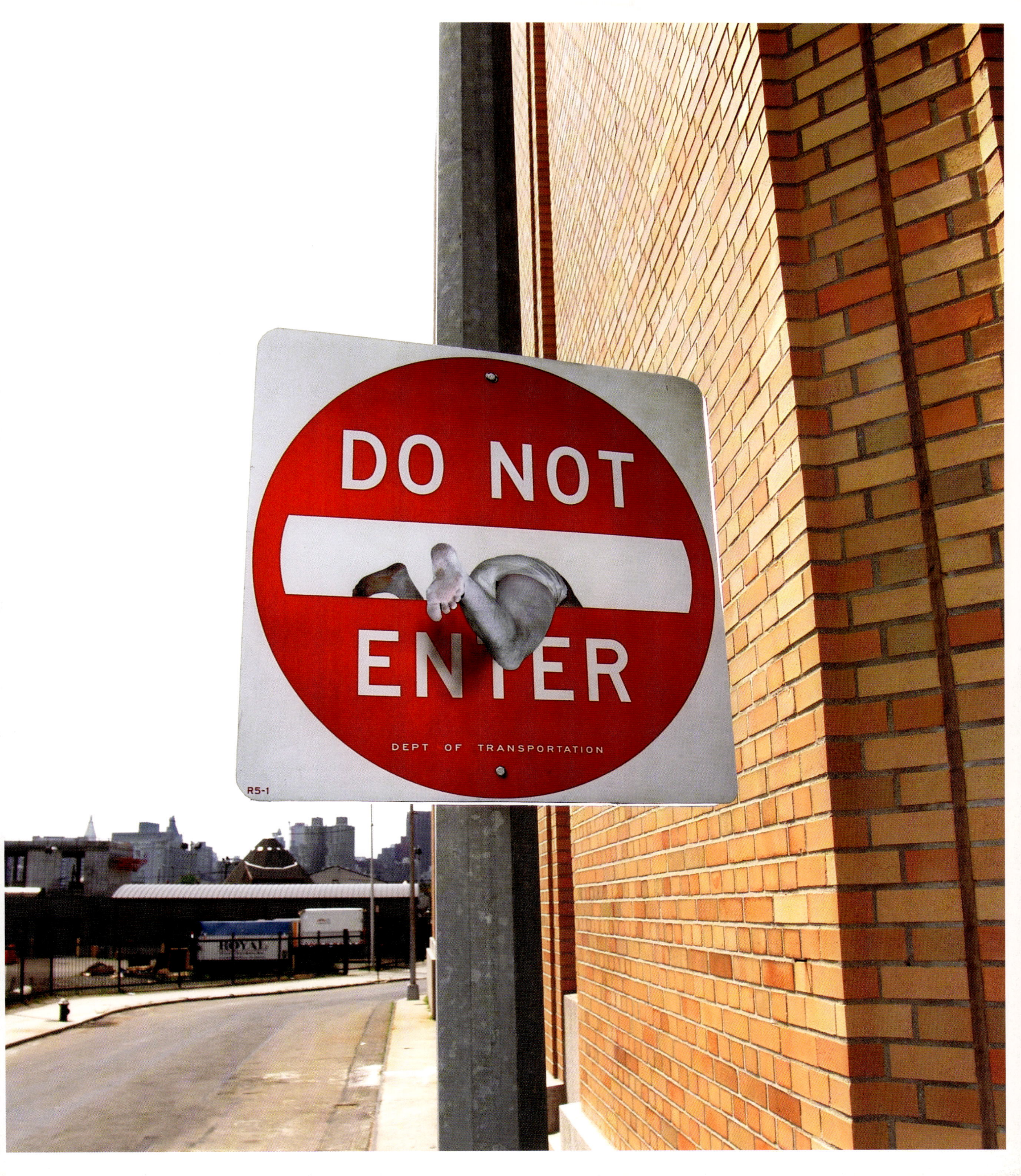
DO NOT
ENTER
DEPT OF TRANSPORTATION
R5-1
ROYAL

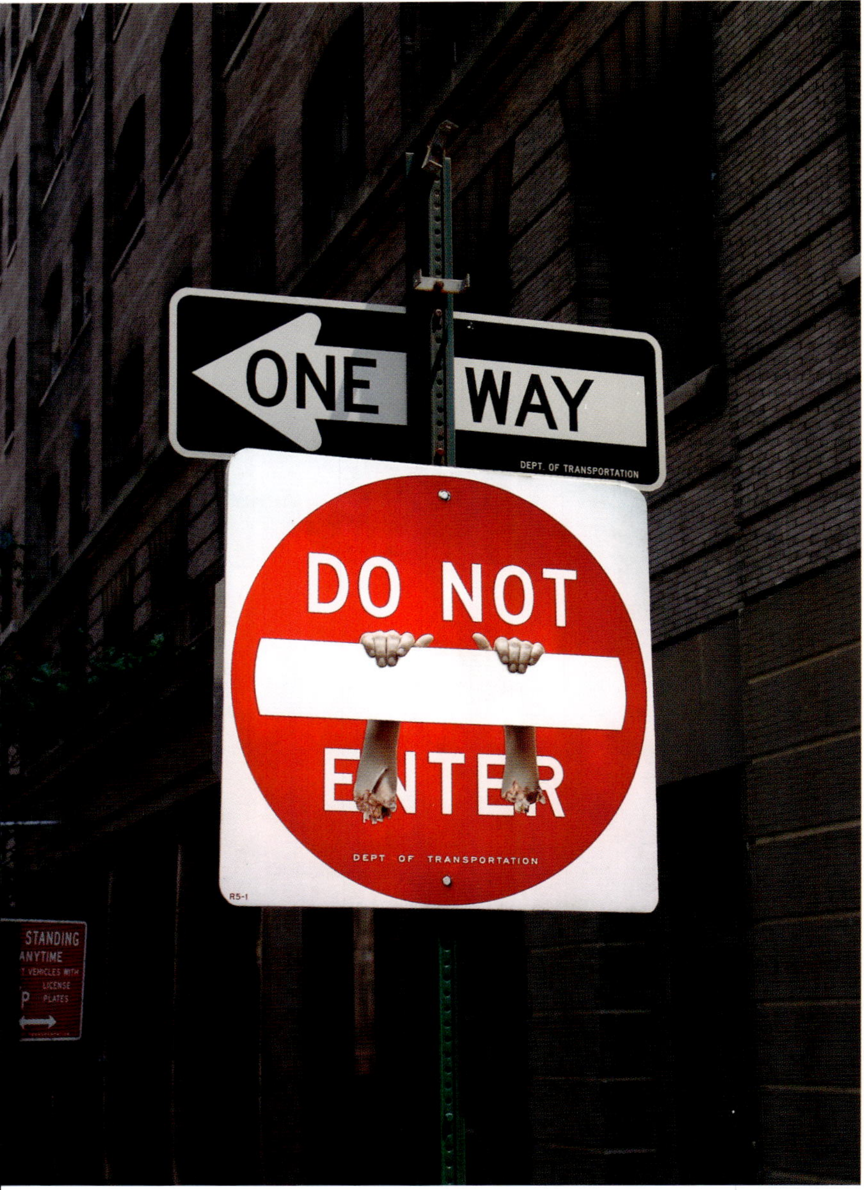

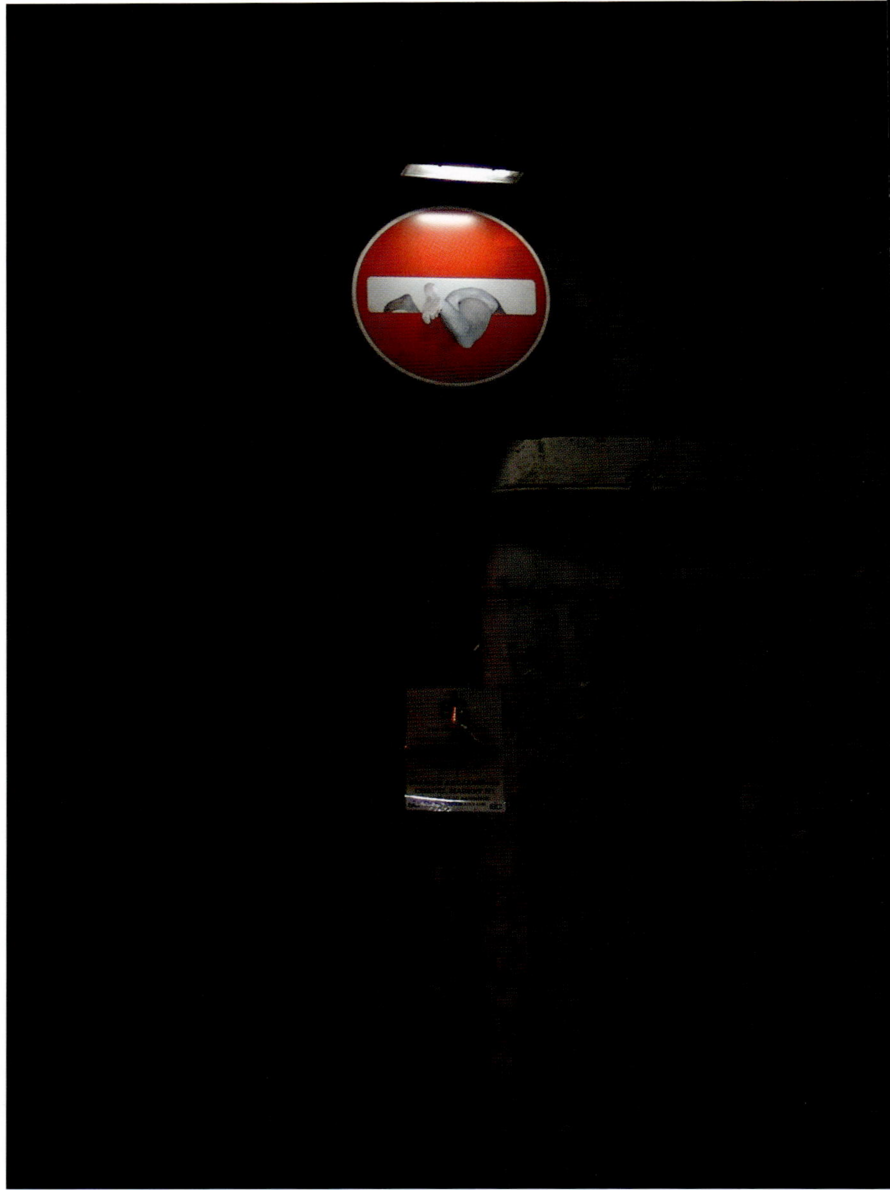

ABOVE:

MANHATTAN, NYC., 2007.
Mixed media plastic affixed to street sign.
A collaboration with the photoshop magician Till Krautkraemer

RIGHT:

BRICK LANE, LONDON, 2007.
Mixed media on street sign. A collaboration with Ian Caskey

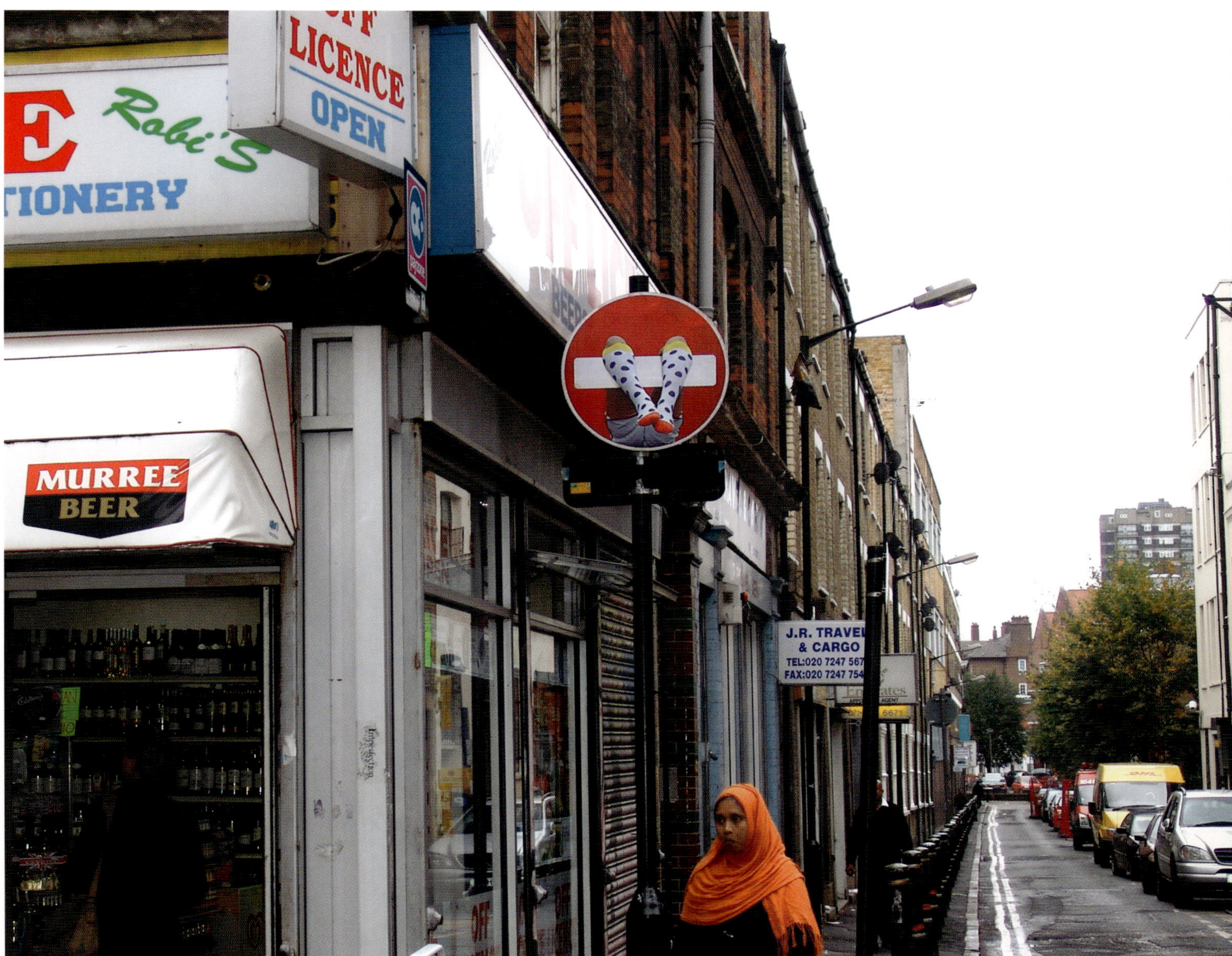

ABOVE:

BRICK LANE, LONDON, 2007.
Mixed media on plastic affixed to street sign.

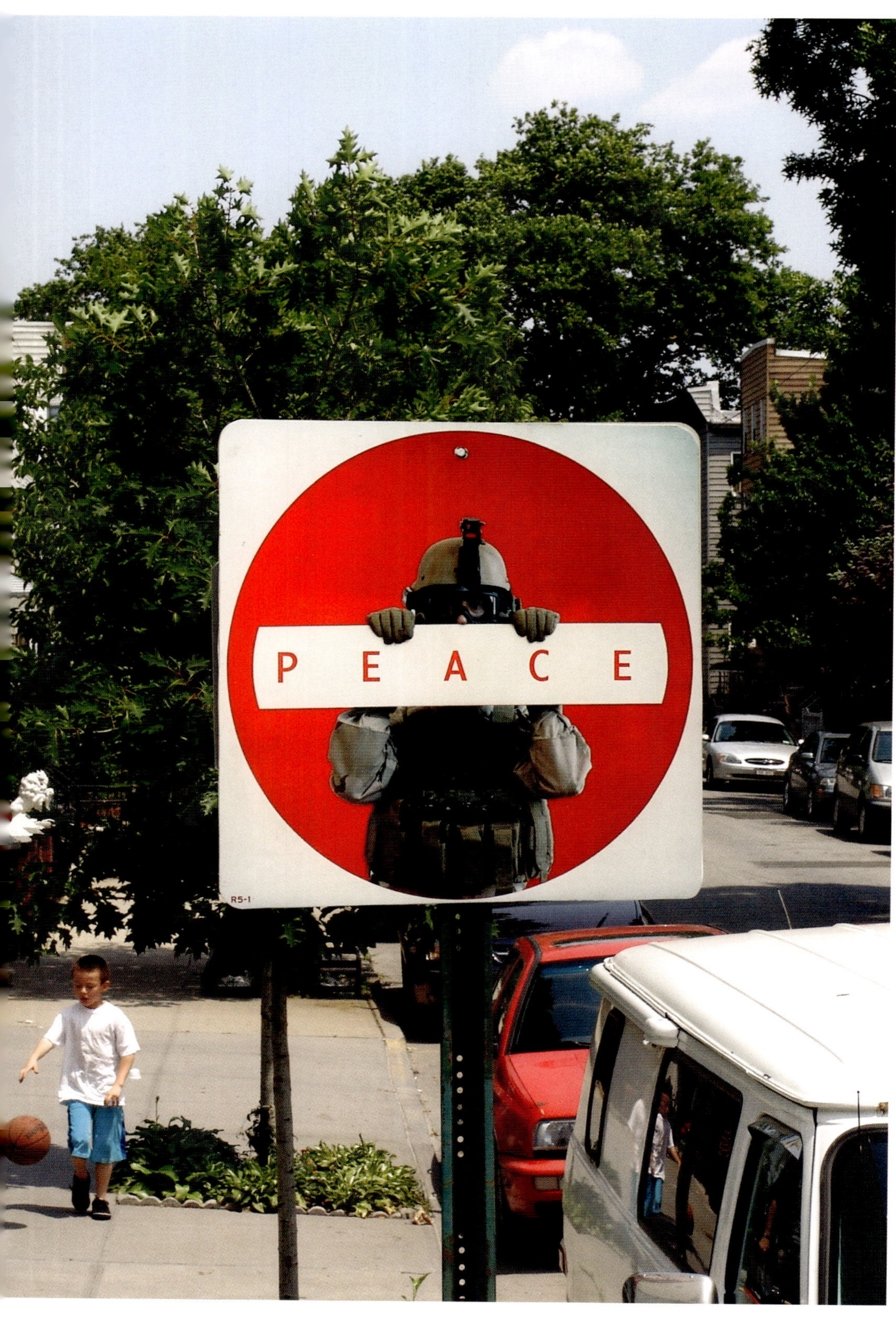
PEACE
R5-1

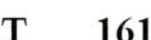

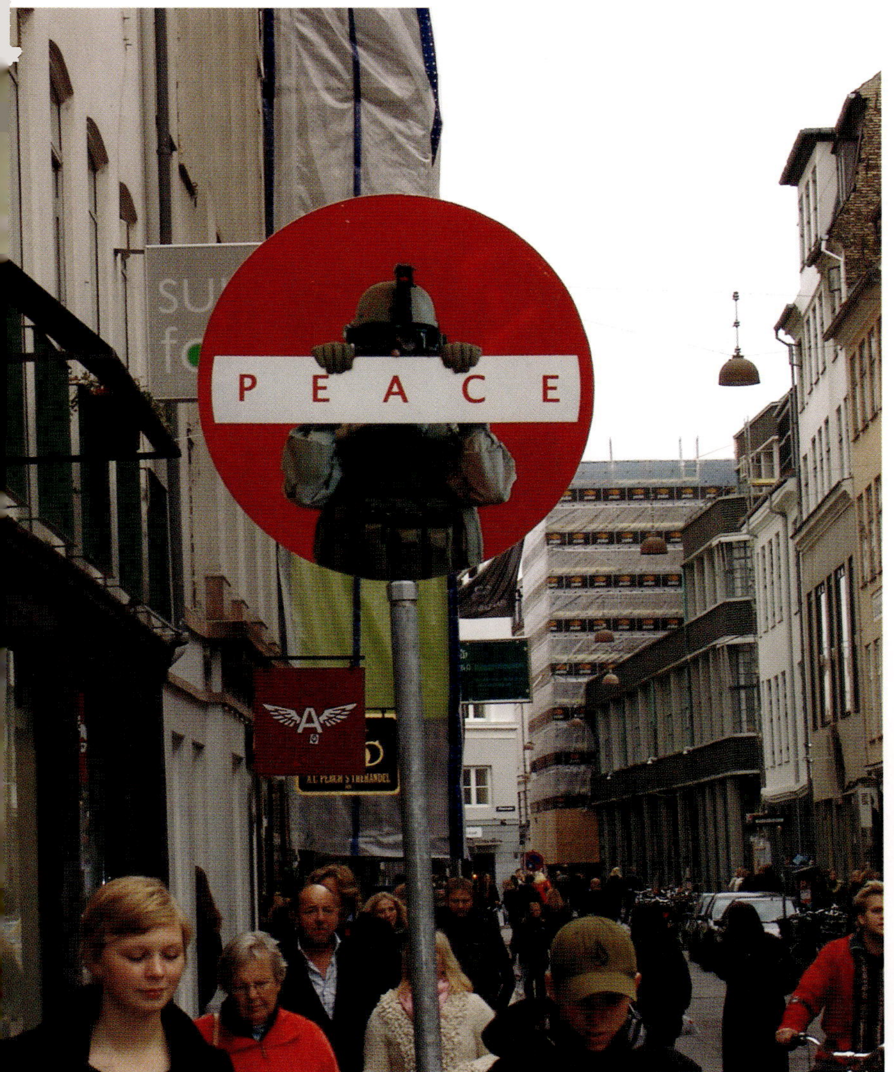

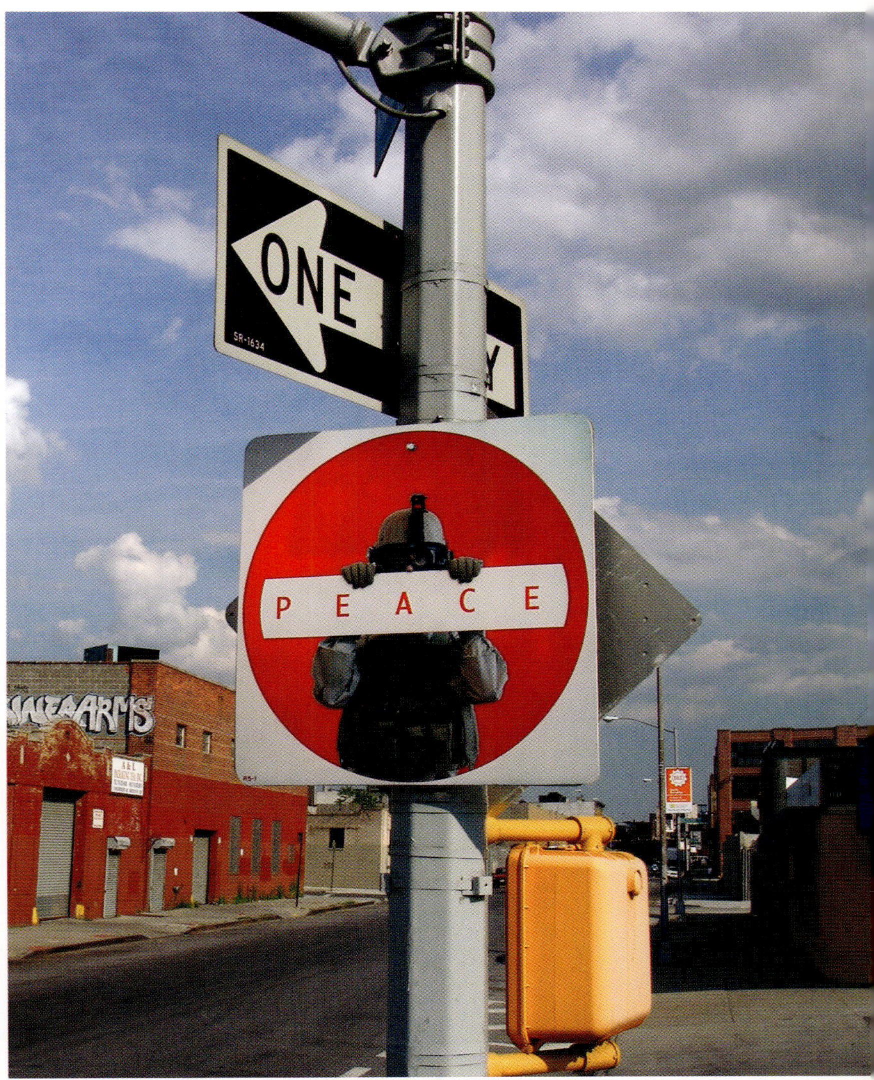

OPPOSITE PAGE:

GREENPOINT, BROOKLYN, 2007.
Mixed media on plastic affixed to street sign.

LEFT:

COPENHAGEN, DENMARK, 2007.
Mixed media on plastic affixed to street sign.

RIGHT:

BUSHWICK, BROOKLYN, 2007.
Mixed media on plastic affixed to street sign.

THE THIRD MAN

2007

Named after the 1948 film with Orson Welles, these originated from my second annual New Years prank. In one of the final scenes of the film the fugitive war profiteer, played by Welles, is being pursued by the police in the Vienna sewers. There's a famous shot of him, trapped, reaching his gloved hands through a sewer grate—an image that's been on my to-do list for years.

I used real gloves. Friends gave me their old gloves which I made rigid and weatherized. Each piece is named after the gloves' original occupant.

SILKE, WILLIAMSBURG, BROOKLYN, 2007.

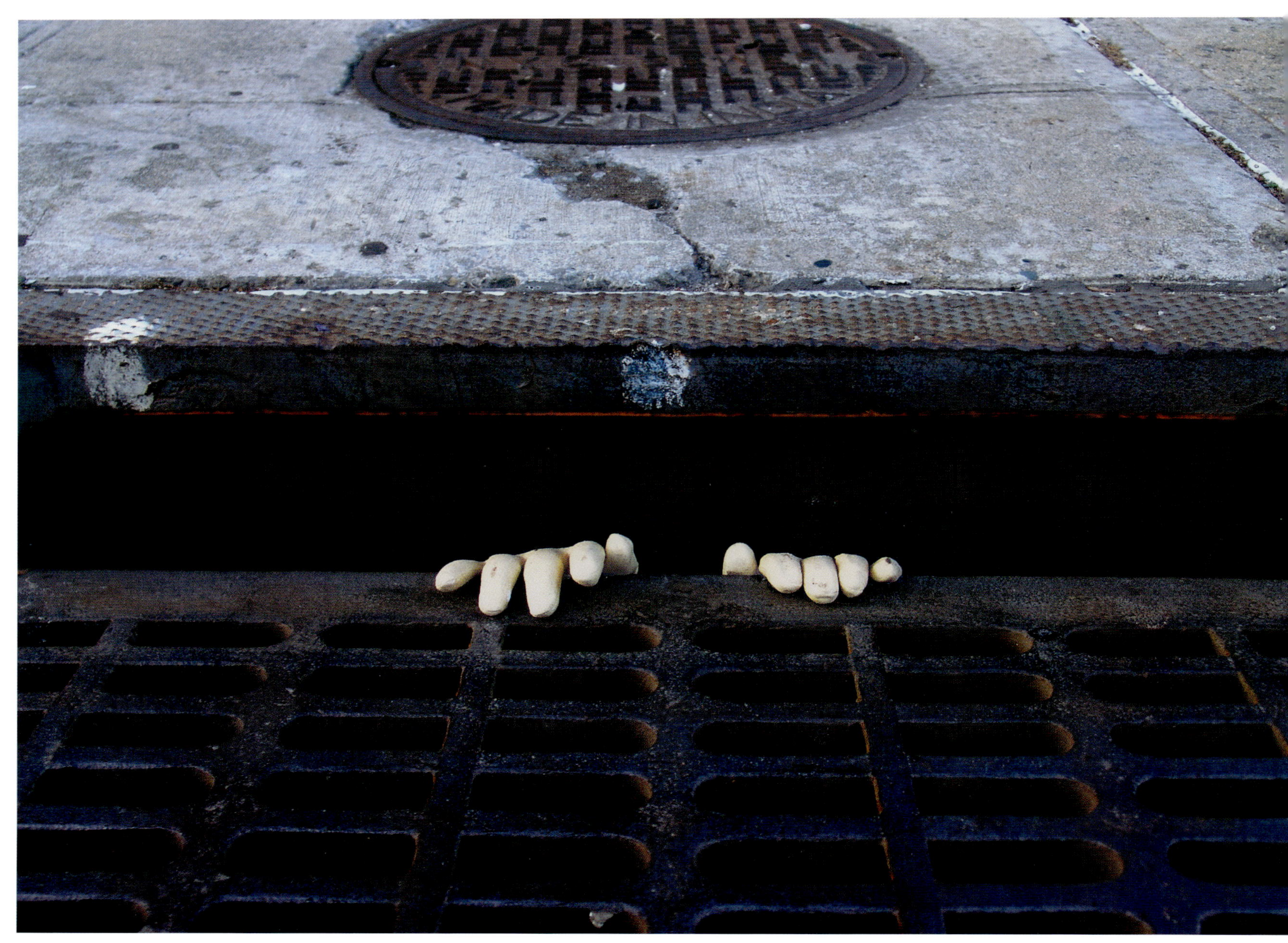

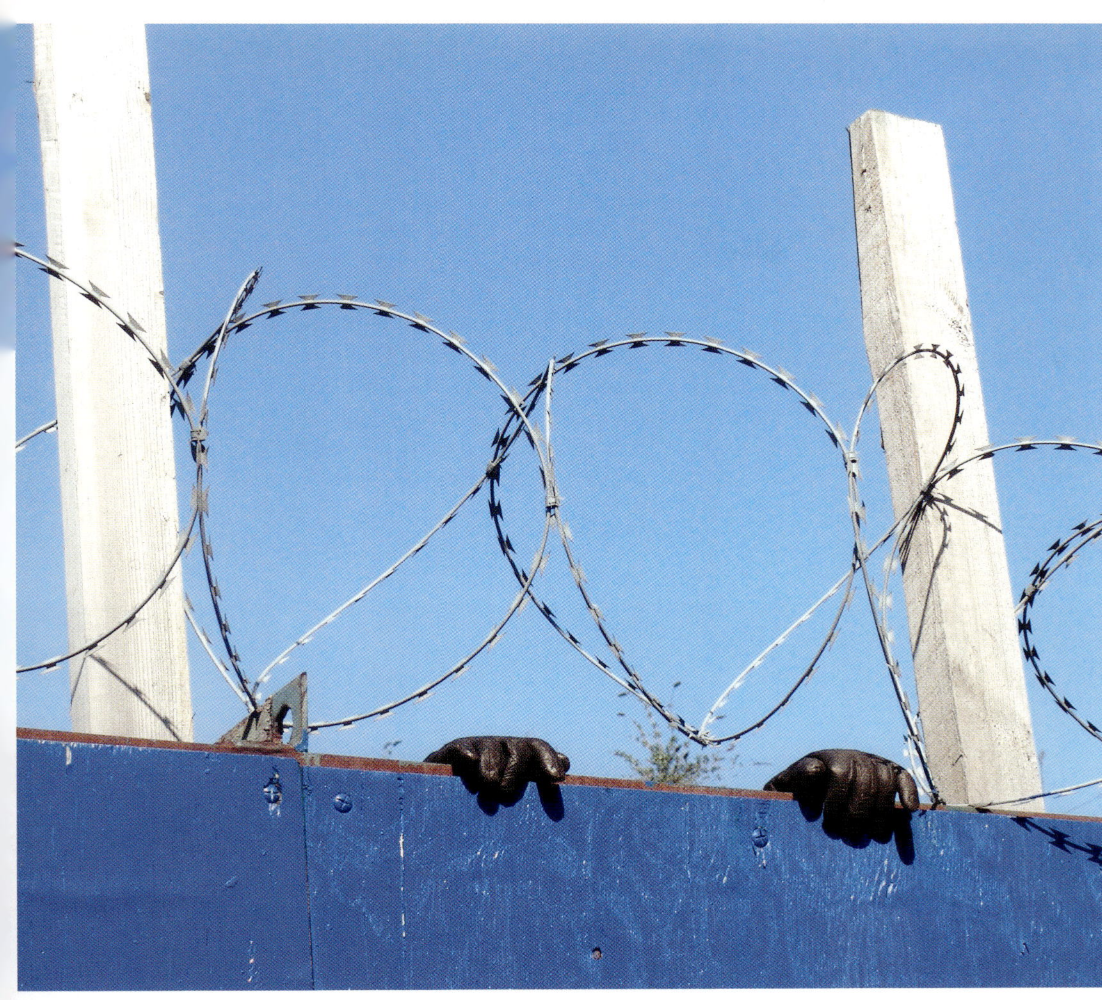

RICH. EAST LONDON, 2007.

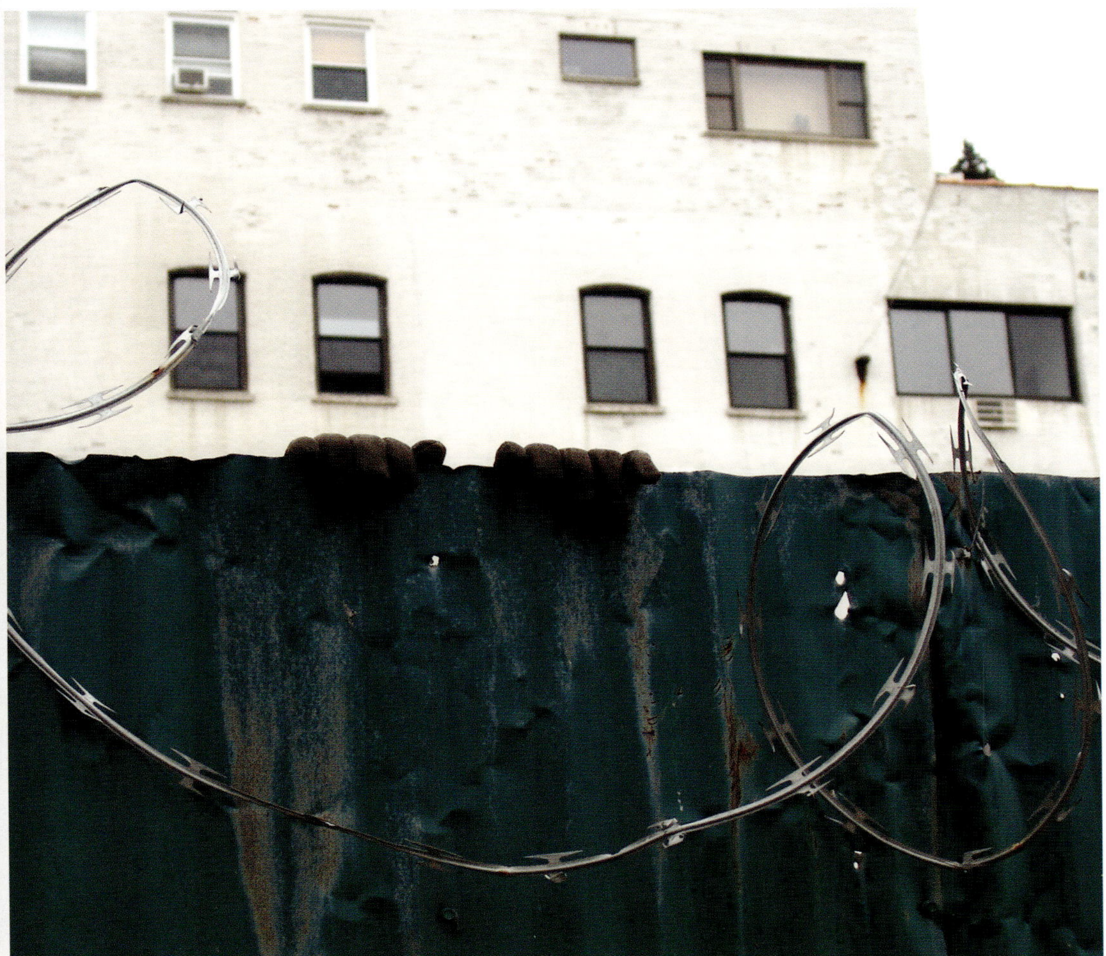

MARY BETH, WILLIAMSBURG, BROOKLYN, 2007.

UGLY NEW BUILDINGS

2008

In the past few years much of my neighborhood in Brooklyn has been torn down to make way for luxury housing. Personally, I can't say I like the new modern architecture very much; it's sterile and so arrogantly disconnected from its surroundings that sometimes it seems like giant alien space ships have landed in the night. But, at the very least, there's some interesting new textures and surfaces to interact with. These are photo-based, heavily re-painted stickers, mounted on plastic and glued to the walls of the Ugly New Buildings. I hit the Lower East Side and East Village in Manhattan, Long Island City, Queens, and Bushwick, Dumbo, Greenpoint and Williamsburg out here in Brooklyn.

BELOW:

WILLIAMSBURG, BROOKLYN, 2008.

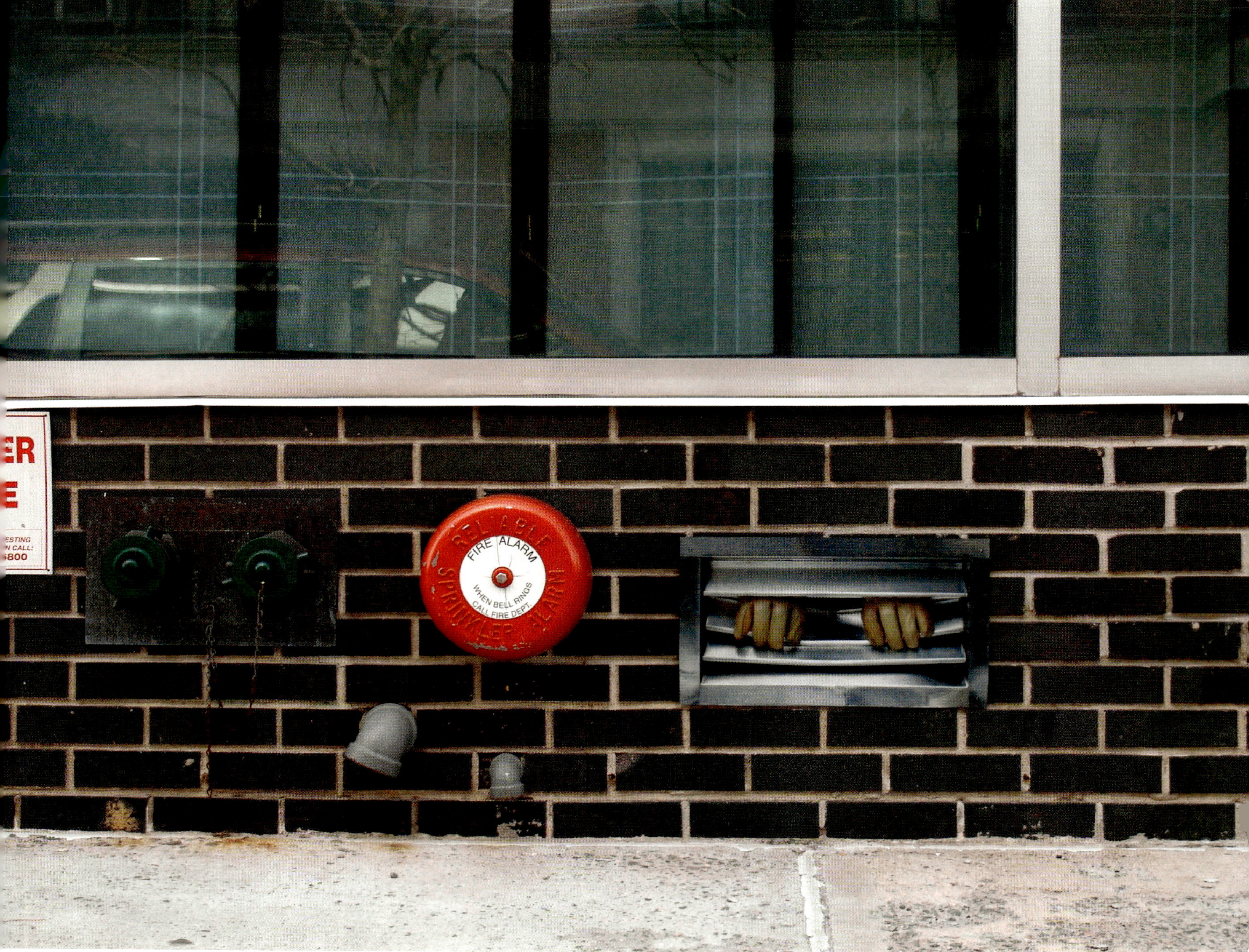

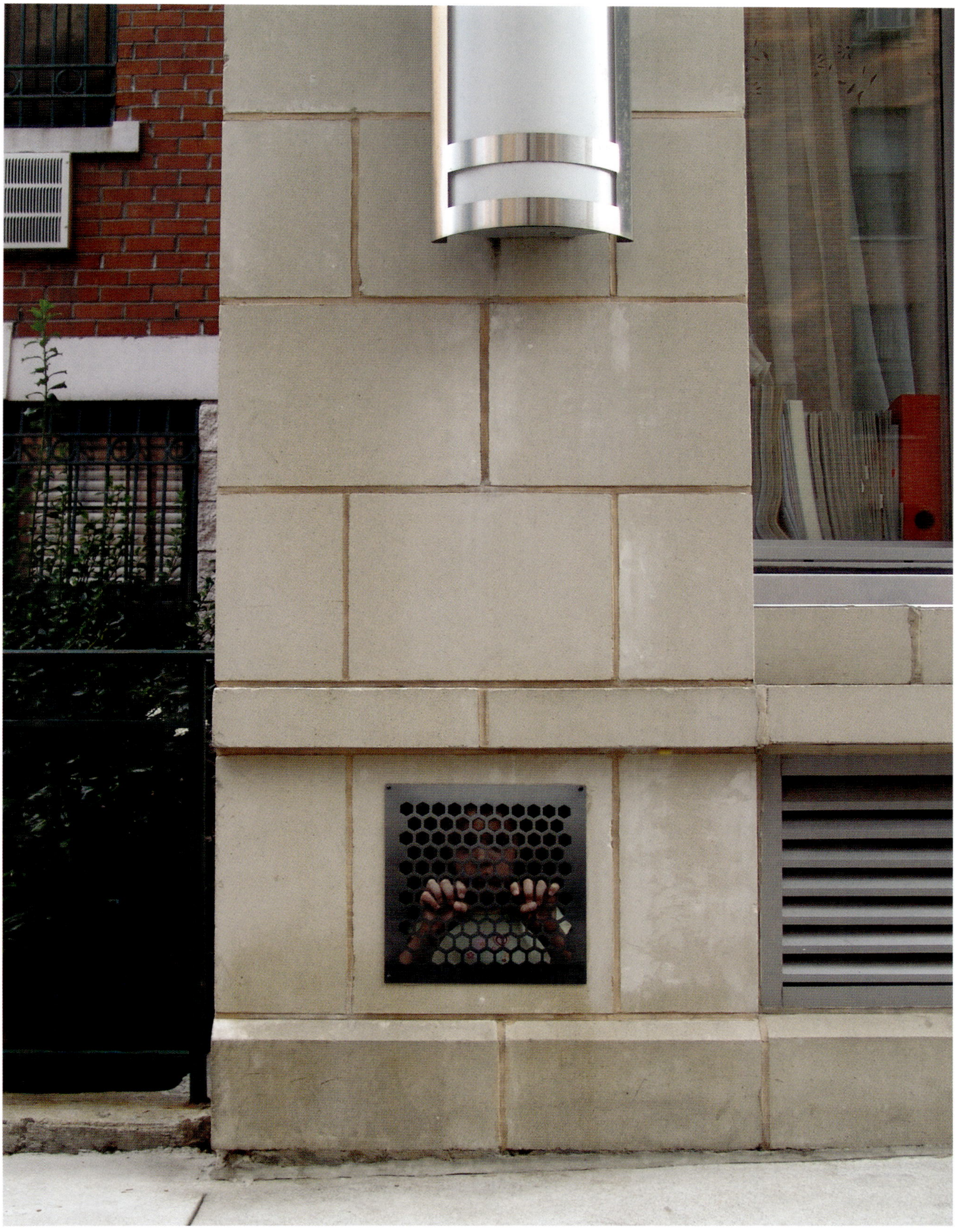

EAST VILLAGE, NYC., 2008.

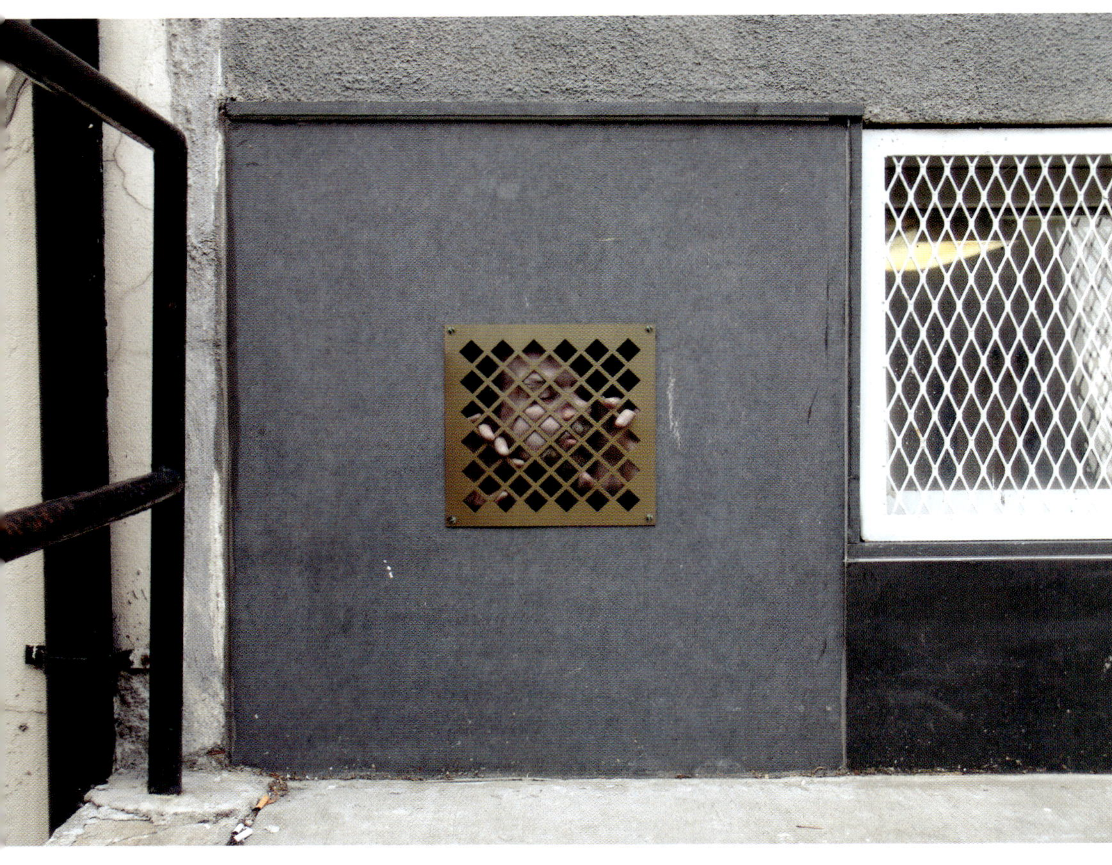

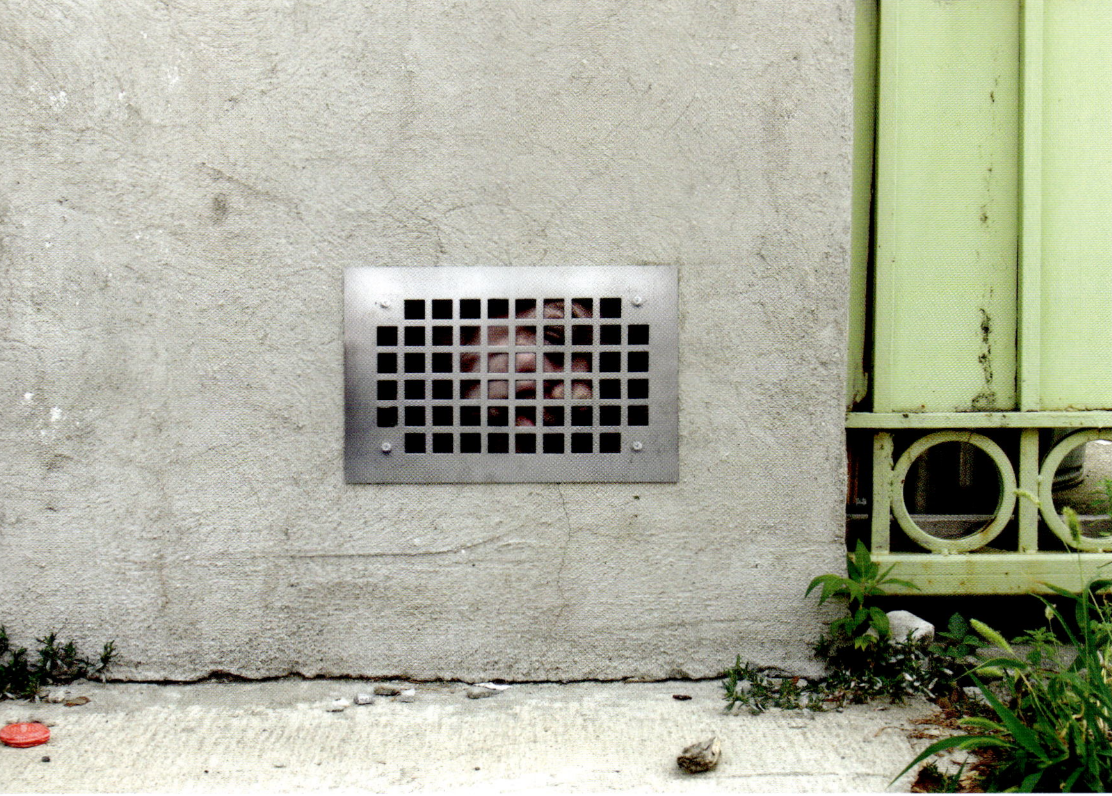

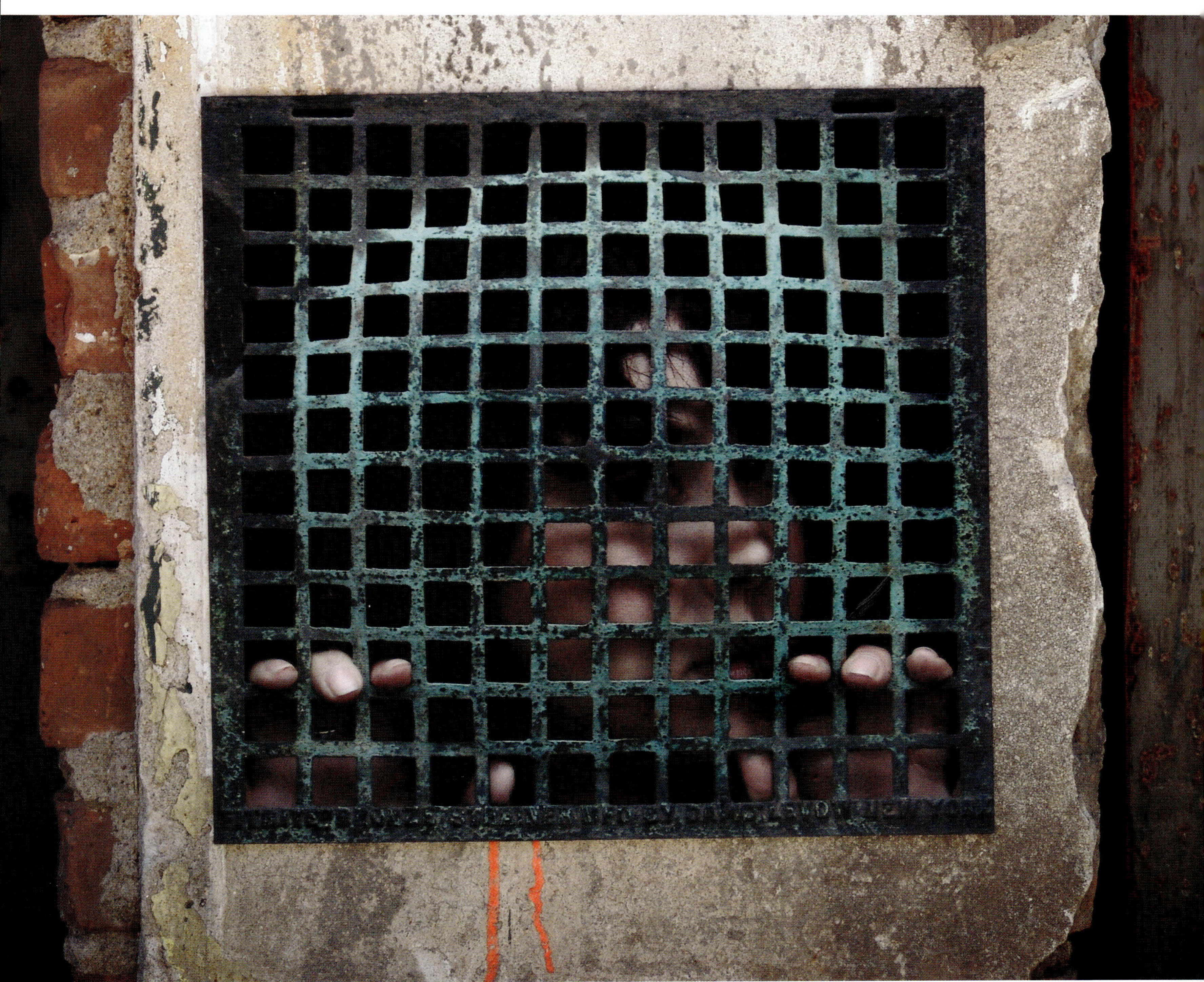

OPPOSITE PAGE, TOP:

EAST VILLAGE, NYC., 2008.

OPPOSITE PAGE, BOTTOM:

WILLIAMSBURG, BROOKLYN, 2008.

THIS PAGE:

LOWER EAST SIDE, NYC., 2008.

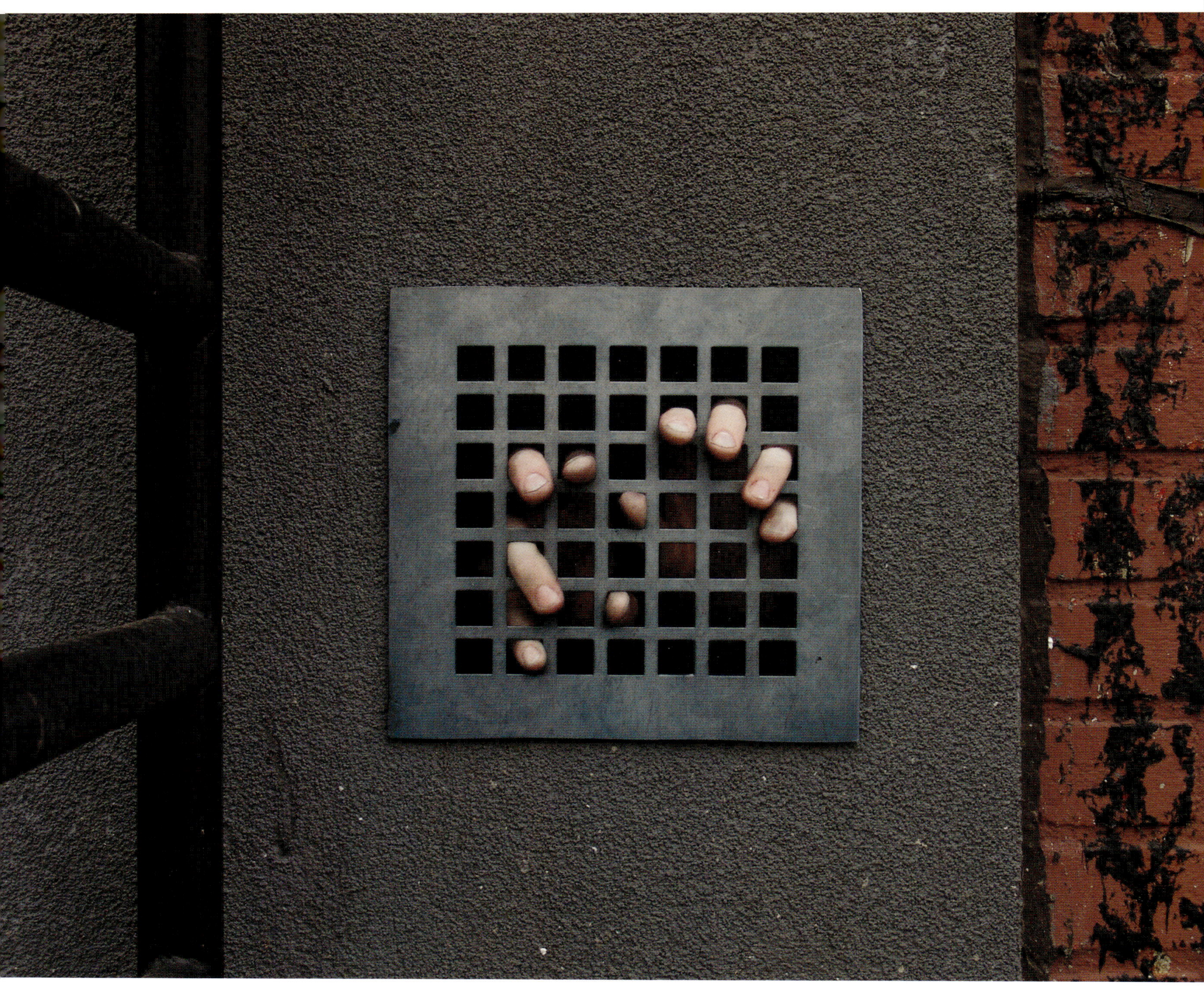

THIS PAGE:

SOUTH WILLIAMSBURG, 2008.

OPPOSITE PAGE, TOP:

WILLIAMSBURG, BROOKLYN, 2008.

OPPOSITE PAGE, BOTTOM:

WILLIAMSBURG, BROOKLYN, 2008.

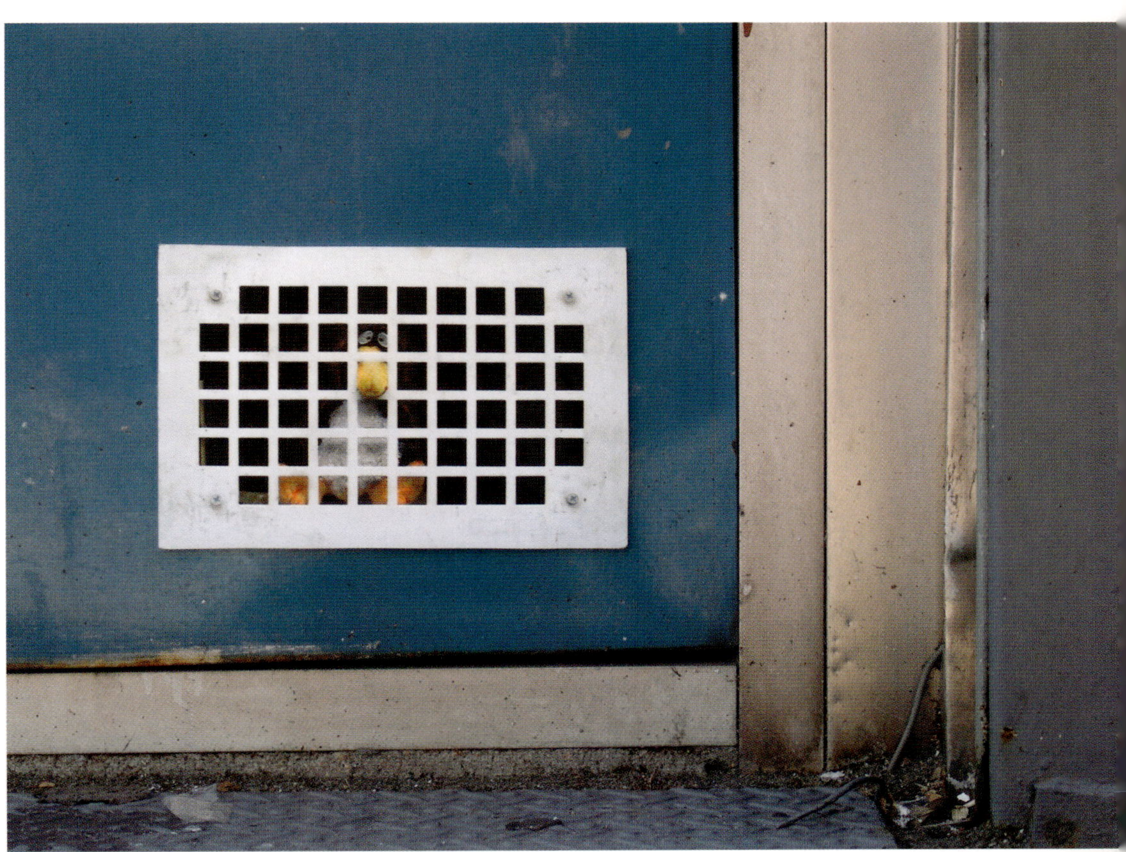

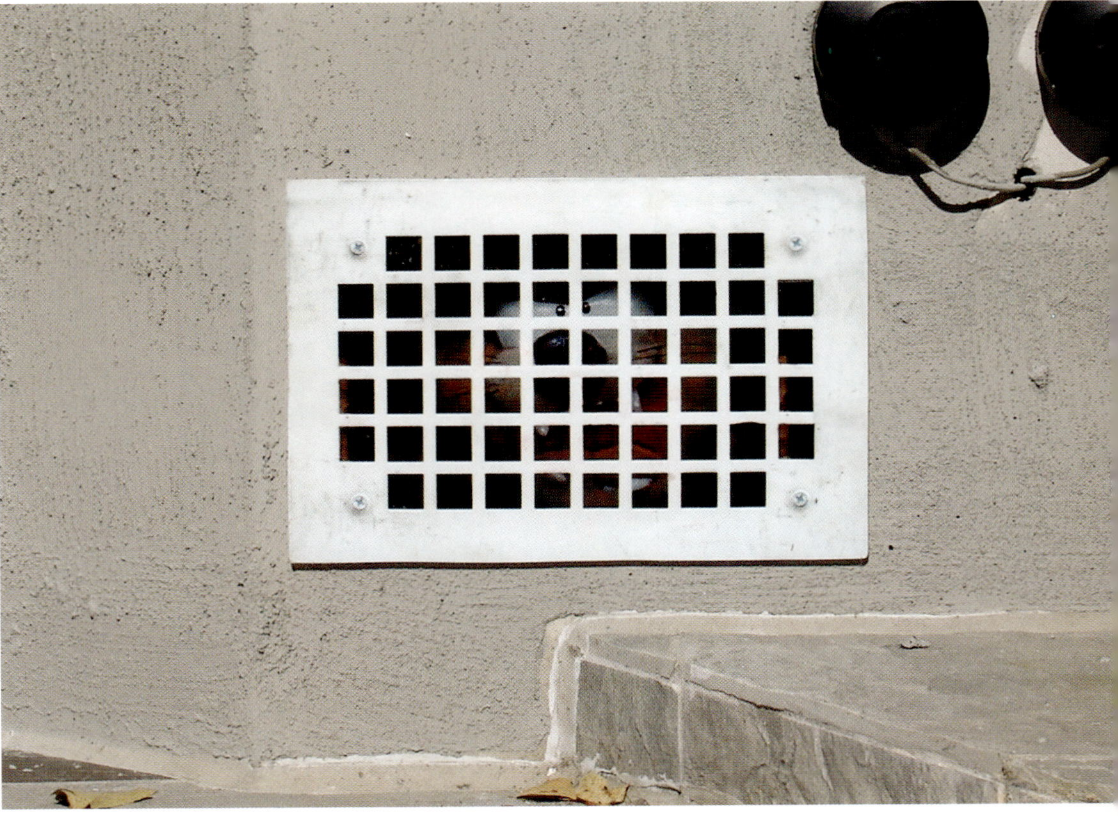

IN PLAIN VIEW

2009

My goal is to make obvious art that most people won't notice. By inserting outrageous things in plain view that most people walk by without seeing. I'm hoping that, eventually when you stumble upon one or find out about it you'll start wondering what else you've been missing.

RIGHT:

WILLIAMSBURG, BROOKLYN.

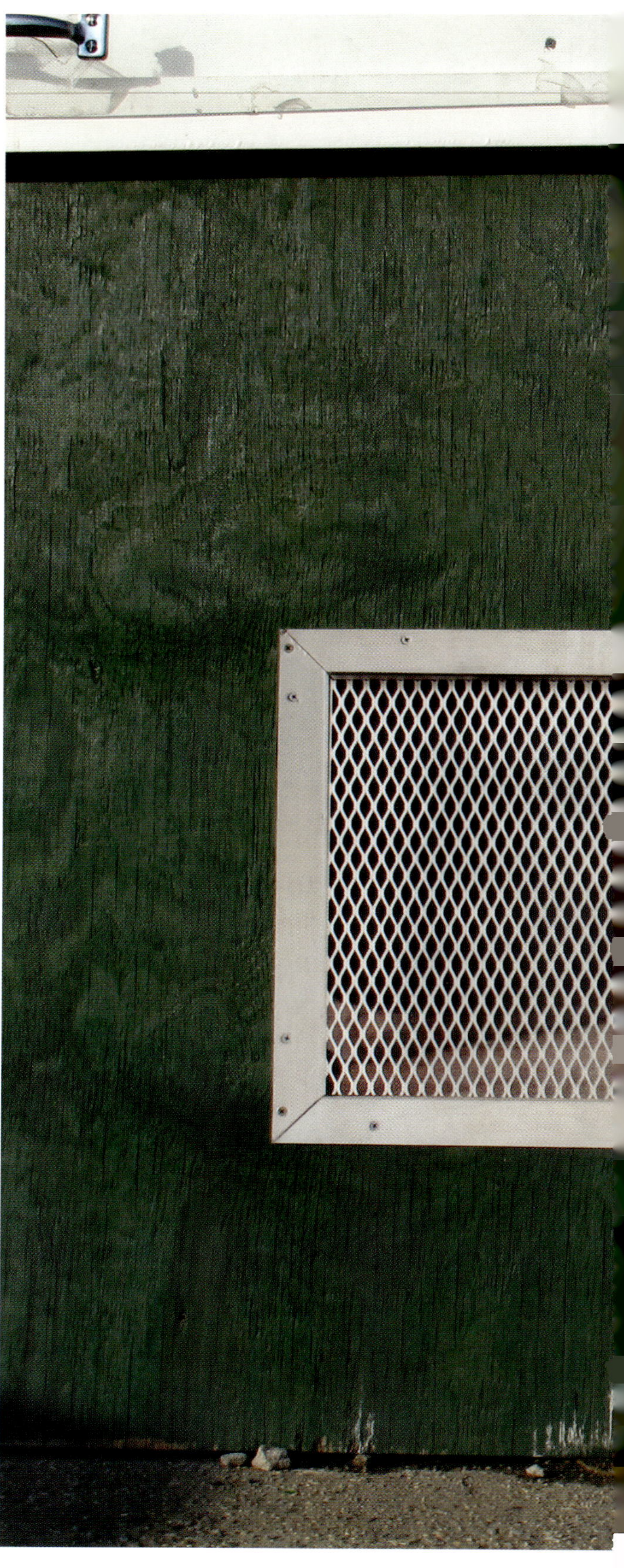

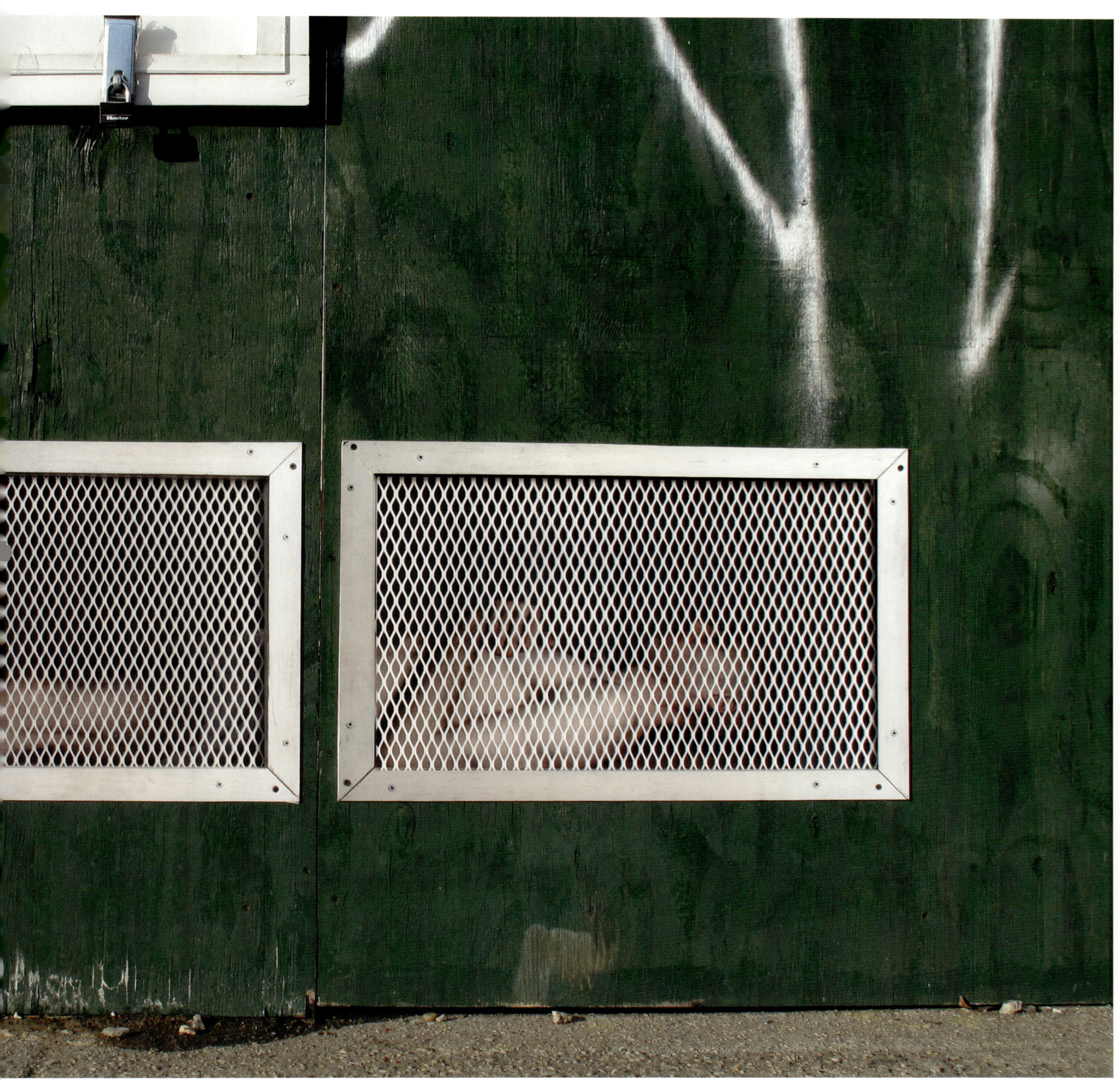

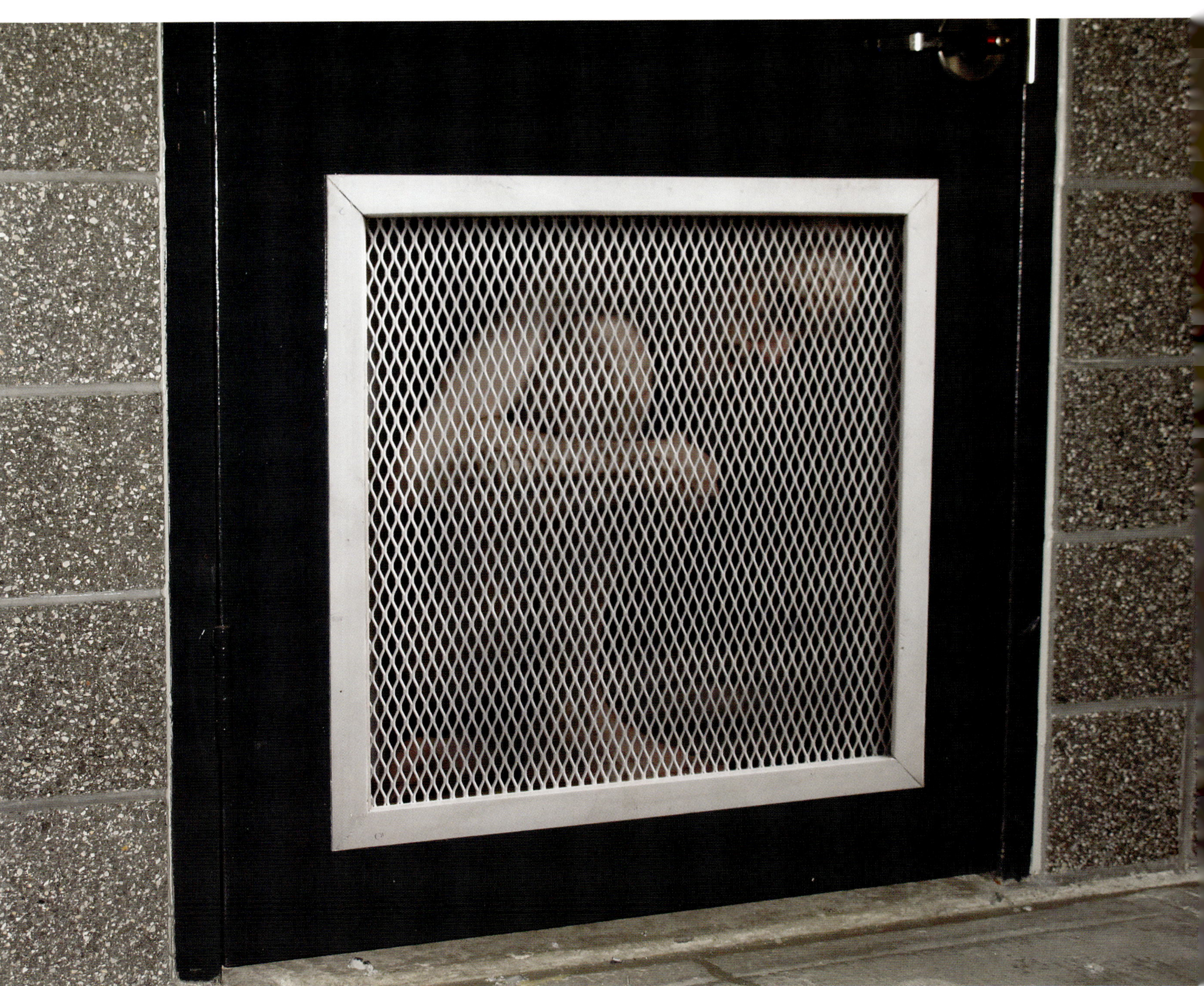

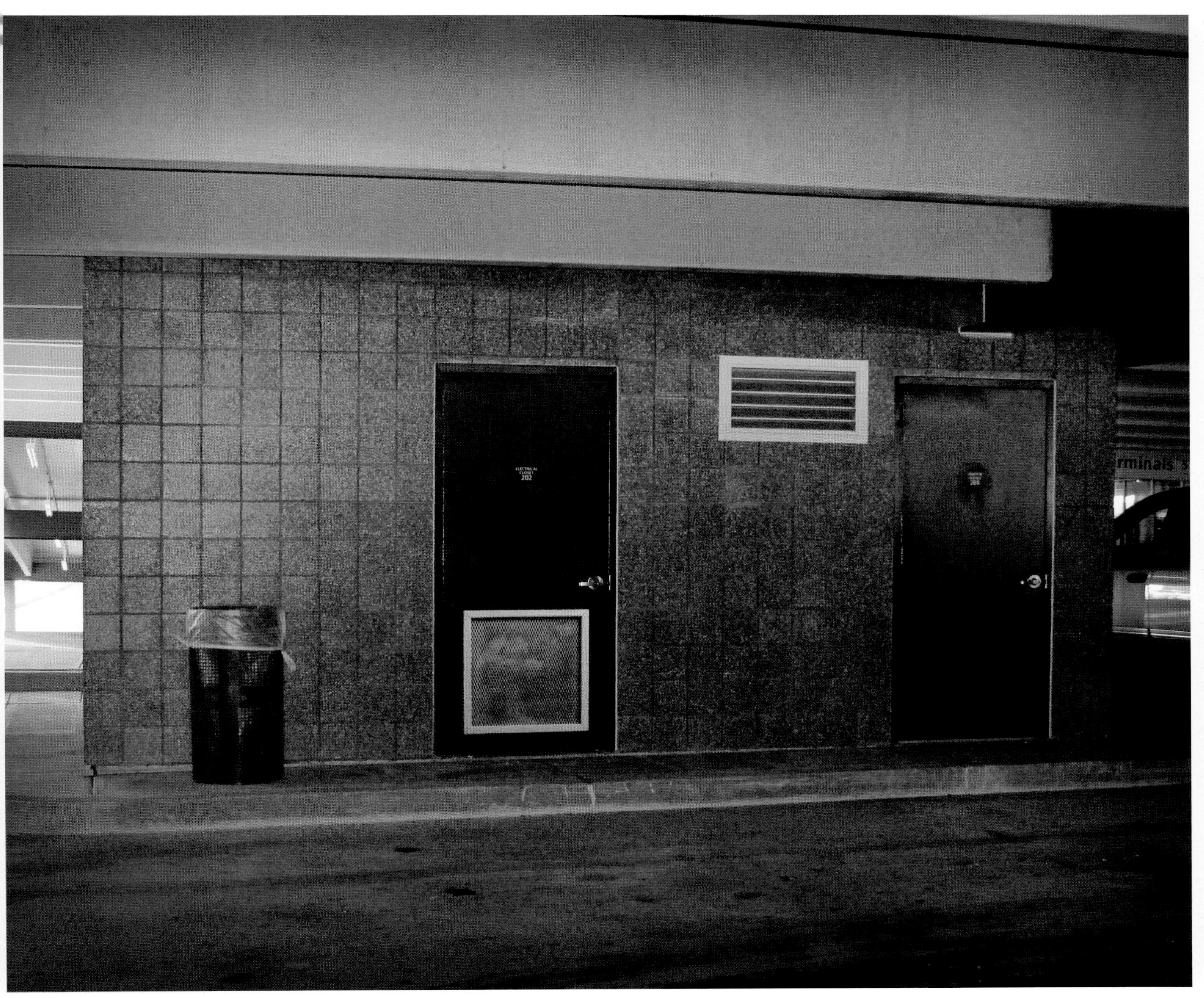

JFK AIRPORT, NYC.

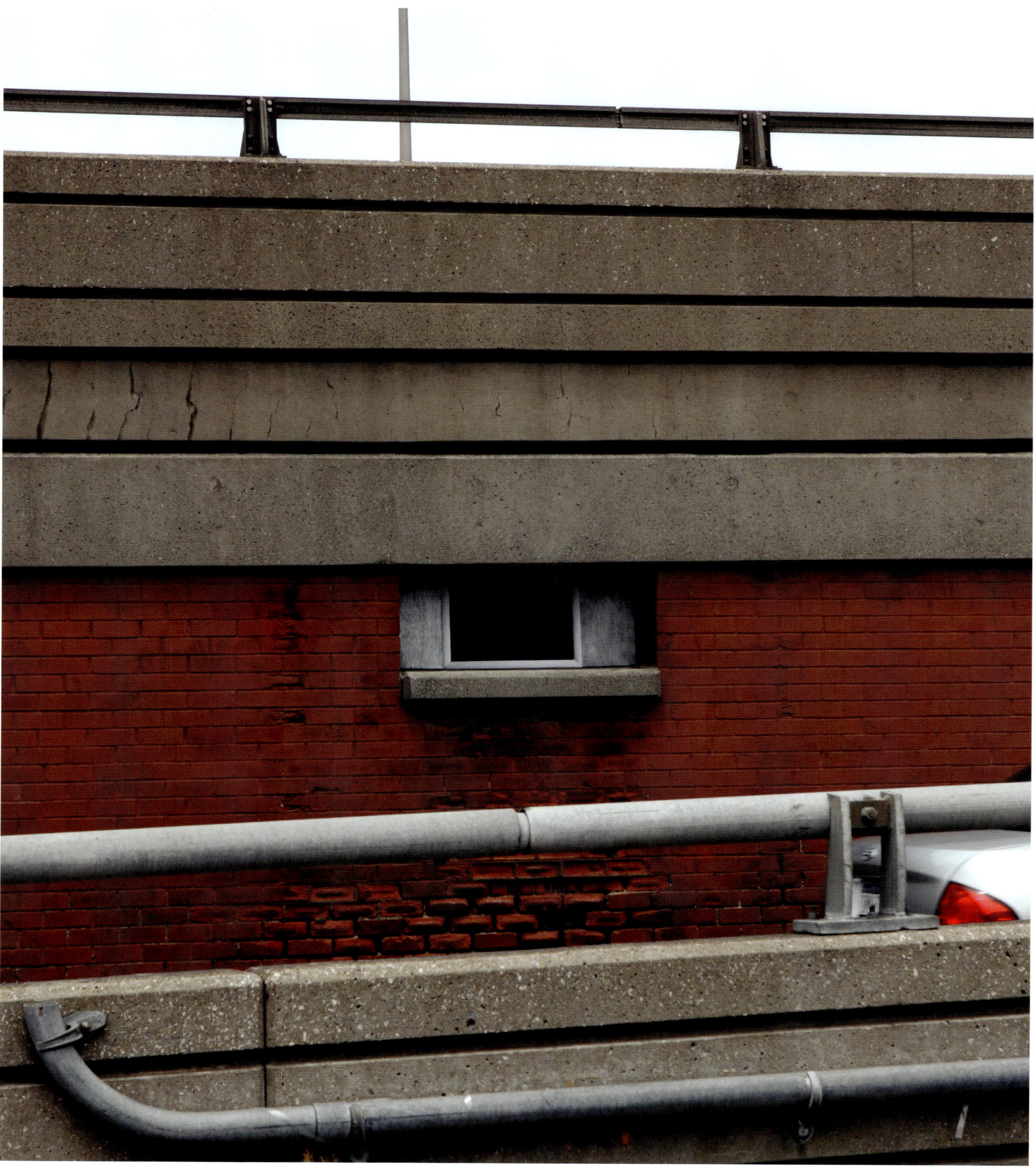

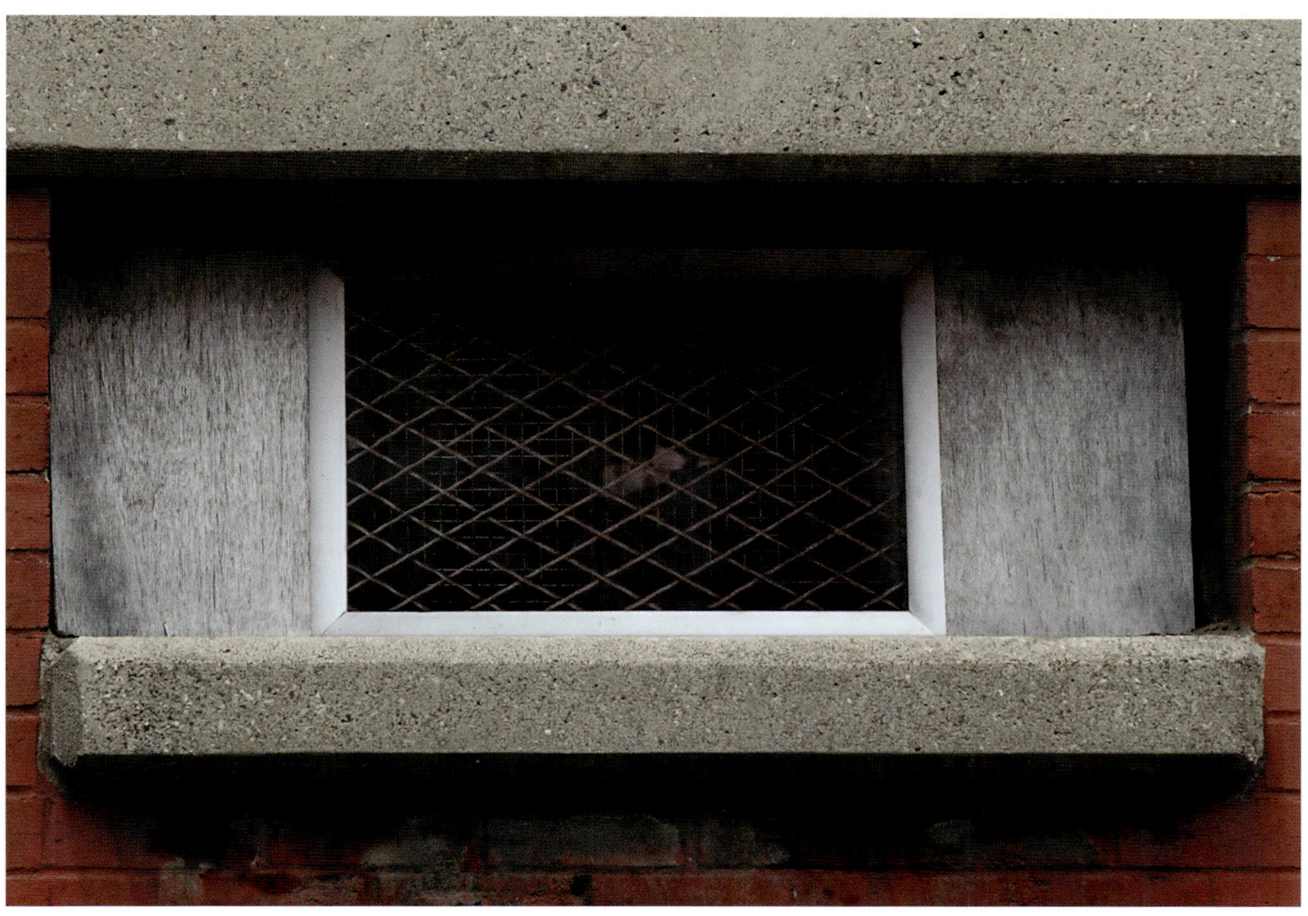

BROOKLYN QUEENS EXPRESSWAY ENTRANCE RAMP.

SNOIDS AND FENESTRATIONS

2009

Acting Globally. Snoids are my homage to the R. Crumb character, Mr. Snoid.

BELOW:

NEW ORLEANS, LOUISIANA.

OPPOSITE PAGE:

AMSTERDAM, HOLLAND.

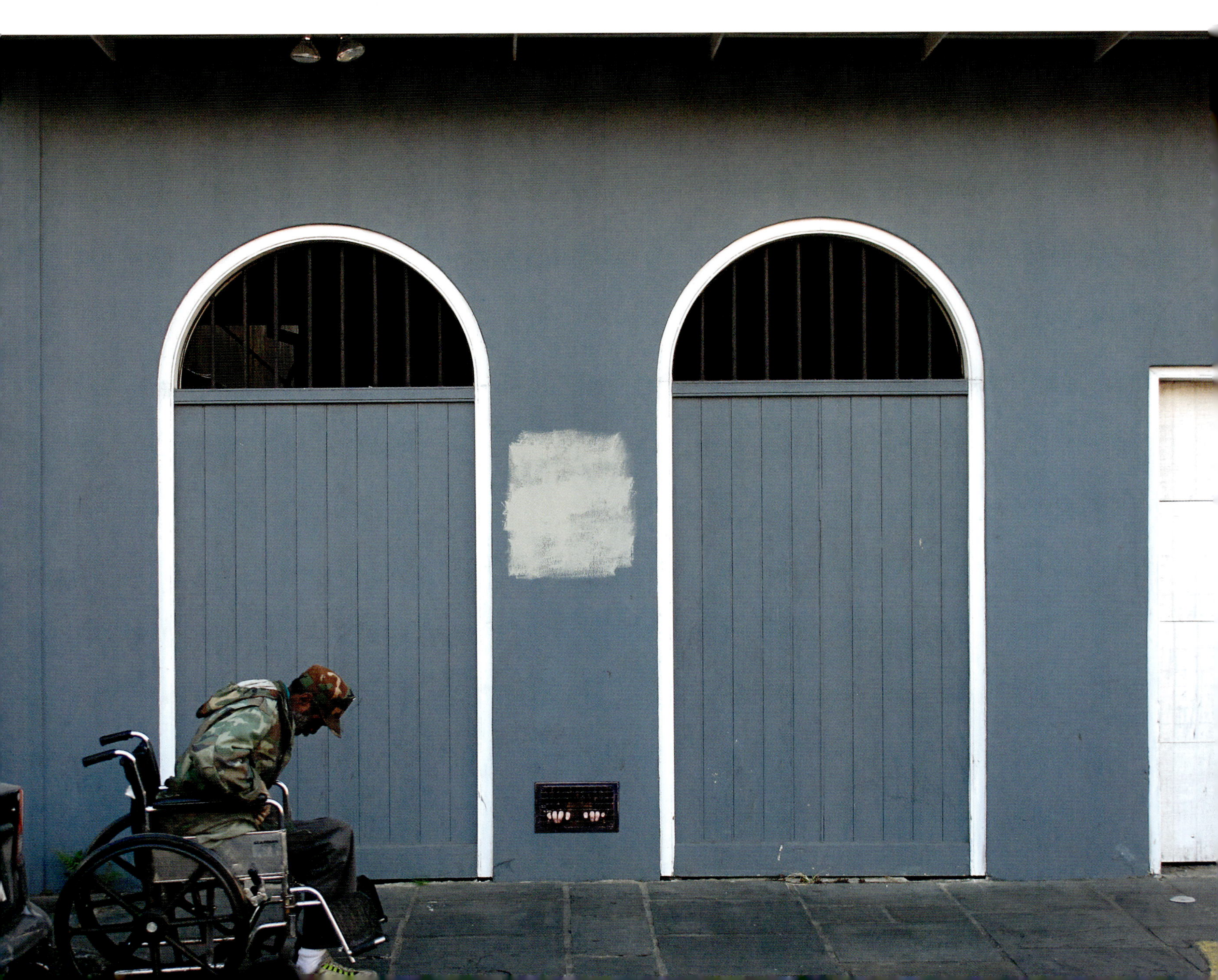

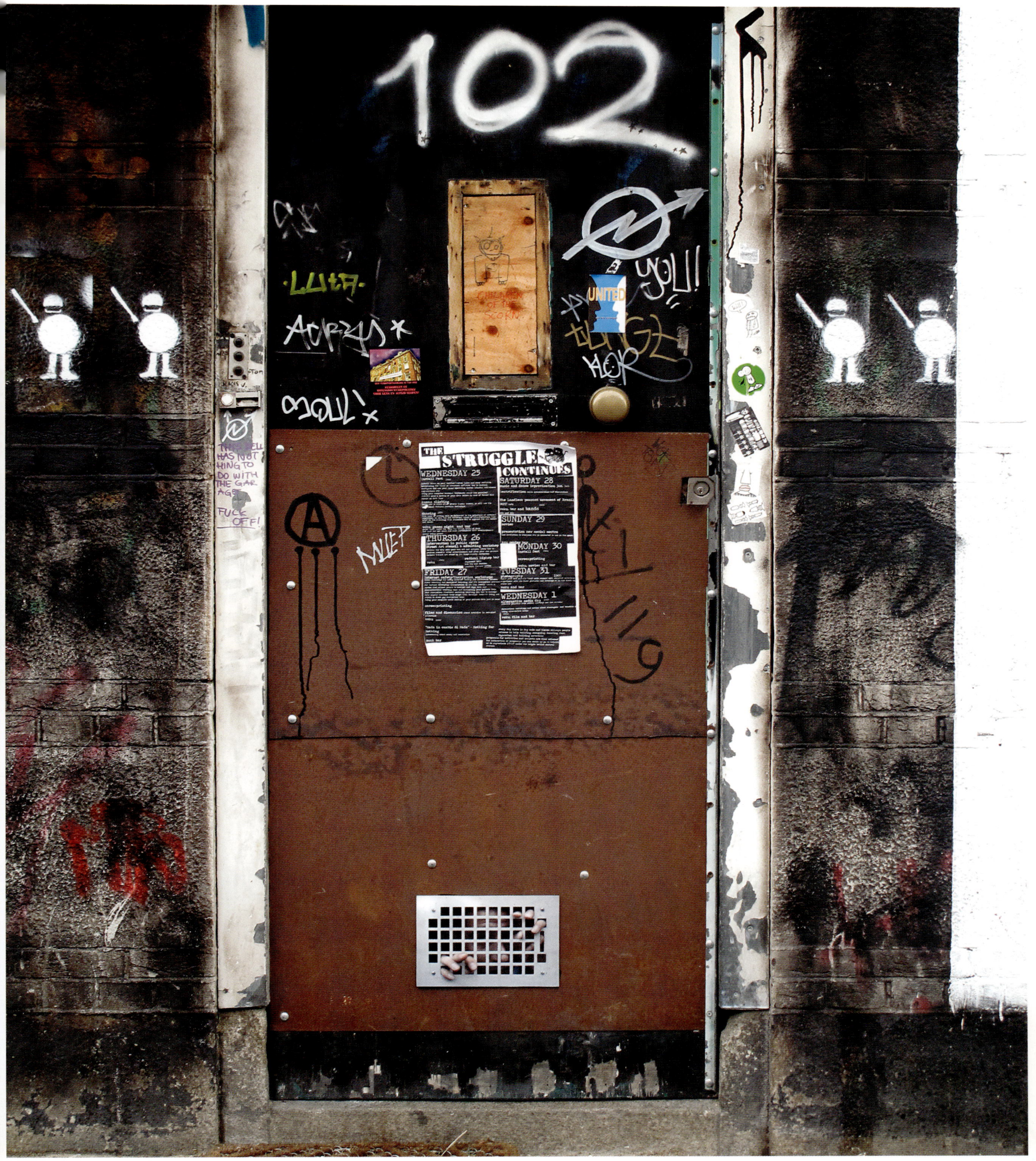
102
THE STRUGGLE CONTINUES
WEDNESDAY 25
SATURDAY 28
SUNDAY 29
THURSDAY 26
MONDAY 30
FRIDAY 27
TUESDAY 31
WEDNESDAY 1
UNITED

DARK DOINGS

2009

Inspired by a visit to Amsterdam's red light district. The window modules are digital and mixed media on vinyl sticker paper embossed onto plastic, then glued to a door. To get the realistic effect I glaze over the vinyl print-out with colored markers, scumble with oil pastels and china markers, then retouch it all with the airbrush.

WILLIAMSBURG, BROOKLYN.

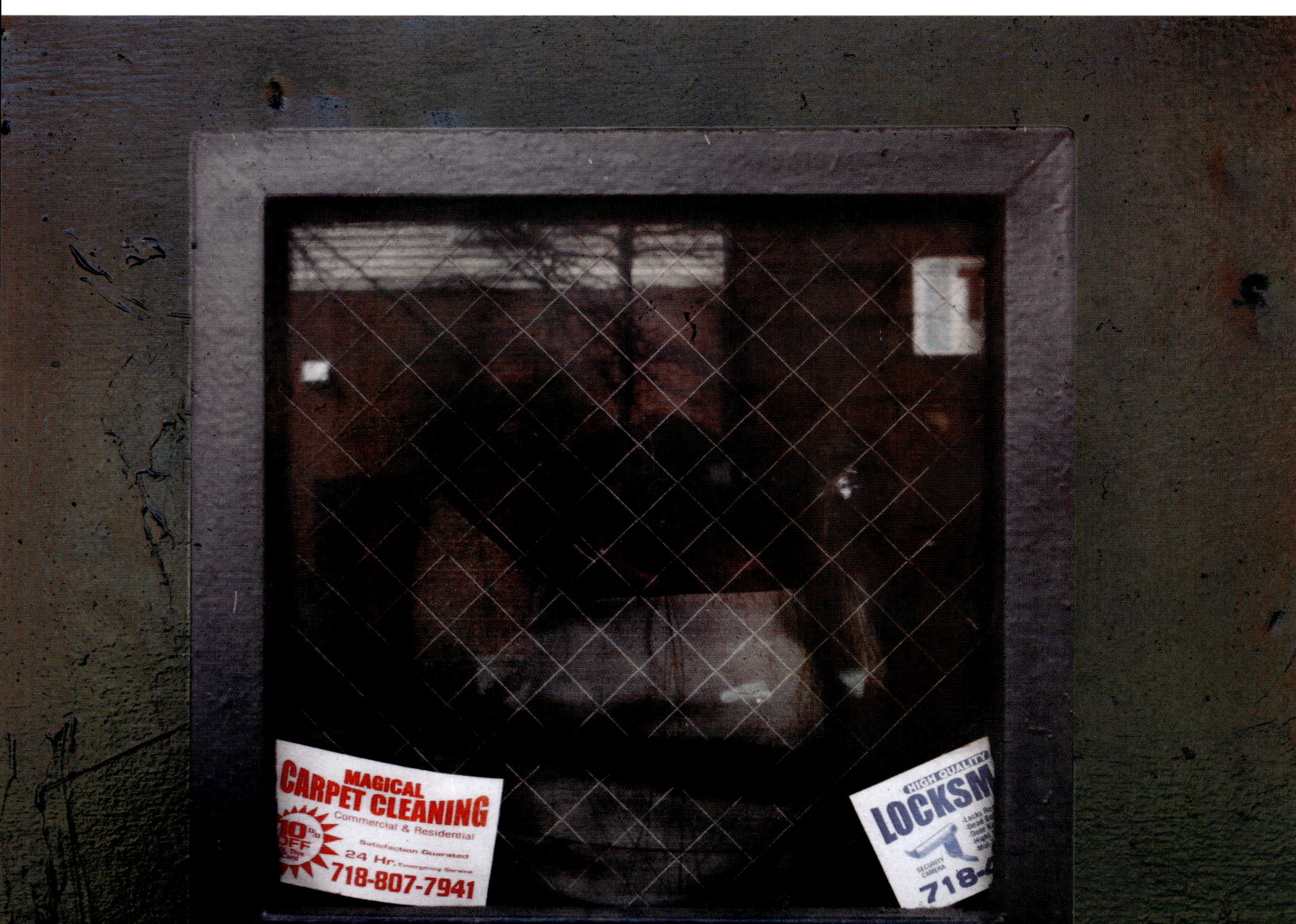

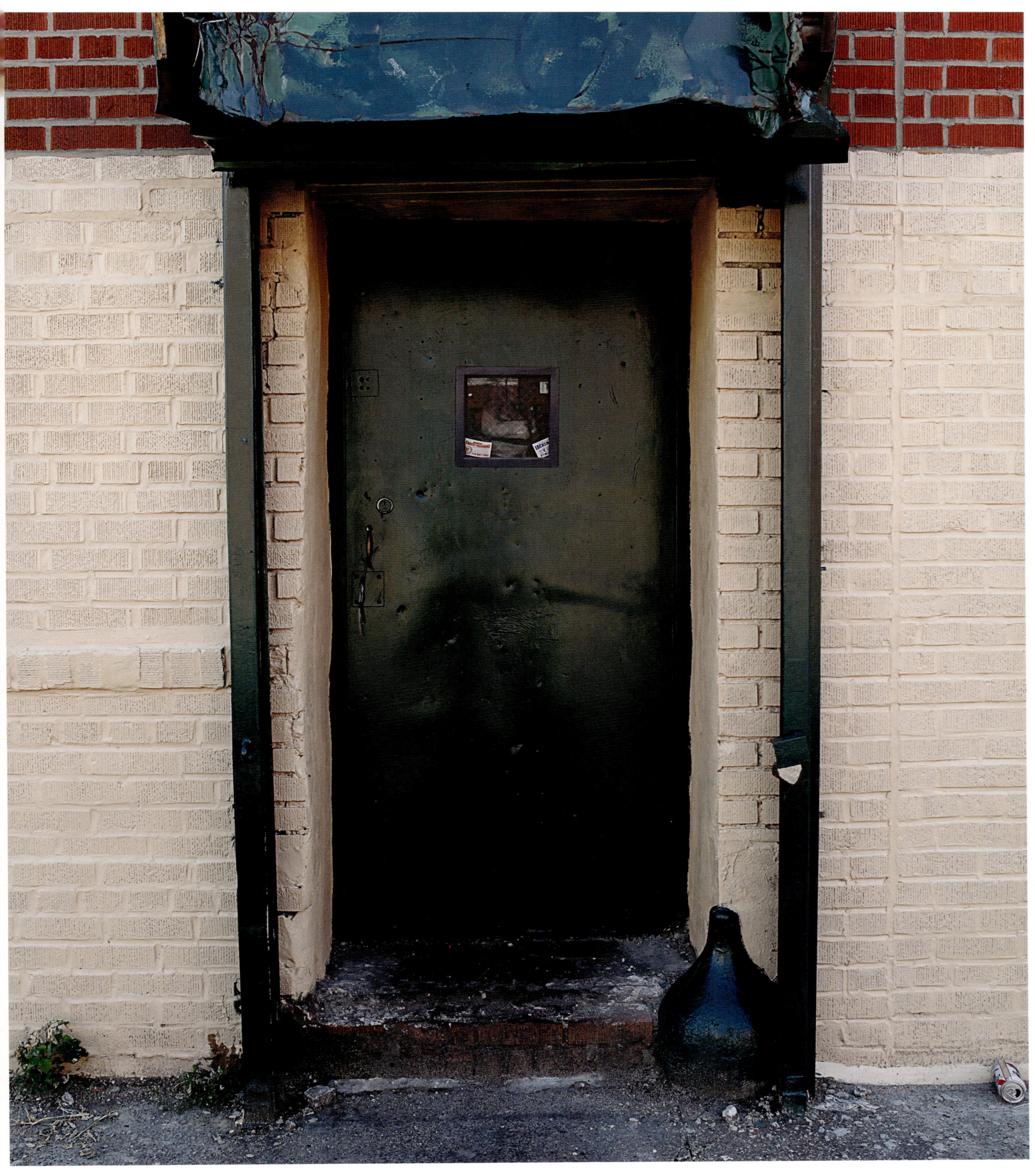

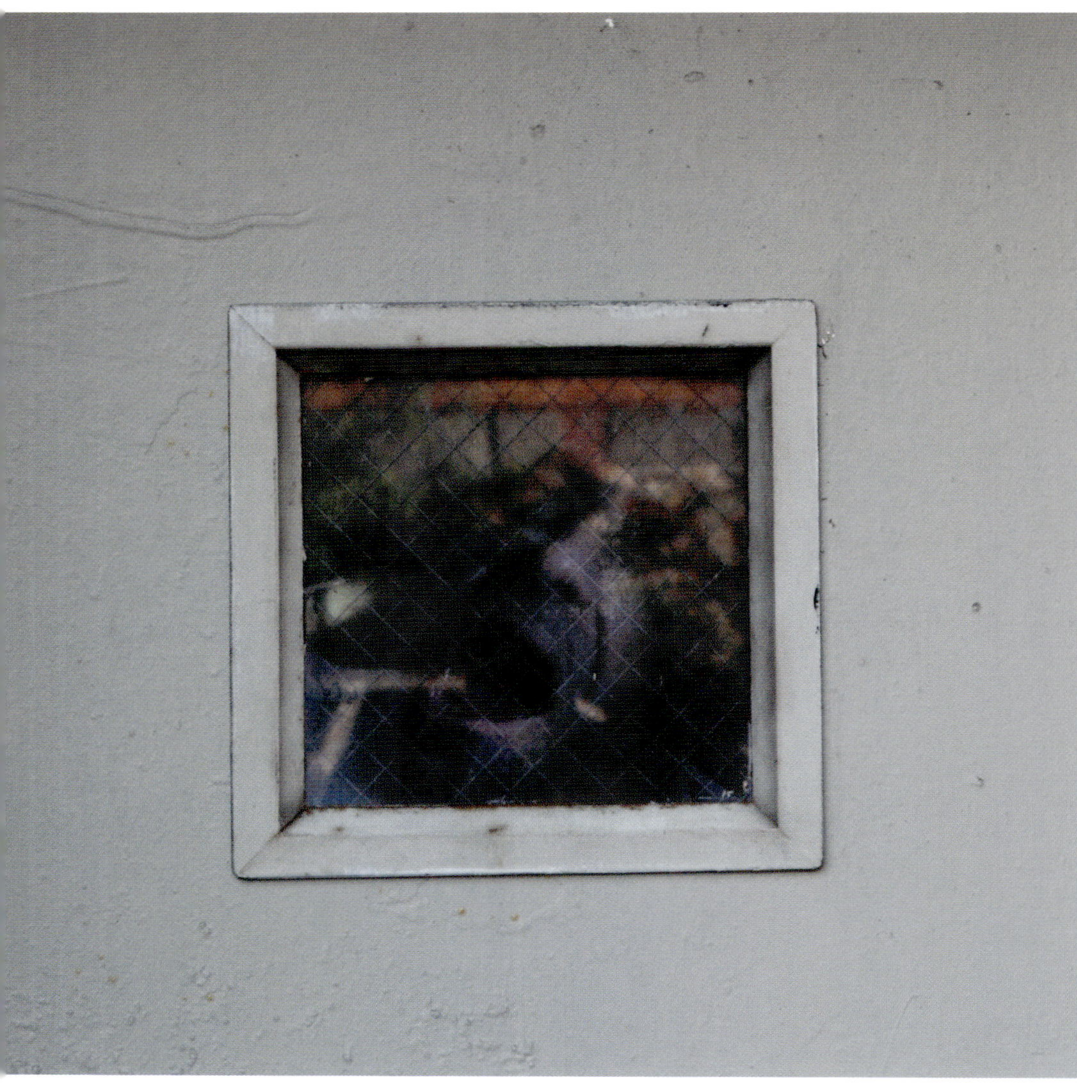

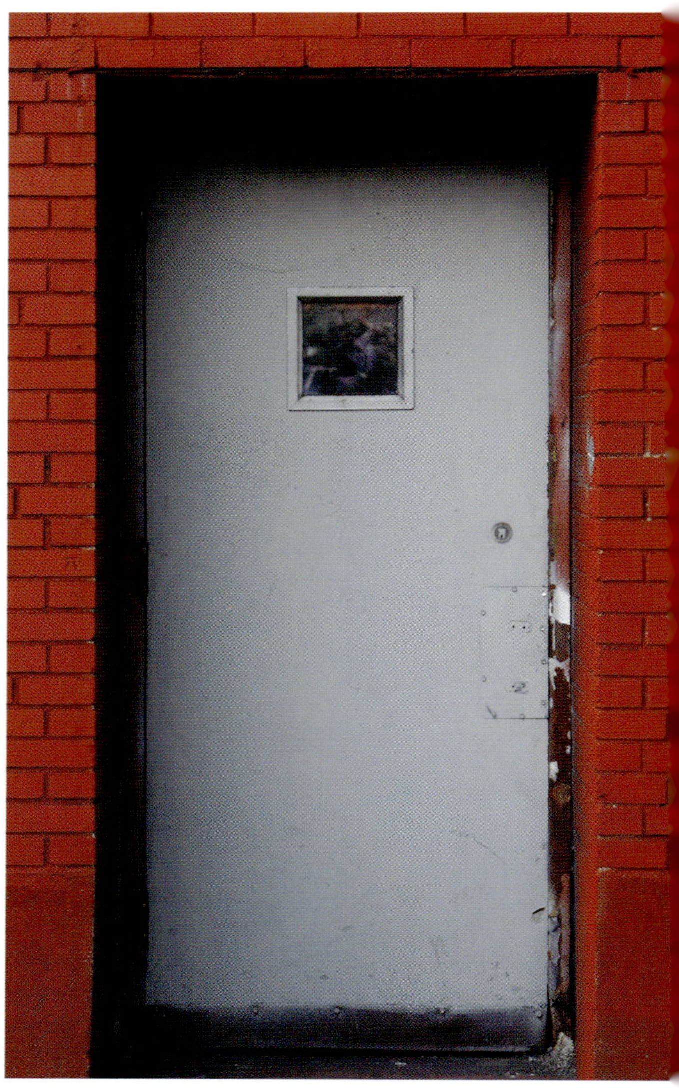

LOWER EAST SIDE, NYC.

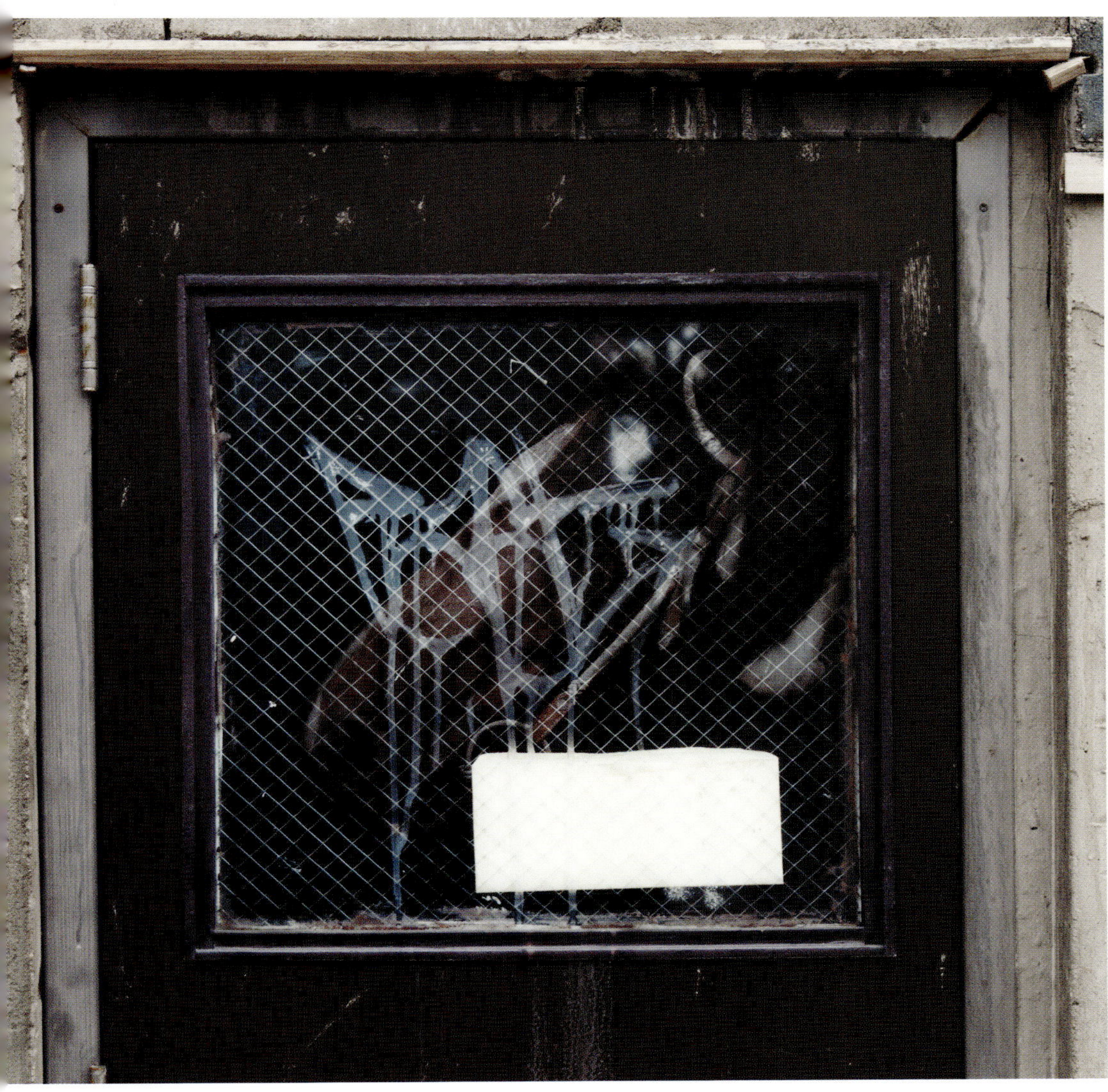

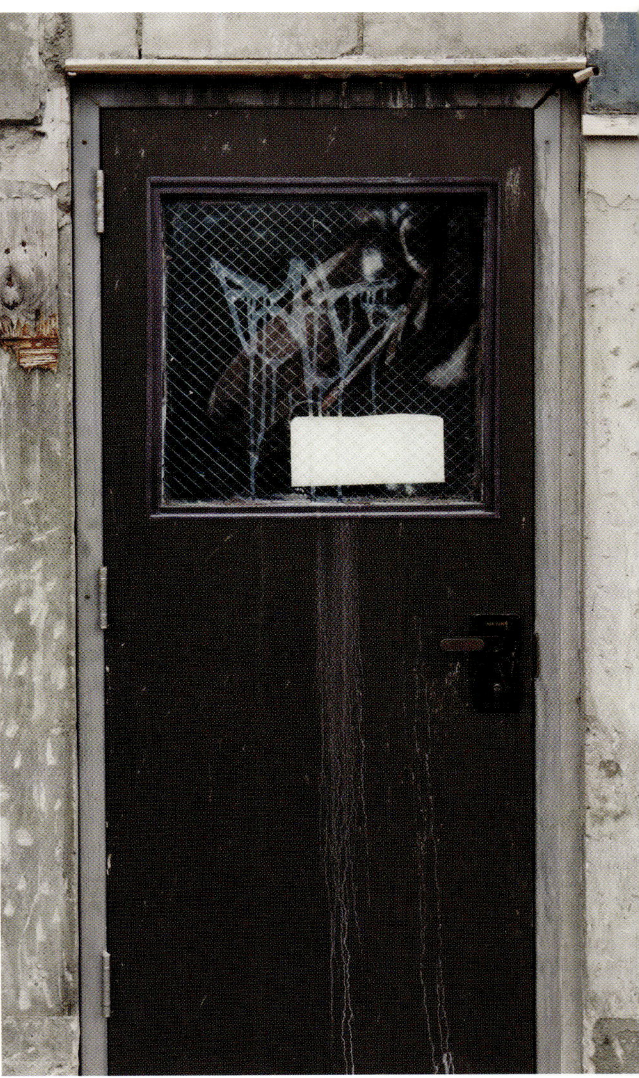

REDHOOK, BROOKLYN.

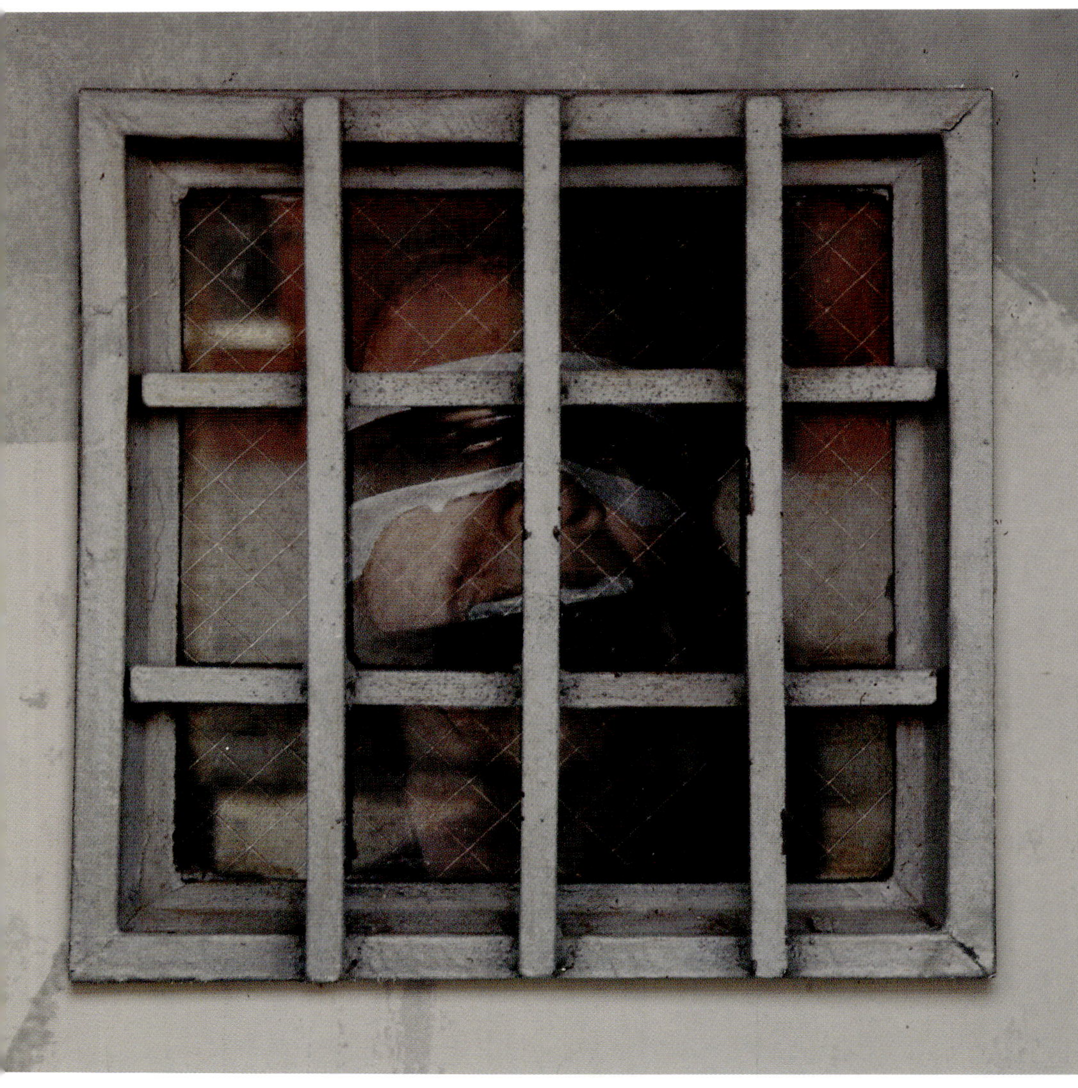

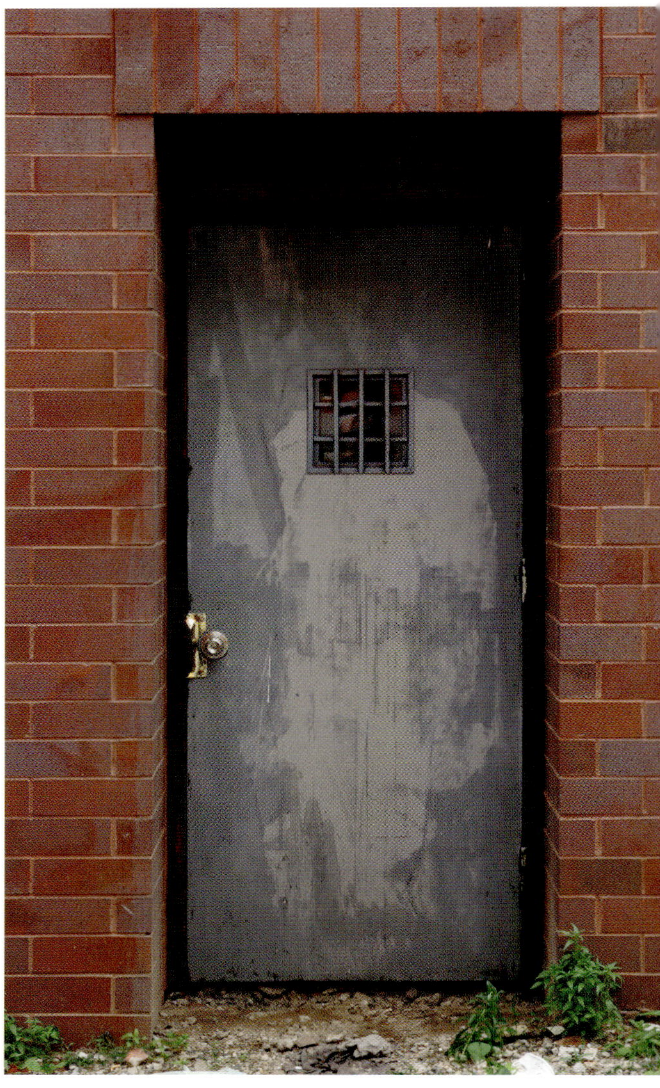

BUSHWICK, BROOKLYN.

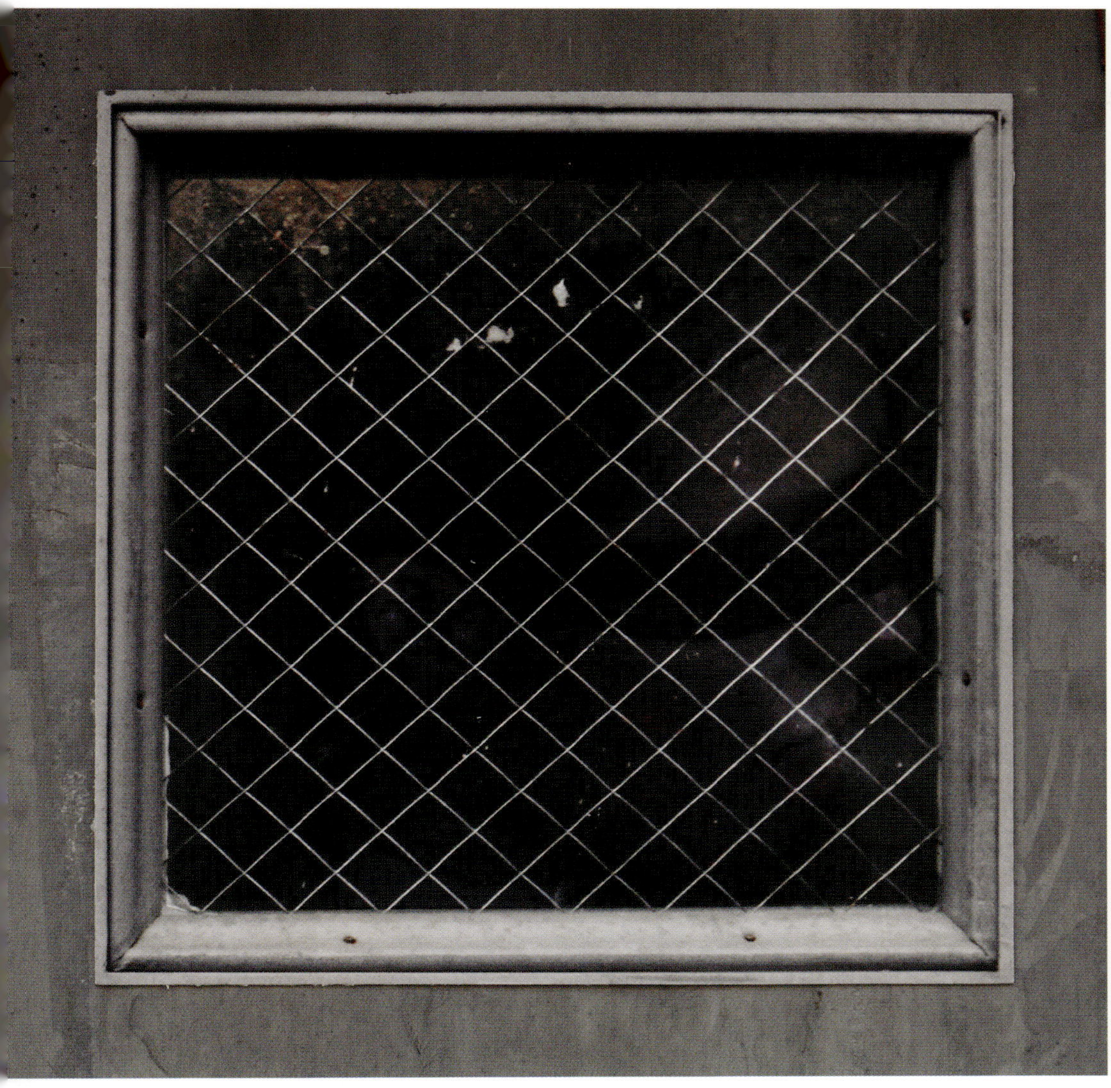

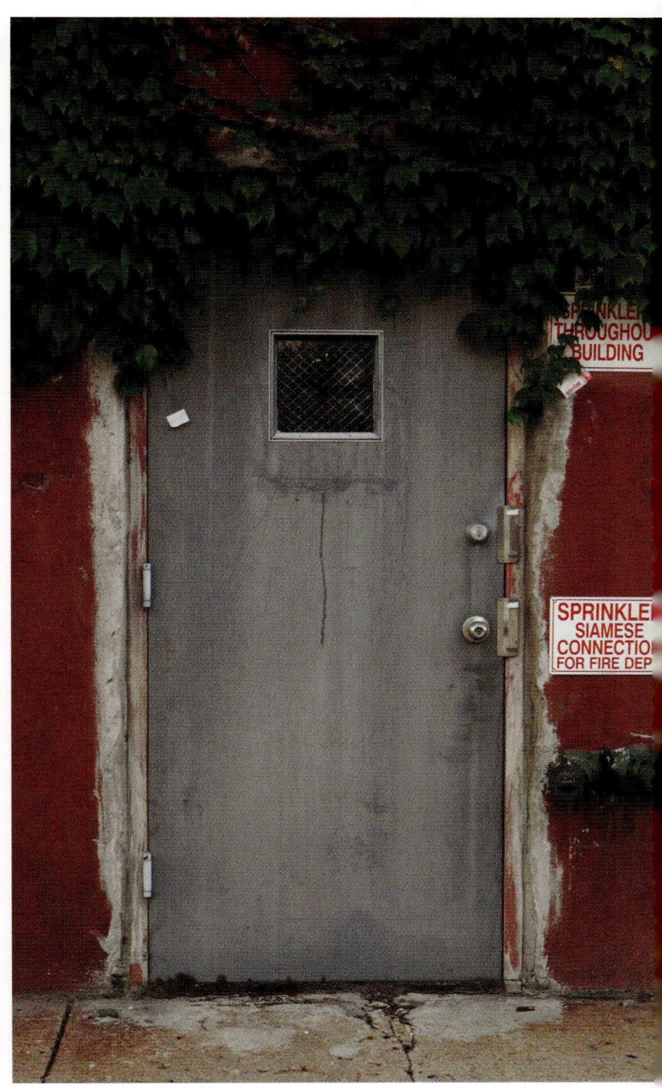

BEDSTUY, BROOKLYN.

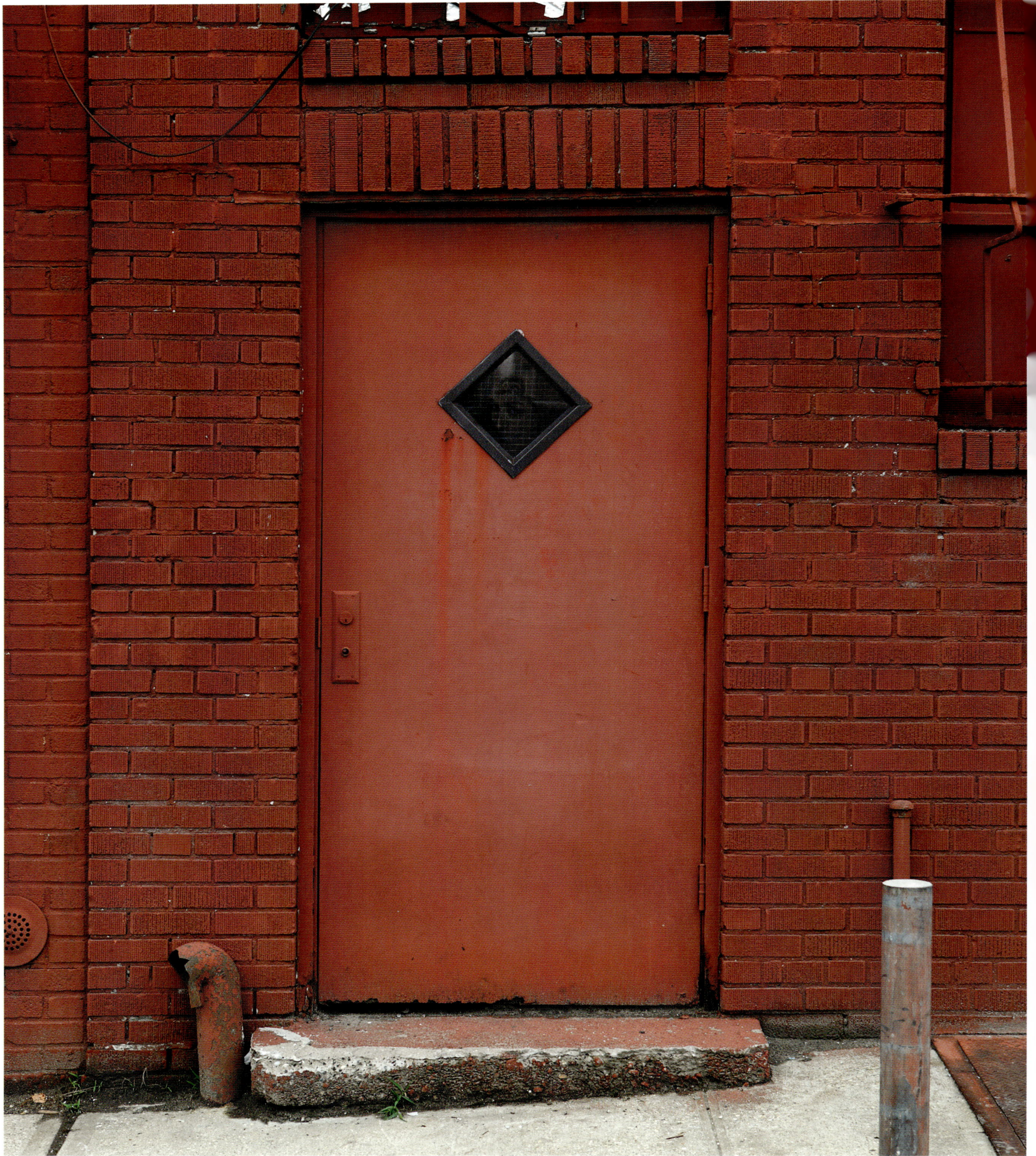

OPPOSITE PAGE:

GREENPOINT, BROOKLYN.

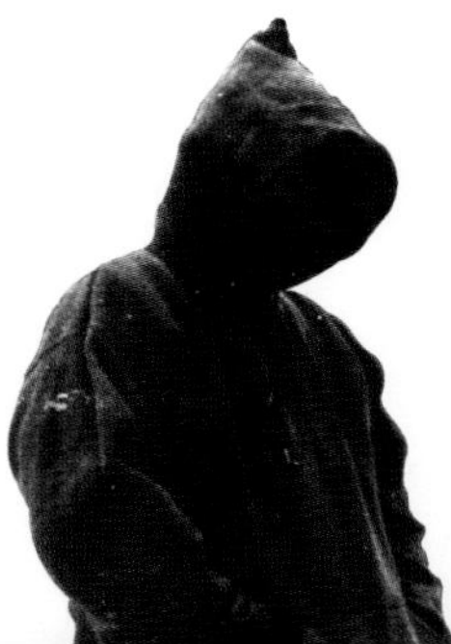

PAINTINGS

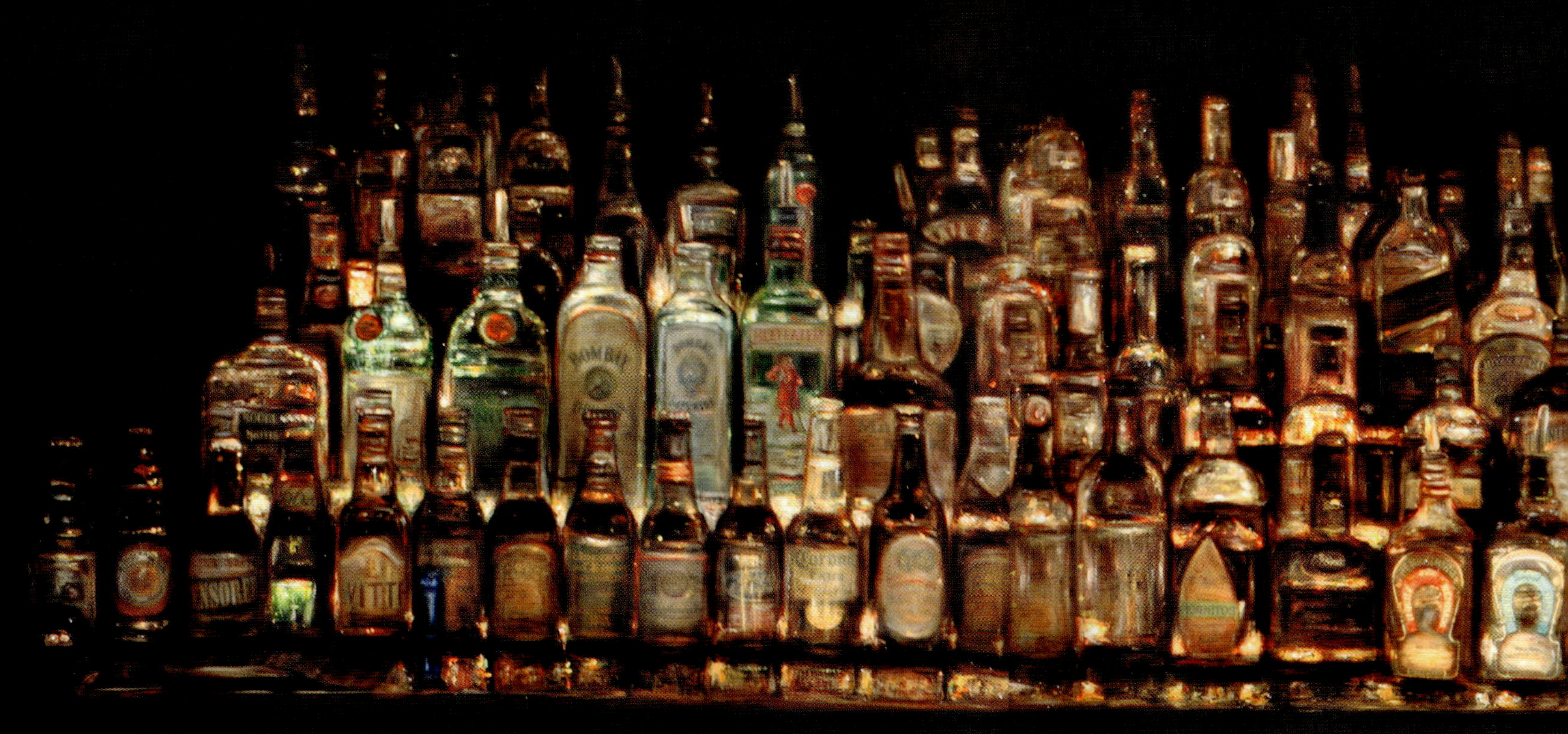

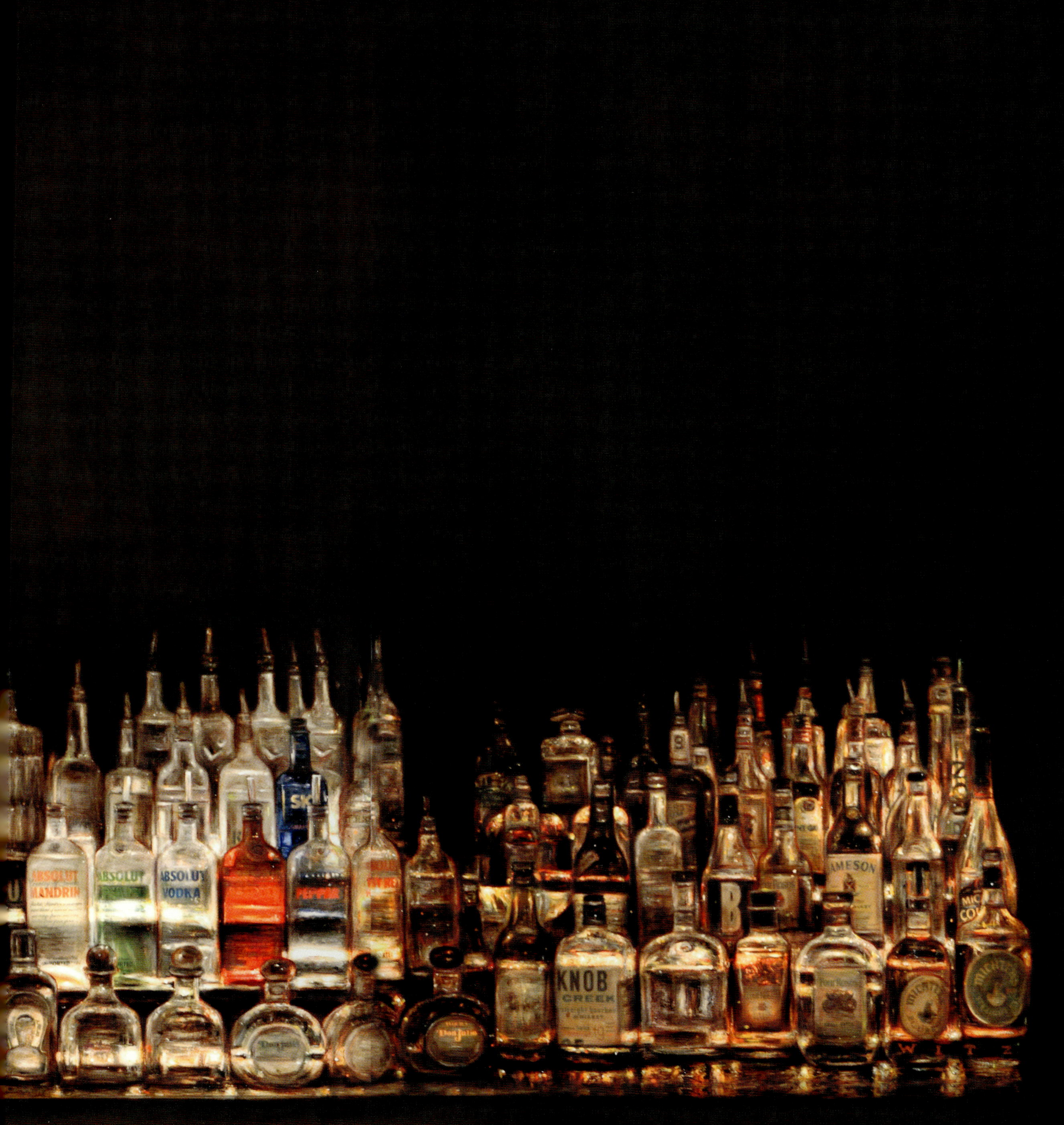
ABSOLUT MANDRIN
ABSOLUT
ABSOLUT VODKA
PEPPER
JAMESON
KNOB CREEK

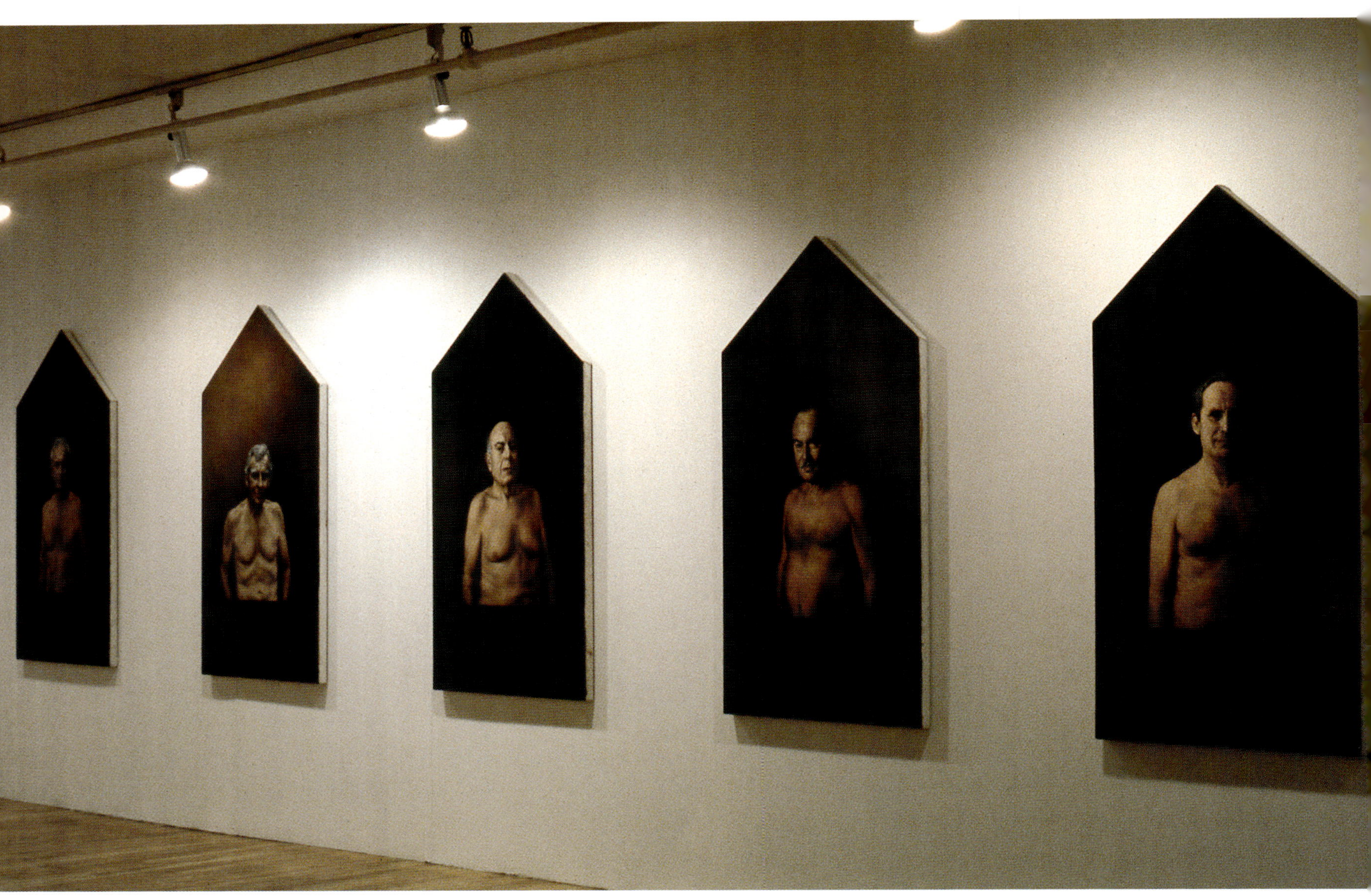

ABOVE:

SEMAPHORE GALLERY, NY., NY., 1985, // Installation shot of my first one man show.

OPPOSITE PAGE:

MAN #5, 1984. // Oil on canvas. Private Collection.

TRIPTYCH, PREVIOUS PAGE:

BAR SHRINE. // Oil and digital media on canvas.

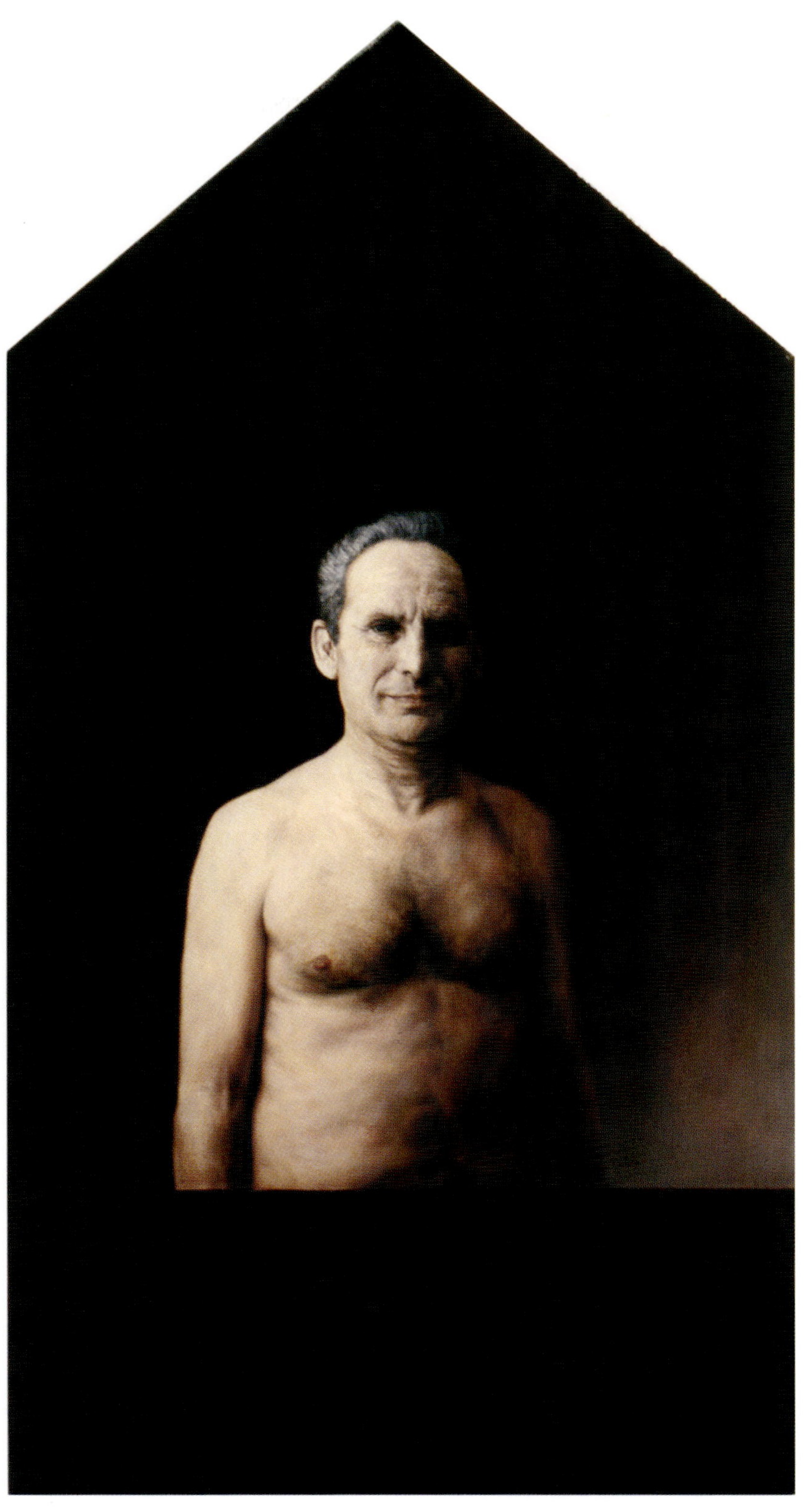

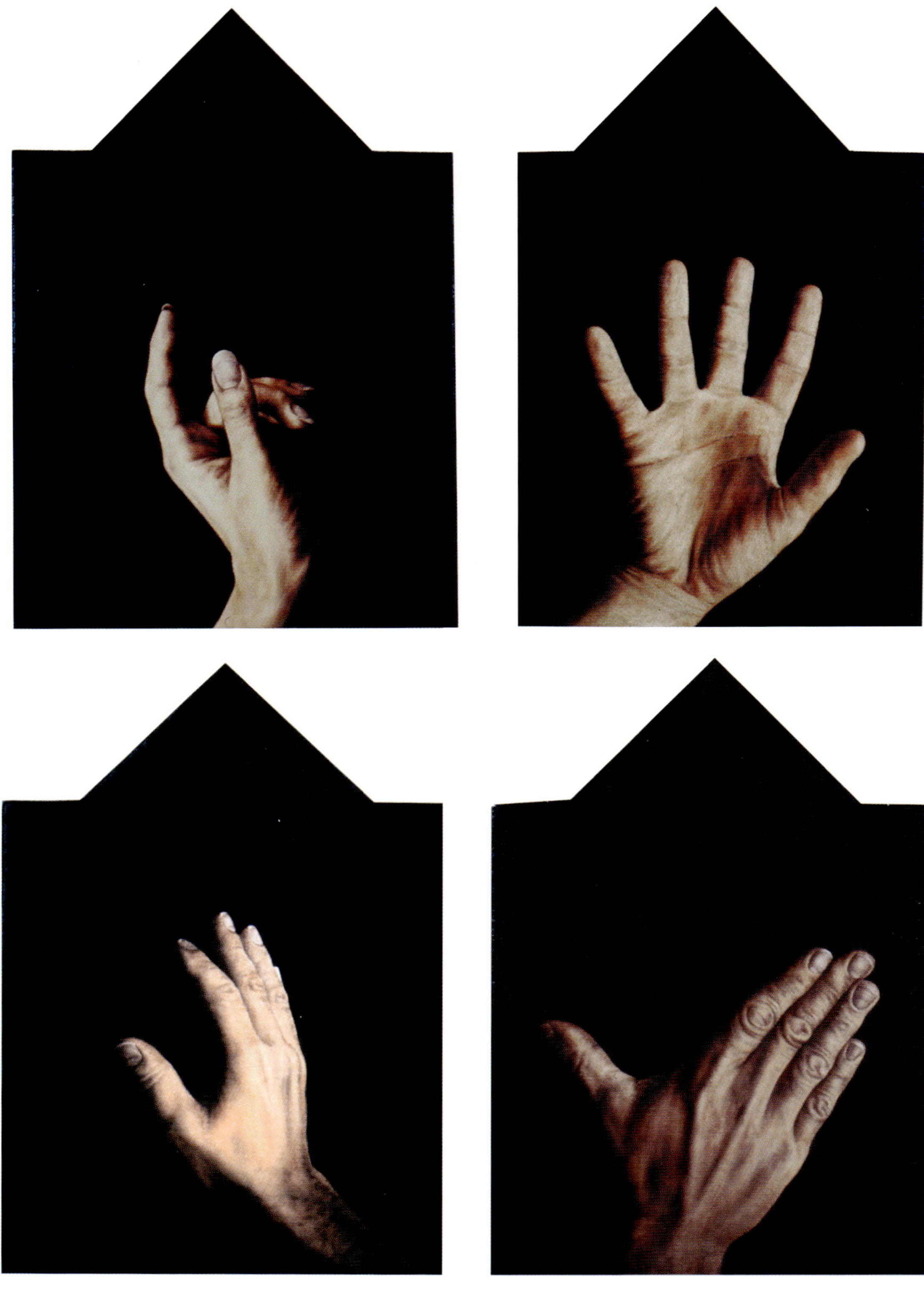

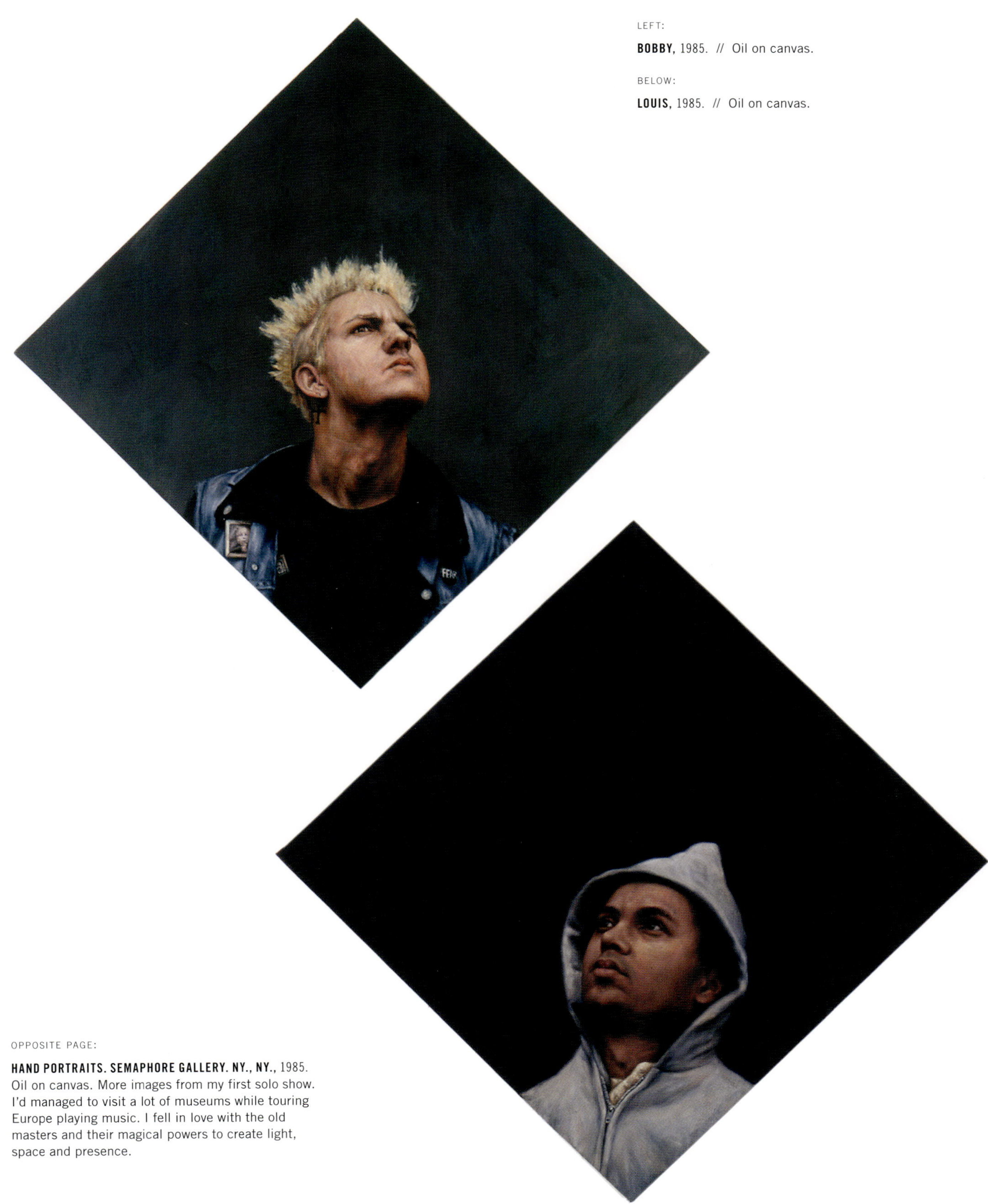

LEFT:

BOBBY, 1985. // Oil on canvas.

BELOW:

LOUIS, 1985. // Oil on canvas.

OPPOSITE PAGE:

HAND PORTRAITS. SEMAPHORE GALLERY. NY., NY., 1985. Oil on canvas. More images from my first solo show. I'd managed to visit a lot of museums while touring Europe playing music. I fell in love with the old masters and their magical powers to create light, space and presence.

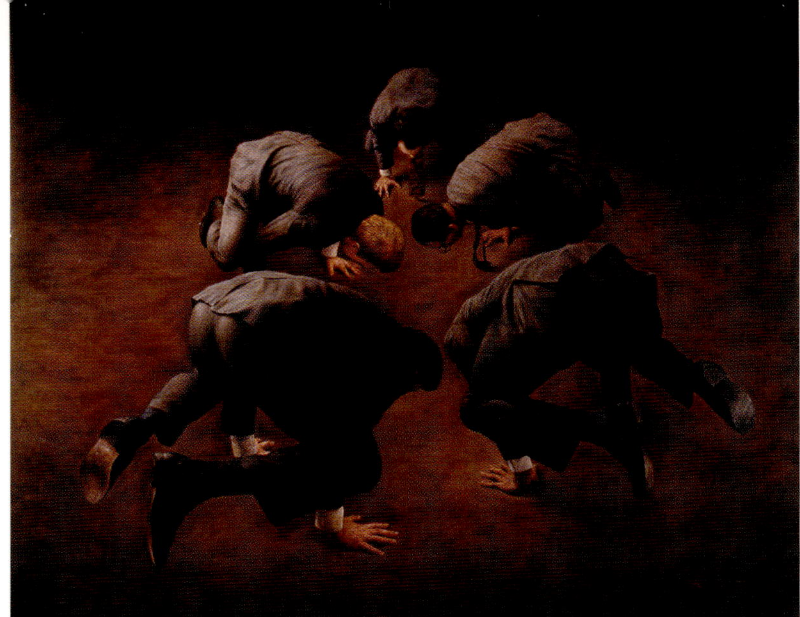

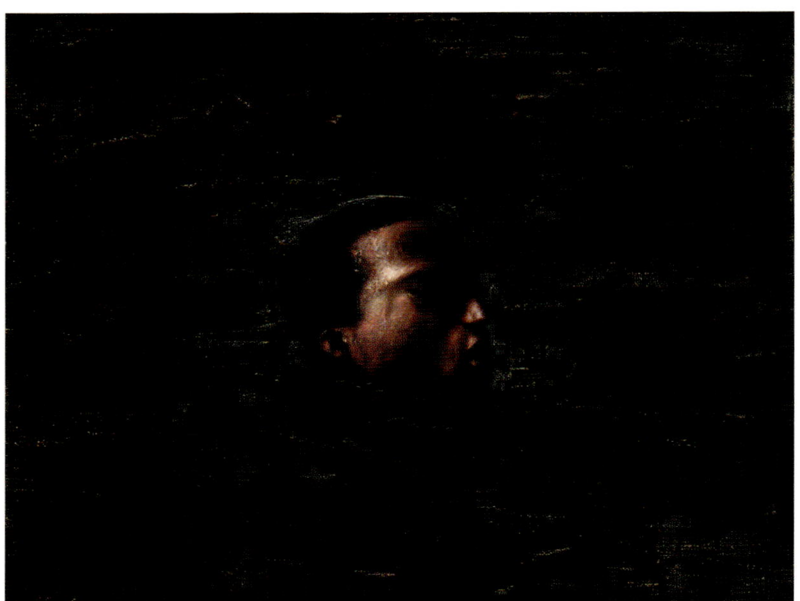

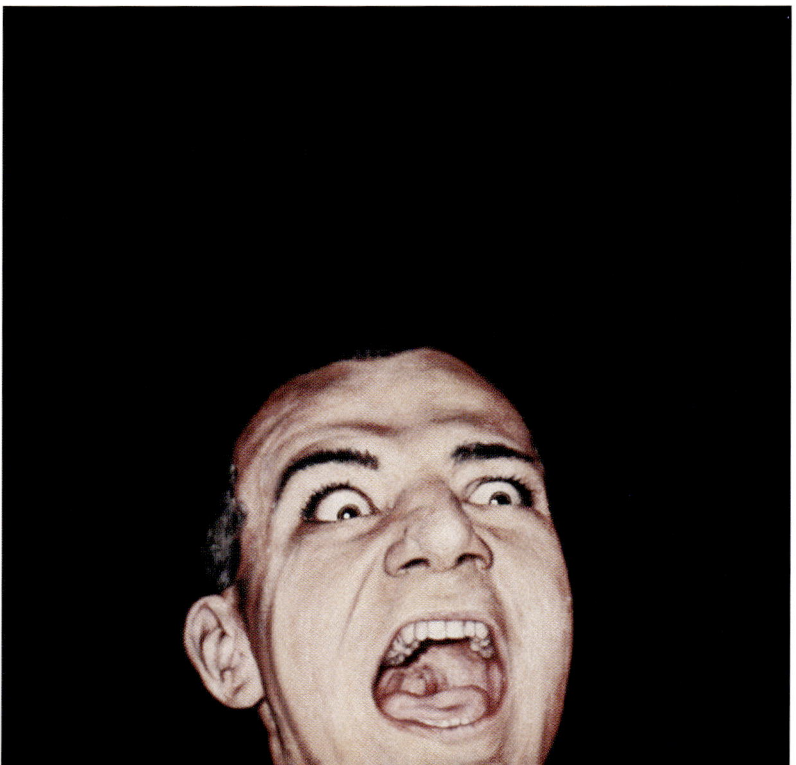

TOP:

UNTITLED (BUSINESSMEN), 1995.
Oil on canvas. Private collection.

MIDDLE:

SWIMMER, 1986.
Oil on canvas. Private collection.

BOTTOM:

DAVID (SCREAMING), 1986.
Oil on canvas. Private collection.

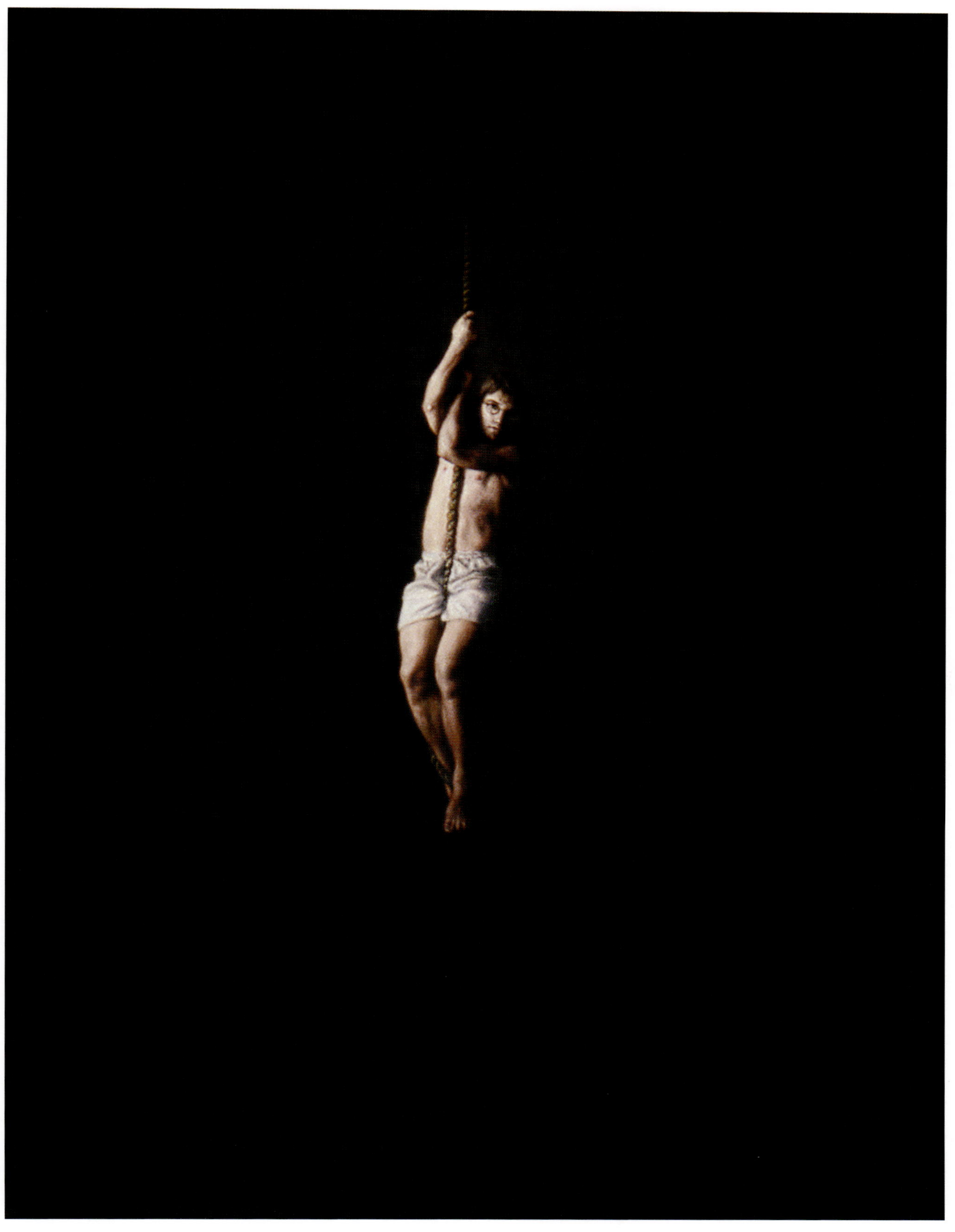

DAVE, 1987. // Oil on canvas. Private collection.

NEXT SPREAD, P.194–195:
RATS, 2003. // Oil on canvas.

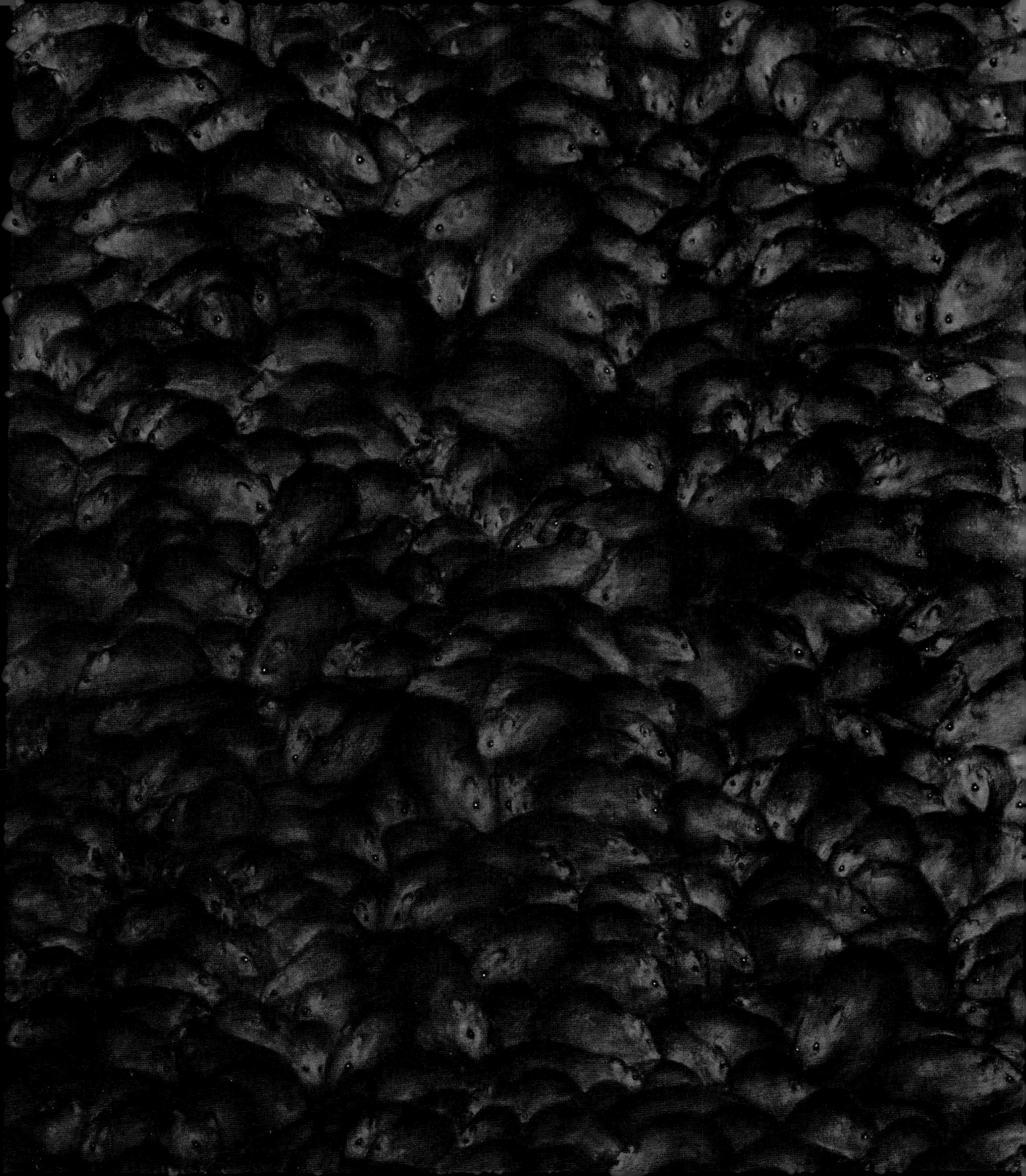

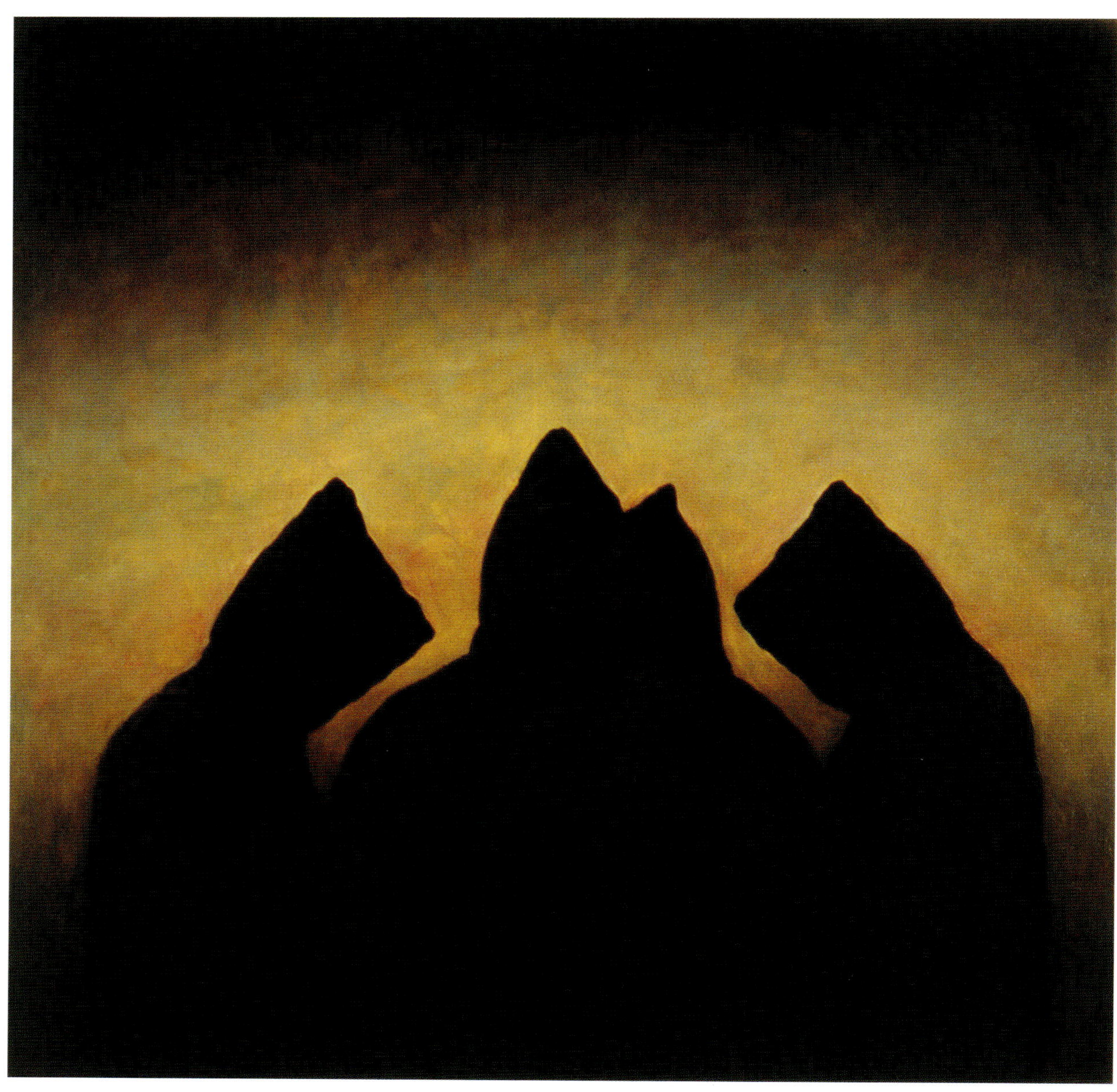

HOODYS, 1995. // Oil on canvas. Private collection. Images from my street works occasionally find their way into my paintings.

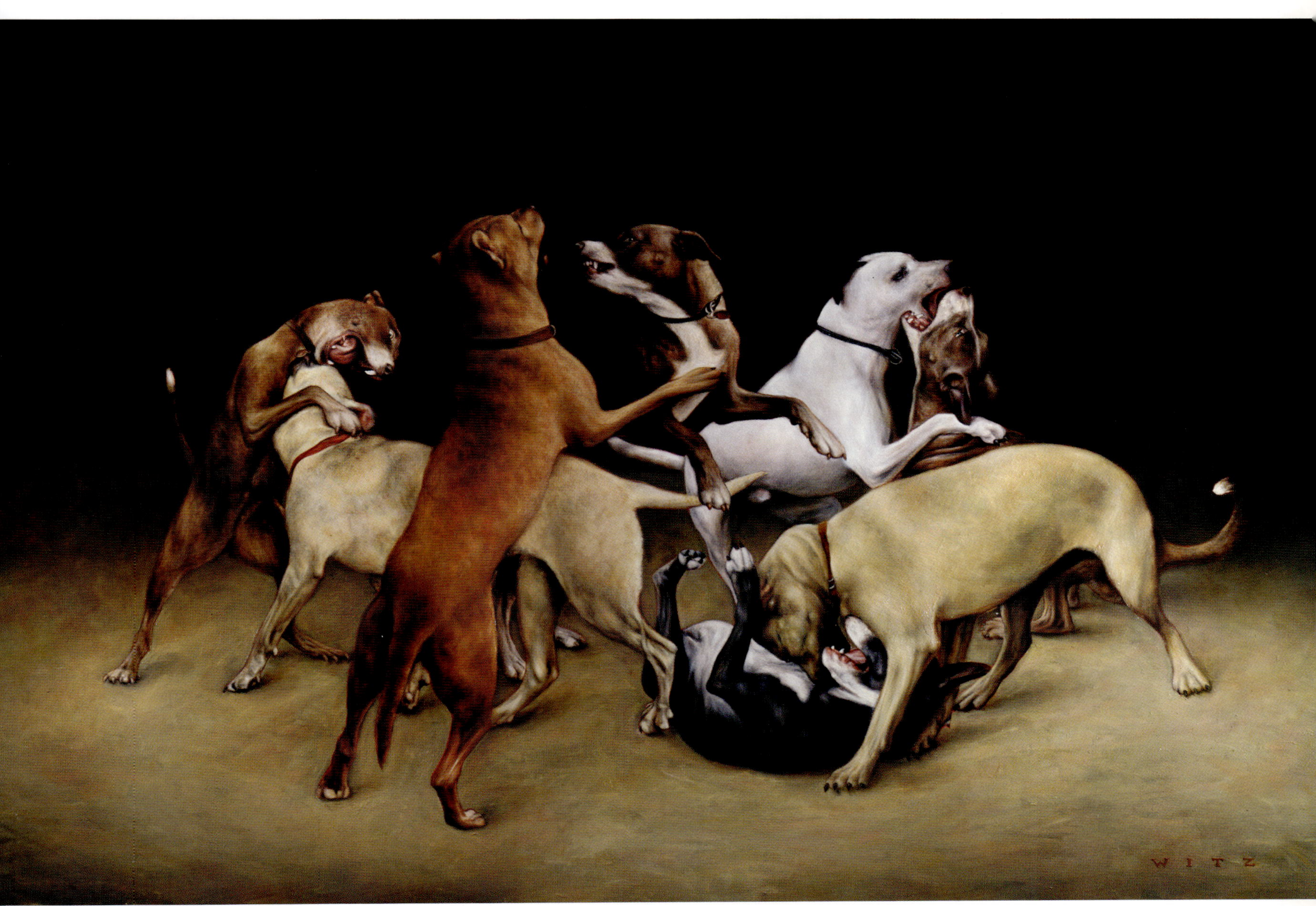

RIGHT:

DOGS FIGHTING, 1996. // Oil on canvas. Private Collection.

NEXT PAGE, DIPTYCH:

DOGS FIGHTING, 2004. // Oil and digital media on canvas.

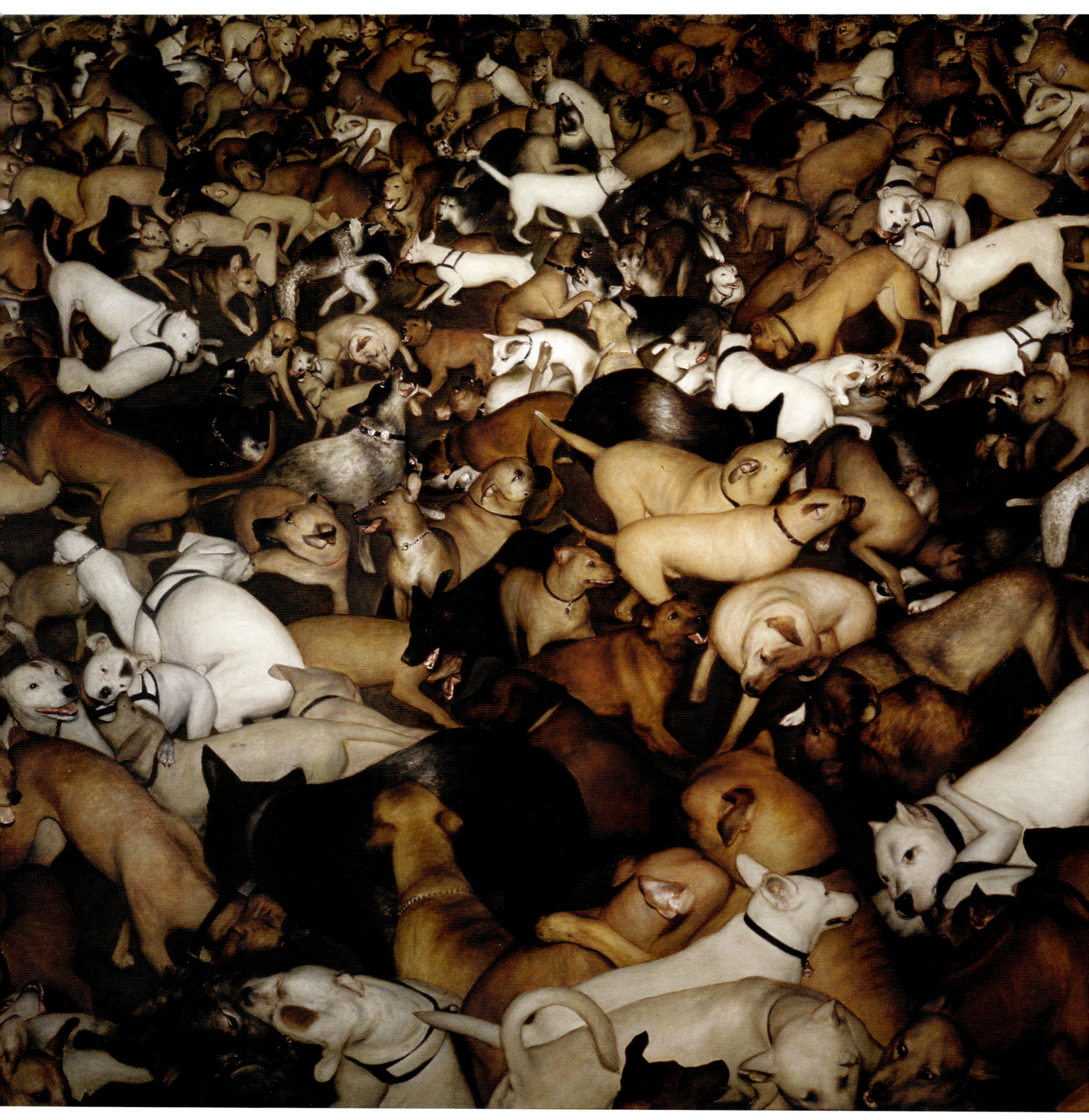

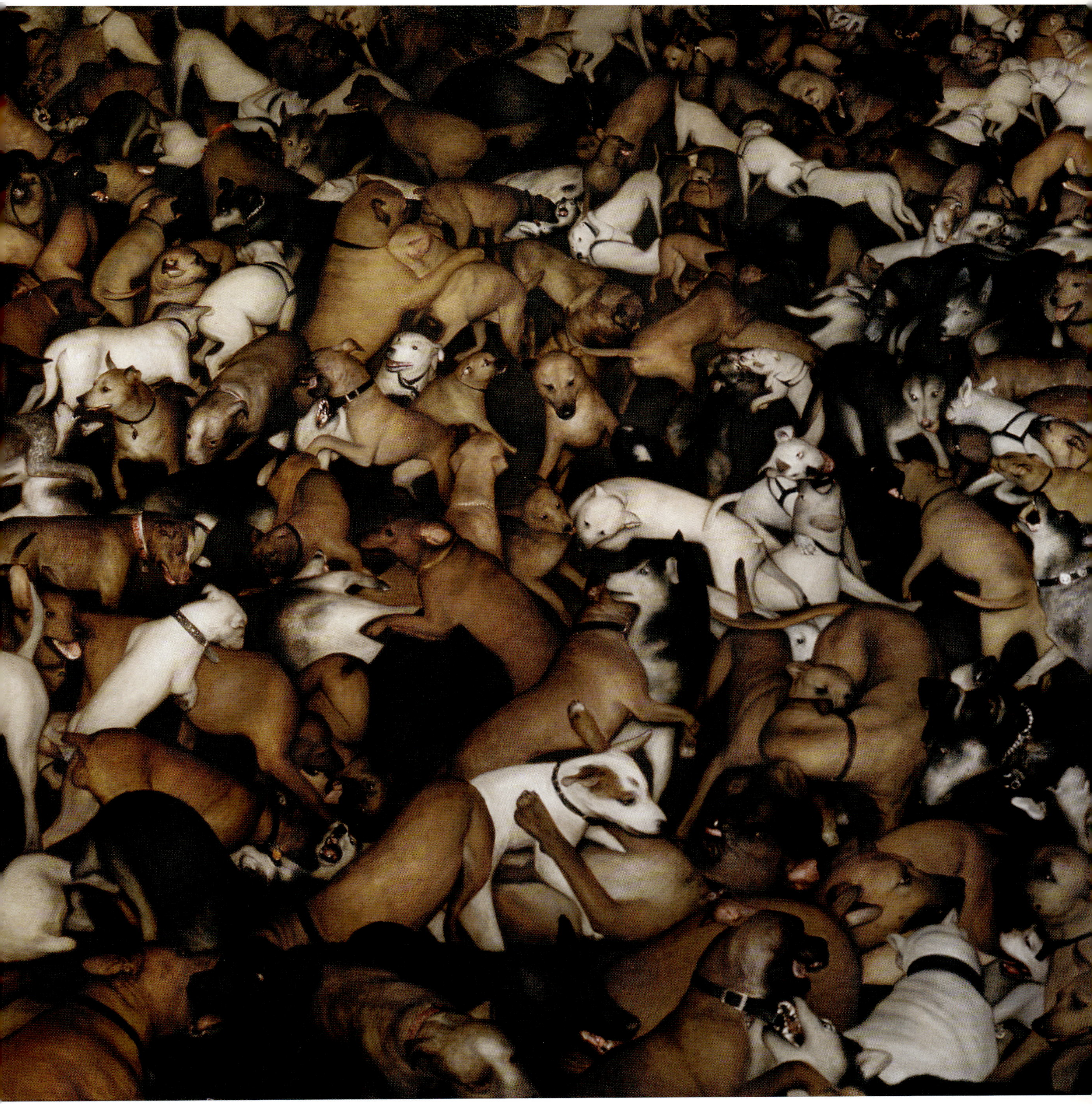

SELF PORTRAITS

1980, 1989

Every year or so I like to do a self portrait. My interest isn't so much in recording a likeness; it's more about examining personal narratives of the time.

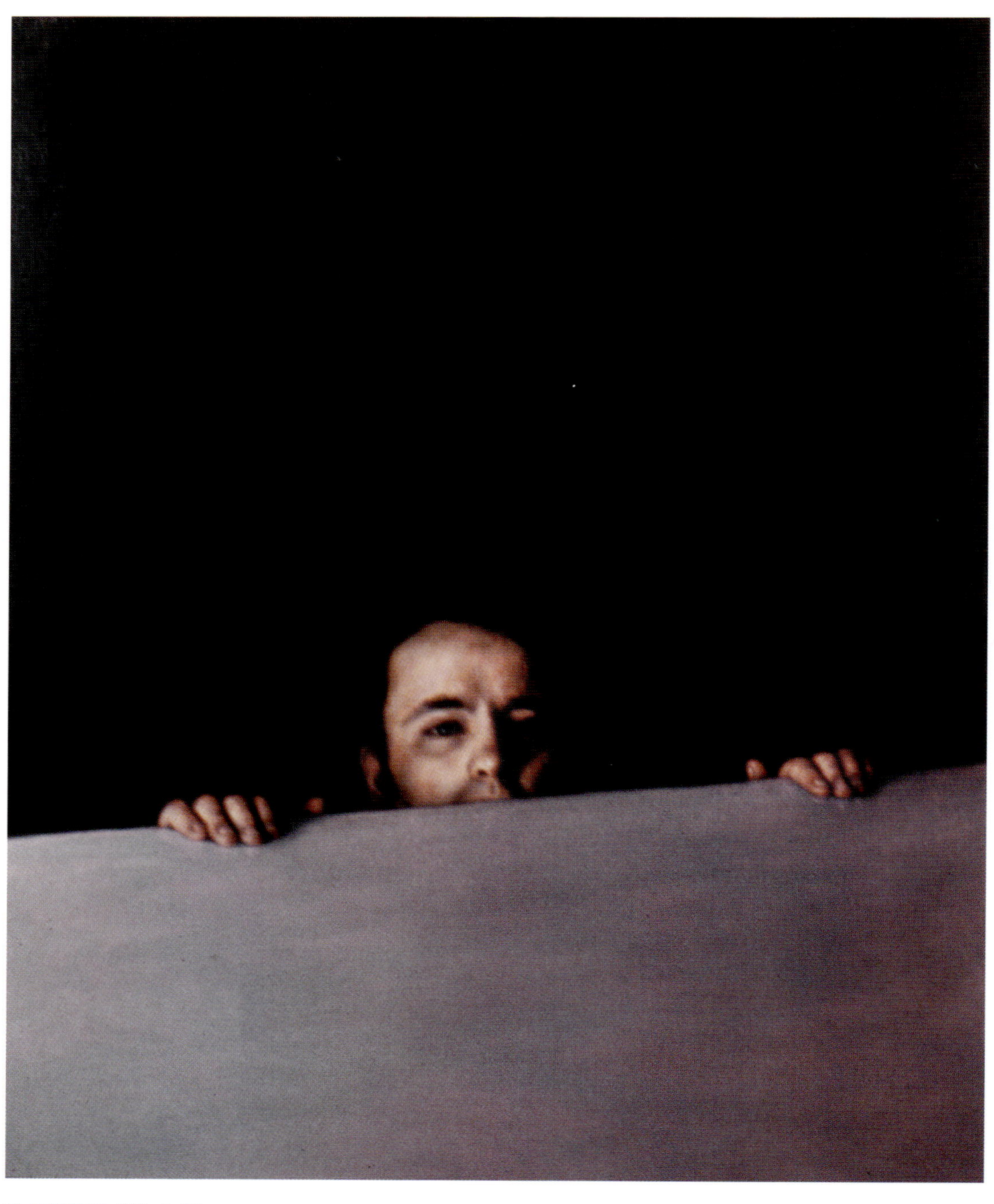

SELF PORTRAIT, 1980. // Oil on canvas.

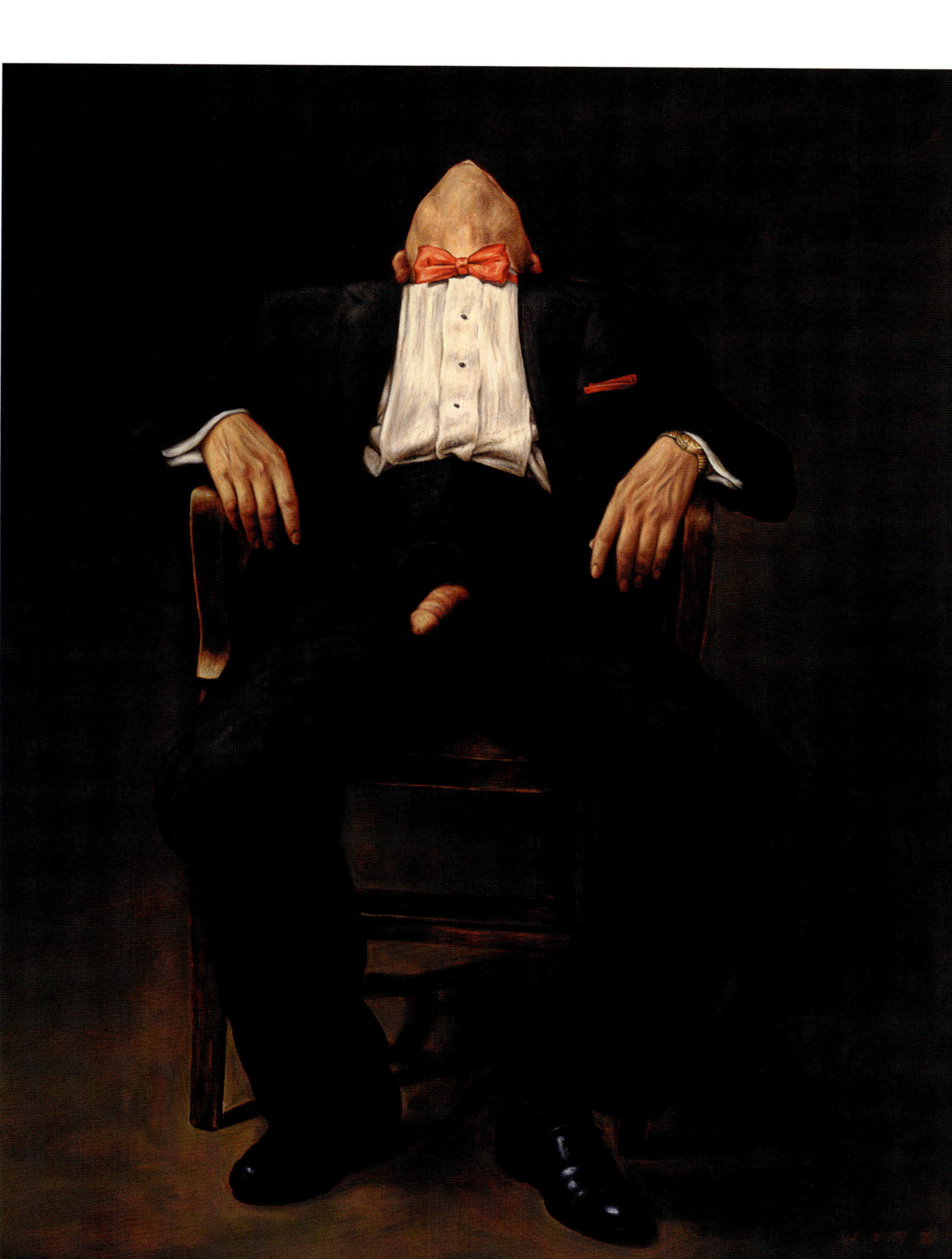

SELF PORTRAIT, 1989. // Oil on canvas. Private collection.

MOSH PITS

2000

Back in the mid 90s I started painting over my photographs so that I could mass produce stickers. Starting in 2001 I adapted a version of that technique for my canvases. It's been a huge boon to my work. Things that would have been impossible or would have taken months of soul crushing labor are now practical and do-able. There came a point where I had to make a decision: Do I use photography and digital sampling to push my representational possibilites further along, even though the purists might dismiss it–do I accept someone else's cut-off point, or do I push ahead and see how far I can go?

Ironically, most of what I was taught about representational painting was about trying to catch up with the past. In school we were always trying to figure out how the old masters got such sophisticated effects. I think that if Vermeer or Rubens or whoever could see what is possible today, they'd be intrigued; they'd accept that advancements in the science are inevitable and good.

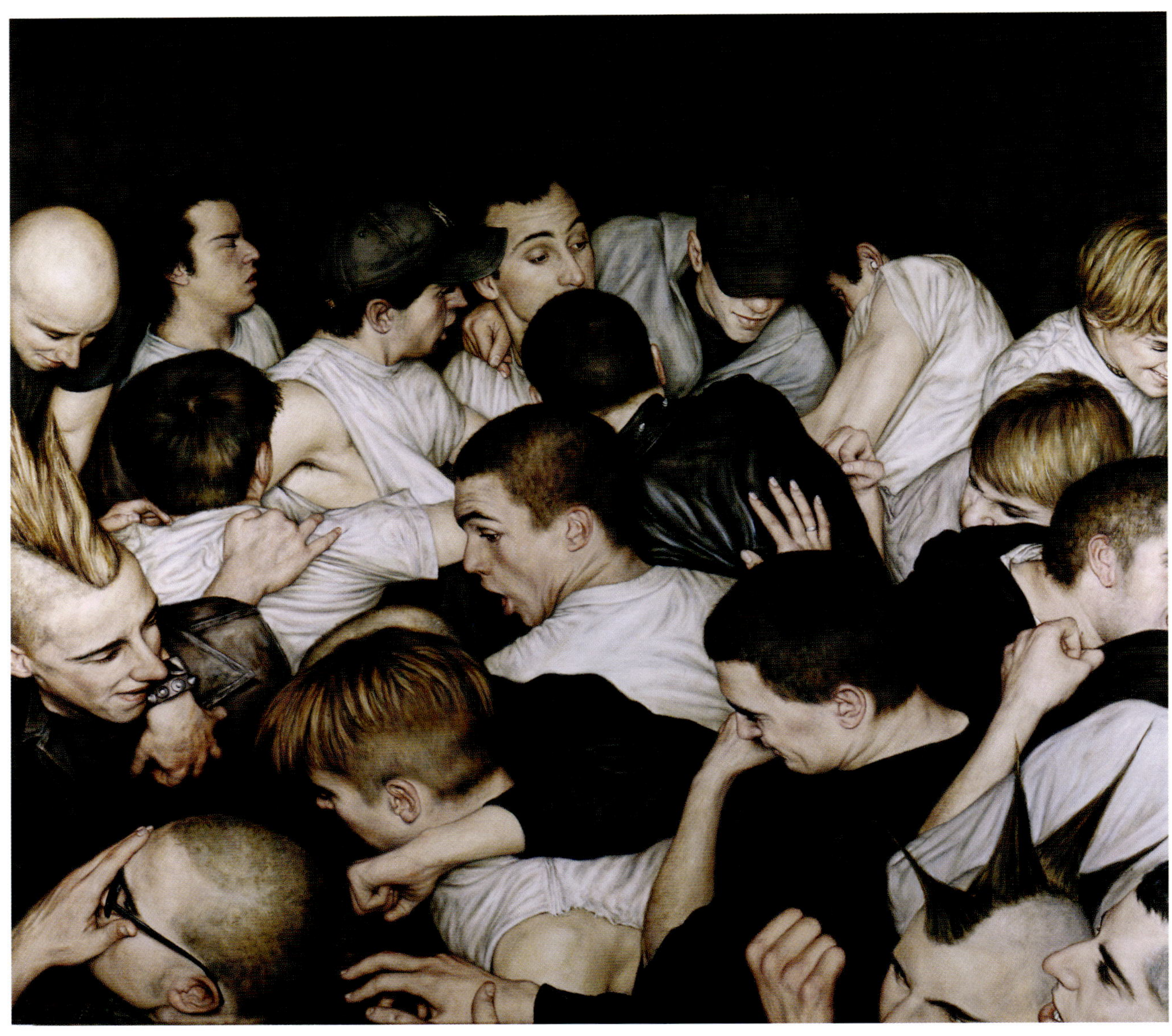

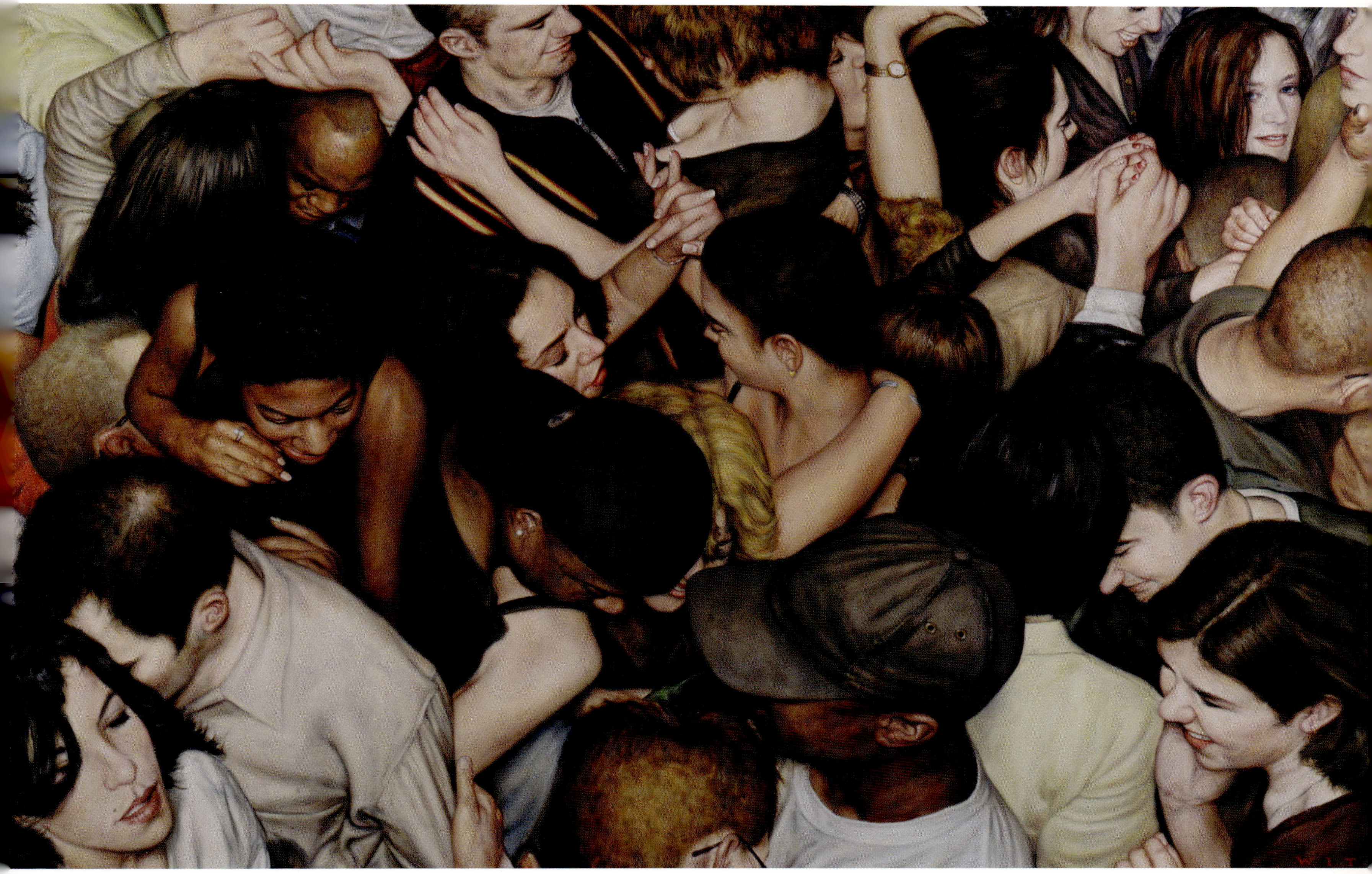

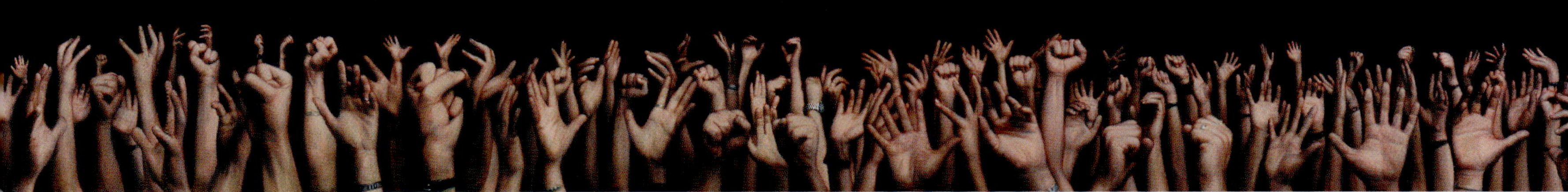

OPPOSITE PAGE:

MOSH PIT, 2000. // Oil on canvas. Private collection. The last of my slide projector compositions.

THIS PAGE, TOP:

SAPPHIRE LOUNGE, 2000. // Oil and canvas.

THIS PAGE, BOTTOM:

HAND FRIEZE, 2001. // Oil and digital media on canvas.

NEXT SPREAD:

BIG MOSH PIT, 2007. // Oil and digital media on canvas.

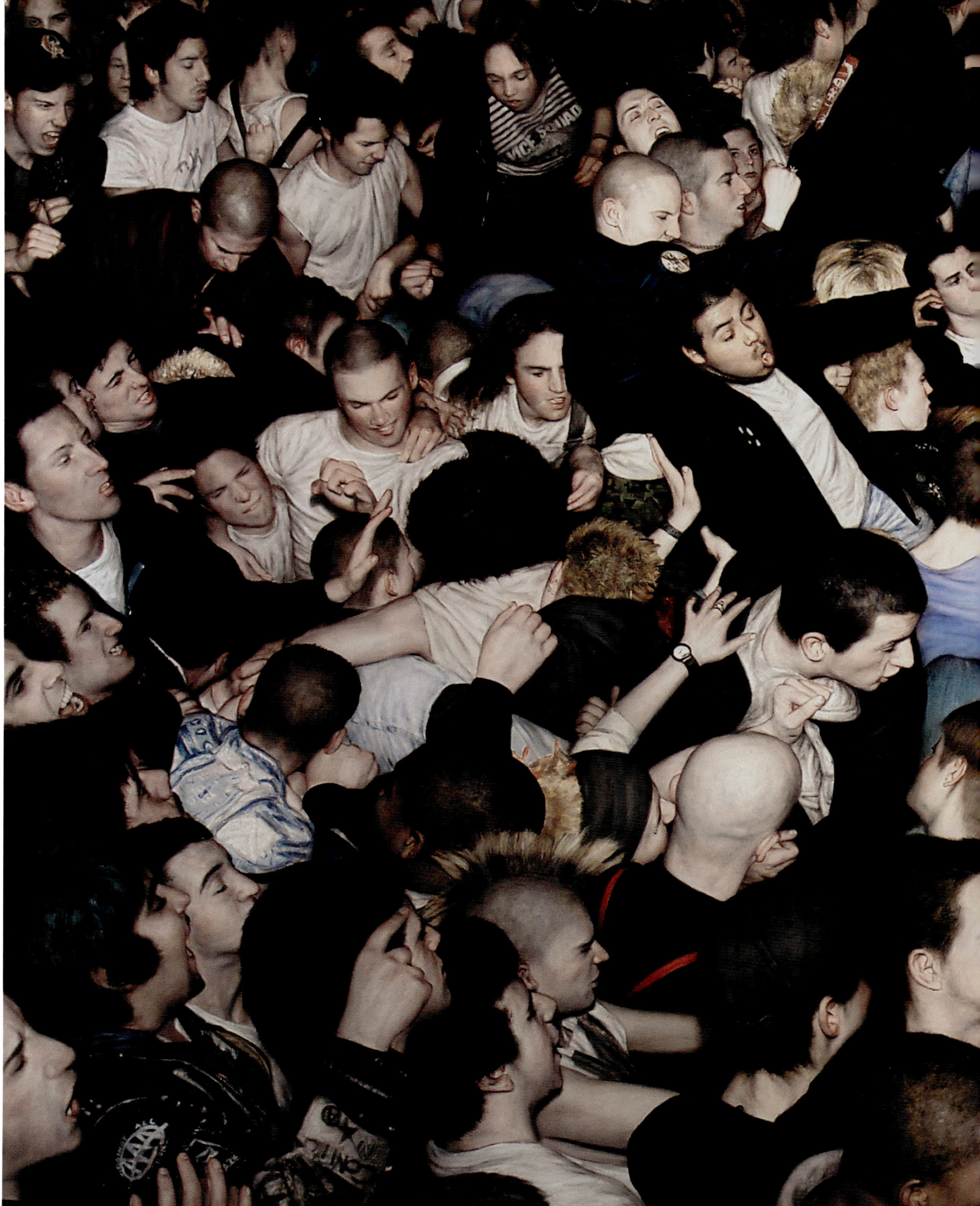
VICE SQUAD

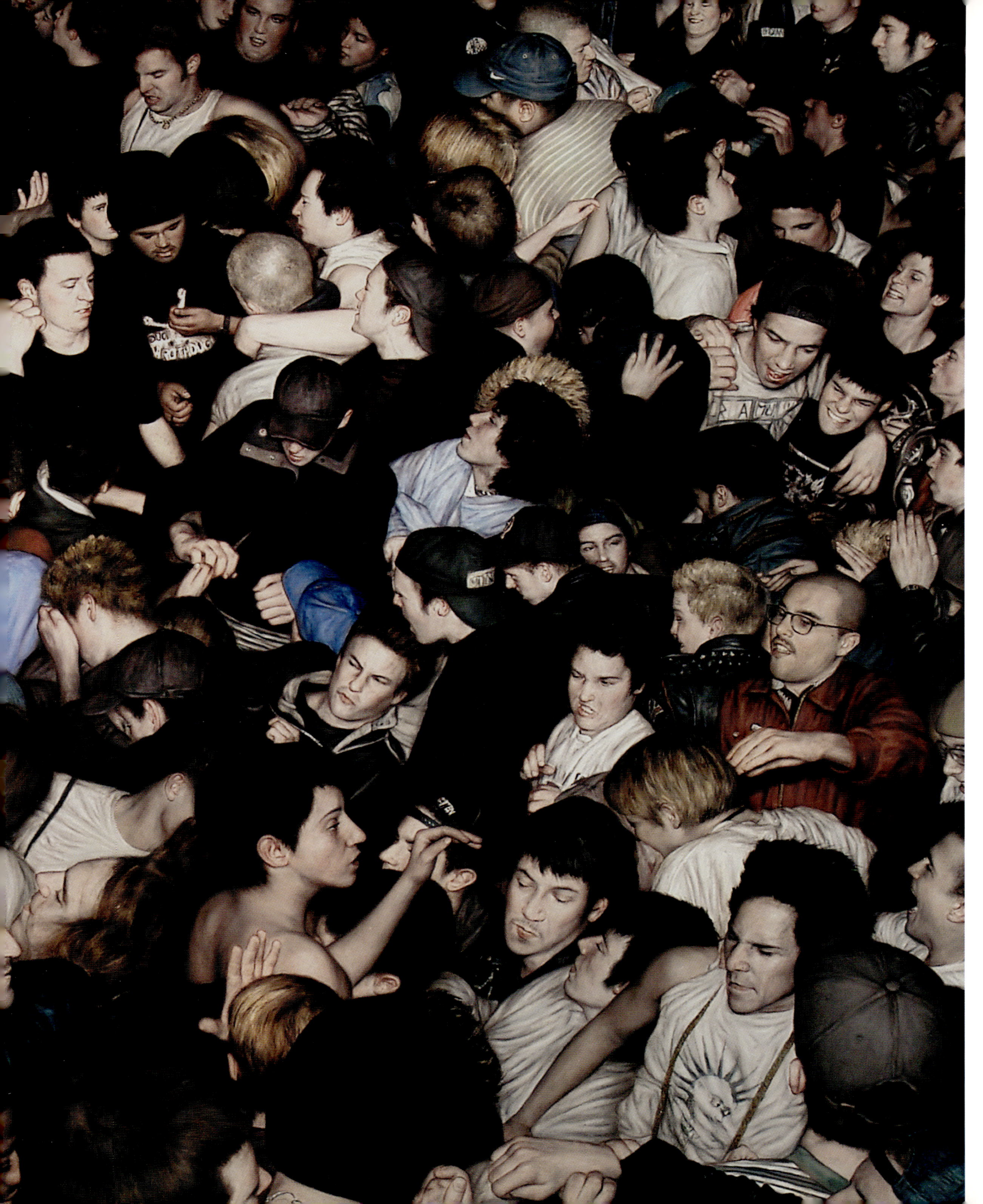

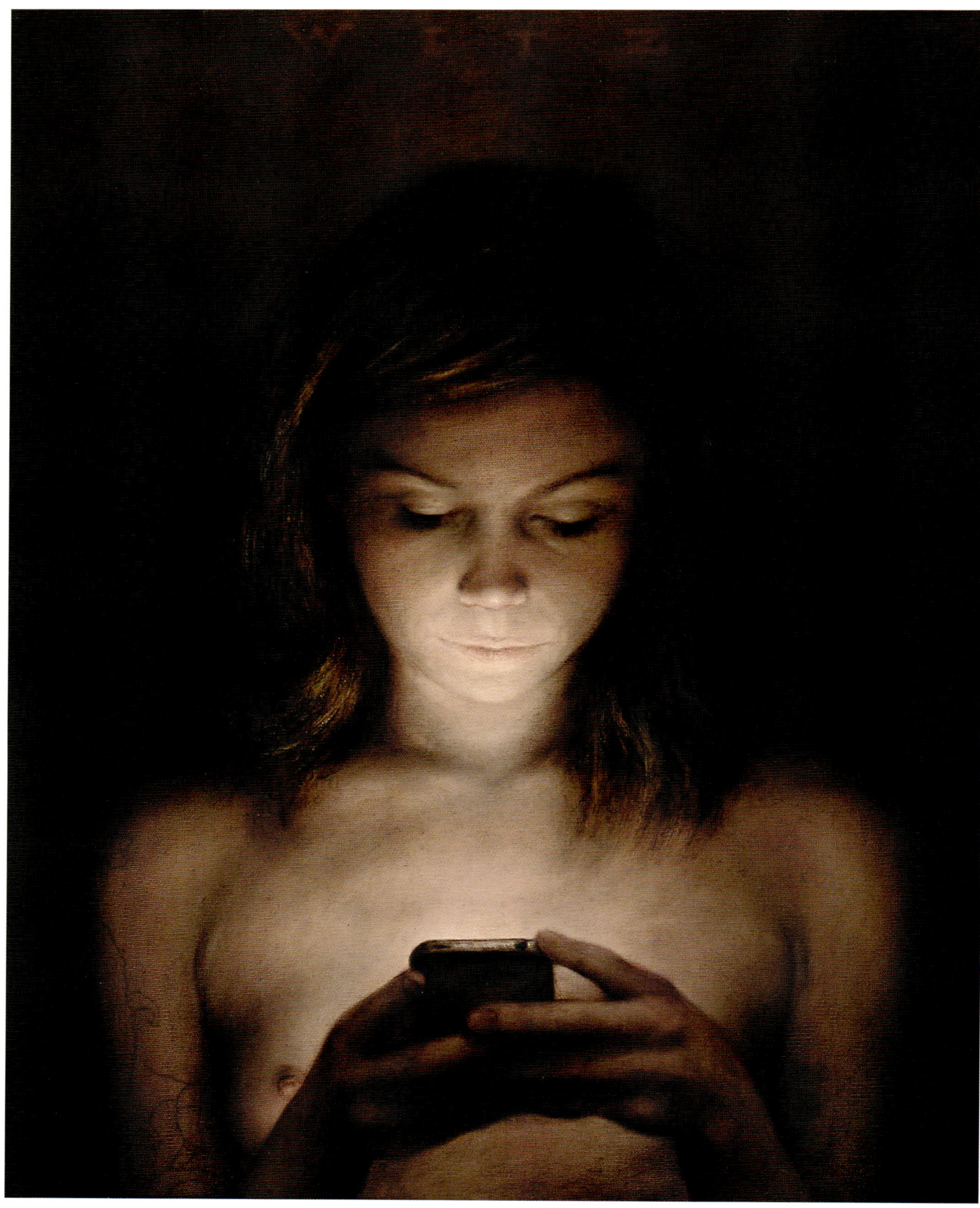

TERESA, 2008. // Oil and digital media on canvas. Private collection.

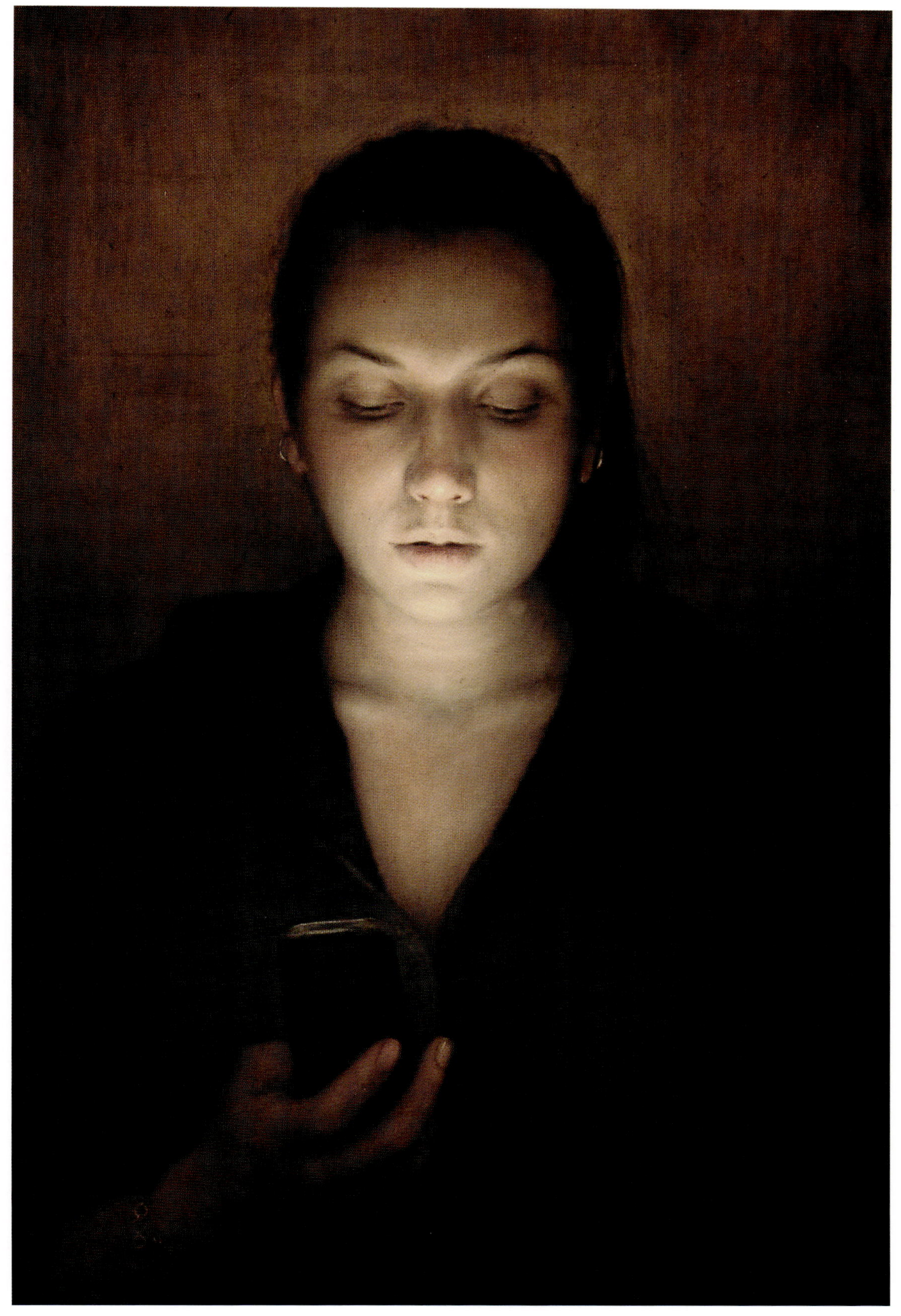

MELISSA, 2007. // Oil and digital media on canvas.

LIGHT 2002

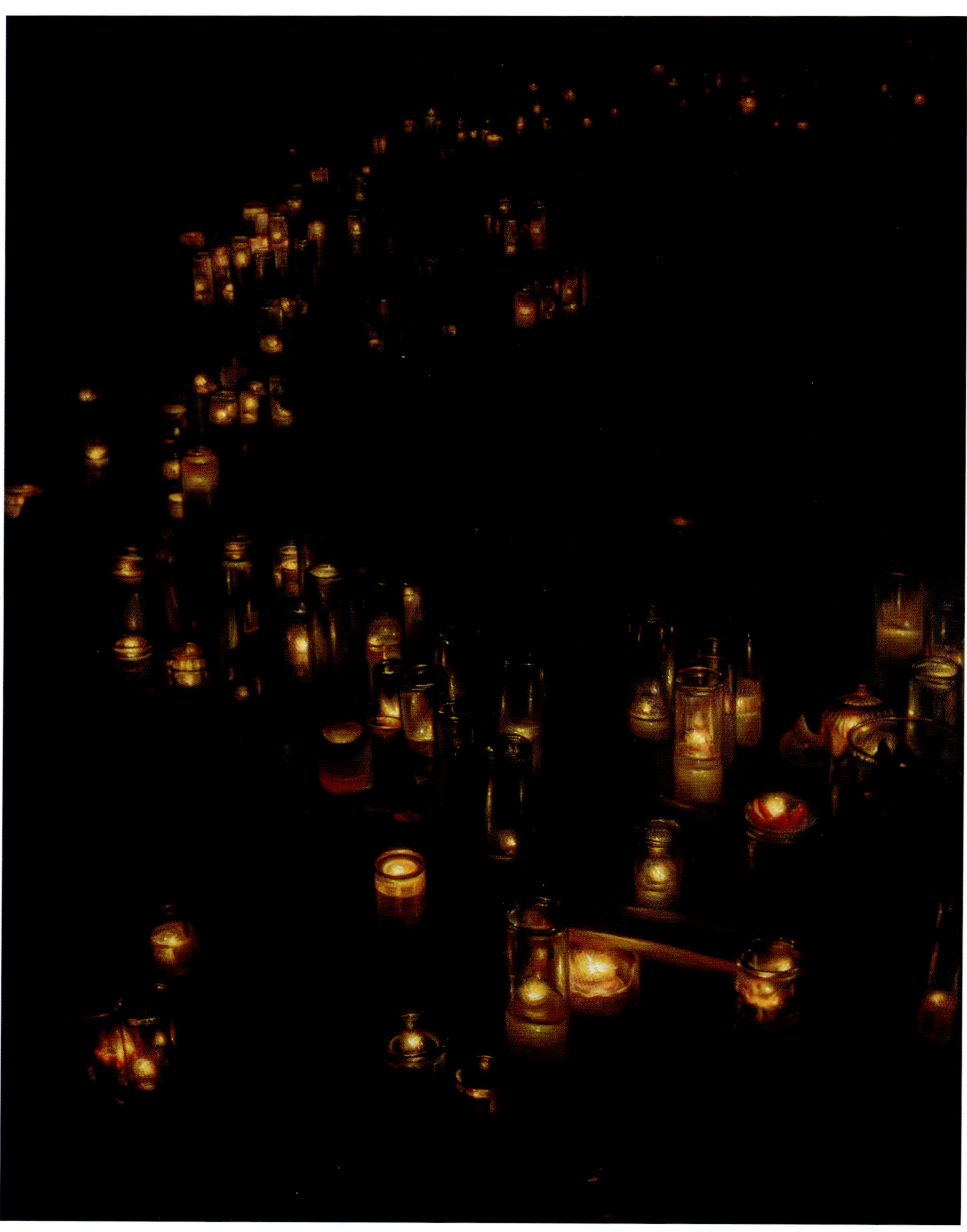

CANDLE FIELD 6, 2002. // Oil and digital media on canvas. Private Collection.

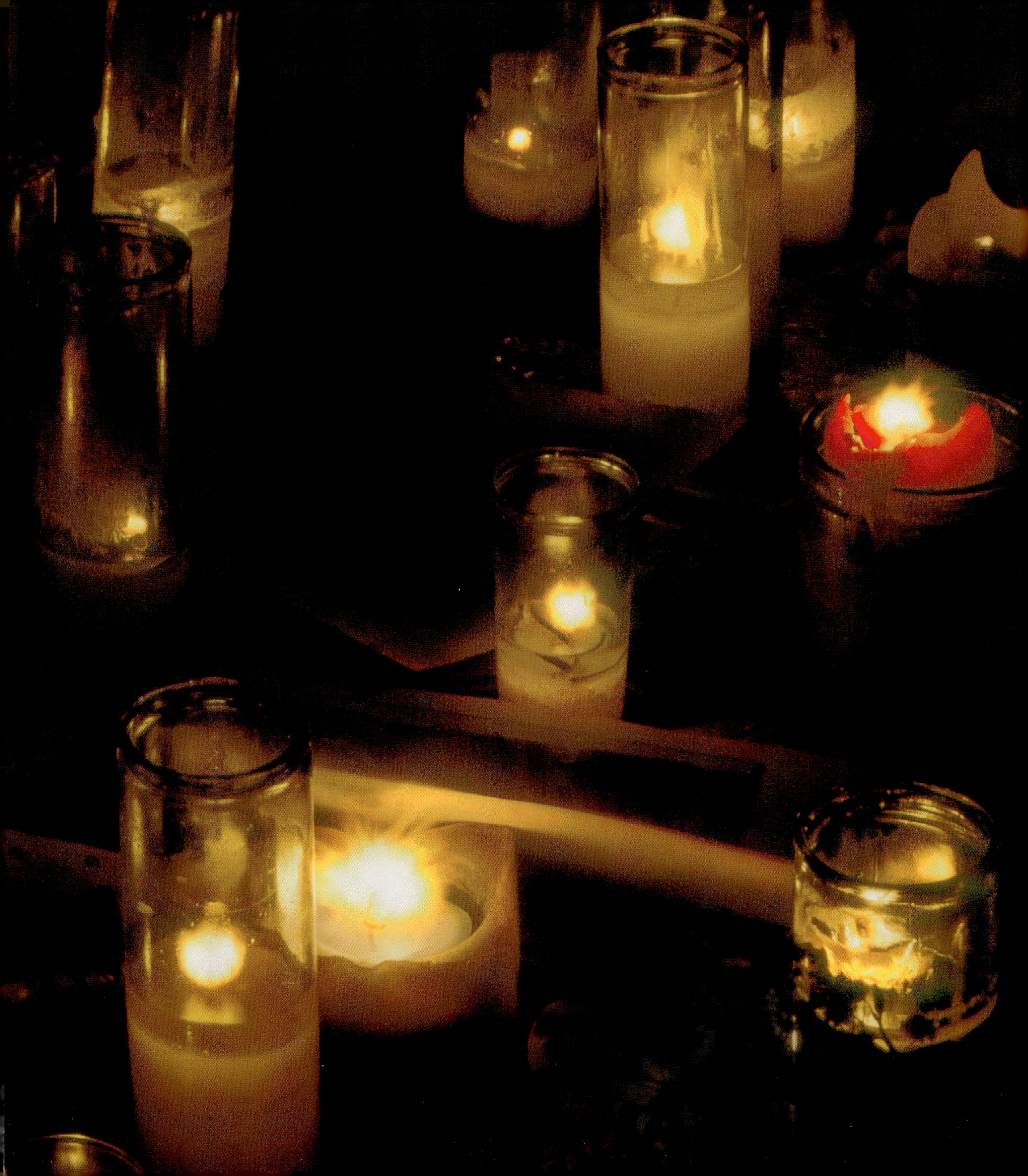

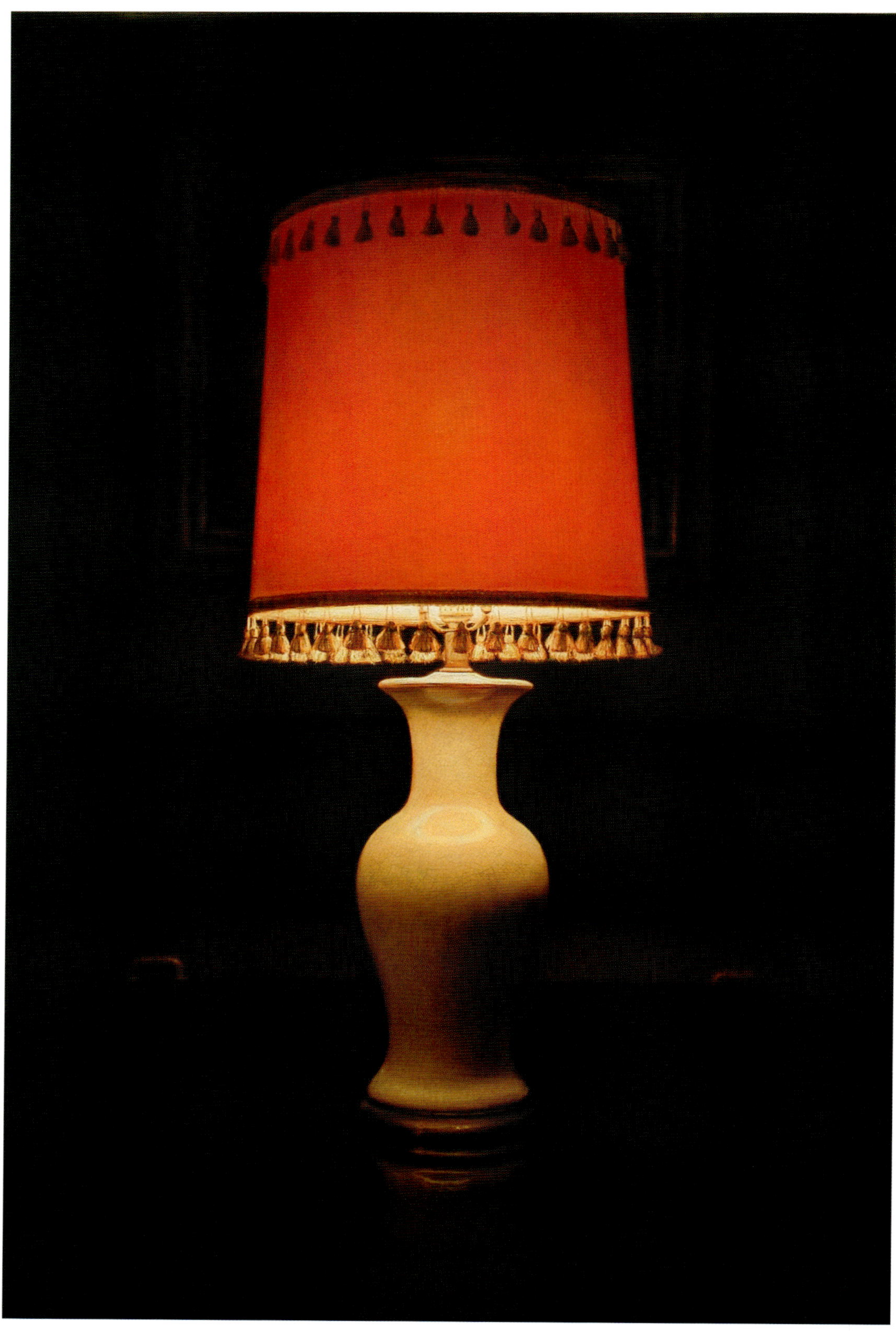

ROSY'S LAMP, 2006. // Oil and digital media. Private Collection.

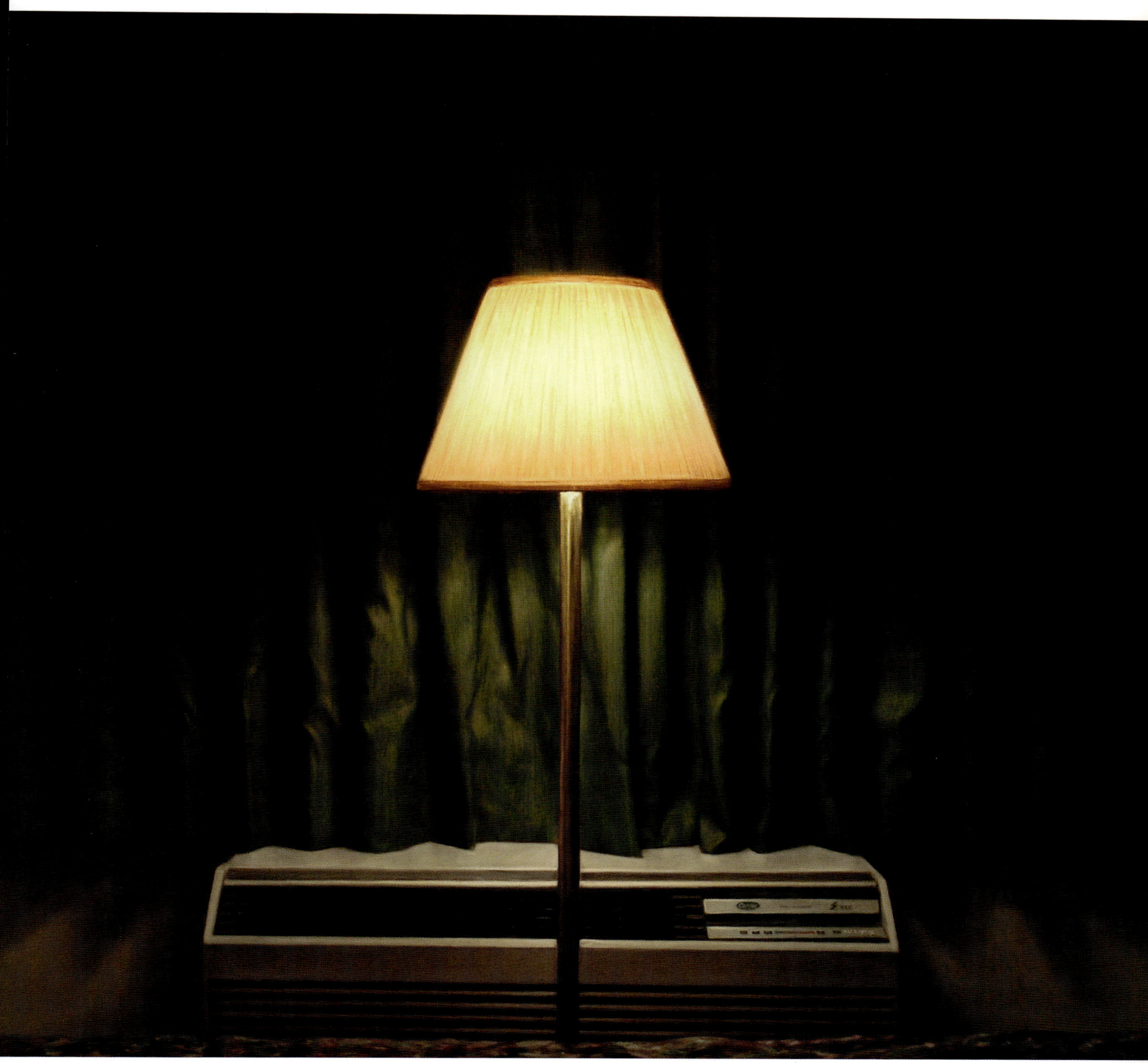

ECONO LODGE LAMP III, 2007. // Oil and digital media.

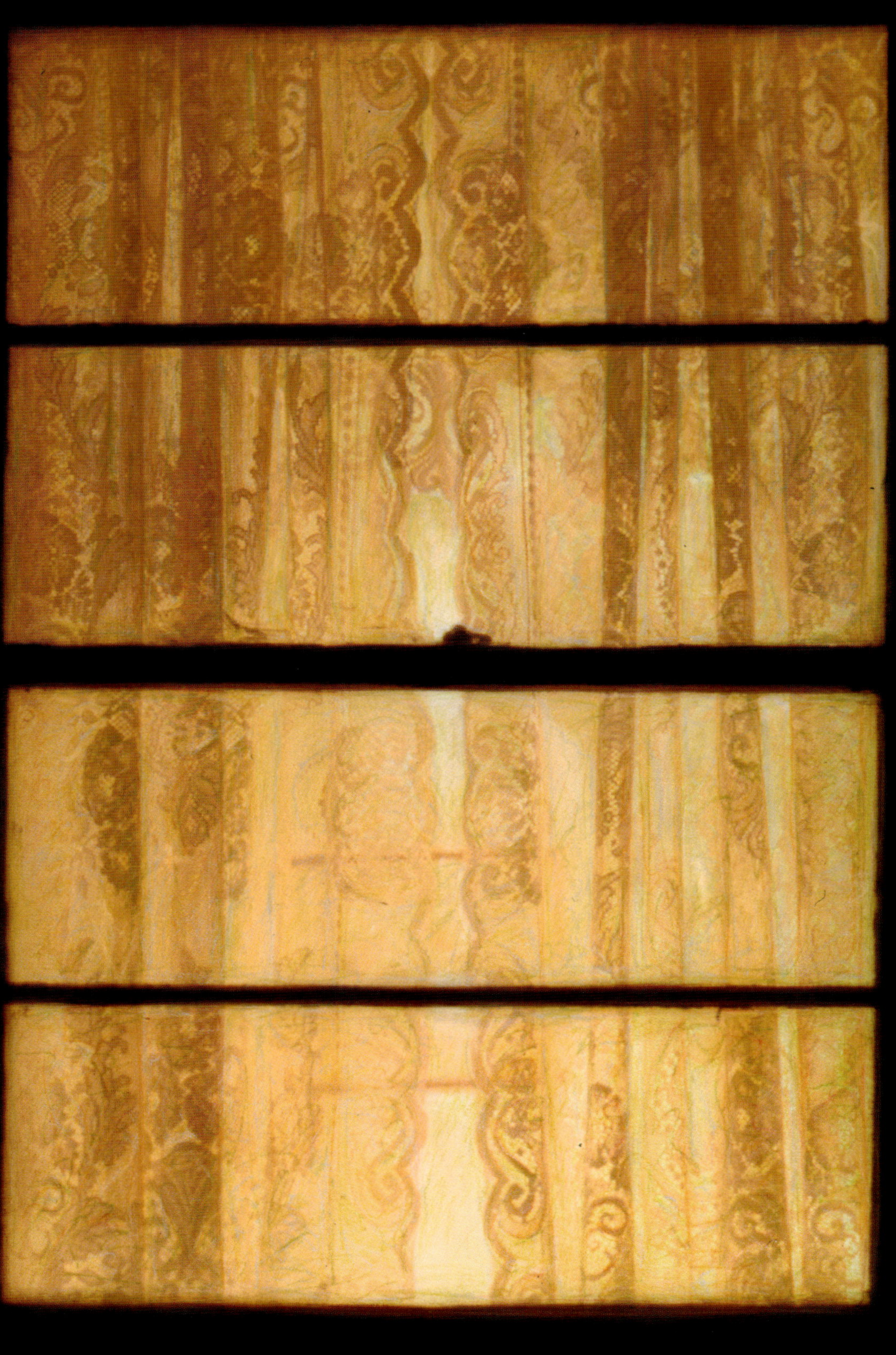

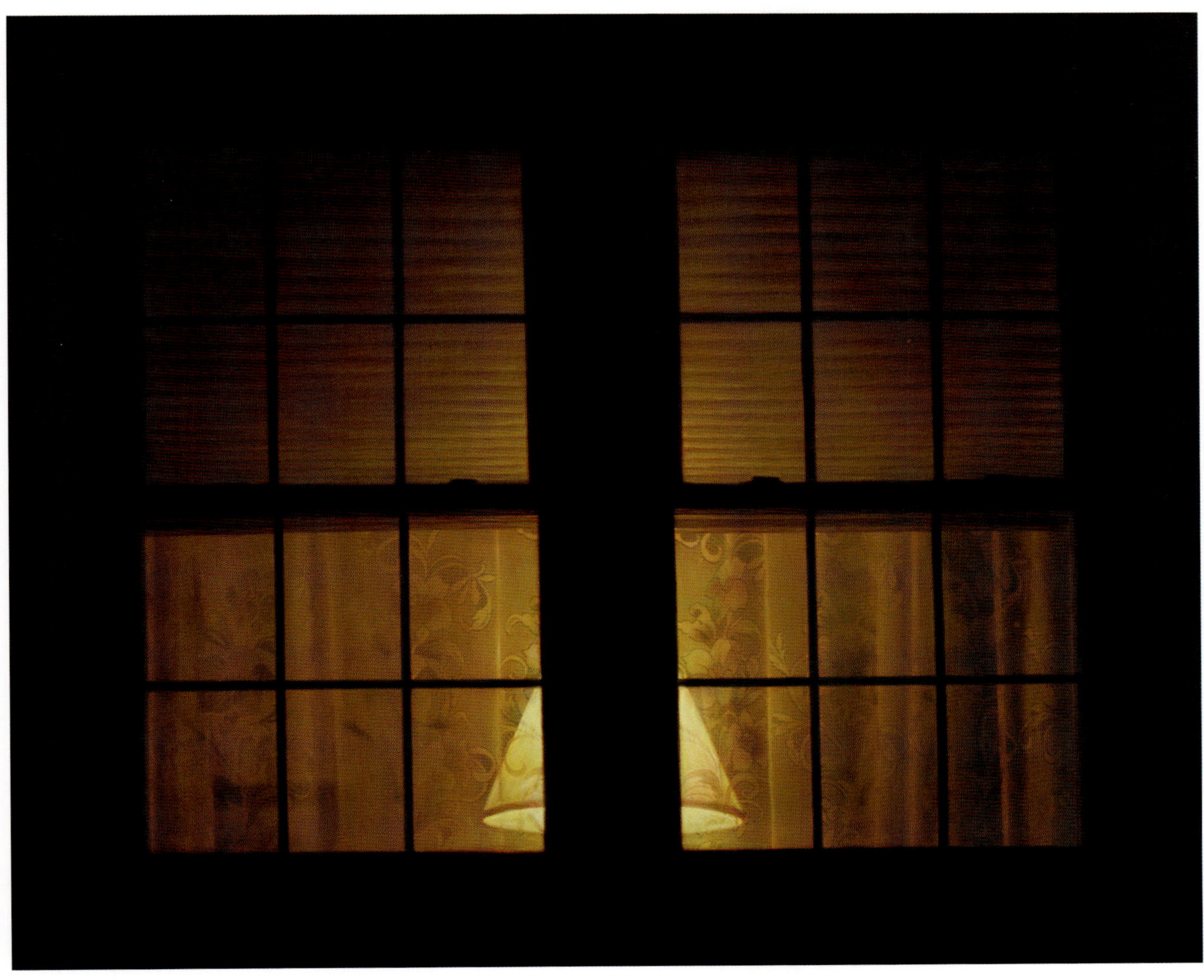

OPPOSITE PAGE:

LACE CURTAIN WINDOW, 2002. // Oil and digital media on canvas, Private Collection. From the Home Sweet Home series. Eviction from my lower east side loft was imminent. I did these paintings while looking for a new place to live.

ABOVE:

FLORAL LACE CURTAIN WINDOW, 2003. // Oil and digital media on canvas. Private Collection From the Home Sweet Home series.

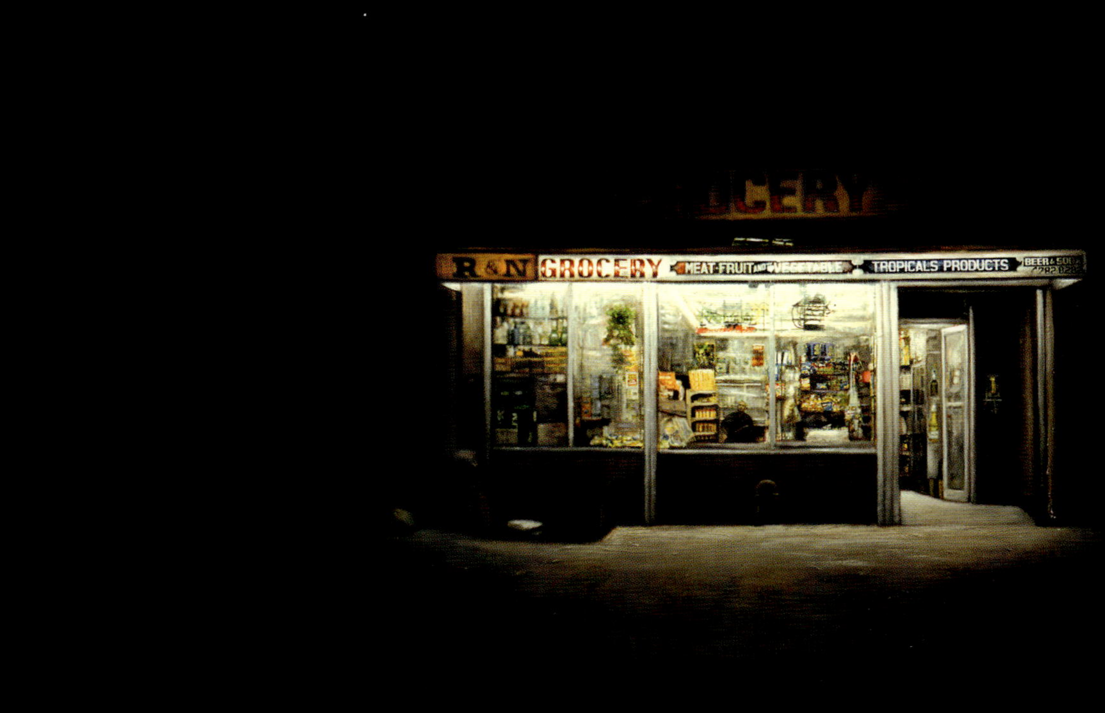

THIS PAGE:

R AND N GROCERY, 2005. // Oil and digital media on canvas. Private Collection.

OPPOSITE PAGE:

NATALIE GROCERY, 2007. // Oil and digital media on canvas. Private Collection.

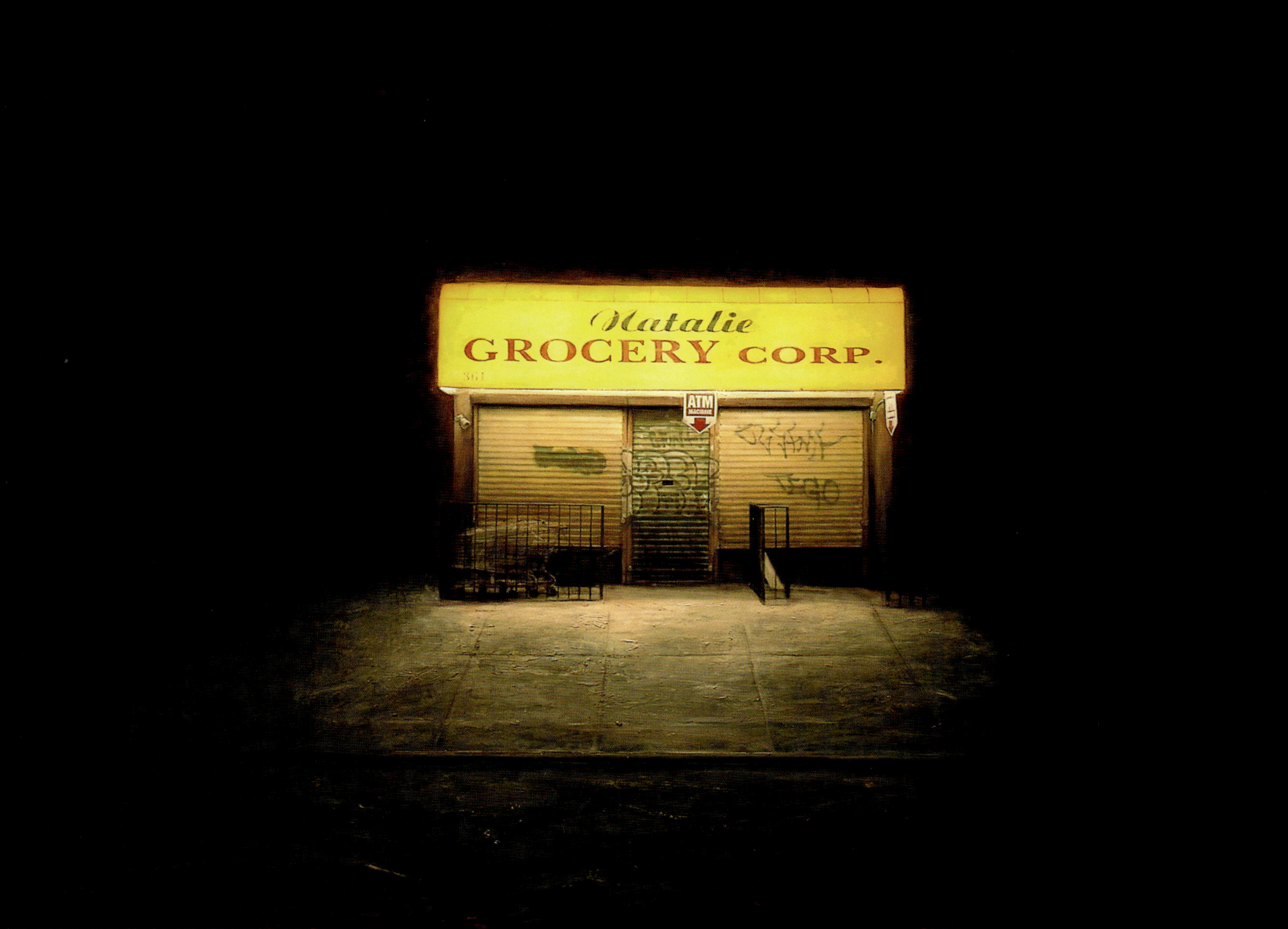

NEXT PAGE, TOP:

LA MINITA GROCERY, 2008. // Oil and digital media on canvas.

NEXT PAGE, BOTTOM:

MET LIQUOR, 2007. // Oil and digital media on canvas.

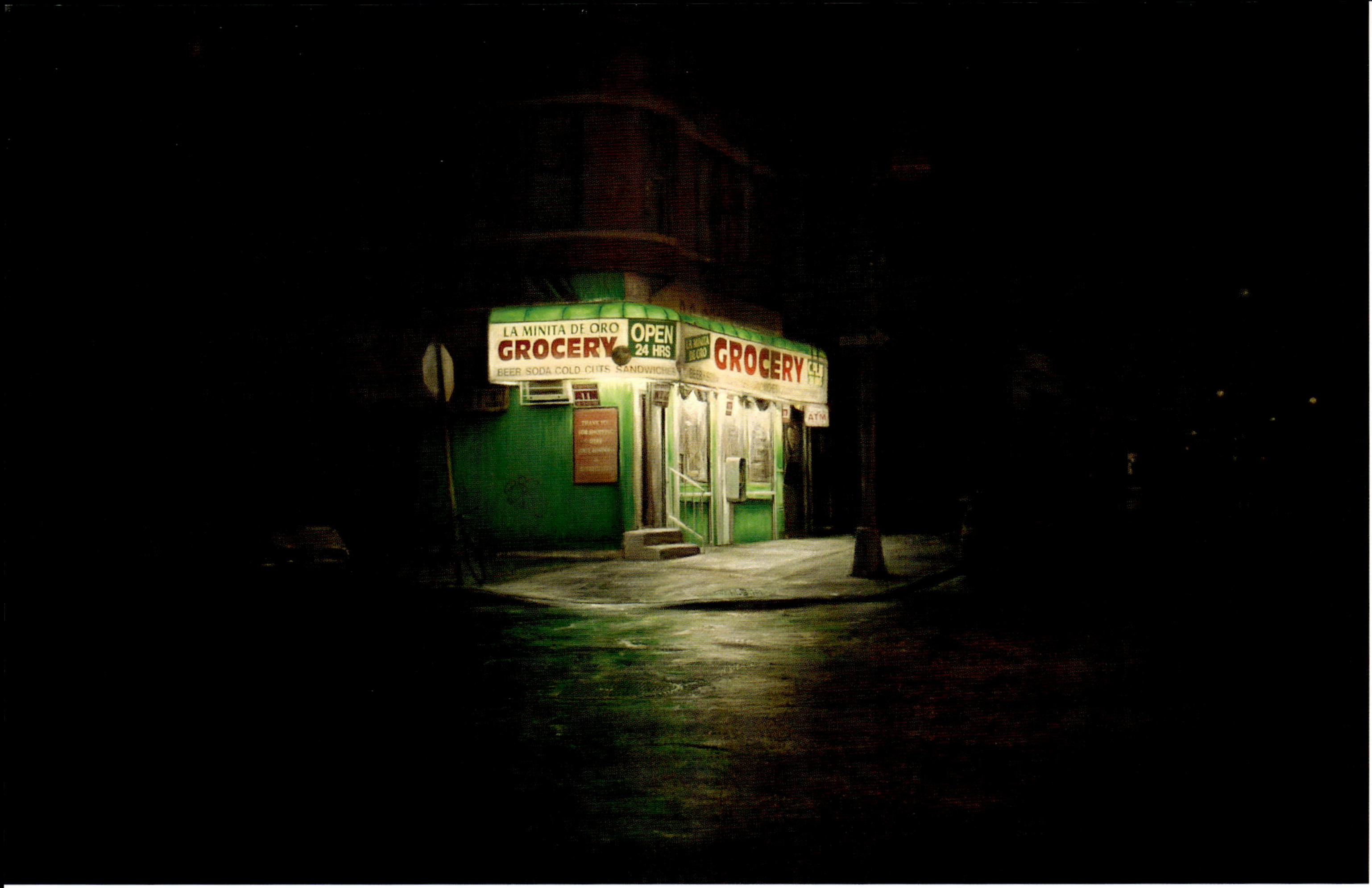

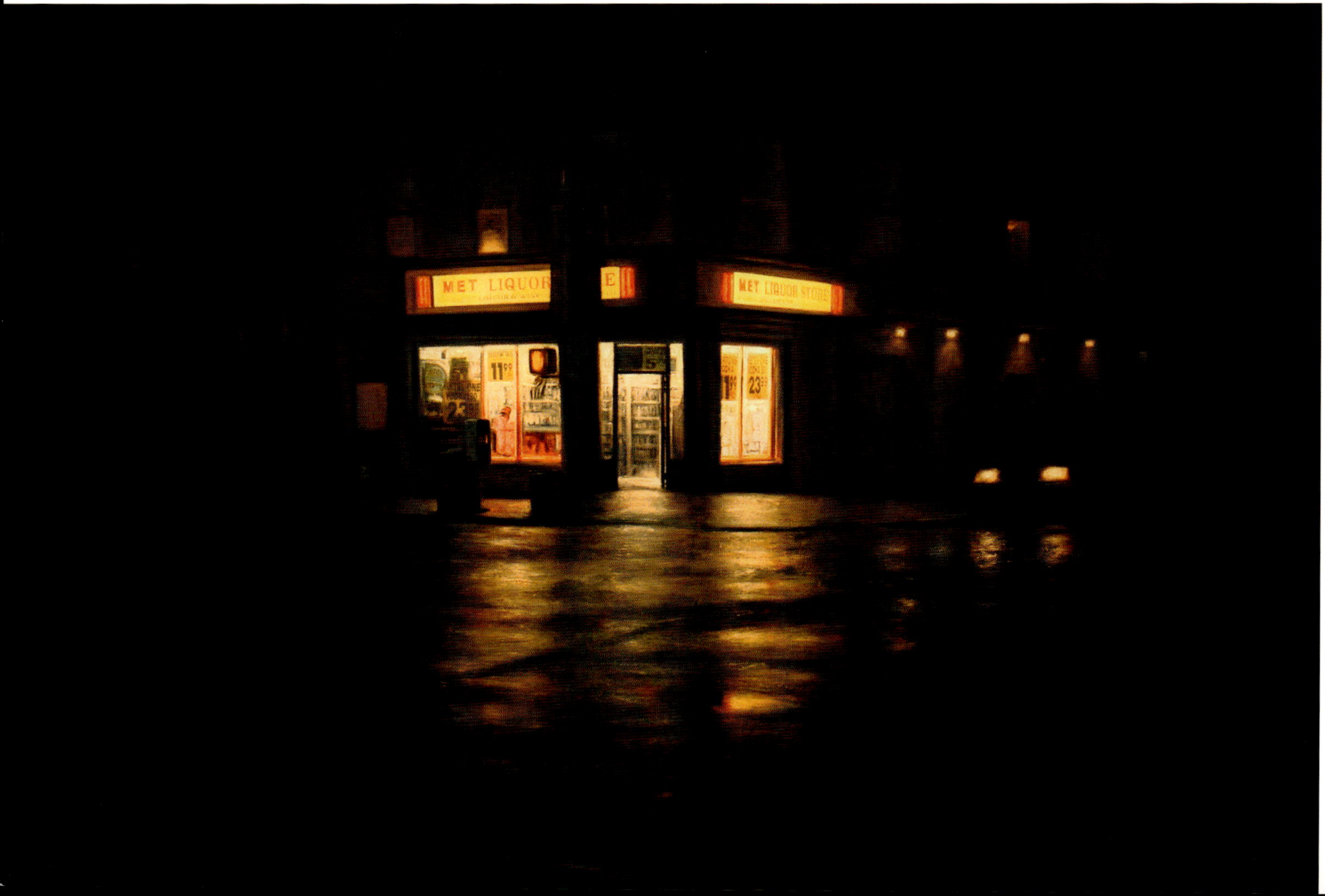

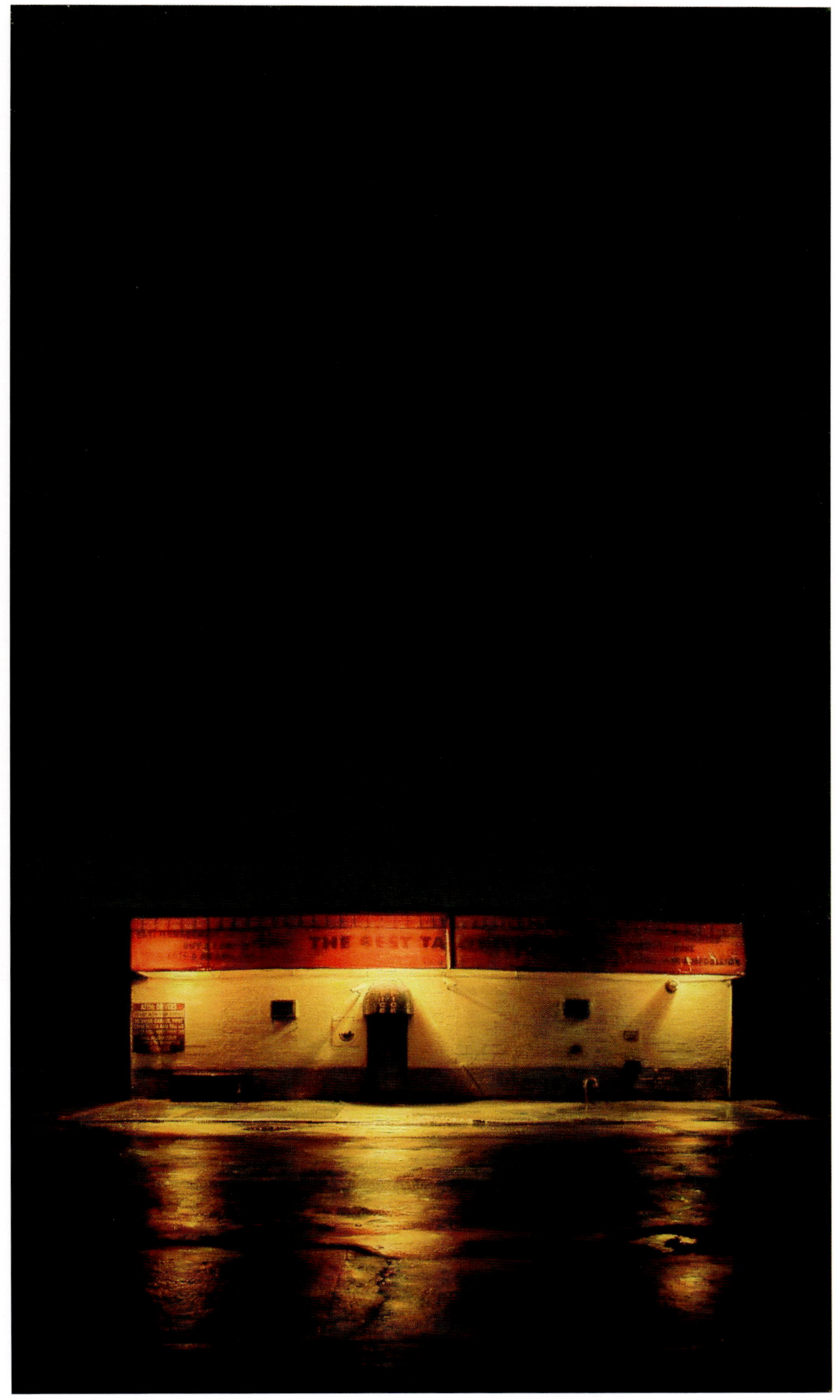

TAXI GARAGE, 2005. // Oil and digital media on canvas. Private Collection.

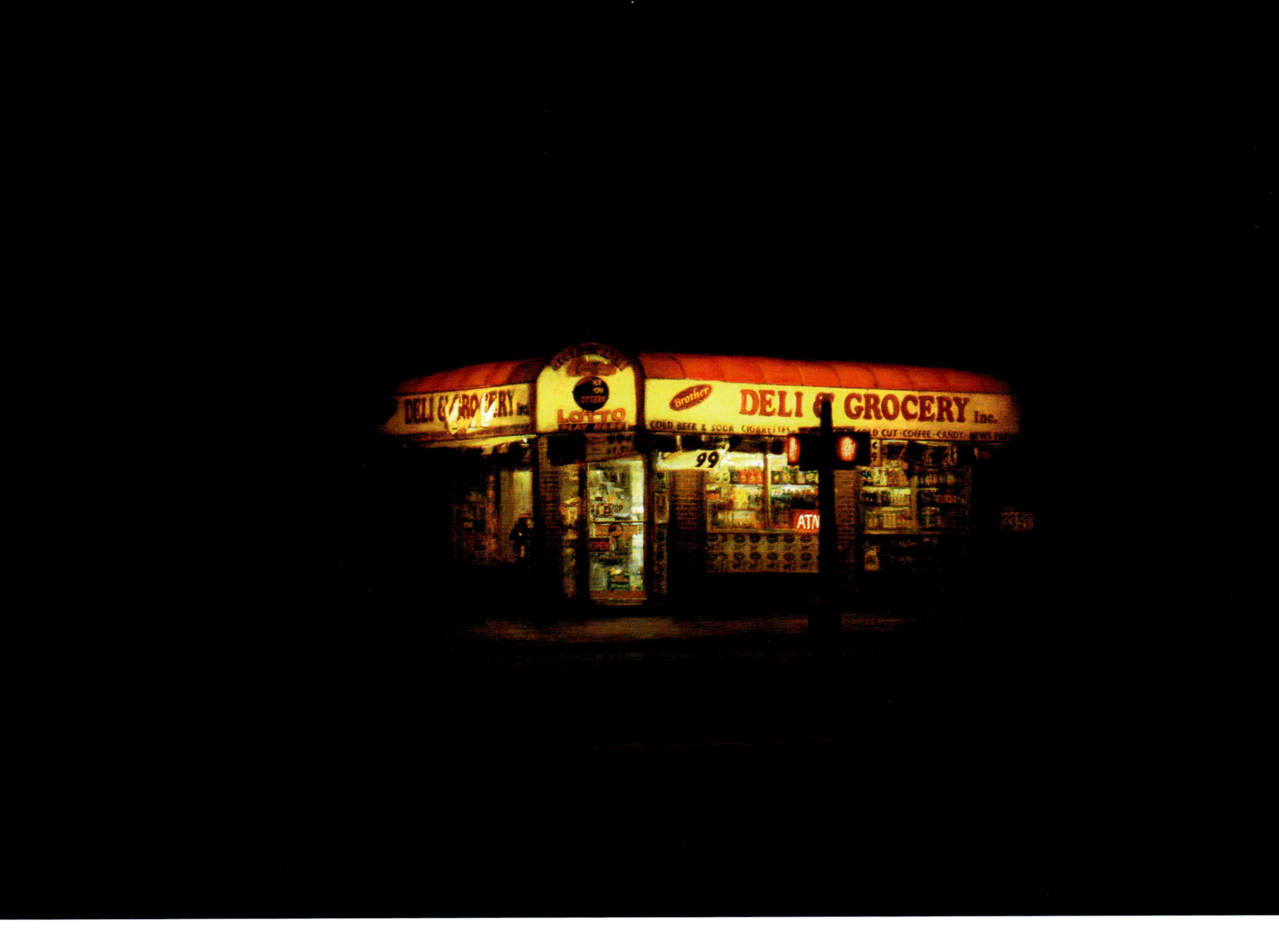

THIS PAGE:

BROTHERS DELI, 2003. // Oil and digital media on canvas. Private Collection.

OPPOSITE PAGE:

DANISH HOT DOG STAND, 2008. // Oil and digital media on canvas.

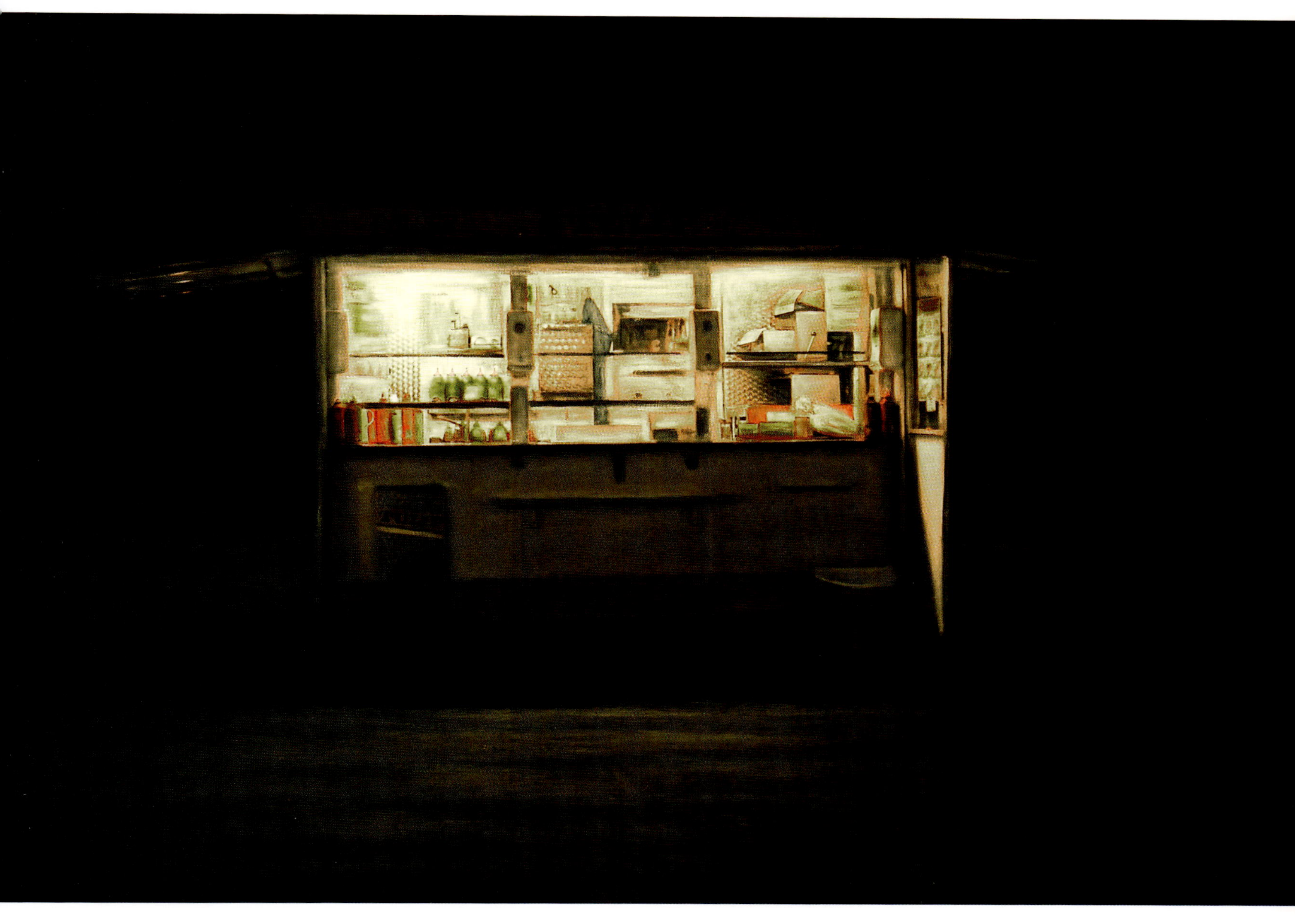

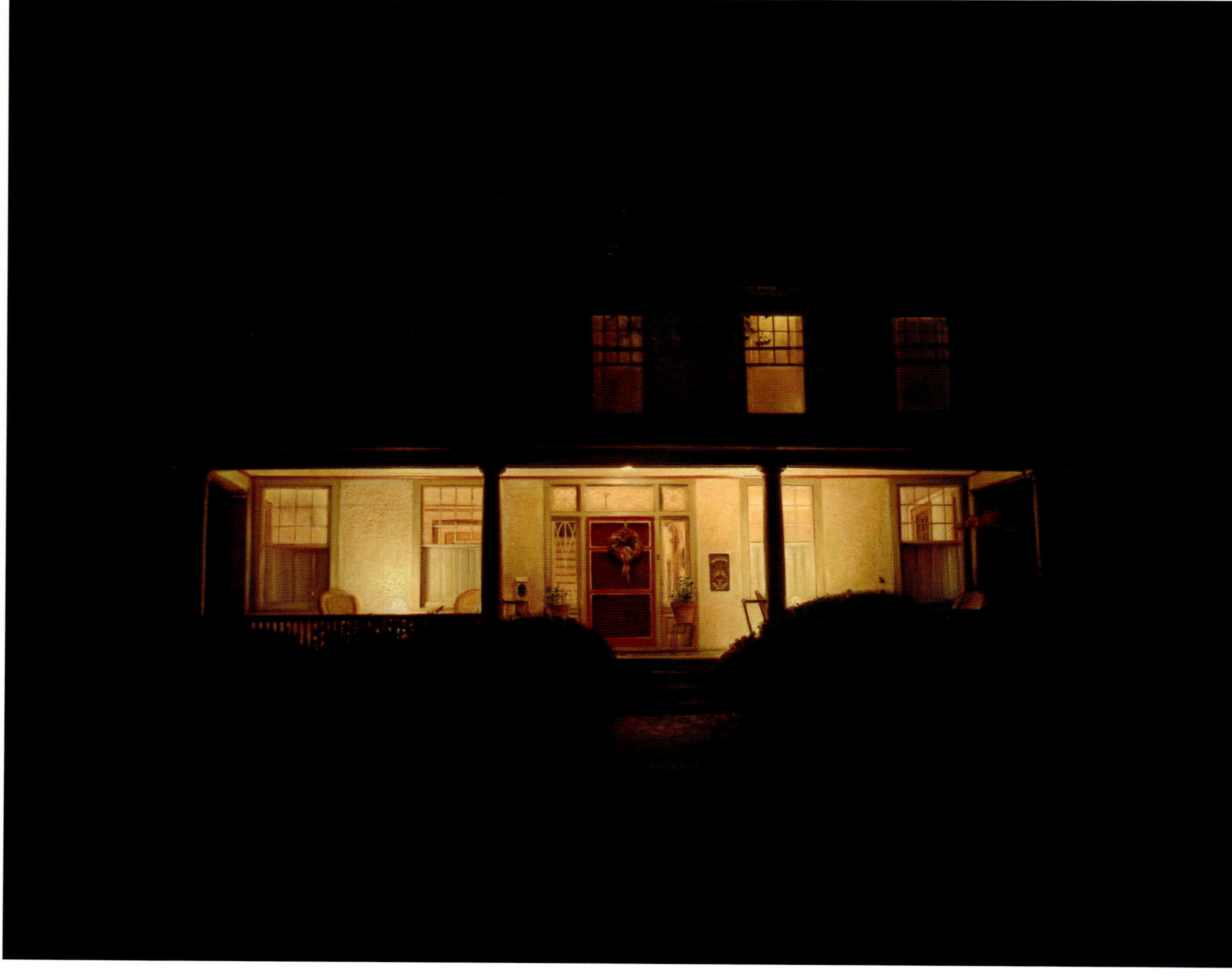

TOP RIGHT:

HIGHLAND PARK, ILLINOIS, 2007. // Oil and digital media on canvas. Private collection.

LOWER RIGHT:

SCHOOL STREET, 2007. // Oil and digital media on canvas. Both paintings are from a series I did of the suburban area outside Chicago where I grew up.

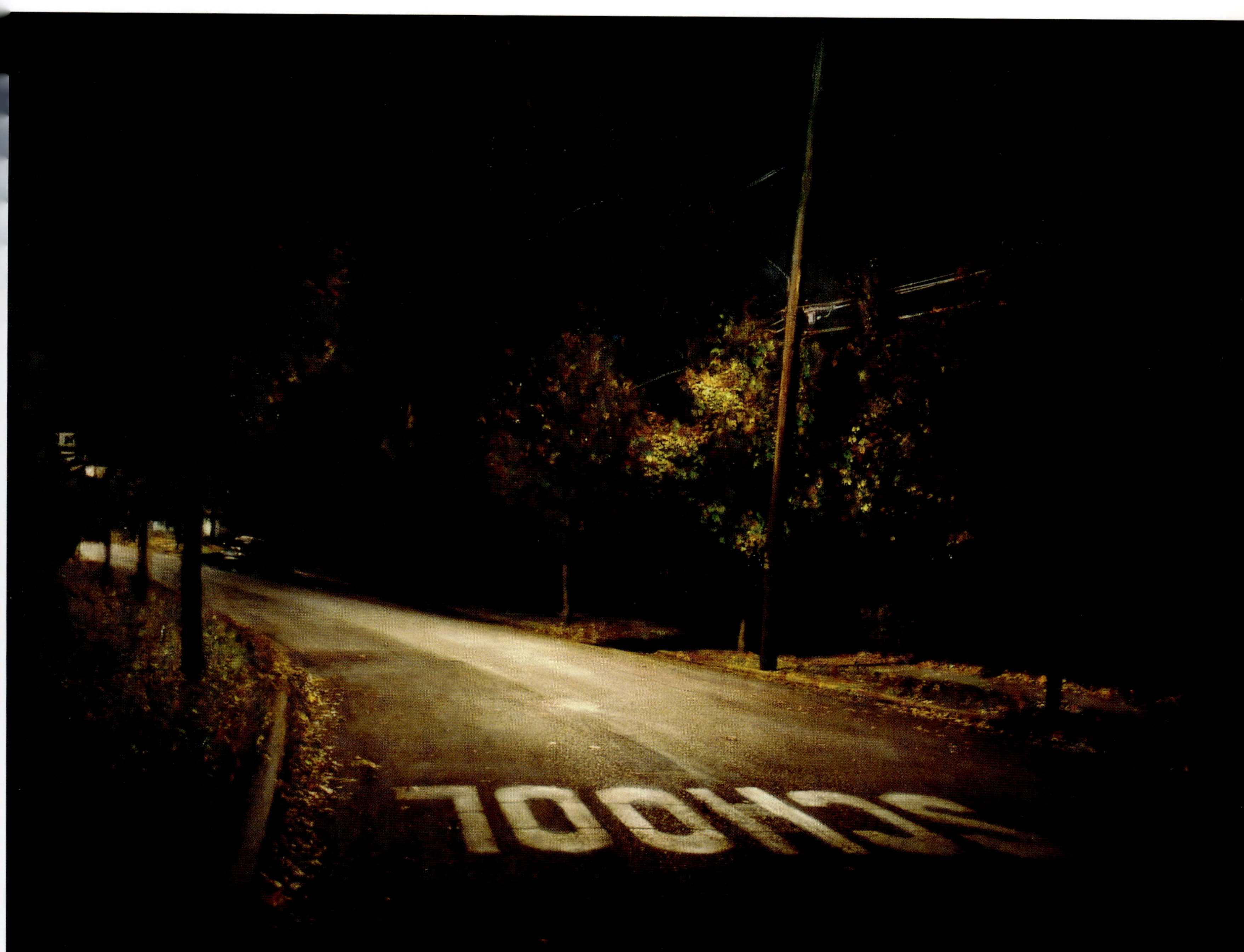
SCHOOL

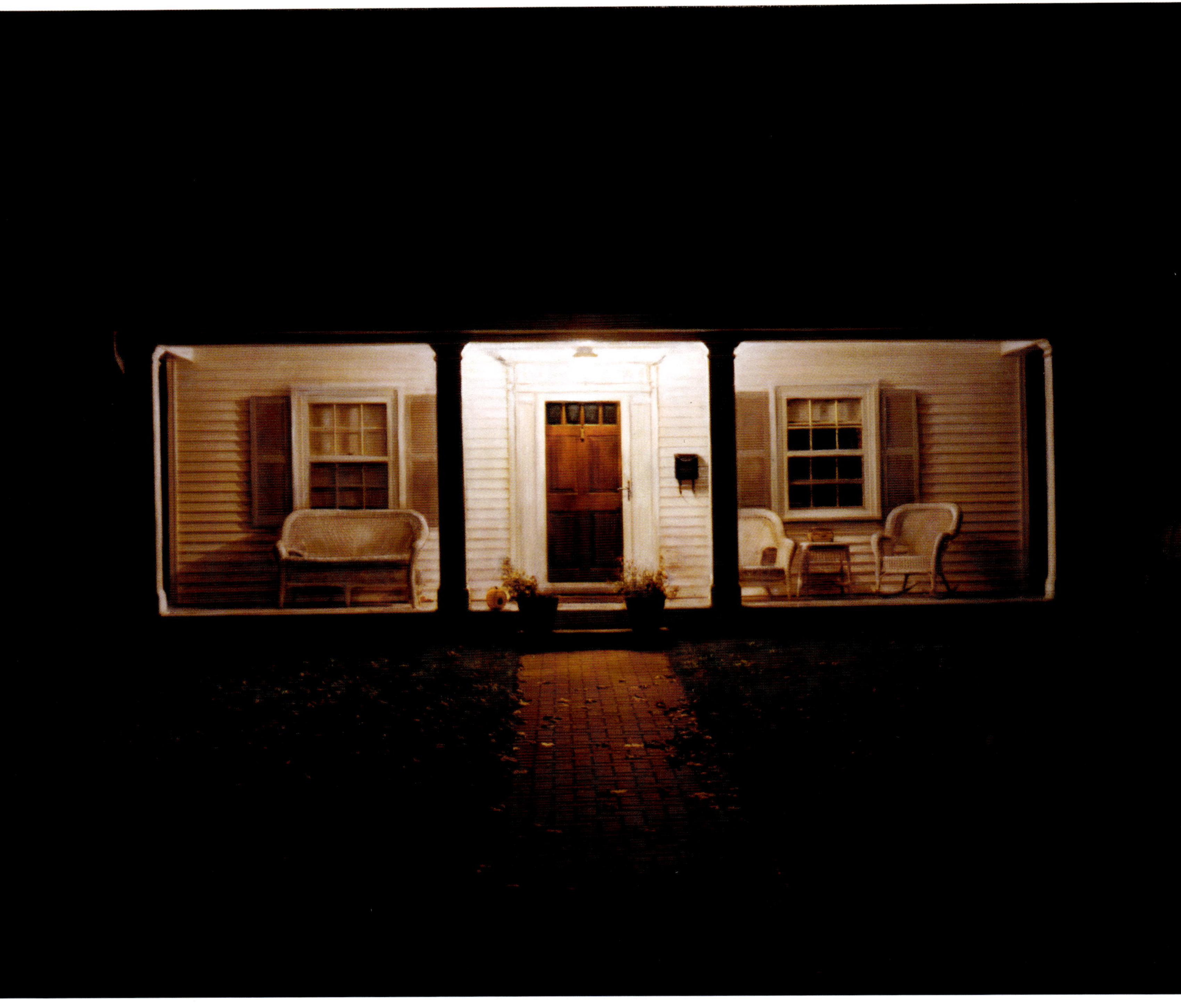

GLENCOE HOUSE, 2007. // Oil and digital media on canvas. Private collection.

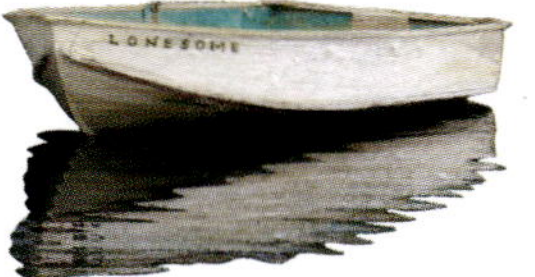
LONESOME

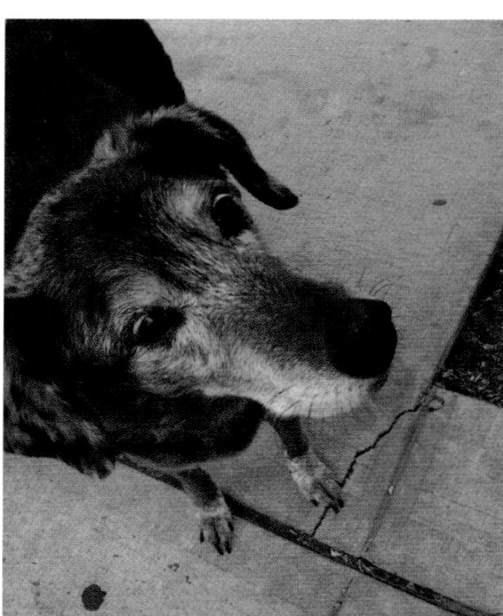

ACKNOWLEDGEMENTS:

So many generous people over the past 30 years have gone out of their way to help me with this work that it would be impossible to thank (or remember) them all. You guys know who you are. Much love. Know that I'm eternally grateful and that I am doing my best to repay this debt in kind.

Camille.

Aug. 1, 1993–March 4th, 2009

March forth.

Photo by John Rauschenberger

DAN WITZ

In Plain View

30 Years of Artworks Illegal and Otherwise

First Edition, June 2010

Gingko Press
1321 Fifth Street
Berkeley, CA 94710
Phone: (510) 898 1195
Email: books@gingkopress.com
www.gingkopress.com

Layout & Design by Kimberly Groebner

All artwork and text © 2010 Dan Witz
(except where specifically noted)

P. 10 Text © Stewart Ewen, from the Alice Arnold film, To Be Seen

P. 16 Text © David Lopes

P. 19 Image © Robert Crumb, 2009

Used by permission, Agence Littéraire Lora Fountain & Associates, Paris, France

P. 20 Images & Photos © Donald Lipski, excepting the top, Photo by Dorothy Zeidman, image Donald Lipski

All rights reserved. No part of this publication may be reproduced, stored in retrieval systems or transmitted in any form or by any means, electronic or mechanical, including photocopying, recording or any information storage and retrieval systems, without permission in writing from the Publisher.

ISBN: 978-1-58423-304-6

Printed and bound in China